MW00755855

PENGUIN BOOKS
MAHARISHI MAHESH YOGI ON THE
BHAGAVAD-GITA

A rediscovery to fulfil the need of our time

MAHARISHI MAHESH YOGI ON THE

BHAGAVAD-GITA

A NEW TRANSLATION AND COMMENTARY
WITH SANSKRIT TEXT

CHAPTERS 1 TO 6

PENGUIN BOOKS

Penguin Books Ltd, Harmondsworth, Middlesex, England
Penguin Books Inc., 7110 Ambassador Road, Baltimore,
Maryland 21207, U.S.A.
Penguin Books Australia Ltd, Ringwood, Victoria, Australia
Penguin Books Canada Ltd,
41 Steelcase Road West, Markham, Ontario, Canada
Penguin Book (N.Z.) Ltd,
182–190 Wairau Road, Auckland 10, New Zealand

First published by International SRM Publications 1967
Published in Penguin Books 1969
Reprinted 1971, 1972, 1973, 1974, 1975
Copyright © Maharishi Mahesh Yogi, 1967

Made and printed in Great Britain by
Hazell Watson & Viney Ltd, Aylesbury, Bucks
Set in Linotype Juliana

TO
THE LOTUS FEET OF SHRI GURU DEVA,
HIS DIVINITY
SWAMI BRAHMANANDA SARASWATI,
JAGADGURU, BHAGWAN SHANKARACHARYA
OF JYOTIR MATH, HIMALAYAS;
AND
AS BLESSINGS FROM HIM
TO THE LOVERS OF LIFE
DESIROUS OF ENJOYING ALL GLORIES,
WORLDLY AND DIVINE

CONTENTS

PREFACE

THE Vedas are the lighthouse of eternal wisdom leading man to salvation and inspiring him to supreme accomplishment.

The omnipresence of eternal Being, unmanifested and absolute; Its status as That, even in the manifested diversity of creation; and the possibility of the realization of Being by any man in terms of himself – these are the great truths of the perennial philosophy of the Vedas.

The Vedas reveal the unchanging Unity of life which underlies the evident multiplicity of creation, for Reality is both manifest and unmanifest, and That alone is. 'I am That, thou are That and all this is That', is the Truth; and this is the kernel of the Vedic teaching, which the rishis extol as teaching 'worthy of hearing, contemplating and realizing'.

The truth of Vedic wisdom is by its very nature independent of time and can therefore never be lost. When, however, man's vision becomes one-sided and he is caught by the binding influence of the phenomenal world to the exclusion of the absolute phase of Reality, when he is thus confined within the ever-changing phases of existence, his life loses stability and he begins to suffer. When suffering grows, the invincible force of nature moves to set man's vision right and establish a way of life which will again fulfil the high purpose of his existence. The long history of the world records many such periods in which the ideal pattern of life is first forgotten and then restored to man.

Veda Vyasa, the sage of enlightened vision and greatest among the historians of antiquity, records the growth of unrighteousness in the families of those who ruled the people about five thousand years ago. It was then that Lord Krishna came to remind man of the true values of life and living. He restored that direct contact with the transcendental Being which alone can give fullness to every aspect of life. He brought to light absolute Being as the basic Reality of life and established It as the foundation of all thinking, which in turn is the basis of all doing. This philosophy of Being, thinking and doing is the true philosophy of the integrated life. It not only helps the doer to gain success in his undertaking, but, at the same time, sets him free from the bondage of action, bringing fulfilment at every level. Such is the teaching of eternal Truth, given by Lord Krishna to Arjuna in the Bhagavad-Gita.

Gradually this teaching came to be forgotten, so that two thousand years later even the principle of Being as the absolute Reality, the source and basis of all creation, was overshadowed by misguided beliefs which glorified only the relative aspects of life. 'The long lapse of time', says Lord Krishna, is the reason for such a loss of wisdom.

When the philosophy of the integrated life restored by Lord Krishna was lost from view, the idea grew that everything which life can offer is present on the obvious levels of existence, and that it would therefore be useless to aspire to anything that might lie deeper than external appearances. Society became dominated by this superficial outlook, insight into Reality was lost, the right sense of values forgotten and the stability of life destroyed. Tension, confusion, superstition, unhappiness and fear prevailed.

Lord Buddha came to remedy this situation. Finding the field of action distorted, He came with a message of right action. Speaking from His level of consciousness established in Being, in eternal freedom (nirvana), Lord Buddha taught the philosophy of action in freedom. He advocated meditation in order to purify the field of thought through direct contact with Being and bring about the state of right action in society. Lord Buddha's message was complete because He incorporated the fields of Being, thinking and doing in His theme of revival. But because his followers failed to correlate these different fields of life in a systematic manner through the practice of transcendental meditation, realization of Being as the basis of a good life became obscured. The whole structure of Lord Buddha's teaching not only became distorted but was also turned upside down. The effect was mistaken for the cause. Right action came to be regarded as a means to gain nirvana, whereas right action is in fact the result of this state of consciousness in freedom.

It has been the misfortune of every teacher that, while he speaks from his level of consciousness, his followers can only receive his message on their level; and the gulf between the teaching and understanding grows wider with time.

The teaching of right action without due emphasis on the primary necessity of realization of Being is like building a wall without a foundation. It sways with the wind and collapses before long. Within three or four hundred years all real connexion between the essential teachings of Lord Buddha and the daily life of His followers had disappeared. Insight into the principle of the integrated life was again lost. Having forgotten the prime importance of realizing Being, society became immersed once more in the superficialities of life.

Nature will not allow humanity to be deprived of the vision of Reality for very long. A wave of revival brought Shankara to re-establish the basis of life and renew human understanding. Shankara restored the wisdom of the Absolute and established It in the daily life of the people, strengthening the fields of thought and action by the power of Being. He brought the message of fulfilment through direct realization of transcendental Being in the state of Self-consciousness, which is the basis of all good in life.

Shankara's emphasis on Self-realization stems from the eternal philosophy of the integrated life expressed by Lord Krishna in the Bhagavad-Gita when He asks Arjuna first to 'be without the three gunas' and then to perform actions while thus established in Being. That all men should at all times live the bliss-consciousness of absolute Being, and that they should live the state of fulfilment in God-consciousness throughout all thought, speech and action; this is the essence of Shankara's message, as it is the essence of Lord Krishna's and of the entire Vedic philosophy.

The greatest blessing that Shankara's teaching has offered to the world is the principle of fullness of intellectual and emotional development in the state of enlightenment, based on transcendental pure consciousness, in which the heart is so pure as to be able to flow and overflow with waves of universal love and devotion to God, while the mind is so refined as to enjoy awareness of the divine nature as separate from the world of action.

The spontaneous expressions of Shankara's mind and heart in this state of freedom and fulfilment have been a source of inspiration both to those who live by the heart and those who live by the mind. His consciousness exemplified the highest state of human development; his heart expressed supreme transcendental devotion to God (para bhakti), while his mind expressed awareness of the Self as separate from the field of action (gyana). This it was that led Shankara's speech to flow into ecstasies of devotion and at the same time into clear expressions of knowledge, the dry and hard-headed truths concerning divine nature as detached from the world. These are the two aspects of the living reality of a life in complete fulfilment.

Shankara not only revived the wisdom of integrated life and made it popular in his day, but also established four principal seats of learning in four corners of India to keep his teaching pure and to ensure that it would be propagated in its entirety generation after generation. For many centuries his teaching remained alive in his followers, who lived the ideal state of knowledge with devotion (gyana and bhakti). But in spite of all his foresight and endeavours, Shankara's message inevitably suffered with time the same misfortunes as those of the other great teachers.

If the occupants of a house forget the foundations, it is because the foundations lie underground, hidden from view. It is no surprise that Being was lost to view, for It lies in the transcendental field of life.

The state of Reality, as described by the enlightened, cannot become a path for the seeker, any more than the description of a destination can replace the road that leads to it. When the truth that Being forms the basis of the state of enlightenment became obscured, Shankara's statements about the nature of the goal were mistaken for the path to realization.

This misunderstanding was increased by the very beauty of Shankara's eloquence. His expressions of deep devotion made in the state of complete surrender and oneness with God, and his intellectual clarifications made in the state of awareness of the divine nature, are both so full and complete in themselves that, seen from the ordinary level of consciousnes, they appeared to present two independent paths to enlightenment: the path of knowledge and the path of devotion.

This is the tragedy of knowledge, the tragic fate that knowledge must meet at the hands of ignorance. It is inevitable, because the teaching comes from one level of consciousness and is received at quite a different level. The knowledge of Unity must in time shatter on the hard rocks of ignorance. History has proved this again and again. Shankara's teaching could not prove an exception to the rule.

The idea of two paths became more predominant owing to the carelessness of the custodians of Shankara's teaching. Since they followed the recluse way of life, they were naturally concerned with thoughts of the separateness of the Divine from the world; and, with the continuance of this situation generation after generation, the aspect of knowledge began to dominate Shankara's tradition while the aspect of devotion gradually lost its importance. The teaching became one-sided and, deprived of its wholeness, eventually lost its universal appeal. It came to be regarded as mayavada, a philosophy of illusion, holding the world to be only illusory and emphasizing the detached way of life.

As the principle of Being began more and more to disappear from view, the paths of devotion and knowledge became more and more separate and finally the link between them was lost. The principle of full development of heart and mind through one process (transcendental meditation) was lost. The integral nature of realization was lost. The true wisdom of life's fulfilment, which lies in the simultaneous development of heart and mind, was lost. The idea that devotion and knowledge are necessarily separate was the greatest blow to Shankara's teaching.

In the absence of the moon, the stars take over and provide as much light as they can. When Shankara's high ideal of transcendental devotion disappeared from sight, Ramanuja, Madhva and other teachers upheld the path of devotion, even though without its proper basis in Being. People followed them, and thus there arose many devotional sects all on the level of emotion and every one founded on the comfortable basis of hope that 'some day our prayer will be heard, some day He will come to us and call us to

Him'. Indeed a comfort to the heart but, alas, such devotion is on the imaginary plane of feeling ! It is far, far away from the reality of actual contact between the devotee and his God. Awareness in the state of Being alone makes the whole field of devotion real.

All these sects hold that transcendental devotion is the last stage of a devotee's achievement. But Shankara's principle of devotion is founded on transcendental consciousness from the very beginning. The first step for Shankara is the last step for these devotional sects, a step which according to their understanding is far above the reach of the ordinary man.

The idea that devotion must start from transcendental consciousness having been lost by the guardians of Shankara's wisdom, entrance into the field of devotion was closed. Seekers of God remained seeking in thin air, and lovers of God remained weeping for Him without finding Him.

As devotion remained merely on the level of thinking and of assuming an attitude of feeling (mood-making), so knowledge met with the same fate once the direct way to the realization of transcendental consciousness had been lost. Understanding of the Unity of life cannot be significant until one has thoroughly understood, by direct experience, that one's inner divine nature is separate from the world of action. If a man has not gained consciousness in Being through the practice of transcendental meditation, he continues to live in ignorance and bondage. Because he has not yet opened himself to the experience of the separateness of the Divine from the world, the thought of Unity has no practical use for such a man. He has nothing to unite.

On the fertile field of transcendental consciousness both knowledge and devotion find their fulfilment. But this principle once forgotten and the technique for developing transcendental consciousness lost, many, many generations have died without seeing the light of God and without gaining fulfilment. That has been the situation for more than a thousand years. Misunderstanding itself has taken the shape of a tradition, unfortunately known as Shankara's tradition. This great loss to human life can hardly be compensated; but that has been the course of history. Time cannot be recaptured. It is no use repenting the past.

In our review of the rise and fall of Truth, we must not lose sight of the great impact that Shankara produced on Indian life. It was the perfection of his presentation that caused Shankara's teaching to be accepted as the core of Vedic wisdom and placed it at the centre of Indian culture. It became so inseparable from the Indian way of life that when, in course of time, this teaching lost its universal character and came to be interpreted as for the recluse order alone, the whole basis of Indian culture also began to be considered in terms of the recluse way of life, founded on renunciation and detachment.

When this detached view of life became accepted as the basis of Vedic wisdom, the wholeness of life and fulfilment was lost. This error of understanding has dominated Indian culture for centuries and has turned the principle of life upside down. *Life on the basis of detachment!* This is a complete distortion of Indian philosophy. It has not only destroyed the path of realization but has led the seekers of Truth continuously astray. Indeed it has left them without the possibility of ever finding the goal.

Not only was the path to enlightenment lost, but the entire art of living disappeared in the clouds of ignorance which obscured every phase of life. Even religion became blind to itself. Instead of directly helping people to gain God-consciousness and act rightly on that basis, religious preachers began to teach that right action is in itself a way to purification and thereby to God-consciousness.

Without Being, confusion of cause and effect invaded every field of understanding. It captured even the most practical field of the philosophy of Yoga. Karma Yoga (attainment of Union by way of action) began to be understood as based on karma (action), whereas its basis is Yoga, Union, transcendental consciousness. The founder of the Yoga philosophy, Patanjali, was himself misinterpreted and the order of stages on his eightfold path reversed. The practice of Yoga was understood to start with yama, niyama, and so on (the secular virtues), whereas in reality it should begin with samadhi. Samadhi cannot be gained by the practice of yama, niyama, and so on. Proficiency in the virtues can only be gained by repeated experiences of samadhi. It was because the effect was mistaken for the cause that this great philo-

sophy of life became distorted and the path to samadhi was
blocked.

With the loss of insight into Yoga, the other five classical systems of Indian philosophy lost their power. They remained on the
theoretical level of knowledge, for it is through Yoga alone that
knowledge steps into practical life.

Thus we find that all fields of religion and philosophy have been
misunderstood and wrongly interpreted for many centuries past.
This has blocked the path to the fullest development of heart and
mind, so precisely revived by Shankara.

Interpretations of the Bhagavad-Gita and other Indian scriptures are now so full of the idea of renunciation that they are
regarded with distrust by practical men in every part of the
world. Many Western universities hesitate to teach Indian philosophy for this reason. The responsibility for this loss of Truth to
the whole world lies with the interpreters of Shankara's teaching;
missing the essence of his wisdom, they have been unable to save
the world from falling ever deeper into ignorance and suffering.

This age has, however, been fortunate. It has witnessed the
living example of a man inspired by Vedic wisdom in its wholeness and thus able to revive the philosophy of the integrated life
in all its truth and fullness. His Divinity Swami Brahmananda
Saraswati, the inspiration and guiding light of this commentary
on the Bhagavad-Gita, adorned the seat of the Shankaracharya of
the North and, glowing in divine radiance, embodied in himself
the head and heart of Shankara. He expounded the Truth in Its
all-embracing nature. His quiet words, coming from the unbounded love of his heart, pierced the hearts of all who heard him
and brought enlightenment to their minds. His message was the
message of fullness of heart and mind. He moved as the living
embodiment of Truth and was addressed as Vedanta Incarnate
by that great Indian philosopher, now President of India, Dr
Radhakrishnan.

It was the concern of Guru Deva, His Divinity Swami Brahmananda Saraswati, to enlighten all men everywhere that resulted
in the foundation of the world-wide Spiritual Regeneration Movement in 1958, five years after his departure from us.

India is a country where Truth matters most and Indians are

a people to whom God matters most. Indian soil has witnessed many times the revival of life's true philosophy. The people of India have never hesitated to return once more to the right path whenever it was convincingly pointed out to them that their way of life had taken a wrong course. This receptiveness to Truth of the Indian people has always been a source of inspiration and a signal of hope to all movements aiming at the revival of true life and living.

May the present commentary on the Bhagavad-Gita produce the desired effect in response to the historical necessity of today.

The purpose of this commentary is to restore the fundamental truths of the Bhagavad-Gita and thus restore the significance of its teaching. If this teaching is followed, effectiveness in life will be achieved, men will be fulfilled on all levels and the historical need of the age will be fulfilled also.

MAHARISHI MAHESH YOGI

The Old Manor, Aldbourne,
Wiltshire, England
12 January 1965

INTRODUCTION

THE Bhagavad-Gita is the Light of Life, lit by God at the altar of man, to save humanity from the darkness of ignorance and suffering. It is a scripture which outlives time, and can be acknowledged as indispensable to the life of any man in any age. It is the encyclopedia of life, and this commentary provides an index to it.

There will always be confusion and chaos in the relative fields of life and man's mind will always fall into error and indecision. The Bhagavad-Gita is a complete guide to practical life. It will always be there to rescue man in any situation. It is like an anchor for the ship of life sailing on the turbulent waves of time.

It brings fulfilment to the life of the individual. When society accepts it, social well-being and security will result, and when the world hears it, world peace will be permanent.

The Bhagavad-Gita presents the science of life and the art of living. It teaches how to be, how to think and how to do. Its technique of glorifying every aspect of life through contact with inner Being is like watering the root and making the whole tree green. It surpasses any practical wisdom of life ever cherished by human society.

The Bhagavad-Gita has a greater number of commentaries than any other known scripture. The reason for adding one more is that there does not seem to be any commentary which really brings to light the essential point of the whole teaching.

Wise commentators, in their attempt to fulfil the need of their times, have revealed the truth of the teaching as they found it. By so doing they have secured a place in the history of human thought. They stand out as torch-bearers on the long corridor of time. They have fathomed great depths of the ocean of wisdom. Yet with all their glorious achievements they have not brought

INTRODUCTION

out the central point of the Bhagavad-Gita. It is unfortunate
that the very essence of this ancient wisdom should have been
missed.

The Bhagavad-Gita needs a commentary which restates in simple
words the essential teaching and technique given by Lord Krishna
to Arjuna on the battlefield. There are commentaries to extol the
wisdom of the paths of knowledge, devotion and action in the
Bhagavad-Gita, but none to show that it provides a master-key
to open the gates of all these different highways of human evolution simultaneously. No commentary has yet shown that
through one simple technique proclaimed in the Bhagavad-Gita,
any man, without having to renounce his way of life, can enjoy
the blessings of all these paths.

This commentary has been written to present that key to mankind and preserve it for generations to come.

The Bhagavad-Gita is the Scripture of Yoga, the Scripture of
Divine Union. Its purpose is to explain in theory and practice all
that is needed to raise the consciousness of man to the highest
possible level. The marvel of its language and style is that every
expression brings a teaching suitable to every level of human
evolution.

Fundamentally there are four levels of consciousness on each
of which the nature of the practice changes: the waking state,
transcendental consciousness, cosmic consciousness and God-
consciousness. Every teaching of the Bhagavad-Gita has its application on each of these planes of development. Every expression
must therefore be interpreted in four different ways to explain,
both in theory and in practice, the ascending progression of the
discourse on each of these four different levels. Thus it is obvious
that the Bhagavad-Gita as a whole must also be interpreted in
four different ways so that the whole path of God-realization
may be explained clearly.

As the Bhagavad-Gita has not yet been interpreted in this
manner, the true message of the scripture has remained dormant.
It is highly important that these four commentaries should be
written, not only to do justice to the scripture but also to present
a straight path to the seeker and bring him the profound wisdom
of this practical philosophy.

Thorough knowledge of any subject requires that its validity be substantiated by the criteria provided by the six systems of Indian philosophy: Nyaya, Vaisheshika, Sankhya, Yoga, Karma Mimansa and Vedanta.

In order to be complete, every aspect of the theory and practice at any stage of development must be verifiable by all these six systems simultaneously. It follows therefore that six interpretations of each of the four commentaries mentioned above are necessary to bring to light the complete significance of the Bhagavad-Gita.

The present commentary should be regarded as a general basis for these twenty-four commentaries. If time allows, these commentaries will be written. But because the world is in such urgent need of the basic principle of spiritual development, it has been thought necessary to bring out the present commentary without further loss of time.

It will be of interest to the reader to know that this commentary is being brought out only after the technique has been verified in the lives of thousands of people of different nationalities throughout the world, under the auspices of the Spiritual Regeneration Movement founded with the sole purpose of spiritually regenerating the lives of all men in every part of the world. It presents a truth that is timeless and universal, a truth of life equally suited to all men, irrespective of differences of faith, culture or nationality.

The overall conception of this commentary is supplementary to the unique vision and profound wisdom of the great Shankara, as set forth in his Gita-Bhashya. The wisdom is a gift from Guru Deva. All glory to Him! It presents the Light of Life and sets the stream of life to find its fulfilment in the ocean of eternal Being, in devotion to God and in the bliss of God-consciousness.

May every man make use of the practical wisdom given in the 45th verse of the second chapter and thereby glorify all aspects of his life and gain eternal freedom in divine consciousness.

CHAPTER I

A VISION OF THE TEACHING IN CHAPTER 1

Verse 1. The chapter opens with a question that demands detailed knowledge of the battlefield of life and the whole range of human evolution.

Verse 2. The answer begins with words that can be interpreted to explain the whole philosophy of the integration of life: not only the philosophy of Yoga, or Divine Union, but all the six systems of Indian philosophy, of which Yoga is only one. The most systematic knowledge of the whole range of life and evolution is here presented in one verse.

Verse 3. The necessity for recognizing that opposing forces on the battlefield of life are one's own creation.

Verses 4-6. An account of the forces that support good.

Verses 7-11. An account of the forces that support evil.

Verses 12, 13. Evil rejoices in challenging good.

Verses 14-19. Good responds to the challenge of evil.

Verses 20-24. The seeker of Truth takes his stand between the opposing forces of good and evil.

Verse 25. His consciousness is raised by a wave of love divinely inspired.

Verses 26-8. He sees the reality of the battlefield of life; he sees the conflict of opposing forces as the very core of life.

Verses 29-46. He probes deep and finds sixteen fundamental problems that form the basis of all conflicts. He seeks for a solution so that life may be lived free from problems.

Verse 47. His appreciation of the fundamental problems inherent in life is so intense that he becomes completely identified with them. He stands silent, deeply absorbed, seeking for a solution on the level of impossibility, where no solution exists.

This is the most extreme situation that could confront a seeker of Truth. Resolving this extreme situation, the Scripture of Divine Union provides one simple solution to all problems in life.

THIS chapter prepares the ground and sets the scene for the glorious dialogue of the Lord's Song, the Bhagavad-Gita. Although it does not contain the actual discourse of the Lord, which really begins in the second chapter, it presents the basic problems of life and gives Lord Krishna the chance to propound the philosophy and practice which enable man to live his life free from suffering. It is of great value for its contribution to the science of living.

It serves as a petition from the representative of human kind to the Incarnation of the Divine – a petition to say that, even though we try our best to live a life of righteousness, suffering does not appear to leave us. The demand is : give us a life free from suffering.

There is one short sentence in this chapter spoken by Lord Krishna to Arjuna on the battlefield. The first word that falls from the lips of the Lord fills Arjuna with love and raises his heart to the elevated plane of his mind. Arjuna's heart and mind, thus established on a high level of alertness, gain a state of such self-sufficiency that communication between them is almost lost, and with it is lost the spur to activity. But inwardly Arjuna's consciousness is raised to that high level of suspension which purifies his heart and mind of all stain and enables him to receive, within a short time, the wisdom of the Absolute, the time-less message of life for the good of all.

Duryodhana, seeing his own army and the army opposing it drawn up on the battlefield, gives the signal for battle. And Arjuna, the greatest archer of his time, thoughtful and conscientious, resolved to oppose evil yet overflowing with a wave of love, visualizes the consequences of war and reaches a state of suspension between the dictates of his heart and mind. This situation, where consciousness is in a state of suspension, where both the mind and the heart are on the highest level of alertness, provides the ideal occasion for the divine intelligence to overtake and shape the destiny of man.

Life is a battlefield of opposing forces. He who, like Arjuna, has recourse to divine intelligence receives the light and shares the cosmic purpose of fulfilment both for himself and others. But he who is trapped by temptation, like Duryodhana, becomes a drag upon life; he retards his own evolution and also hinders the progress of others.

This chapter presents the mechanics of nature and reveals the fundamentals of life and society. While remaining on the human level, it portrays the heights of human consciousness through which the Divine descends on earth. It provides a firm foundation for the edifice of Lord Krishna's teaching – the wisdom of eternal freedom in life.

The chapter opens with Dhritarashtra in his royal palace at Hastinapur asking Sanjaya to tell him about the battle.

VERSE 1

धृतराष्ट्र उवाच।

धर्मक्षेत्रे कुरुक्षेत्रे समवेता युयुत्सवः॥
मामकाः पाण्डवाश्चैव किमकुर्वत सञ्जय॥१॥

Dhritarashtra said:

Assembled on the field of Dharma,
O Sanjaya, on the field of the
Kurus, eager to fight, what did
my people and the Pandavas do?

'Dharma' is that invincible power of nature which upholds existence. It maintains evolution and forms the very basis of cosmic life. It supports all that is helpful for evolution and discourages all that is opposed to it.

Dharma is that which promotes worldly prosperity and

spiritual freedom. In order to understand the role of dharma in life, we have to consider the mechanics of evolution.

When life evolves from one state to another, the first state is dissolved and the second brought into existence. In other words, the process of evolution is carried out under the influence of two opposing forces – one to destroy the first state and the other to give rise to a second state. These creative and destructive forces working in harmony with one another maintain life and spin the wheel of evolution. Dharma maintains equilibrium between them. By maintaining equilibrium between opposing cosmic forces, dharma safeguards existence and upholds the path of evolution, the path of righteousness.

Man's life is so highly evolved that he enjoys freedom of action in nature. This enables him to live in any way he desires, either for good or for evil. As he behaves, so he receives. When the good increases in life and the positive forces tend to overbalance the normal state of existence, then the process of dharma, restoring equilibrium, results in feelings of happiness in the heart and satisfaction in the mind. In the same way, when evil increases in life and the negative forces predominate, the power of dharma, restoring the balance, produces sensations of pain and suffering.

Life is as we want it – either suffering or joy. When we allow the positive and negative forces to remain in their normal state of equilibrium, we live through normal periods of life. Assisting the growth of negative forces results in suffering; when we help the positive forces to increase we share the joy of life. 'As you sow, so shall you reap', expresses the role of dharma in practical life.

Calamities, crises and catastrophes in a community or country are caused by the increase of negatives forces resulting from the evil deeds of a majority of their people. A high degree of concentration of negative forces, without positive forces to balance them, ends in suffering and destruction of life. Similarly, a high degree of concentration of positive forces fails to maintain life in its normal state. The life of an individual under the influence of increasing positive forces enters into a field of increasing happiness and is eventually transformed into bliss-consciousness, in which state it gains the status of cosmic existence, eternal life.

In this way, we find that the increase of negative forces ends in passivity or extinction of life, whereas the increase of positive forces results in life eternal. Our individual life moves backwards and forwards automatically as we direct it under the influence of dharma. Positive and negative forces, as we develop them, play their role on the field of dharma and shape the destiny of life.

The two armies of the Kauravas and Pandavas on the battlefield of Kurukshetra represent the negative and positive forces on the field of dharma. This is what made Dhritarashtra say : 'Assembled on the field of Dharma, on the field of the Kurus.'

Dhritarashtra, as an old experienced head of the royal family, knows that the battlefield of Kurukshetra lying within the Dharmakshetra, the land between the rivers Yamuna and Saraswati, always maintains its sanctity and brings victory to the righteous.

He is anxious to hear details of the happenings and curious to find out whether the good influence of the land has had any effect on the destructive tendencies of his evil-minded sons; or whether it stimulated the righteousness of the Pandavas and encouraged them to forgive the evildoers.

This is the only time that Dhritarashtra speaks in the text of the Bhagavad-Gita. He only appears in order to ask this question.

The 'Kurus' are the members of the Kuru family, a leading clan of the time.

'The field of the Kurus' is a vast plain near Hastinapur in the neighbourhood of Delhi. As it belonged to the Kurus at the time of this battle it is called Kurukshetra.

'My people and the Pandavas': Dhritarashtra was the blind king of the Kuru family. His younger brother Pandu was managing the affairs of the kingdom for him. When Pandu died, Dhritarashtra wanted to give the reins of the kingdom to Yudhishthira, the eldest of the five sons of Pandu, who was called Dharmaraj, the embodiment of righteousness, for his noble qualities; but Duryodhana, the eldest of the hundred evil-minded sons of Dhritarashtra, by trick and treachery secured the throne for himself and began attempting to destroy Yudhishthira and his four brothers.

Lord Krishna, as head of the Yadava clan, tried to bring about a reconciliation between the cousins; but when all his attempts failed and the treachery of Duryodhana continued and increased, war between the Kauravas and Pandavas became inevitable. It brought kings and warriors from all over the globe to take sides, according to the level of their consciousness, with the righteous Pandavas or the evil-minded Kauravas. The good and evil of the whole world formed the two armies. Lord Krishna's main mission, which was to destroy evil and give protection to righteousness, had been simplified.

'Sanjaya' is the charioteer of the blind king Dhritarashtra. The word, however, means one who has conquered the senses and the mind. Sanjaya was asked to narrate the details of the battle because he was clairvoyant and clairaudient and at the same time impartial. The whole of the Bhagavad-Gita is Sanjaya's answer to Dhritarashtra.

VERSE 2

सञ्जय उवाच ।
दृष्ट्वा तु पाण्डवानीकं व्यूढं दुर्योधनस्तदा ॥
आचार्यमुपसङ्गम्य राजा वचनमब्रवीत् ॥२॥

Sanjaya said:

Then Duryodhana the prince, seeing
the army of the Pandavas drawn up
in battle array, approached his
master and spoke these words:

'Master' is one who understands the meaning of the scriptures, teaches it to others and practises the teaching[1] himself. The master here is Dronacharya, who had taught the art of war to both Kauravas and Pandavas.

It is a crucial moment, so it is natural for Duryodhana to approach his master, Dronacharya, for blessings and strength.

1. See Appendix: The Six Systems of Indian Philosophy.

VERSE 3

पश्यैतां पाण्डुपुत्राणामाचार्य महतीं चमूम् ॥
व्यूढां द्रुपदपुत्रेण तव शिष्येण धीमता ॥३॥

Behold, O Master, this great army of
the sons of Pandu, arrayed by your wise
pupil, the son of Drupada.

'The son of Drupada', Dhrishtadyumna, is the commander-in-chief of the Pandavas' army.

Duryodhana points out to his master that the opposing army is certainly large and powerful but that this does not matter because his own army is graced by the master, while the other is supported only by the disciple. Although wise, he remains after all a disciple, and since he is so ready to fight against his master, his morale will be weak and his strength will fail him. At the same time, by saying 'your wise pupil', Duryodhana creates an effect to excite the master's mind against the disciple who has organized the front against him.

VERSE 4

अत्र शूरा महेष्वासा भीमार्जुनसमा युधि ॥
युयुधानो विराटश्च द्रुपदश्च महारथः ॥४॥

Here are men of valour , mighty
archers, the equals of Bhima and
Arjuna in battle – Yuyudhana,
Virata and Drupada, the maharathi.

'Bhima' is the second son of Pandu, the mightiest warrior of the Pandavas' army and virtually in control of it, even though the office of commander-in-chief is held by Dhrishtadyumna.

'Arjuna', the hero of the Mahabharata, is the third son of
Pandu. He is the greatest archer of his time and a close friend of
Lord Krishna.

'Maharathi' means a great warrior proficient in military
science who, single-handed, can fight ten thousand archers.

'Yuyudhana' is Lord Krishna's charioteer, also called Satyaki.

'Virata' is the prince in whose territory the Pandavas lived for
some time in disguise after losing a dice-match with Duryodhana.

VERSE 5

धृष्टकेतुश्चेकितानः काशिराजश्च वीर्यवान् ॥
पुरुजित् कुन्तिभोजश्च शैब्यश्च नरपुङ्गवः ॥५॥

Dhrishtaketu, Chekitana and the
valiant king of Kashi, also Purujit,
Kuntibhoja and Shaibya, chief among
men.

'Dhrishtaketu' is the king of the Chedis.

'Chekitana' is a famous warrior in the army of the Pandavas.

'Purujit' and 'Kuntibhoja' are two brothers.

'Shaibya' is a king of the Shibi tribe.

VERSE 6

युधामन्युश्च विक्रान्त उत्तमौजाश्च वीर्यवान् ॥
सौभद्रो द्रौपदेयाश्च सर्व एव महारथाः ॥६॥

Yudhamanyu, the brave; the
valiant Uttamauja; also the son
of Subhadra and the sons of Draupadi —
all of them maharathis.

Duryodhana seems to accomplish several aims in naming these
great warriors in the opposing army. It strengthens his own

mind, awakens a deep sense of responsibility in the mind of his master and produces alertness in all those who are listening to him.

Having created these effects, this atmosphere, Duryodhana, in the following verse, draws the attention of his master to the great heroes of his own army.

VERSE 7

अस्माकं तु विशिष्टा ये तान्निबोध द्विजोत्तम ॥
नायका मम सैन्यस्य संज्ञार्थं तान् ब्रवीमि ते ॥७॥

Know well, O noblest of the twice-born,
those who are pre-eminent among us. I
speak to you of the leaders of my army
that you may know them.

'Twice-born' is a term that Duryodhana uses in addressing the master, Dronacharya. This is to flatter him and at the same time to arouse in him a sense of responsibility, so that he shall remain true to the cause that he has undertaken.

The term 'twice-born' is generally used for one born in a brahmin family, although other castes are also eligible for the ceremony of purification according to Vedic rites.

A brahmin is said to be twice-born because after his birth, when he is about eight years old, he undergoes a Vedic ceremony of purification, and this qualifies him for the study of the Vedas – the main function of a brahmin. Thus the ceremony is referred to as the second birth.

This second birth is important in life because it gives a man, born of flesh, entry into the field of spirit. This is the main purpose of the study of the Vedas, which opens the door to the inner kingdom of man and enables him to see the light of God.

By recalling to his master the names of the heroes of his army, Duryodhana reviews his own strength and creates an awareness of the mighty power which belongs to him and to everyone who is there to support him.

VERSE 8

भवान् भीष्मश्च कर्णश्च कृपश्च समितिञ्जयः ।।
अश्वत्थामा विकर्णश्च सौमदत्तिर्जयद्रथः ।।८।।

Thyself and Bhishma and Karna
and Kripa, victor in battle;
Ashvatthama and Vikarna and
also the son of Somadatta.

'Bhishma' is the grandsire (grandfather's step-brother) of both the
Kauravas and Pandavas. He brought up Dhritarashtra and
Pandu. He is the most experienced of all the assembled warriors.
On him, Duryodhana chiefly relies.
    'Karna' is half-brother to Arjuna.
    'Kripa' is the brother-in-law of Dronacharya.
    'Ashvatthama' is the son of Dronacharya.
    'Vikarna' is the third of the hundred sons of Dhritarashtra.
    'Somadatta' is the king of the Bahikas.

VERSE 9

अन्ये च बहवः शूराः मदर्थे त्यक्तजीविताः ।।
नानाशस्त्रप्रहरणाः सर्वे युद्धविशारदाः ।।९।।

And many other heroes there are,
armed with various weapons, all
skilled in warfare, who have
risked their lives for me.

Having recounted the names of the heroes of his own army,
Duryodhana stresses their might and in the following verse com-
pares the strength of the two sides.

VERSE 10

अपर्याप्तं तदस्माकम् बलं भीष्माभिरक्षितम् ॥
पर्याप्तं त्विदमेतेषां बलं भीसाभिरक्षितम् ॥१०॥

Unlimited is that army of ours,
commanded by Bhishma, whereas this
their army commanded by Bhima is
limited.

Duryodhana had to rouse his own commander, Bhishma, against
the mighty Bhima, chief of the Pandavas' army. At the same
time he reminded Bhishma that, as commander, victory or defeat
was his responsibility.

Having proclaimed that he is more powerful than his opponent,
Duryodhana, in the following verse, pronounces his final order
of battle.

VERSE 11

अयनेषु च सर्वेषु यथाभागमवस्थिताः ॥
भीष्ममेवाभिरक्षन्तु भवन्तः सर्व एव हि ॥११॥

Therefore, stationed in your
respective positions on all
fronts, support Bhishma alone,
all of you!

This verse brings out Duryodhana's shrewdness. He knows that
most of the warriors assembled on his side are not there primarily
for his sake but because of their love for Bhishma. This is why
he speaks as he does; and by so doing he wins their sympathy
and confidence along with that of Bhishma.

VERSE 12

तस्य संजनयन्हर्षं कुरुवृद्धः पितामहः ॥
सिंहनादं विनद्योच्चैः शङ्खं दध्मौ प्रतापवान् ॥१२॥

The aged Kuru, the glorious grandsire
(Bhishma), gave a loud roar like a
lion and blew his conch, gladdening
the heart of Duryodhana.

Having heard the words of Duryodhana, Bhishma, encouraging
him, begins to give the signal for battle.

The following verse describes how the whole army of Duryodhana joined Bhishma in making an uproar to show their
readiness to fight.

VERSE 13

ततः शङ्खाश्च भेर्यश्च पणवानकगोमुखाः ॥
सहसैवाभ्यहन्यन्त स शब्दस्तुमुलोऽभवत् ॥१३॥

Then quite suddenly conches,
horns, kettledrums, tabors and
drums blared forth, and the sound
was tumultuous.

'Quite suddenly' gives expression to the way in which nature
functions. Nature ensures great flexibility for the growth of good
or evil in the atmosphere. But when an influence grows beyond
elastic limits, nature will no longer sustain it; suddenly the
breaking-point is reached. The sudden burst of the lion roar of
Bhishma and the tumultuous noise produced by the whole army
symbolized the great cry of nature announcing the breaking-

point of the immeasurable evil that Duryodhana and his supporters had accumulated for themselves.

Wars in history have resulted from the cumulative effect of
aggression on the innocent; individuals continue to oppress
others, not knowing that aggression is growing in the atmosphere,
eventually to break upon them as their own disaster. One reaps
the consequences of one's own actions.

The following verses describe the effect of this upon the opposing army.

VERSE 14

ततः श्वेतैर्हयैर्युक्ते महति स्यन्दने स्थितौ ॥
माधवः पाण्डवश्चैव दिव्यौ शङ्खौ प्रदध्मतुः ॥१४॥

Then, seated in a great chariot
yoked to white horses, Madhava
(Lord Krishna) and the son of
Pandu (Arjuna) also blew their
glorious conches.

In this verse the word 'then' has a special significance, for it
shows that the Pandavas – Arjuna and his party – are not taking
the lead in the battle but are only responding to the Kauravas'
actions.

This is the natural behaviour of righteous people – they are
never aggressive. If they appear to be so, they are only playing
their role as instruments of the divine plan. The Pandavas are
challenged, and they have to accept the invitation as it comes;
but they do not give the first signal for war. Only when they
have received the signal from the other side are they obliged to
answer it. And when they do answer, their reply is more powerful
because it has the power of righteousness behind it.

The word 'chariot' has a special metaphysical connotation. The
'chariot' is the physiological structure, the body. It stands on the
battlefield of life as a vehicle for the natural process of evolution.

The senses are the horses to which the body-chariot is yoked.

'Yoked to white horses': 'white' symbolizes 'sattva', or purity, meaning thereby that the chariot was driven under the influence of purity or righteousness. When the Self guides, the body moves under the influence of sattva. Lord Krishna symbolizes the Self, and the chariot He drives must be yoked to white horses. The very appearance of the chariot expresses its purpose. It stands and moves to safeguard and protect purity and righteousness.

'Madhava' means Lord of fortune and also slayer of the demon Madhu. The use of this name indicates Lord Krishna's power over nature. It indicates that He will prove to be the Lord of fortune to those who are supporting positive forces and the slayer of demons to those who are promoting evil. Lord Krishna stands neutral between the two armies, blowing His conch to proclaim that He is there for anyone to derive advantage from His presence.

VERSE 15

पाञ्चजन्यं हृषीकेशो देवदत्तं धनञ्जयः ॥
पोण्ड्रं दध्मौ महाशङ्खं भीमकर्मा वृकोदरः ॥१५॥

Hrishikesha (Lord Krishna) blew
Panchajanya, Dhananjaya (Arjuna)
blew Devadatta, Bhima of powerful
deeds blew his great conch Paundra.

'Hrishikesha' has two meanings, according to the two different ways in which the word may be derived from the root. It means the Lord of the senses and also one with long hair. Both meanings are significant. Long hair has to do with control of the senses. Cutting the hair produces some subtle energy which tends to release the senses from control. So the word reveals not only the appearance of Lord Krishna on the battlefield but also the inner strength of the charioteer who, being the Lord of the senses, can control any situation.

'Panchajanya' is the conch made from the bone of the demon Panchajana.

'Devadatta' means given by God – this conch was received by Arjuna from his divine Father, Indra.

'Dhananjaya' means the winner of wealth, Arjuna.

The words 'Hrishikesha blew Panchajanya' reveal many significant points. They convey first that Lord Krishna's breath was absorbed by the demon element in the conch which produced the sound. This left Lord Krishna neutral in the battle, as He had promised.

Lord Krishna was revered both by the Kauravas and the Pandavas. He was approached for help at the same time both by Arjuna and Duryodhana, when each was preparing for war. As Lord Krishna could not say yes to either in the presence of the other, He resolved the situation by asking them to decide between themselves.

Lord Krishna said : 'I will be on one side, and my army will be on the other, but I shall not fight, though my army will. Now decide between yourselves who would like to have me and who would like my army.'

The first choice was given to Duryodhana, who preferred to take the army. Lord Krishna thus came out to help Arjuna, but as He had promised not to fight He became Arjuna's charioteer and guided the destiny of battle.

The Lord of the senses blowing the signal for war through the demon's conch has a further meaning. It indicates that Lord Krishna created a powerful demoniac force against the devilish Kauravas. The reason is that the force of righteousness is always positive. It is always creative and constructive; it cannot destroy. Destruction can be brought about only by negatives forces. Because they had the power of righteousness, it was hard for the Pandavas to destroy the Kauravas. So Lord Krishna, through the sound of Panchajanya, excited the negative powers in all those present in both armies. The excitement of the negative forces in the Pandavas' army gave that army much more power to destroy evil because of the support from the great power of righteousness, whereas the excitement of the negative forces in the Kauravas' army hastened their destruction owing to an over-

concentrated negative element without the support of any positive force.

There is yet another implication. Lord Krishna blew Panchajanya to declare aloud that the Pandavas' response to the war
signal did not belong to their righteousness. It was only the
resonance of the devilish uproar of the Kauravas echoing from
Panchajanya. It was a devil echoing the voice of a devil, and if
there was anything original in the sound, it was Panchajanya's
sigh for the pain and iniquities which the Pandavas had suffered
for many long years under the Kauravas' oppression.

The Lord of the senses did not use His senses : He only breathed
out through Panchajanya. The occasion was too far beneath the
divinity of Lord Krishna for Him to respond. The Lord of the
senses is neutral, ever established in His eternal state of Being,
while all things around Him react to the prevailing atmosphere.
As the Lord of the senses, His status transcends the highest
righteousness, and the Kauravas were on the lowest level of evil.
It was because of the great difference between Lord Krishna's
status and the level of the Kauravas' consciousness that He
promised at the beginning that He would not fight in the battle.

All these implications are contained in the first phrase of this
verse. It is the glory of Vyasa, the sage of enlightened vision who
wrote down the Bhagavad-Gita, that the implications of any one
word in it are inexhaustible.

The recounting of the names of warriors and of the conches
that they blew continues through the next three verses.

VERSE 16

अनन्तविजयं राजा कुन्तीपुत्रो युधिष्ठिरः ।।
नकुलः सहदेवश्च सुघोषमणिपुष्पकौ ।।१६।।

Prince Yudhishthira, the son of
Kunti, blew his conch Anantavijaya;
Nakula and Sahadeva blew Sughosha
and Manipushpaka.

'Kunti' is the mother of the five Pandavas, the sons of Pandu.
'Yudhishthira' is the eldest of the five Pandavas.
'Nakula' is the fourth, skilled in the art of training horses.
'Sahadeva' is the fifth and youngest, skilled in the management
of cattle.
'Anantavijaya' means eternal victory.
'Sughosha' means sweet-toned.
'Manipushpaka' means gem-flowered.

VERSE 17

काश्यश्च परमेष्वासः शिखण्डी च महारथः ॥
धृष्टद्युम्नो विराटश्च सात्यकिश्चापराजितः ॥१७॥

The King of Kashi, the great archer,
and Shikhandi, the maharathi, Dhrishtadyumna
and Virata and Satyaki, the unsubdued.

VERSE 18

द्रुपदो द्रौपदेयाश्च सर्वशः पृथिवीपते ॥
सौभद्रश्च महाबाहुः शङ्खान्दध्मुः पृथक् पृथक् ॥१८॥

Drupada, as well as the sons of
Draupadi, and the mighty-armed son
of Subhadra, O Lord of earth, all
blew their different conches.

'O Lord of earth': Sanjaya is addressing Dhritarashtra, the king.

VERSE 19

स घोषो धार्तराष्ट्राणां हृदयानि व्यदारयत् ॥
नभश्च पृथिवीञ्चैव तुमुलोऽभ्यनुनादयन् ॥१६॥

That tumultuous uproar, reverberating
through earth and sky, rent the hearts
of Dhritarashtra's men.

The Pandavas announced their readiness for war by the blowing
of the conches, which thrilled the air and vibrated through everything in earth and sky. A stir was created in the universe.

A cosmic process is revealed here. The evil doings of the
Kauravas had saturated the atmosphere and had, as it were, pervaded everything with an evil influence. This evil influence was
shaken when righteousness, having gained strength, rose to accept
its challenge. The force of destruction in the world was to be
destroyed by the rising wave of life.

VERSE 20

अथ व्यवस्थितान् दृष्ट्वा धार्तराष्ट्रान् कपिध्वजः ॥
प्रवृत्ते शस्त्रसम्पाते धनुरुद्यम्य पाण्डवः ॥२०॥

Then, seeing the sons of Dhritarashtra
drawn up in battle order, as missiles
were about to fly, the son of Pandu
(Arjuna), whose banner bore the image
of Hanuman, took up his bow.

'The sons of Dhritarashtra drawn up in battle order' represents
evil prepared to annihilate righteousness.

When Arjuna 'took up his bow', he expressed the readiness of
righteousness to resist evil and restore harmony on earth.

This is a cosmic process. Whenever evil arises and threatens to overtake life, nature moves to balance it. A wave of righteousness rises to neutralize the evil. Those who are the medium through which vice enters the world perish from the rise of such a wave, and those who have borne suffering under the influence of evil, becoming the instrument of righteousness, begin to enjoy.

'Banner bore the image of Hanuman': Hanuman symbolizes devotion and service to the supreme Lord. Arjuna's life was dedicated to the divine cause. His skill and art of archery were useful for the cause of righteousness. Therefore his chariot had a sign which bore the image of Hanuman.

VERSE 21

हृषीकेशं तदा वाक्यमिदमाह महीपते ॥
सेनयोरुभयोर्मध्ये रथं स्थापय मेऽच्युत ॥२१॥

Then, O Lord of earth, he spoke these
words to Hrishikesha (Lord Krishna):
Draw up my chariot between the two armies,
O Achyuta.

'Lord of earth': through this expression Sanjaya draws Dhritarashtra's attention to the fact that he had the influence to intervene and stop the two armies from involving themselves in destruction. Already in verse 18 Sanjaya has addressed Dhritarashtra as 'Lord of earth'. The repeated expression indicates that he wants to make Dhritarashtra see the seriousness of the situation – both the armies have declared their readiness to fight, and now Arjuna is moving to the forefront. Every moment is vital and significant. The destruction seems inevitable.

'Achyuta' means immovable. Arjuna calls Lord Krishna 'Achyuta'. He wants the immovable to start moving for him! 'Achyuta' also means one who has never fallen. Thereby Arjuna wants to suggest to Lord Krishna that He will never fail him.

Arjuna asks for the chariot to be placed between the two

armies, so that both himself and Lord Krishna shall be there. By
placing Lord Krishna midway, Arjuna desires to present a picture
on the screen of time – absolute Being present between the opposing forces – a picture expressing the inner mechanics of nature
which will explain the fundamentals of life and clarify the basic
principles of war and peace for the generations to come.

Lord Krishna symbolizes the absolute Being, which is the field
of dharma and which, by remaining between the negative and
positive powers in nature, balances them. Although remaining
neutral, It always supports righteousness. Although Lord Krishna
is neutral, He is with Arjuna, who enjoys His support.

In the following verse Arjuna explains why he himself wishes
to be placed between the two armies.

VERSE 22

यावदेतान्निरीक्षेऽहं योद्धुकामानवस्थितान् ।
कैर्मया सह योद्धव्यमस्मिन्रणसमुद्यमे ।।२२।।

So that I may observe those who stand
here eager for battle and know with whom
I should fight in this toil of war.

The skill of battle lies first in locating the strategic points of the
enemy line.

Arjuna's power of concentration was so great that if he correctly located the positions of the enemy leaders his arrows would
fly straight at them.

'Eager for battle' shows that Arjuna wanted carefully to pick
off only those who were eager for battle. He would not concern
himself with those who were not eager to fight. This illustrates
Arjuna's bravery and self-confidence; it also expresses his readiness for battle.

VERSE 23

योत्स्यमानानवेक्षेऽहं य एतेऽत्र समागताः ॥
धार्तराष्ट्रस्य दुर्बुद्धेर्युद्धे प्रियचिकीर्षवः ॥२३॥

Let me look on those who are assembled
here ready to fight, eager to accomplish
in battle what is dear to the evil-minded
son of Dhritarashtra.

The tone of this verse shows the strength of Arjuna's indignation
against the evil which the supporters of Duryodhana wish to
accomplish by fighting. The contempt is so great that Arjuna
does not even speak Duryodhana's name – and by naming his
father, Dhritarashtra, he brings shame on him also.

Arjuna is sure of his position, sure that he is making a stand
to safeguard virtue and resist corruption. He does not think that
all those assembled in the opposing army are evil in themselves,
but they are supporters of evil.

In verse 21 Sanjaya addressed Dhritarashtra as 'Lord of earth',
yet here he reports Arjuna's insinuation that Dhritarashtra is
being brought to shame by the actions of his sons. This shows
that, as father of his evil-minded sons, Dhritarashtra is ultimately
responsible for the threatened destruction of the whole community.

When the collective karma (action) threatens national destruction, it is beyond the power of the individual to check it; this is
even more true when it has reached the ultimate limit and is
about to break into catastrophe. Therefore it is wise for people
of every generation to be cautious and not to tolerate an increase
of wrong-doing in their surroundings, but to nip it in the bud.
For it is the cumulative influence of these small wrongs done by
individuals in their own little spheres of activity that produces
national and international tensions and leads to catastrophe.

There is a way of transcendental meditation,[2] taught by Lord

2. See II, 45 and Appendix.

Krishna, to be practised by each individual daily in order to infuse the transcendental divine consciousness into his own mind,
so that by nature man may become freed from wrong tendencies
and may become the source of good influence in all spheres of life.

Had Dhritarashtra, as a king, educated his sons in the art of
transcending and gaining divine consciousness, the royal family
of the Kauravas would not have been the cause of this great war,
which brought disaster on the civilization of the time.

This is a message which should be heeded in every generation.
It is for the world's rulers and for those in public life, who have
the welfare of mankind at heart, to organize education in such a
way that everyone has an opportunity of learning how to cultivate divine consciousness. No generation should be allowed to
leave behind an evil influence, the accumulated consequences of
which will be reaped by future generations.

VERSE 24

सञ्जय उवाच ।
एवमुक्तो हृषीकेशो गुडाकेशेन भारत ॥
सेनयोरुभयोर्मध्ये स्थापयित्वा रथोत्तमम् ॥२४॥

Sanjaya said:

*O Bharata, thus invoked by Gudakesha
(Arjuna), Hrishikesha (Lord Krishna),
having drawn up the magnificent chariot
between the two armies,*

Sanjaya is reporting to Dhritarashtra what is happening on the
battlefield. Here he addresses him as 'Bharata', descendant of the
great king of Bharata – greater India.

Arjuna, the hero of the Mahabharata, drives out between the
two armies to see with whom he has to fight. Sanjaya here uses
the name Gudakesha to refer to him. This is to symbolize an
essential quality of Arjuna's, for Gudakesha means the Lord of
sleep, one who has mastery over sleep, over dullness of mind.

Arjuna's one-pointedness of mind is thus expressed. As an un-failing archer, Arjuna has a mind which is fully alive; Sanjaya uses the word Gudakesha to depict the character and quality of the hero.

Such is Vyasa's narrative skill; he uses exact and concise ex-pressions with great fullness of meaning to tell the story. It only needs a mind to understand them in order to enjoy his writings and derive the maximum from them.

Vyasa has used the adjective 'magnificent' to describe Arjuna's chariot. This one word, which in the Sanskrit text reads 'utta-mam', conveys a world of glory. It indicates magnificence, com-fort, stability, lightness and strength; in fact, all the qualities of a chariot that is designed to meet the fiercest enemy there could be. Again, the chariot is magnificent not only for its quality but also for its charioteer and the hero within it. Hrishikesha, the Lord of the senses, is the charioteer and Gudakesha, the con-queror of sleep, is the hero.

VERSE 25

भीष्मद्रोणप्रमुखतः सर्वेषां च महीक्षिताम् ।।
उवाच पार्थ पश्येतान्समवेतान् कुरूनिति ।।२५।।

Before Bhishma and Drona and all
the rulers of the earth, said:
Partha (Arjuna)! behold these
Kurus gathered together.

Lord Krishna had seen that Arjuna was outraged.[3] Anger is a great enemy;[4] it reduces one's strength. And his charioteer does not like to see Arjuna's strength waning. Lord Krishna is required to do something to restore Arjuna to his normal stature. But this alone will not suffice; something more is necessary to make Arjuna really strong. Anger in him indicates that he is not really strong, for anger is a sign of weakness. Lord Krishna knows that

3. See verse 23.   4. See III, 37, commentary.

Arjuna, although the greatest archer of his time, has not been given the real secret of warfare. He has been taught the art of archery, but he has not been trained to shoot his arrows while remaining firm in himself. If an archer shoots while he is angry, his anger will make him weak.

Arjuna has called Lord Krishna 'Achyuta',[5] which means firm and unmoved. This is what Lord Krishna has to teach Arjuna to be. But wisdom cannot be given to a man unless he asks for it and shows his readiness to receive it. It is therefore necessary for Lord Krishna to arouse in Arjuna the need and desire to learn.[6] It would have been demoralizing if Arjuna had been told on the battlefield that he needed to know the art of being firm. He had to recognize this for himself; only then could Lord Krishna help him. To produce the desired result in Arjuna, the Lord speaks one short sentence:

'Partha! behold these Kurus gathered together.' This is the first utterance of Lord Krishna in the Bhagavad-Gita, the first word of advice to Arjuna on the battlefield.

The miracle it produced in Arjuna has for centuries escaped the attention of practically every commentator, and in consequence Arjuna is portrayed as a confused mental wreck. A close study of the commentary on the following verses will reveal the true nature of Arjuna's condition.

Lord Krishna addresses Arjuna as 'Partha', the son of Pritha. With this expression He reminds Arjuna of his mother and thereby creates a warm wave of love in his heart, the warmth of love that connects son and mother. It is this tender bond of love that develops into all family and social relationships, that maintains a family, a society, a nation and a world.

Having created this wave of love in Arjuna's heart, Lord Krishna desires to strengthen it; and for this He says: 'behold these Kurus gathered together.' This quickens all the ways of the heart, where different relationships are held in different shades of love. Seeing all his dear ones 'together' in one glance, his whole heart swells with love.

5. See verse 21.   6. See II, 7.

VERSE 26

तत्रापश्यत् स्थितान् पार्थः पितॄनथ पितामहान् ॥
आचार्यान् मातुलान् भ्रातॄन् पुत्रान् पौत्रान् सखींस्तथा ॥२६॥

The son of Pritha (Arjuna) saw there
before him uncles and grandfathers,
teachers, maternal uncles, brothers,
sons and grandsons and many friends
as well.

'The son of Pritha saw' indicates that when Arjuna gazed on the
opposing army his vision was coloured by love and not by enmity
or bravery. Had he seen with the vision of the 'scorcher of
enemies', this is what he would have been called.

   This indicates the power of control that Lord Krishna possesses.
He said, 'Partha behold', and Arjuna became as a son before his
mother, full of love and reverence.

VERSE 27

श्वशुरान् सुहृदश्चैव सेनयोरुभयोरपि ॥
तान्समीक्ष्य स कौन्तेयः सर्वान्बन्धूनवस्थितान् ॥२७॥

Fathers-in-law and well-wishers also
in both the armies. Then that son
of Kunti (Arjuna), seeing all these
kinsmen thus present,

Arjuna stands up to behold his opponents but he fails to see
opponents; instead he sees his dear ones. This is because his vision
has been coloured with love by Lord Krishna's calling him Partha.
With this the whole scene takes a critical turn. Arjuna, who was

about to go into battle, is overtaken by pity, as the following
verses show.

VERSE 28

कृपयापरयाविष्टो विषीदन्निदमब्रवीत् ॥
दृष्ट्वेमं स्वजनं कृष्ण युयुत्सुं समुपस्थितम् ॥२८॥

Possessed by extreme compassion, spoke
this in grief: Seeing these my kinsmen,
O Krishna, gathered, eager to fight,

This verse presents the basis of the problems that Arjuna is going
to lay before Lord Krishna.

He expresses his thoughts aloud to Lord Krishna, who is close
at hand. One thinks aloud with someone who is close to one's
heart and mind and wise enough to further the thought. Lord
Krishna is like this to Arjuna. He can share his thoughts and
feelings and think intimately with Him.

'Possessed by extreme compassion' and 'kinsmen' indicate the
basic principle of 'grief'. It is born of the condition of the individual and his relationship with others.

This verse not only depicts Arjuna's condition but lays open
the fundamental principle of suffering in human society and
seeks a solution to it.

Compassion is among the most glorious qualities of the heart.
'Extreme compassion' expresses fullness of heart. But once disso-
ciated from the qualities of the mind, the heart as such can no
longer be effective in supporting action in life. Even good qualities
of heart or of mind fail to uphold life in the absence of coordination between them. This verse proclaims 'extreme compassion' as
the source of all the problems confronting Arjuna, a most
balanced man of noble character.

The whole discourse of Lord Krishna in the Bhagavad-Gita is
designed to give the wisdom of life and the technique of living
which enable man to live all the good qualities of life with full

coordination of heart and mind. By this wisdom and this technique the individual is raised to a high level of consciousness where he gains eternal contentment within himself. He lives a life in fulfilment, useful to himself and society. Such a life supports surrounding nature; all becomes harmonious, resulting in ideal relationships with others.

Here is the glory of the Bhagavad-Gita – it records for all time and for the use of all men the wisdom of life and the technique of living. So that everyone may live a life free from suffering, it selects the most noble character, Arjuna, leading the most balanced life, and places that life completely under the influence of the most cherished qualities of heart and mind. On this high level of glory and grace, where heart and mind are at their best, it locates the basic cause of all suffering at a point between the heart and mind. The heart is full of feeling, saturated with love; the mind is completely alert, full of the sense of righteousness and the call of duty. Both are at their full stature. No suffering can possibly touch either of them taken separately, but as the Upanishad says: 'Dvitiyad vai bhayam bhavati: Certainly fear is born of duality.' Whenever and wherever there is a sense of two, fear or suffering can exist.

Within man there is mind and there is heart. These, by their very existence as two, hold the possibility of suffering. When they are united, when there is harmony between a heart and mind full of righteousness and noble inspiration, suffering cannot arise. But when there is a lack of coordination or a conflict between them, suffering automatically results. Arjuna's 'grief' is born of the basic difference between the heart and the mind.

Religious scriptures prescribe a mode of conduct to save man from falling into error and suffering. They induce man to do good and to spurn evil.

The Bhagavad-Gita, the scripture of the eternal religion of realization, in its diagnosis of suffering is not satisfied by the rejection of evil or the acceptance of virtue alone; it finds that suffering can result even from two good qualities. For a life to be free from suffering, it is not enough for heart and mind to be free from the stain of sin and established in righteousness.

The Bhagavad-Gita undertakes to solve the problem of suffering completely. It locates the ultimate cause of suffering and provides a means to eliminate it. The seed of suffering in life is located in the duality inherent in the characteristic difference between the qualities of heart and mind. The Bhagavad-Gita therefore takes Arjuna, already most noble, sinless and most highly developed in both heart and mind, and sets him down in an environment which further stimulates his heart [7] and his mind.[8] As both continue to grow more active in their respective domains, the basic difference in their structure becomes greater. When heart and mind are both at their best, each is full in itself and is no longer concerned with the other; there is no link left between them. The heart, fully saturated with love, naturally becomes sufficient unto itself and oblivious to the decisions of the mind. Likewise, the mind becomes oblivious to the cry of the heart. Separately they are each in a state of fulfilment. But because there is no communication between them, both cease to contribute to activity in life. That is why Arjuna is in a state of suspension without activity.

Activity starts with the flow of desire. When the heart feels the lack of something and the mind responds to it, or when the mind feels the lack and the heart responds, then a stream of desire arises from between them and flows towards the object in view, engaging different faculties of heart, mind and body as well as the available material in the surroundings. This makes it clear that communication between heart and mind must exist for desire to arise. And if the flow of desire is in the direction of the natural current of evolution, it is further supported by the invisible influence of nature and will find fulfilment.

Arjuna is in a state where the mind and heart are held high in the fullness of their respective qualities with no link between them. In the fullness of heart and mind, where both are contented in themselves, neither feels the lack of anything, and hence there exists no room for desire to arise. Absence of desire leaves Arjuna in a state of suspension in which the entire personality loses its dynamic structure and is faced with seemingly insuperable problems whenever the need for action arises in any sphere of life.

Thus the Bhagavad-Gita portrays a situation in which life can

7. See verses 26–35.   8. See verses 36–46.

be full of problems, even while it is established in fulfilment of
heart and mind. By resolving such an extreme situation, it brings
to light the wisdom and technique of living life without suffering
at any level. It establishes that life must be without suffering.
No one should ever suffer in life: this is the teaching of the
Bhagavad-Gita.

Duality is the fundamental cause of suffering. But when the
entire field of life is dual in nature, how can life be free from
suffering? This has always been a serious problem of metaphysics
and indeed of practical life as well. The solution lies in the infusion into the field of duality of a non-dual element which blesses
man's life with a status unaffected by suffering, even while he
remains in the field where suffering is possible. This will be
appreciated as the discourse advances.

Arjuna starts placing his problems before Lord Krishna.

VERSE 29

सीदन्ति मम गात्राणि मुखं च परिशुष्यति ॥
वेपथुश्च शरीरे मे रोमहर्षश्च जायते ॥ २६॥

My limbs fail and my mouth is parched,
my body quivers and my hair stands on end.

A great strength of noted warriors lies in their concern for
their fellow men, which has moved them to become the saviours of
their societies. Arjuna was filled with a concern for others which
enabled him to accept the challenge of his time when evil threatened. Because this concern for others formed the basis of his
acceptance of battle, it comes as no surprise that the power of
love overwhelms his heart and brings it to fullness. In this state
of self-contentedness the heart becomes oblivious to the need of
the mind – the call of duty. Arjuna is caught between the power
of love and the call of duty. He finds he cannot yield to either.

The call of righteousness and the tide of love rising in the heart
– both are dear to him because life, as he understands it, is all
love of righteousness.

But as he is placed now, suspended between the heart and mind, he is not in a position to undertake activity. Even if, by some miracle, he tries to initiate action, he is faced with a terrible situation. If he follows the call of righteousness, he must rebel against love and kill all his dear ones assembled for battle. And if he follows the call of love, he must sacrifice the cause of righteousness and yield to evil. From this viewpoint we find that Arjuna is divided between the two forces which have so far been the essential components of his life. He stands like a child who is being called with love by his mother and at the same time is being summoned by his father from the other side. If he goes towards one, the other pulls him. He swings both ways. That is why he begins to feel shaken in body and mind.

When one is deeply absorbed in thinking, the attention no longer remains outside on the level of the senses, and the coordination of the body and mind becomes weak. If at this time the heart is not supported by the mind, that coordination is weakened still further. If this process goes far enough, the body does not function properly. This is why Arjuna felt his limbs failing, his mouth parched, his body quivering. His physical state indicates that the power of love is dominating Arjuna and challenging the call of duty by throwing his body out of balance. The consequences of a further rise in this power of love are described in the following verses.

VERSE 30

गाण्डीवं संसते हस्तात्त्वक्‌ चैव परिदह्यते ॥
न च शक्नोम्यवस्थातुं भ्रमतीव च मे मनः ॥३०॥

Gandiva (the bow) slips from my hand and
even my skin burns all over; I am unable
to stand and my mind seems to whirl.

'Gandiva slips from my hand': Arjuna's fast grip on Gandiva has been in response to the call of righteousness. His mind was

completely dominated by the call of duty, and it was this which
made him hold Gandiva fast. But now, after the wave of love
created by Lord Krishna, the power of love has filled his heart
and in its fullness equals the power of his mind. They balance
each other, and therefore the power of mind no longer remains
dominant. Consequently, his grip becomes loose, and Gandiva
slips from his hand. Never before had the bow slipped from
Arjuna's hand. The wave of love causes this to happen.

'My skin burns': Arjuna has been overwhelmed with the
power of love. The warmth of love is soothing and comforting.
What then burns his skin? We have seen that the power of
dharma upholds existence and evolution. As long as love is on the
level of dharma or on the path of righteousness, it helps evolution, supports life and is soothing and comforting. But when the
innocent power of love stands without supporting the path of
righteousness, it is influenced by negative forces and becomes a
means of destruction, misery and suffering. In thinking that he
could avoid fighting, Arjuna is deserting the cause of righteousness, and so he feels his skin burning in the warmth of love.

'Unable to stand': love with the power of righteousness makes
a man strong but without it leaves him weak. Arjuna has been
overcome with love, which threatens to overthrow the cause of
righteousness. Therefore it is no surprise that he feels weak,
'unable to stand'.

'Mind seems to whirl': Arjuna is overtaken by the qualities of
the heart. But Arjuna's mind is strong. It has the essential qualities of a brave man. Even when his heart is overwhelmed by the
force of love, his mind is active and alert. The alert mind puts
out a great force to change the course of the heart. It is as if
the car of Arjuna's life were being driven with great speed on the
road of love, and there came a great force of mind to reverse the
direction. This attempt at reversing the flow of the life-stream
produces the impression that his mind is whirling.

VERSE 31

निमित्तानि च पश्यामि विपरीतानि केशव ।।
न च श्रेयोऽनुपश्यामि हत्वा स्वजनमाहवे।।३१।।

And I see adverse omens, O Keshava (Lord
Khrishna), nor can I see good from killing
my kinsmen in battle.

Arjuna in this verse gives expression to the feeling of the whole
of nature at that perilous moment of war.

'Killing my kinsmen' is an expression which contains the cry
of both Arjuna's heart and mind. 'Killing' comes from the mind,
for it is dedicated to Truth and righteousness and the destruction
of evil. 'My kinsmen' is the cry of the heart. Arjuna's heart, full
of love, allows him to see his opponents only as his 'kinsmen' and
not as the aggressor and the enemy. Seeing them thus, he is right
in saying : 'nor can I see good from killing my kinsmen in battle.'

In his present state of deep concern, Arjuna feels love for all
his kinsmen standing before him and, at the same time, grief for
their destruction in battle. His heart is torn between these two
feelings. Deep within himself, immersed in feeling the situation
and its consequences, he visualizes 'adverse omens'. The cries of
anguish and the terrible sufferings that follow destruction in war
flash through his mind. Arjuna's vision of omens reveals the
purity of his heart and the deep state of concentration of his mind.

The future casts its image on the sanctuaries of pure hearts.

'Good' here means spiritual comfort. The Sanskrit word used
is *shreyas*, which means evolution or fulfilment – the security
and accomplishment that lies in spiritual freedom. Arjuna sees
that spiritual comfort does not lie in killing his kinsmen. But this
is the act that awaits him. Under the circumstances he finds he
can do nothing but reject all that could possibly be desired.

Verse 32

न कांक्षे विजयं कृष्ण न च राज्यं सुखानि च ॥
किं नो राज्येन गोविन्द किं भोगैर्जीवितेन वा ॥३२॥

I desire not victory, O Krishna, nor a
kingdom, nor pleasures. Of what avail
will a kingdom be to us, or enjoyments,
or even life, O Govinda?

Desire presents no problem if it is allowed to flow freely. Problems arise when a desire is checked or encounters resistance.
Arjuna's words express this fact. He challenges the validity of
victory, pleasures, kingdom and even life in which desire has no
chance of fulfilment.

The desire of a great man rises to support others and rejoices
in the happiness that others derive from such support.

Having found the cause of battle to be damaging to body,[9]
mind[10] and surroundings,[11] Arjuna now looks at the situation
from the point of view of usefulness to his own aims in life. He
finds that nothing in the outside world is of interest to him
personally because, as he sees life, it is for others. So, from this
point of view also, he sees no reason for fighting.

Arjuna raises his voice against the corrupting influences of a
kingdom, pleasure and power. He has seen in the case of Duryodhana how they can blind a man's vision and cause the destruction of a whole civilization.

In the previous verse Arjuna has said that he can see no good
from killing his kinsmen. Here he gives expression to the possible
advantages that could come from the battle and weighs them in
terms of their validity in life. This shows his presence of mind and
the unbiased manner in which he is analysing the situation. He
rejects the validity of victory, a kingdom and pleasures if they are
for selfish ends. He expresses not only indifference but positive

9. See verse 29.   10. See verse 30.   11. See verse 31.

aversion towards them. He makes it clear that 'even life' has no significance for him.

Arjuna uses the word 'us', which can imply either that he wants to verify his views with Lord Krishna, or that he is sure that Lord Krishna's views are in accord with his own.

'Govinda' means master of the senses. In using this word Arjuna is also silently suggesting that Lord Krishna, as master of the senses, naturally also has little use for the objects of the senses and the pleasures derived from them.

In his present state of deep contemplation, what Arjuna finds significant is a dedicated way of life. In the next verse he says clearly that his whole life is dedicated to others.

VERSE 33

येषामर्थे कांक्षितं नो राज्यं भोगाः सुखानि च ॥
त इमेऽवस्थिता युद्धे प्राणांस्त्यक्त्वा धनानि च ॥३३॥

*Those for whose sake we desire a
kingdom, enjoyments and comforts
are here on the battlefield, having
resigned their lives and riches.*

This brings to light the greatness of Arjuna's heart and mind. His vision is clear: he views the situation with a serene and deep insight. His logic is profound. His thought is balanced and noble. His feeling is for others: when he thinks, it is in terms of others; if he wants to fight and gain sovereignty, it is for the sake of others; if he wants to amass enjoyments and pleasures, it is for the sake of others; if he wants to live, it is for others. Such is his developed consciousness, devoid of any thought of self-interest. This is the status of truly great men – living, they live for others; dying, they die for others.

The question may be asked: If Arjuna's character shows such greatness of heart and mind, why does he come on to the battlefield prepared to fight? A close study of Arjuna's utterances reveals that he is bent upon resisting evil; he is not interested in killing people. He wants to destroy the evil without destroying the evil-doer. It is a noble ideal. His aim is to destroy the evil on earth, if possible without bringing down upon society the untold suffering and destruction of war. Only a man of such an ideal character can speak as does Arjuna in the next two verses.

VERSE 34

आचार्याः पितरः पुत्रास्तथैव च पितामहाः ॥
मातुलाः श्वशुराः पौत्राः श्यालाः संबन्धिनस्तथा ॥३४॥

Teachers, uncles, sons and likewise
grandfathers, maternal uncles, fathers-
in-law, grandsons, brothers-in-law and
other kinsmen.

This portrays the state of Arjuna's heart. It is full of love, full of life. From all sides he finds different channels of love pouring life into his heart and leaving it full. When love is full, life is full like the ocean. It is full like a silent ocean, for it ceases to flow in any direction. It just is. It is free from any desire. That is why Arjuna could only mention the names of relationships to portray the different fields of love and give expression to the condition of his heart.

This verse, coming in the midst of verses which express many problems, presents a vast field of life in love and silently proclaims that there are no problems in this field. The field of love is an innocent field of life. Problems arise when attachment[12] or detachment[13] overshadows pure love.

12. See verse 33.   13. See verse 35.

VERSE 35

एतान्न हन्तुमिन्छामि घ्नतोऽपि मधुसूदन ॥
अपि त्रैलोक्यराज्यस्य हेतो: किं नु महीकृते ॥३५॥

O Madhusudana (Lord Krishna), these
I do not wish to kill — though killed
myself — even for the sake of
sovereignty of the three worlds, how
much less for this world.

'Madhusudana' means the slayer of the demon Madhu. By using
this name, Arjuna suggests to Lord Krishna that, as the slayer of
the demon, He may rise to kill the Kauravas if He finds that they
are demoniacal; but as far as he himself is concerned, he finds
that they are dear relatives and noble elders whom he would do
anything to protect. Whatever the cost of letting them live, he
cannot think of killing them. Arjuna speaks as only a conscientious, deeply thoughtful and brave man will speak. This is his
character. He stands for principle. Nothing can tempt him to
deny the high ideals of life. That is why his thinking is so
uncompromising.

The words 'even for the sake of sovereignty of the three worlds'
indicate that Arjuna's vision was not restricted to the field of
man's life on earth. Only such a man as he could challenge the
value of sovereignty over the three worlds. Such is the height of
human consciousness which upholds Arjuna even at this hour
of his great concern.

VERSE 36

निहत्य धार्तराष्ट्रान्नः का प्रीतिः स्याज्जनादेन ॥
पापमेवाश्रयेदस्मान्हत्वैतानाततायिनः ॥३६॥

What happiness could come to us
from slaying the sons of Dhrita-
rashtra, O Janardana (Lord Krishna)?
Only sin would come upon us through
killing these aggressors.

This verse presents another change in Arjuna's vision. In the
opposing army, he has been seeing just his own kinsmen; now,
once again, they are the 'sons of Dhritarashtra', 'these aggressors'.
Arjuna has so far looked at the situation from the aspect of love
but has arrived at no solution to his problem. He therefore decides
to consider it from the mind – with discrimination and intuition
– yet cannot suddenly abandon the fullness of love in his heart.
Maintaining that fullness of heart, he begins to make more use
of his mind.

As he gives himself over to reason, the call of duty begins to
gain ground. With this his vision changes. He begins to see his
kinsmen as 'aggressors'; the reality begins to dawn. Seeing them
in this light, Arjuna asks : 'What happiness could come to us
from slaying the sons of Dhritarashtra?' And when he starts
thinking in these terms, he finds killing is sin.

The act of killing does not produce life-supporting influences
for anyone at any time. Killing is a sin for all time. No matter
who is killed, killing is sin. The pain and suffering caused in the
act of killing produce negative influences in creation, and the
reaction recoils on the killer. So Arjuna says : 'Only sin would
come upon us'.

The killing of aggressors is supposed to be a right action. The
aggressor's life is put to an end, and thereby he is prevented from
producing more negative influences for himself and others. But
this justification of killing arises from a completely different con-

sideration. The act of killing as such is sinful. And this is Arjuna's main concern here.

Arjuna can see killing as sin even when he is on the battlefield. This indicates that his mind is clear and his vision not obstructed either by feelings of the heart or by the call of duty. He is deep in thought, evaluating the situation from every side. Arjuna is at a high pitch of mental and emotional activity. Both his alertness of mind and fullness of heart are displayed in the innocent utterance of truth: 'Only sin would come upon us through killing these aggressors.'

The expressions: 'What happiness could come to us' and 'Only sin would come upon us' indicate that happiness and suffering are considered as well as sin and virtue. For suffering results from sin, and happiness from virtue.

Verse 37

तस्मान्नार्हा वयं हन्तुं धार्तराष्ट्रान् स्वबान्धवान् ॥
स्वजनं हि कथं हत्वा सुखिनः स्याम माधव ॥३७॥

Therefore it would not be right
for us to kill the sons of
Dhritarashtra, our own kinsmen.
How should we be happy after
killing our own people, O Madhava?

Arjuna's arguments have gone further. Previously it was only his 'wish' not to kill, but now he finds that it is not 'right' for him to engage in killing.[14]

In this verse Arjuna seems to weigh the killing of his kinsmen in terms of the happiness which could be derived from it: could any happiness remain after killing them? This does not mean that happiness is the criterion of action for Arjuna. He only wants to emphasize that he does not even see any happiness to justify it.

Happiness has certainly to be taken into account while con-

14. See verse 31, commentary.

sidering the performance of any action, because the aim of any
action is the increase of happiness – the very purpose of creation
and of evolution is expansion of happiness. So if happiness does
not result from an action, then that action defeats the very purpose of action, and its performance cannot be justified. That is
why Arjuna says killing 'would not be right for us'.

VERSE 38

यद्यप्येते न पश्यन्ति लोभोपहतचेतसः ॥
कुलक्षयकृतं दोषं मित्रद्रोहे च पातकम् ॥३८॥

Although, their minds clouded
by greed, they see no wrong
in bringing destruction to the
family and no sin in treachery
to friends,

VERSE 39

कथं न ज्ञेयमस्माभिः पापादस्मान्निवर्तितुम् ॥
कुलक्षयकृतं दोषं प्रपश्यद्भिर्जनार्दन ॥३९॥

How should we not know to turn
away from this sin, we who
clearly see the wrong in bringing
destruction upon the family,
O Janardana?

'Know' shows Arjuna's chief concern at this moment. He tries
to understand why he is unable to take a right course of action
when he sees the truth of the situation and, even more so, when
he knows what is right.

Arjuna expresses his concern over the influence of greed that
has blinded the vision of his kinsmen and has prevented them

from seeing 'the wrong'. This again shows that Arjuna's vision is clear.

The tone of the verse indicates that he does not give as much importance to the actual 'destruction' as to 'the wrong' that will result from it. But, for all his purity and clarity of vision, Arjuna fails to see the right way out of this sin of killing that awaits him. He turns to the Lord to receive the light.

Such moments in life make a man fall at the feet of God – moments when he sees and yet does not see, moments when he wants to act yet is unable to act.

When we investigate the invisible mechanics of nature, we find that everything in the universe is directly connected with everything else. Everything is constantly being influenced by everything else. No wave of the ocean is independent of any other. Each certainly has its individuality, but it is not isolated from the influence of other waves. Every wave has its own course to follow, but this course is dependent on that of every other wave. The life of any individual is a wave in the ocean of cosmic life, where every wave constantly influences the course of every other.

Certainly man is the master of his own destiny. He has free will – the greatest of God's gifts to him – whereby he has complete freedom of action. But having performed an action he has to bear its consequence, for reaction is always equal to action.

When people behave rightly, a corresponding atmosphere is naturally produced, and when such an influence is dominant, the individual's tendencies are affected by it. If in such an atmosphere of grace and glory an individual is tempted to follow a wrong path, he is protected by the unseen influence of righteousness which surrounds him. Similarly when a man fails in his efforts, the unseen working of nature is behind that failure. No amount of intellectual analysis can reveal to him why the failure occurs. He must rise to another level and realize the working of nature and the power behind it. He must rise to understand the laws of nature and the cosmic law which underlies all of them.

Arjuna fails to understand why his decision to refrain from battle produces no result, and he continues to be drawn into the battle. It is not because he is in a state of confusion, but because no amount of intellectual clarity can provide anyone with insight into the complex workings of diverse nature.

Arjuna, although his consciousness is pure, has not yet fathomed the absolute Being which is the field of the cosmic law. This is why he fails to see that he is living in an atmosphere saturated with evil influence, in which it is not possible for virtue to survive for long. Arjuna is trying to refrain from fighting out of consideration for family and caste dharmas; he is not aware of the absolute state of dharma whose power is leading him to fight. In consequence he fails to see why he is unable to act according to his feelings.

The following verse presents Arjuna's argument on how the path of evolution becomes extinct and bears witness to his concern for society.

VERSE 40

कुलक्षये प्रणश्यन्ति कुलधर्माः सनातनाः ॥
धर्मे नष्टे कुलं कृत्स्नमधर्मोऽभिभवत्युत ॥४०॥

The age-old family dharmas are
lost in the destruction of a
family. Its dharma lost, adharma
overtakes the entire family.

'Dharmas', the plural of dharma, signifies the different powers of nature upholding different avenues of the way of evolution. They take expression as specific modes of activity or different ways of righteousness, which keep the whole stream of life in harmony – every aspect of life being properly balanced with every other aspect – and moving in the direction of evolution. As these specific modes of activity are passed on from generation to generation, they form what we call traditions. It is these traditions which are referred to here as family dharmas.

'Adharma' means absence of dharma. When adharma prevails, the great power of nature, which maintains the equilibrium between positive and negative forces, is lost, and the process of evolution is thereby obstructed.

Arjuna uses the word 'age-old' because the ideals of life that have withstood the test of time represent the genuine path of evolution, the upward current in nature. Nothing that is against evolution lasts long. Therefore the tradition which has survived the ages has certainly proved itself to be the right one, the one nearest to the Truth, which is Life Eternal. That is why Arjuna is afraid to break this path of evolution for the generations to come.

In the process of analysing the quality of the act of fighting, Arjuna shows great foresight and a highly developed mind. It is clear that his thinking is extremely logical and correct, and that it certainly does not come from the superficial level of consciousness. Its basis is dharma, the basic power of evolution. Arjuna's vision is not restricted; the boundaries of his foresight lie far in the future.

As a great man of his time, Arjuna, before entering upon an undertaking, gauges its influence on succeeding generations. Only such a heightened state of consciousness could inspire the dawn of great wisdom on earth.

Arjuna's chief concern is the preservation of the path of evolution. With this in view he places great value on dharma and on the conduct of society, which supports it and is upheld by it.

Arjuna continues his argument in the following verse.

VERSE 41

अधर्माभिभवात् कृष्ण प्रदुष्यन्ति कुलस्त्रियः ॥
स्त्रीषु दुष्टासु वार्ष्णेय जायते वर्णसङ्करः ॥४१॥

When adharma prevails, O Krishna,
the women of the family become
corrupt, and with the corruption
of women, O Varshneya, intermixture
of castes arises.

A mother's life is the expression of the creative power of nature. Creative intelligence has to be pure in order to be effective. Impurity brings ineffectiveness, and when ineffectiveness increases, destruction is the result. For the creation of more effective people, the purity of the mother's life is of great concern.

'Intermixture of castes' is of concern to Arjuna because he understands how difficult and dangerous it is to shift from one boat to another in a fast current. All beings, under the tremendous influence of the mighty force of nature, are held fast in the current of evolution. Each has his own specific course to follow. If a man deviates from his own natural course, his own dharma, then it is like changing boats in a fast current. He has to struggle hard to maintain life – a struggle which is experienced as sorrow and suffering and which gives rise to all problems on the path of evolution.

The answer to every problem is that there is no problem. Let a man perceive this truth and then he is without problems. This is the strength of knowledge – the strength of Sankhya – the strength of the wisdom that offers instantaneous realization. This is the knowledge that Lord Krishna is going to reveal to Arjuna in answer to all the basic problems of life that Arjuna is posing in these verses 28 to 46.

VERSE 42

सङ्करो नरकायैव कुलघ्नानां कुलस्य च ॥
पतन्ति पितरो ह्येषां लुप्तपिण्डोदकक्रियाः ॥४२॥

This intermixture leads only to
hell, both for the family and its
destroyers. Their forefathers fall
as well, when the offerings of the
Pindodaka cease.

Purity of blood is at the basis of long life for a family and a society. And this purity depends upon the preservation of ancient family traditions. Destruction of the social order is the greatest

loss to a nation. Arjuna is viewing the battle with this vital consideration in mind, taking into account the life of many future
generations. His vision is perfect and his concern is genuine. The
depth of his thought, his foresight and love for human life and
society inspire Lord Krishna to strengthen him with the wisdom
of eternal liberation. Lord Krishna quietly listens to what he is
saying in order to prepare him more thoroughly for this great
blessing.

Every sentiment expressed by Arjuna, every doubt raised by
him and every inquiry of his into the field of knowledge is being
sympathetically received by Lord Krishna and will be answered
by Him to Arjuna's satisfaction.

'Pindodaka': according to the Vedic Karma Kanda, the exposition of karma, or action, sons and grandsons are expected
to perform certain rites and ceremonies in the name of their
departed father and grandfather. The performance of these rites by
the direct blood relations, according to the law of affinity, brings
goodwill, peace and satisfaction to the departed forefathers wherever they may be in the field of evolution. Not only this, but
as a child receives blessings and comforts from his parents, so
the departed also bless their children. The Vedic performance of
the Pindodaka connects the departed parents with their children
on earth and serves as a channel through which the blessings flow.

Having shown his concern for the life of individuals, Arjuna,
in the following verse, again expresses his concern for the path
of evolution and for the whole of society.

VERSE 43

दोषैरेतैः कुलघ्नानां वर्णसङ्करकारकैः ॥
उत्साद्यन्ते जातिधर्माः कुलधर्माश्च शाश्वताः ॥४३॥

*Through the wrongs done by the
destroyers of the family in
causing the intermixing of castes,
the immemorial dharmas of caste
and family become extinct.*

The laws maintaining the well-being of the whole body consist
of a collection of the laws maintaining its different parts, together
with others added to co-ordinate different limbs. The laws of the
evolution of the body likewise are the sum total of those governing the evolution of different limbs, along with those coordinat-
ing them.

In a similar way, there are dharmas governing individual evolution and there are dharmas which connect and coordinate
different individuals. These latter are said primarily to govern
the evolution of the society or caste. In verse 40 Arjuna was
thinking in terms of the dharma of the family. In this verse he
is considering the dharma of the caste, that is, a collection of
families upholding similar dharmas.

The intermixing of castes destroys the ideals preserved by the
immemorial traditions and has the direct result of upsetting the
social equilibrium. What happens to a life which is not based on
ancient traditions is shown on the following verse.

VERSE 44

उत्सन्नकुलधर्माणां मनुष्याणां जनार्दन ॥
नरके नियतं वासो भवतीत्यनुशुश्रुम ॥४४॥

Men whose family dharmas have lapsed,
so we have heard, O Janardana (Lord
Krishna), necessarily live in hell.

'Family dharmas' are the powers of different principles which
uphold the coordination between different members of a family,
at the same time enabling every member, consciously or unconsciously, to help every other member on his path of evolution. Such
family dharmas are, for example, those that go to make the relationship of a mother with her son or daughter, or of a brother
with his brother or sister, and so on. Family dharmas are maintained in the family traditions. If the family traditions are broken,
people living together do not know how to live in such a manner

that their way of life naturally helps each of them to evolve. The result is the loss of the path of evolution and the increase of disorder and chaos in the family. Life in such a family is a life in hell, and those fallen into such a degenerate pattern of life remain off the path of evolution and continue to mould their destinies in wretchedness. This is what Arjuna means when he says 'necessarily live in hell'.

Here is a great teaching of vital importance which has been missed for centuries. It sets a standard for any society.

'Family dharma' is an established tradition where people born in a particular family engage in the profession of that family. Because of their parental heritage they work efficiently, produce better material for society and improve in their profession. Working with all ease and comfort in their profession, they do not exhaust themselves in work and find time to be regular in their practice for spiritual unfoldment, which is the basis of all success in life. This is how family dharmas and traditions help both the individual and society.

Arjuna addresses Lord Krishna as 'Janardana', which is a reminder that He established law and order by destroying the demon Jana. Now, as a result of battle, greater chaos will prevail, for family dharmas will be lost – the world will become hell.

Arjuna's concern over the destruction of dharmas indicates that he is reviewing the whole situation from the point of view of the working of nature.

This verse establishes a fundamental principle of action: the action should be such that it does not stray from the invisible power of dharma.

The following verse indicates how one's wisdom could fail one and wrong decisions result.

VERSE 45

अहो बत महत्पापं कर्तुं व्यवसिता वयम् ।।
यद्राज्यसुखलोभेन हन्तुं स्वजनमुद्यताः ।।४५।।

Alas! We are resolved to commit
great sin in that we are prepared
to slay our kinsmen out of greed
for the pleasures of a kingdom.

Arjuna feels sorrowful because he is going to sacrifice a greater
end for a smaller gain – family and caste dharmas are going to be
sacrificed for the sake of his individual dharma.

Arjuna calls it a great sin because he is aware that the establishment of righteousness, the Kingdom of God on earth, is a co-
operative enterprise. All men have to play their part in it, and
this can be done only when family and caste dharmas are properly maintained by the individuals firmly established in their
individual dharmas. The loss of family and caste dharmas is a
calamity for the social order, a destruction of righteousness; it is
a sin against God. That is why Arjuna calls it 'great sin'.

Arjuna begins in the following verse to express the line of
action he would like to take.

VERSE 46

यदि मामप्रतीकारमशस्त्रं शस्त्रपाणयः ।।
धार्तराष्ट्रा रणे हन्युस्तन्मे क्षेमतरं भवेत् ।।४६।।

It were better for me if the sons
of Dhritarashtra, weapons in hand,
should slay me, unresisting and
unarmed in battle.

Arjuna sees that he would be committing great sin by fighting.
As a warrior, once having come on to the battlefield he can
neither hold back from fighting nor can he flee; but if he fights,
there remains that fear of great sin. He sees no way of escape
from this situation, so he says that he were better killed in battle.
Because he cannot be killed while armed and alert, he wishes
to be unarmed and unresisting. In this way he will not incur
great sin against God. This is the faultless mind of the greatest
archer of all time, this is bravery and nobility of character. Arjuna
considers it better to die than to commit sin.

VERSE 47

सञ्जय उवाच ।

एवमुक्त्वाऽर्जुनः संख्ये रथोपस्थ उपाविशत् ॥
विसृज्य सशरं चापं शोकसंविग्नमानसः ॥४७॥

Sanjaya said:

Having spoken thus at the time of
battle, casting away arrow and bow,
Arjuna sat down on the seat of the
chariot, his mind overwhelmed with
sorrow.

'Having spoken thus': in the previous verses, Arjuna has described the consequences of battle as they presented themselves
to his developed heart and mind. Now, still unable to decide his
course of action, he becomes aware of himself standing with
bow and arrow in his chariot, apparently prepared for war.
Arjuna may have thought that by standing armed for battle he
did not allow himself to be impartial in his consideration and so
decided to cast away arrow and bow, abandon his battle posture
and sit down to reflect more deeply in order to find an answer
which would satisfy both sides of his problem – love for dear
ones and the demand of duty.

Arjuna's mind was 'overwhelmed with sorrow': the hour of

duty was at hand, but his heart prevented him from responding. With his clear mind he could visualize the far-reaching effects of the destruction the battle would bring. This overwhelmed his thought with sorrow. Fortunate are they whose minds are distressed for the misfortunes of others. More fortunate still are they who are able to relieve the misfortunes of others, themselves remaining undisturbed.

In the following chapter, Arjuna will receive the light which will enable him, without a trace of distress and established in the blissful freedom of God-consciousness, to alleviate the evil overshadowing the world.

Thus, in the Upanishad of the glorious
Bhagavad-Gita, in the Science of the Absolute,
in the Scripture of Yoga, in the dialogue
between Lord Krishna and Arjuna, ends the
first chapter, entitled: The Yoga of
the Despondency of Arjuna.

CHAPTER II

A Vision of the Teaching in Chapter II

Verse 1. The seeker of Truth is held in a state of suspension, for he sees no solution to the basic problems of life.

Verses 2, 3. From the point of view of the Divine, problems do not exist. Impurity overshadows the dignity that naturally belongs to life.

Verses 4-9. This statement about the nature of life appears meaningless to one who clearly knows that problems do exist at the basis of individual and social life. As a practical man, he does not wish to turn a blind eye to them.

Verses 10-38. To him the teaching comes, giving insight into life. There are two aspects of life, the changing body and the unchanging self, whose real nature is absolute Being. Until Being is realized, life is without a stable foundation and remains based solely on the fundamental problems of existence, even though it may be in accord with almighty Nature and the force of evolution. Knowledge of the self and Being brings equanimity of mind.

Verses 39-44. Equanimity is made permanent by gaining absolute consciousness: the mind gains absolute consciousness naturally and easily, but the man who is immersed in sensory enjoyment misses it.

Verses 45-8. The technique lies in allowing the mind to arrive naturally at absolute consciousness and then, having become acquainted with the fullness of life, to engage in action.

Verses 49-52. The advantages are improved efficiency and greater success in all fields of life, relief from problems and complete liberation from bondage.

Verses 53-72. A description of life established in equanimity and of precautions to safeguard that blessed state of freedom in divine consciousness.

THIS chapter is the soul of the Bhagavad-Gita, while all those that follow form the body. Hope and fulfilment are the blessings of this glorious chapter. It gives a direct way to peaceful, energetic and successful life in the world, together with spiritual comfort and freedom from bondage.

The chapter expounds Brahma Vidya in its completeness – the wisdom of the Absolute both in its theoretical and practical aspects – and presents the central idea of the entire theme of the Bhagavad-Gita. It has seed-ideas which are developed in all the following chapters.

At the same time this chapter is self-contained. It is in itself powerful enough to uplift any mind, however low its level. It presents a complete philosophy of life, starting from the state of a seeker and ending in the state of fulfilment.

The thought of the first chapter continues to flow into the early part of this one. The potential force underlying Arjuna's state of suspension finds an outlet in the ocean of the eternal wisdom of Lord Krishna.

Arjuna's condition, which inspired Lord Krishna to reveal the secret wisdom of integrated life, is portrayed at the beginning of the chapter, and the key to this wisdom is revealed in the 45th verse.

VERSE 1

सञ्जय उवाच ।
तं तथा कृपयाविष्टमश्रुपूर्णाकुलेक्षणम् ॥
विषीदन्तमिदं वाक्यमुवाच मधुसूदनः ॥१॥

Sanjaya said:

To him thus overcome by compassion,
full of sorrow, his eyes distressed
and filled with tears, Madhusudana
(Lord Krishna) spoke these words:

'Madhusudana': the slayer of the demon Madhu. The use of
this word indicates that a mighty power is rising to put an end
to Arjuna's paralysing state of suspension.

Even a mind as highly alert and intelligent as was Arjuna's
had become caught in a situation which was out of control. His
heart could not be reconciled with his mind – his love of kinsmen with the call of duty to destroy evil. On the practical level,
this is like wanting to remain in darkness and yet be in the light.
Arjuna has set himself a task which is impossible unless he attains a state of consciousness which will justify any action of his
and will allow him even to kill in love, in support of the purpose of evolution.

Arjuna could not reconcile killing and loving. This is no weakness on his part and does not detract from his greatness. Any
man of similar high development would arrive at this state of
suspension between heart and mind.

Arjuna was a man of dynamic nature. His heart was full of
love, yet he could not at this time love his dear ones. His mind
was clear, alert and full of purpose, yet he could not at this
time act according to its dictates. Held in suspension as he was,
he could not fight and satisfy his mind, nor could he love his
dear ones and satisfy his heart. For this reason he was 'full of
sorrow'.

Arjuna was not confused, as commentators in general have

portrayed him. His heart and mind were at the height of alertness, but they could not show him a line of action to fulfil their
contradictory aspirations. Even this could not throw Arjuna off
his balance, for Sanjaya says: 'eyes distressed and filled with
tears.' Had he been off his balance, his eyes would have been
vacant. But they had life in them: distress is seen in them, and
they express the heart through tears. The 'distress' seen in the
eyes gives expression to his great concern, and this shows mental alertness.

The sequence of the expressions used in this verse is of great
significance in arriving at the truth of Arjuna's condition. 'Overcome by compassion' shows that his heart is filled with compassion alone. The expression that follows is 'full of sorrow'. If
the heart is full of compassion, then there is no place in it for
an emotion of such a dissimilar quality as sorrow. This makes
it clear that the phrase 'full of sorrow' does not refer to Arjuna's
heart. It does not describe an emotion, but only the state of his
mind.

Thus Arjuna's heart was full of compassion and his mind full
of sorrow. His state should not be misunderstood as indicating
weakness or confusion. This verse shows Arjuna in his full
stature, at the height of his intelligence, sensitivity and alertness, and at the same time without any line of action to follow.

This condition of suspension is of value, for it provides a real
basis for divine intelligence. At first sight it appears to be the
result of circumstances, but it is in fact produced by the first
word of Lord Krishna on the battlefield.[1] The purity of Arjuna's
life, receiving a wave of love from Lord Krishna, developed into
a state of suspension and prepared the ground for the divine
wisdom to dawn.

Here is the picture of a man of the world who is going to receive the greatest divine wisdom ever revealed to man. In order
to find the real Arjuna on whom the blessing came, we must
look beyond the appearance of tears and distress. The outer structure of tears and distress serves to protect the inner glory of consciousness in a state of suspension. It is like the bitter skin of an
orange which contains sweet juice within it. The apparent pheno-

1. See I, 25, commentary.

menal phase of the world is not so attractive, but within it is
the altar of God whose light sustains our life.

Lord Krishna will not allow even the outer aspect of Arjuna's
life to look 'sorrowful'. He will improve the appearance also. And
with that in view He shocks Arjuna as He begins His speech.

VERSE 2

श्रीभगवानुवाच ।

कुतस्त्वा कश्मलमिदं विषमे समुपस्थितम् ॥

अनार्यजुष्टमस्वर्ग्यमकीर्तिकरमर्जुन ॥२॥

The Blessed Lord said:
Whence has this blemish, alien to
honourable men, causing disgrace and
opposed to heaven, come upon you,
Arjuna, at this untimely hour?

Problems are not solved on the level of problems. Analysing a
problem to find its solution is like trying to restore freshness to a
leaf by treating the leaf itself, whereas the solution lies in watering the root.

Arjuna, in the previous twenty-one verses, has raised, basically, all the problems that may confront any life at any time.
When the Lord begins to answer, He does not devote a moment
to Arjuna's arguments. He simply dismisses everything that
Arjuna has said without analysing it, because by analysing each
statement it would not be possible to resolve the situation.

All problems of life arise from some weakness of mind. All
weakness of mind is due to the mind's ignorance of its own essential nature, which is universal and the source of infinite energy
and intelligence. This ignorance of one's own self is the basis
of all problems, sufferings and shortcomings in life. In order to
root out any problem of life it is only necessary to be brought
out of ignorance, to be brought to knowledge.

In order to bring anyone to knowledge, it is first necessary to
bring him to a state of mind where he will listen. Arjuna being

in a state of suspension, the Lord said something to him which would shake his mind and make him capable of hearing and understanding.

In this verse the Lord appraises Arjuna's situation in words which suggest its solution. The first word spoken by Lord Krishna in this discourse expresses the whole philosophy of life, the whole of Vedanta: the world of forms and phenomena in its ever-changing nature, and the absolute never-changing Reality of transcendental nature, both are full – 'purnamadah purnamidam'. Whence then has come this blemish of ignorance, which causes sorrow? Again, as the present is composed of the two 'fulls', the blemish does not belong to any present time; that is why it is 'untimely' at any 'hour'.

Arjuna has presented his problems in verses 28–46 of the first chapter; how Lord Krishna sees the situation and disapproves of it is clear from the expressions of this verse.

'Whence' indicates the baselessness of the whole argument. This word runs parallel to verse 28 which provides a basis for Arjuna's argument.

'Blemish' refers to the content of verses 29–31.

'Alien to honourable men' expresses the nature of verses 32–5.

'Causing disgrace' refers to verses 36–9.

'Opposed to heaven' refers to verses 40–6.

The Lord exclaims to Arjuna: 'Whence has this blemish ... come upon you?' He speaks with surprise and uses the word 'blemish' to epitomize Arjuna's overall state and way of thinking. The word 'blemish', accompanied by 'alien to honourable men, causing disgrace and opposed to heaven' and 'untimely hour', hit Arjuna hard. His alert mind and heart received a severe shock, which jolted him out of the state of suspension. Immediately he lost confidence in the way he was thinking. This made him look to the Lord.

The following verse brings another shock to Arjuna and strengthens the effect produced by this verse. The Lord implies that, whether surroundings and circumstances are favourable or unfavourable, men of honour and grace always act in a way that leads them to glory here on earth and in heaven.

VERSE 3

क्लैब्यं मास्म गमः पार्थ नैतत्त्वय्युपपद्यते ॥
क्षुद्रं हृदयदौर्बल्यं त्यक्त्वोत्तिष्ठ परन्तप ॥३॥

Partha! Yield not to unmanliness.
It is unworthy of you. Shake off
this paltry faintheartedness. Stand
up, O scorcher of enemies!

Again this verse shows psychological skill in handling a problem. Here the Lord uses the word 'unmanliness', at the same
time reminding Arjuna of his honourable heritage by calling him
Partha, the son of Pritha. This is to neutralize in Arjuna what
Lord Krishna calls 'faintheartedness'.

Lord Krishna realized that when He first addressed him as
Partha, asking him to behold the Kurus assembled in the battle,[2]
He awoke in him the love of his mother Pritha, and He knew
that the great wave of love instilled by Him in Arjuna's heart
was responsible for his present state of suspension. Therefore, to
bring Arjuna back to his initial preparedness to fight, it was
necessary to expand the one-sided nature of the love produced
by the word Partha. This is the reason why Lord Krishna here
again uses 'Partha' and associates it with 'faintheartedness'.

Having produced this effect in the heart, it was at once necessary to direct the flow of Arjuna's mind away from the state
of suspension towards action; so the Lord tells him to 'stand up'.
In this way, the Lord sets up an impulse in his mind towards
fighting and immediately supplements it by reminding him of
his status as a 'scorcher of enemies'.

The Lord wants to stop Arjuna at once from thinking in a
manner that will lead him nowhere. He tells Arjuna that this
way does not belong to him, for he has always been a dynamic
personality – 'It is unworthy of you'.

2. See I, 25.

This saying of the Lord's also has a deeper meaning. 'It is unworthy of you' reminds Arjuna of his essential nature. 'That
thou art', declare the Upanishads – unbounded eternal Being.
You should breathe universal life and not fall prey to 'faintheartedness', for that belongs to the field of ignorance.

Asking him to shake off his 'faintheartedness', the Lord qualifies it by 'paltry'. By this He means to encourage Arjuna: the
weakness he has to overcome is not great but just a failing of
the heart. Lord Krishna wants to convey to Arjuna that when
love grows in man's heart, his outlook becomes more universal,
and he should become stronger and more dynamic, but that in
his case this has not happened. Arjuna has not gained a universal
outlook.

This expresses a great metaphysical truth: ignorance has no
material substance. It is just an illusion which should be easy to
shake off. Unfortunately this ignorance has deprived Arjuna of
the strength that the wave of love should naturally bring.

Certainly, as a great warrior, Arjuna is brave by nature. That
is why the Lord seems only to remind him of what he is: unbounded and eternal in his absolute nature and the 'scorcher of
enemies' in his relative nature, in his human form.

A close study of these two verses, which form the Lord's first
exhortation, shows that they contain in essence the entire teaching of the Bhagavad-Gita.

VERSE 4

अर्जुन उवाच ।
कथं भीष्ममहं संख्ये द्रोणं च मधुसूदन ॥
इषुभिः प्रतियोत्स्यामि पूजार्हावरिसूदन ॥४॥

Arjuna said:
How shall I fight Bhishma and Drona
with arrows on the battlefield,
O Madhusudana? Worthy of reverence
are they, O slayer of enemies!

Arjuna addresses Lord Krishna as Madhusudana, slayer of the demon Madhu, while recounting the names of Bhishma and Drona. Thereby he silently suggests to Lord Krishna: You are the slayer of demons; how can you ask me to slay these noble elders? You are the slayer of enemies; how can you ask me to kill those who are worthy of reverence?

This shows Arjuna's alertness of mind even in this state of suspension. If one is alert and awake in heart and mind, there is always hope of rising above any time of trial.

Arjuna presses his point further in the next verse.

VERSE 5

गुरूनहत्वा हि महानुभावान्
    श्रेयो भोक्तुं भैक्ष्यमपीह लोकें ॥
हत्वार्थकामांस्तु गुरूनिहैव
    भुञ्जीय भोगान् रुधिरप्रदिग्धान् ॥५॥

It is surely better to live even
on alms in this world than to slay
these noble-minded masters; for
though they are desirous of gain,
having killed them I should enjoy
only blood-stained pleasures in
this world.

This shows Arjuna's greatness, nobility of character and far-sightedness. It shows the quality of his human heart. Arjuna, as a great archer, was aware of the pathetic records of blood-stained conquests in history. He could foresee great damage to the civilization of his time. He could picture in his mind ruins of war everywhere; he could hear within himself the cries of children and lamentations of women, tales of calamity and oppression. Arjuna, a hero with a good human heart, would do anything to hold back from the situation that seems imminent.

He goes so far as to say that it is 'better to live even on alms in this world than to slay these noble-minded masters' and 'enjoy only blood-stained pleasures'.

In the following verse he continues his argument.

VERSE 6

न चैतद्विद्मः कतरन्नो गरीयो
    यद्वा जयेम यदि वा नो जयेयुः ॥
यानेव हत्वा न जिजीविषाम-
    स्तेऽवस्थिताः प्रमुखे धार्तराष्ट्राः ॥६॥

We do not know which is better for us:
that we should conquer them or they
should conquer us. The sons of
Dhritarashtra stand face to face with
us. If we killed them we should not
wish to live.

This shows Arjuna's selfless view of life. If he is to enjoy the kingdom, he wants the joy of it to be shared by all those who are dear to him; and if he cannot share it with them, he prefers to forgo the kingdom altogether. The verse brings to light the way of thinking of a man of evolved consciousness. Arjuna, realizing the gravity of the situation, is concerned over the responsibility that rests upon him. He thinks about the consequences of victory or defeat and finds no justification even for a victory of his own side, if that will deprive him of his dear ones.

Placed in a helpless situation, Arjuna decides that it cannot be resolved on any level of human thinking or feeling. He therefore looks to the Lord for divine guidance.

The following verse records the helplessness of the greatest archer of all time, the most innocent and sincere feelings of surrender of a great and wise man.

VERSE 7

कार्पण्यदोषोपहतस्वभावः
    पृच्छामि त्वां धर्मसंमूढचेताः ॥
यच्छ्रेयः स्यान्निश्चितं ब्रूहि तन्मे
    शिष्यस्तेऽहंशाधि मां त्वां प्रपन्नम् ॥७॥

My nature smitten with the taint of
weakness, confused in mind about dharma,
I pray Thee, tell me decisively what is
good for me. I am Thy disciple; teach
me for I have taken refuge in Thee.

Arjuna has persisted in his attitude, and when he has gone as
far as he possibly can in that direction, he suddenly feels unable
to think any more. He stops, his intellect rebounds and he falls
at the feet of the Lord.

It generally happens that as long as a man feels that he can
think and do for himself, he sees no need to listen to others. When
he is at his wits' end, he looks for refuge. If he finds a refuge, he
approaches it in all humility and puts his trust in it. When he has
surrendered himself completely, it takes full care of him. This is
the impartial divine nature: I am to them as they are to Me.

'Tell me decisively' reveals Arjuna's character. He is a practical man who does not want to remain on the level of idealistic
talk. He asks for a clear line of action, which he can follow
without doubt and which will prove to be right for him, his aim
being the good of all. If a man has dedicated his life to the service
of others and is conscientious about his responsibilities, he has all
the greater need to be right in the course of action he adopts.

This situation does not in any way reflect on Arjuna's character. It is the integrity of his inner life that makes him see
weakness in himself. His greatness is revealed when he says: 'confused in mind about dharma'. On one side he has his family
dharma (duty of a householder) impelling him to protect and

love his kinsmen, and on the other his caste dharma (duty of a kshatriya, protector of society) demanding that he kill the aggressors. He is is not able to decide for himself which dharma to follow and looks upon this as his weakness. In reality it is the circumstances that are responsible. No man of heart and mind would consider it to be Arjuna's weakness; but he calls it his weakness. His greatness of character makes him too humble in analysing his condition before Lord Krishna.

When Arjuna surrenders himself to gain wisdom as a disciple, the Lord accepts him, and it is from this point that Lord Krishna's teaching commences. This is really the beginning of the Bhaga-vad-Gita.

It is an established natural law that action and reaction are equal to one another. In order that the reaction may take place, the action has first to begin. In the same way, in order that the teaching may begin, the pupil has first to approach the teacher. When he has done this he is considered serious, and the teacher feels a responsibility to teach him.

As long as Arjuna was talking to Lord Krishna on a friendly basis, Lord Krishna answered in the same manner. But when Arjuna became serious and said : I submit myself to you as a disciple, show me the way, guide me to the light, for I am un-able to see for myself — when Arjuna became quiet and turned completely to Lord Krishna, then the Lord took him seriously and began to enlighten him with the practical wisdom of life.

When a patient will not keep still, the surgeon cannot start the operation; only when the patient submits himself to the surgeon to do as he wishes does he feel free to operate.

This is a great secret of success when guidance is sought from another in any walk of life. And the wisdom of peace and happiness in life, the wisdom of success in the world and free-dom from bondage is the greatest secret of life. It is Brahma Vidya, the knowledge of the Ultimate. Naturally it can be im-parted only to those who are at least willing to receive it. Their willingness is judged by their readiness to receive, and this in turn by their one-pointed attention in faithful devotion to the master.

Faith makes the student a good assimilator of knowledge. Devotion sets him free from resistance and at the same time influences the heart of the master, whence the spring of wisdom pours forth. Devotion on the part of the disciple creates affection in the heart of the master. When a calf approaches its mother, the milk begins to flow from her udder, ready for the calf to drink without effort. Such is the glory of devotion and faith in a disciple. He surrenders at the feet of the master and cuts short the long path of evolution.

The result of Arjuna's sincere surrender to Lord Krishna was seen without delay. By His teaching, both theoretical and practical, He helped Arjuna to free himself from his state of suspension. At the end of a short discourse on a battlefield, Arjuna had become a yogi,[3] a bhakta[4] and a gyani.[5] He had become established in the fullness of resolute intellect, in great skill in action and in the eternal freedom of existence.

To reach that state, Arjuna had only to surrender at the feet of the Lord. Surrender does not mean blind passivity. Throughout the Bhagavad-Gita, Arjuna continues to ask questions, for the student gains complete freedom to ask anything, once he has impressed the master with his sincerity. In a relationship of this quality between the teacher and the taught, the task of both becomes easy and free from resistance. Wisdom flows spontaneously from one to the other.

Having surrendered himself, Arjuna, in the next verse, shows clearly the present state of his mind. The path of surrender does not allow any reservations.

3. An integrated man.   4. A devotee of God.
5. An enlightened man.

VERSE 8

न हि प्रपश्यामि ममापनुद्याद्
        यच्छोकमुच्छोषणमिन्द्रियाणाम् ।।
अवाप्य भूमावसपत्नमृद्धं
        राज्यं सुराणामपि चाधिपत्यम् ।।८।।

Indeed I do not see what could dispel
the grief that dries up my senses,
though I should obtain an unrivalled
and prosperous kingdom on earth and
even lordship of the gods.

'Dries up my senses': by reason of Arjuna's state of suspension, the coordination between the mind and the senses is lost.
A plant becomes dry because it has received no nourishment
from the root, and there is no way of giving it nourishment from
outside. Without coordination with the mind, the senses have no
chance of remaining alert and cannot enjoy even the greatest
pleasures on earth.

If the surrender described in the previous verse had been complete, Arjuna should have been silent about his grief from that
moment. But he expresses it even after declaring that he has
surrendered. This shows that even the sense of surrender cannot
immediately free him. It can happen that even the ocean fails to
subdue a volcanic eruption. Nothing in the outer world can dispel the grief in Arjuna's mind, for he is overtaken by a suspension so profound that it renders him incapable of action.

Study of this verse brings out a fundamental principle of
spiritual life. The true state of surrender does not leave one
suffering; one casts off all difficulties, and the relief brings one
to silence.

This and the previous four verses summarize the basic problems of life that Arjuna put before the Lord in verses 28–46 of
Chapter I.

VERSE 9

सञ्जय उवाच ।
एवमुक्त्वा हृषीकेशं गुडाकेशः परन्तपः ॥
न योत्स्य इति गोविन्दमुक्त्वा तूष्णीं बभूव ह ॥६॥

Sanjaya said:
Gudakesha, oppressor of the foe,
having spoken thus to Hrishikesha,
said to Govinda (Lord Krishna):
'I will not fight' and fell silent.

Arjuna has been called 'Gudakesha' (the conqueror of sleep)
and 'oppressor of the foe'. These expressions indicate that at this
point, when Arjuna says: 'I will not fight', he is free from dullness and his strength is not failing him.

The use of 'Hrishikesha' or 'Govinda', the lord and master of
the senses, expresses Lord Krishna's position in relation to Arjuna.
With all his strength and alertness of mind, Arjuna stands as a
child before the greatness of Lord Krishna. His words: 'I will
not fight', are like the words of a child who says: 'I will not
go there', and yet looks to his father to find out his intentions.
Once Arjuna has surrendered [6] himself at the feet of the Lord, he
becomes as a child before Him.

Arjuna is justified in saying that he will not fight, because
he has surrendered himself. Arjuna is a warrior; when he says
he has surrendered, he means it and begins to behave accordingly. Now his heart, body and mind all belong to Lord Krishna;
therefore he cannot fight or do anything unless he receives
orders. He knows that the problem must be expressed clearly, and
then the solution will come easily. Arjuna has had his say;
now Lord Krishna will speak.

6. See verse 7.

Verse 10

तमुवाच हृषीकेशः प्रहसन्निव भारत ।।
सेनयोरुभयोर्मध्ये विषीदन्तमिदं वचः ।।१०।।

To him, O Bharata (Dhritarashtra),
sorrowing in the midst of the two
armies, Hrishikesha smilingly spoke
these words:

'Hrishikesha smilingly spoke': this expression is used to indicate that lifting Arjuna out of his state of silence and hesitancy
and releasing him from the benumbed condition of the senses
was not a big task for one who is the Lord of the senses. 'Smilingly' may also be understood as indicating the technique of
enlightening a disciple by encouraging him at the very start.

The disheartened seeker becomes encouraged by the first sign
of the master's smile, which shows him without a word that his
problems are neither so serious as he thinks nor so difficult as to
be insurmountable. The contrast brought out is significant. It
shows Arjuna in despair, while Lord Krishna smiles in His usual
divine, playful, blissful mood. The two aspects of existence are
represented here: on the one hand, unmanifested absolute bliss-
consciousness, symbolized by Lord Krishna; and on the other,
the height of human consciousness represented by Arjuna. The
darkness is on the point of being illumined by the celestial light;
the silence of Arjuna is about to be broken and made melodious
by the celestial song, as his grief is transformed into the smile
of the Lord.

The word 'smilingly' also refers to the unshakeable nature of
Lord Krishna. Anyone but the Lord would have been overwhelmed to find that, with the two great armies drawn up ready
to fight, the hero on his side was sinking into despair.

In the following verse Lord Krishna begins his glorious discourse. But it should be noted again[7] that He does not enter

7. See verse 2, commentary.

into Arjuna's arguments; He dismisses them all with the first
word that He speaks.

VERSE 11

श्रीभगवानुवाच।
अशोच्यानन्वशोचस्त्वं प्रज्ञावादांश्चभाषसे ॥
गतासूनगतासूंश्च नानुशोचन्ति पण्डिताः ॥११॥

The Blessed Lord said:
You grieve for those for whom
there should be no grief, yet
speak as do the wise. Wise
men grieve neither for the dead
nor for the living.

The Lord tells Arjuna that he speaks in the language of the
wise, and in saying this He also shows him how wise men think.
The first mark of such men is that they do not grieve over
anything, for they know that everything is in its essence everlasting. From the point of view of real existence, Bhishma and
Drona and all those for whom Arjuna is concerned have infinite
life. It is wrong for Arjuna to grieve for them. Can there be grief
in the mind of a wise man either for the living or for the dead?
He does not grieve over the past, nor can anything in the present
make him unhappy, for he is established in Truth, the unchangeable Reality.

This verse reveals the wisdom of the master: he makes the
aspirant aware of his own position and at the same time makes
clear to him his goal. Lord Krishna makes Arjuna see his present
state of mind, in which he is grieving over nothing, and his goal,
the state of wisdom, in which he would not grieve over anything.

This also illustrates a principle of the relationship between
master and pupil: the master is only concerned with taking the
disciple from his present state to the goal. The Lord does not

bring Himself into the picture here; He only describes Arjuna's present position and the state to which He wishes to lead him. He has only hinted at the goal but has made Arjuna clearly aware of his condition, His purpose being to bring Arjuna to that complete dependence which will enable him to receive His skilful guidance to the fullest advantage. The disciple is not asked to be alert and listen, yet this effect is produced in his mind at the beginning of the discourse by making him aware of his position.

This verse begins the first part of Lord Krishna's discourse, which is known as 'Sankhya'. From here to verse 38, Lord Krishna gives Arjuna this wisdom of full life, the wisdom of both the absolute and the relative aspects of existence, which He calls Sankhya.

A close study suggests that the questions raised by Arjuna in five verses[8] are answered by the five expressions contained in this verse:

1. You grieve for those for whom there should be no grief.
2. Yet speak as do the wise.
3. Neither for the living nor for the dead.
4. Grieve not.
5. Wise men.

VERSE 12

न त्वेवाहं जातु नासं न त्वं नेमे जनाधिपाः ॥
न चैव न भविष्यामः सर्वे वयमतः परम् ॥१२॥

There never was a time when I was not,
nor you, nor these rulers of men. Nor
will there ever be a time when all of
us shall cease to be.

8. II, 4–8. These verses, in turn, contain in essence all the questions Arjuna had put in I, 28–46.

Here the Lord presents to Arjuna the permanent nature of the inner man, the inner Reality of individual life. The nature of this spirit in man is imperishable. Despite the continual change of bodies in the past, present and future, it ever remains the same. The permanent nature of the inner aspect of life, the Self, is an abstract conception and so, in order to make it as concrete as possible the Lord speaks about it in terms of Himself, Arjuna and those present. This illustrates an important aspect of teaching: abstract theories are explained by concrete illustrations.

The Lord says we shall all continue to exist even after the death of these bodies, for the self is eternal – life continues to be, it is everlasting. Here follows an illustration which illumines the wisdom of Sankhya.

VERSE 13

देहिनोऽस्मिन् यथा देहे कौमारं यौवनं जरा ॥
तथा देहान्तरप्राप्तिर्धीरस्तत्र न मुह्यति ॥१३॥

As the dweller in this body passes
into childhood, youth and age, so also
does he pass into another body. This
does not bewilder the wise.

The wise are not taken aback by changes of the body; the death of the body is like the change that takes place when children become grown-up, or when the young become old. Phenomenal changes continue to take place, while the never-changing Reality of life, the dweller in the body, remains ever the same.

It is not possible for a man who knows this to feel great concern about the death of the body, but even with this knowledge he still feels heat and cold, pleasure and pain. How this situation should be met is explained in the next verse.

These verses express the vital content of the wisdom of Sankhya.

VERSE 14

मात्रास्पर्शास्तु कौन्तेय शीतोष्णसुखदुःखदाः ॥
आगमापायिनोऽनित्यास्तांस्तितिक्षस्व भारत ॥१४॥

Contacts (of the senses) with their
objects, O son of Kunti, give rise to
(the experience of) cold and heat,
pleasure and pain. Transient, they
come and go. Bear them patiently,
O Bharata!

Firmly established in the understanding of the unchangeable, the
wise are never affected by the changing conditions of the body
during life or after death. The experience of the objects of the
senses and their effects, the experience of pleasure and pain, are
just phenomena which come and go. Here the Lord wants to
show Arjuna that things which are not of a permanent nature
should not weigh heavily. It is as if He were saying: Take it
lightly, for things will naturally go in the same way in which they
came. Your life should be based on something which is of lasting
nature, Arjuna ! Do not give importance to the consideration of
the fleeting and impermanent phases of life. Rise to the understanding that the permanent Reality of existence will continue to
be, while that which is temporary will go on changing. So take
life as it comes. This alone befits you, for you are called Bharata,
the descendant of the great Bharata, who was established in the
light, the Reality of life.

The result of remaining even-minded in pleasure and pain is
shown in the following verse.

VERSE 15

यं हि न व्यथयन्त्येते पुरुषं पुरुषर्षभ ॥
समदुःखसुखं धीरं सोऽमृतत्वाय कल्पते ॥१५॥

That man indeed whom these (contacts)
do not disturb, who is even-minded in
pleasure and pain, steadfast, he is fit
for immortality, O best of men!

The Lord emphasizes to Arjuna that, once a man has become
established in the understanding of the permanent Reality of life
as explained in verse 13, his mind rises above the influence of
pleasure and pain. Such an unshakable man passes beyond the
influence of death and lives in the permanent phase of life; he
attains eternal life. It is the Lord's purpose that Arjuna shall
gain this state where he will be above all considerations in the
relative field, even death, and all problems of life and death.

The unlimited state of the ocean is not affected either by the
inflow of rivers or the process of evaporation. In the same way, a
man established in the understanding of the unlimited abundance of absolute existence is naturally free from influence of
the relative order. This is what gives him the status of immortal life.

At the present time it is generally found that people try to
make a mood of equanimity in pleasure and pain, in loss and
gain – they try to create a mood of equable behaviour and un-
affectedness while engaged in the diverse activities of the world.
But trying to make a mood on the basis of understanding is
simply hypocrisy. Many seekers become trapped in such an attitude. This will become clearer as we proceed.

The understanding does not become ripe as a result of mood-
making. It is only necessary to understand the meaning of this
and the previous three verses once, in order to live the Reality
of the relationship between the inner eternal life and the outer
ever-changing phases of existence. When once a man knows that

he is king and the state belongs to him, he immediately begins
to make use of his relationship with the state, begins to behave
as a king. He is not required to cultivate kingship by practice
and by constant thought about his position, just as a child is
not required to remember always that his mother is his mother.
He just knows it once and lives the relationship at all times. So
simple is the path of understanding which results in freedom
from bondage.

The whole truth of life is that there is nothing substantial to
bind the never-changing to the ever-changing sphere of life. And
nothing to keep them bound together. It is only ignorance of the
natural state of freedom existing between these spheres that
results in binding them together. This ignorance, and the bondage born of it, keep life in motion – the inner aspect remaining never-changing and the outer ever-changing. The outer ever-
changing aspect continues eternally by virtue of the inner. Thus
life flows onward in the natural state of eternal freedom – on
the basis of ignorance!

The knowledge contained in these verses – the wisdom of
Sankhya – cuts asunder the bonds of ignorance and allows life
to be in its natural state of eternal freedom.

The following verses further expound this wisdom.

VERSE 16

नासतो विद्यते भावो नाभावो विद्यते सतः ॥
उभयोरपि दृष्टोऽन्तस्त्वनयोस्तत्त्वदर्शिभिः ॥१६॥

The unreal has no being; the real
never ceases to be. The final truth
about them both has thus been perceived
by the seers of ultimate Reality.

The indestructibility of human essence is explained here. Ultimate Reality has been defined as that which never changes.
Opposed to it is the unreal, which is ever-changing; for clearly

that which always changes has no substance, no real existence.

Here in this verse the Lord brings Arjuna to see the Reality at the basis of the multiplicity of creation. This is the next step, following logically upon that of the previous verse. Here the seer of Truth perceives clearly the difference between the permanent, never-changing absolute state of life and its ever-changing states of diversified phenomenal existence. It is this which gives him that stability and heightened state of consciousness by which he rises above the binding influence of activity in the phenomenal world.

Arjuna is being led step by step towards the vision of a realized man.

VERSE 17

अविनाशि तु तद्विद्धि येन सर्वमिदं ततम् ॥
विनाशमव्ययस्यास्य न कश्चित्कर्तुमर्हति ॥१७॥

Know That to be indeed indestructible
by which all this is pervaded. None
can work the destruction of this
immutable Being.

The Lord presents to Arjuna the indestructibility of the inner Reality, the Being of the phenomenal objective world, which pervades everything.

It may be made clear here that the omnipresent Being and the spirit within man are not two different entities. They are found to be different because of the different individual nervous systems. As the same sun appears as different when shining on different media, such as water and oil, so the same omnipresent Being, shining through different nervous systems, appears as different and forms the spirit, the subjective aspect of man's personality. When the nervous system is pure, Being reflects more and the spirit is more powerful, the mind more effective. When the nervous system is at its purest, then Being reflects in all its fullness, and the inner individuality of the spirit gains the level

of unlimited eternal Being. Thus it is clear that in its essential
nature the spirit is undying and omnipresent. This explains the
universality of individuality.

In the previous verses, step by step, and each a step of profound wisdom, the everlasting nature of the spirit was brought
home to Arjuna. In this verse its indestructible nature is stressed. In the verses which follow, the impermanence of phenomenal life will be emphasized and with it the principle that the
phenomenal world is just the manifested phase of eternal unmanifested Being. The conclusion is that, from both points of
view – that of the permanence of Being and that of the impermanent level of life – Arjuna's duty is not to worry about
anything, but to rise up and do what he has to do.

Verse 18

अन्तवन्त इमे देहा नित्यस्योक्ताः शरीरिणः ॥
अनाशिनोऽप्रमेयस्य तस्माद्युध्यस्व भारत ॥१८॥

These bodies are known to have an end;
the dweller in the body is eternal,
imperishable, infinite. Therefore,
O Bharata, fight!

It is obvious that at every moment the body is changing. The
body of a child is not the body of a youth; and the body of
a youth is not the body of an old man. So if death is inevitably
going on, even during what is said to be life, nothing new seems
to happen when one body dies and another body is taken. There
is no point therefore in lamenting the death of the body – and
even less in lamenting it in anticipation.

'Dweller in the body': this verse brings out a distinction between the body and the spirit that dwells within it. There is no
aim here of classifying the different aspects of the spirit within,
but only of drawing a line between the unchangeable inner content of life and the destructible nature of the outer body.

It can, however, be explained that the inner spirit may be understood in two ways : first, as the ego, together with the mind
and senses, which constitutes the doer and the experiencer, the
enjoyer and the sufferer; secondly, as the 'dweller in the body',
which is the individual aspect of cosmic existence, of eternal
Being, and which is known in Sanskrit terminology as 'jiva'.

Jiva, then, is individualized cosmic existence; it is the individual spirit within the body. With its limitations removed,
jiva is Atman, transcendent Being.

When the individuality of the jiva and the universality of
the transcendent Self, the Atman, are united and found together on one level of life, then there is Brahman, the all-
embracing cosmic life.

As the individual jiva in its essence is Atman,[9] it is here called
'eternal, imperishable, infinite'.

VERSE 19

य एनं वेत्ति हन्तारं यश्चैनं मन्यते हतम् ॥
उभौ तौ न विजानीतो नायं हन्ति न हन्यते ॥१९॥

He who understands him to be the slayer,
and he who takes him to be the slain,
both fail to perceive the truth. He
neither slays nor is slain.

It has been made clear that the self, or spirit, in its essential
nature, knows no change or variation, is free from any attributes,
is neither the doer nor the doing. All attributes belong to the
relative, the manifested field of life; therefore the spirit cannot
be regarded as either the subject or the object of any action. The
activity assumed by an ignorant man to belong to himself – to
the subjective personality that he calls himself – does not belong
to his real Self, for this, in its essential nature, is beyond activity.
The Self, in its real nature, is only the silent witness of every-

9. See verse 17, commentary.

thing. That is why the Lord says: 'He who understands him to
be the slayer, and he who takes him to be the slain, both fail
to perceive the truth.'

VERSE 20

न जायते म्रियते वा कदाचि-
    न्नायं भूत्वा भविता वा न भूयः ॥
अजो नित्यः शाश्वतोऽयं पुराणो
    न हन्यते हन्यमाने शरीरे ॥२०॥

He is never born, nor does he ever die;
nor once having been, does he cease to
be. Unborn, eternal, everlasting,
ancient, he is not slain when the body
is slain.

The eternal unmanifested absolute nature of the spirit, or self,
is ever unaffected by happenings in the relative field. It is ever
the same, beyond the limits of time, space and causation. Without beginning or end, it knows no birth or death. Whether in
this or that body, the self continues to be. The immutable eternal life remains through the ever-changing phases of the bodies
which it takes.

VERSE 21

वेदाविनाशिनं नित्यं य एनमजमव्ययम् ॥
कथं स पुरुषः पार्थ कं घातयति हन्ति कम् ॥२१॥

One who knows him to be indestructible,
everlasting, unborn, undying, how can
that man, O Partha, slay or cause anyone
to slay?

In these verses Lord Krishna provides the intellectual conception of that state to which He wants Arjuna to rise – the state where he will be established in his real, eternal Self. Once established in It, he will attain to the Reality of existence and thus rise above the influence of the action of fighting and, indeed, of all actions in life. For action is in the field of ever-changing existence, and his consciousness will be established in the changeless existence of Being. Therefore he will quite naturally be above the influence of action.

The discourse is presented with marvellous skill. Since the Lord wants to give Arjuna the intellectual conception of Reality, not only does He continue to describe that which has no attributes, but He also questions Arjuna to attract his attention and to awaken his wits so that the description will be more clearly understood. It is obvious, the Lord tells him, that anyone who knows the Reality of life as never-changing eternal Being would not – how could he? – attribute to It anything of the perishable order.

VERSE 22

वासांसि जीर्णानि यथा विहाय
    नवानि गृह्णाति नरोऽपराणि ॥
तथा शरीराणि विहाय जीर्णा-
    न्यन्यानि संयाति नवानि देही ॥२२॥

As a man casting off worn-out garments
takes other new ones, so the dweller
in the body casting off worn-out
bodies takes others that are new.

This is an illustration to make clear the idea contained in the previous verse. It presents a picture of the unchanging nature of the dweller in the body, the spirit or jiva, which is enlarged upon in the following verse.

VERSE 23

नैनं छिन्दन्ति शस्त्राणि नैनं दहति पावकः ॥
न चैनं क्लेदयन्त्यापो न शोषयति मारुतः ॥२३॥

*Weapons cannot cleave him, nor fire
burn him; water cannot wet him, nor
wind dry him away.*

The intention here is to bring home to Arjuna the immortality,
the never-changing nature of the self, and to make him see clearly
that nothing can possibly affect it in any way. One thing was
deep-rooted in Arjuna's mind : the feeling that his sharp arrows
would pierce and mutilate the bodies of those he held dear and slay
them. That is why the Lord begins by making him understand
that their existence would not, in the real sense, be destroyed by
his weapons. Reality is one, omnipresent, devoid of any duality,
without components – that is why It cannot be slain. The body is
composed of different parts – that is why it can be slain.

To make the idea still clearer, the Lord explains that even the
elements of air, water and fire, which are much more refined and
powerful than Arjuna's weapons, are unable to disturb the self.
The Lord mentions weapons, fire, air and water as symbolic of the
entire creation. His aim is to show Arjuna that the self, being
transcendental, remains ever untouched by anything in this relative field. This idea is developed in the verses that follow, so as to
leave Arjuna in no doubt regarding the permanent nature of
the self.

VERSE 24

अच्छेद्योऽयमदाह्योऽयमक्लेद्योऽशोष्य एव च ॥
नित्यः सर्वगतः स्थाणुरचलोऽयं सनातनः ॥२४॥

He is uncleavable; he cannot be burned;
he cannot be wetted, nor yet can he be
dried. He is eternal, all-pervading,
stable, immovable, ever the same.

The teacher may start, as in this verse, by explaining Reality in
terms of the negation of common experience. When the mind of
the pupil begins to rise to something abstract, beyond the sphere
of his present experience, he is then told of what may be called
the positive attributes of Reality. It is true that absolute Reality
is without any attribute, but even so, expressions have to be used
to convey some sense of It.

Here the Lord uses both means of enlightenment, negation and
affirmation, beautifully in one stroke. The teacher has to be alert
enough not to miss a single reaction of the pupil's mind to every
word he speaks. Only by striking at the right moment are the
desired results achieved.

The sequence of words is important: being eternal, Reality is
all-pervading; being all-pervading, It is stable; being stable, It is
immovable; and being immovable, It is ever the same.

VERSE 25

अव्यक्तोऽयमचिन्त्योऽयमविकार्योऽयमुच्यते ॥
तस्मादेवं विदित्वैनं नानुशोचितुमर्हसि ॥२५॥

He is declared to be unmanifest,
unthinkable, unchangeable; therefore
knowing him as such you should not
grieve.

It was essential for Lord Krishna to impart to Arjuna a vivid intellectual conception of the soul, the real Self, transcendent and without attributes, and He had to do this when Arjuna's mind was 'full of sorrow'. It was therefore all the more necessary to present the conception of the unknowable through attributes of the already known world.

Arjuna had to be given this clear intellectual conception of Reality in order to prepare him for the state of enlightenment. He could not be given the direct vision but had to be shown the intellectual conception first and then be led to experience step by step. Otherwise Arjuna could not have understood that behind obvious phenomenal existence there lies eternal Being, and that he himself is That, and everything is That.

VERSE 26

अथ चैनं नित्यजातं नित्यं वा मन्यसे मृतम् ।
तथापि त्वं महाबाहो नैनं शोचितुमर्हसि ॥२६॥

*Even if you think of him as constantly
taking birth and constantly dying, even
then, O mighty-armed, you should not
grieve like this.*

Up to this stage in the dialogue, the Lord has explained life from the viewpoint of the indestructibility of the self. In this verse He begins on a different argument.

Even if Arjuna remains unconvinced of the immortality of the dweller in the body, this does not justify his grieving; even if the dweller in the body is seen as repeatedly dying with the death of the body and repeatedly being born with the birth of the body, Arjuna still has no need to grieve.

So perfect is the Lord's logic that one argument is given and a statement established, and then, even when quite contrary reasoning is applied, the same conclusion is reached. This is the glory that belongs to the teaching of the Absolute: It is found to be the same whatever one's angle of vision. Only the Absolute can be known in this manner.

While this is the glory of the Absolute, it is also the glory of the master's mind that can deduce the same conclusion from two diametrically opposed lines of reasoning. If Arjuna is not convinced by one line of reasoning, the Lord does not leave him to his fate but tries to convince him through another. This is the situation between Arjuna and the Lord that was created by his surrender[10] at His feet.

VERSE 27

जातस्य हि ध्रुवो मृत्युर्ध्रुवं जन्म मृतस्य च ॥
तस्मादपरिहार्येऽर्थे न त्वं शोचितुमर्हसि ॥२७॥

Certain indeed is death for the born
and certain is birth for the dead;
therefore over the inevitable you
should not grieve.

Change is inevitable in the field of relative existence; it is going on even in the present, as it was in the past and will be in the future. Therefore birth and death are natural events about which one should not feel much concern.

The phenomenon of birth and death is the expression of the eternal process of evolution, which in its turn expresses the purpose of creation. Life evolves with a view to the realization of perfection. Development through change is the natural course of this cosmic process. Every change is significant, for it provides a step to perfection. The manner in which change takes place is also in line with the cosmic purpose of evolution, for it too is governed by the eternal laws of cause and effect. This is how, through birth and death, the plan of life finds its fulfilment.

Man has freedom of action; thereby he can adopt any channel, good or bad, through which he wants the course of his life to

10. See verse 7.

flow. This is in his hands. But change is inevitable, and it is for the sake of life that this is so: 'therefore over the inevitable you should not grieve.' On the contrary, change should be welcomed for it opens new vistas of life towards fulfilment.

VERSE 28

अव्यक्तादीनि भूतानि व्यक्तमध्यानि भारत ॥
अव्यक्तनिधनान्येव तत्र का परिदेवना ॥२८॥

Creatures are unmanifest in the beginning,
manifest in the middle state and unmanifest
again at the end, O Bharata! What
grief is there in this?

Here again, and from yet another angle, the same conclusion is reached: the phenomenal presents the manifested state of life, while Being is of unmanifested transcendental nature.

According to the findings of modern physics, all matter has only phenomenal existence and is in reality formless energy. Both in its previous state and in its present obvious form, matter is nothing but pure energy, and on dissolution of the present form it will remain the same energy. Similarly, the present phenomenal phase of existence is seen to have no permanent significance, and it is this that the Lord is impressing upon Arjuna.

VERSE 29

आश्चर्यवत्पश्यति कश्चिदेन-
माश्चर्यवद्वदति तथैव चान्यः ॥
आश्चर्यवच्चैनमन्यः शृणोति
श्रुत्वाप्येनं वेद न चैव कश्चित् ॥२९॥

One sees him as a wonder, another
likewise speaks of him as a wonder,
and as a wonder another hears of him.
Yet even on (seeing, speaking and
hearing) some do not understand him.

Because the self is of unmanifested nature, and because man's
life is always in the field of the manifested, it is not to be won-
dered at if some people hear about it with great surprise and
others are not able to understand it at all. The purpose of this
verse is simply to give a picture of the dissimilar nature of the
ephemeral and eternal aspects of life. Although Arjuna is obviously unfamiliar with eternal Reality, it is not the Lord's aim
to stress the difficulty of understanding It. It is a wonder to some
because, although omnipresent, It is found as the individual self,
and although eternal, It is found dying and being born. That is
why it is difficult to comprehend Its full nature by mere intellectual process. It needs a direct experience for the abstract Reality
to be properly understood.

There is yet another implication. Up to this verse, the Lord has
been trying in different ways to make Arjuna understand that he
should not grieve. But he is not free from grief, and therefore, as
an additional step in the task of enlightening him, the Lord
points out that his response to what he has heard is a feeling of
strangeness. In order to encourage him, the Lord seems to be
saying that this feeling of strangeness does not matter, for it is
natural with regard to knowledge of eternal life. Many marvel
at it and find it a wonder.

One can take a different point of view and conclude that the
Lord means to show that Reality is difficult to attain, for many
having heard of It and spoken about It are not able to understand
It. Nevertheless it is wiser to hold that the purpose of the verse is
not to convince Arjuna of the difficulty of attainment, but to
give him hope that, although many find it difficult, it is going to
prove easy for him.

This verse speaks of eternal Reality, which is strange to many
in many different ways, because everyone looks at It from his own
level of consciousness. For this reason, many who seek It find It
impossible to attain on the level of the senses and the intellect,
since these are concerned only with the temporary, phenomenal
phases of life.

The next verse brings to an end the intellectual description of
the two aspects of life, the ever-changing and the never-changing.

VERSE 30

देही नित्यमवध्योऽयं देहे सर्वस्य भारत ॥
तस्मात्सर्वाणि भूतानि न त्वं शोचितुमर्हसि ॥३०॥

He who dwells in the body of everyone
is eternal and invulnerable, O Bharata;
therefore you should not grieve for
any creature whatsoever.

This is the conclusion of all that has been said by the Lord from
the eleventh verse onwards. Every creature is on the path to
perfection. Through births and deaths of bodies, everyone is pro-
gressing towards fulfilment. No one should grieve over the death
of another. Arjuna, having acquired understanding of the permanent nature of the dweller in the body and the impermanence
of the body, should respond to the call of duty, for that alone will
help his own evolution and that of others.

The following verse begins the argument on the level of duty.
This is to deepen the understanding of life after the absolute and
relative aspects of existence have been made clear.

VERSE 31

स्वधर्ममपि चावेक्ष्य न विकम्पितुमर्हसि ॥
धर्म्याद्धि युद्धाच्छ्रेयोऽन्यत्क्षत्रियस्य न विद्यते ॥३१॥

Even if you consider your own dharma
you should not waver, for there is
nothing better for a kshatriya than
a battle in accord with dharma.

The event of war is a natural phenomenon. It is a process of
restoring the balance between the negative and positive forces of
nature. To rise to the call of a war to establish righteousness is to
respond to the cosmic purpose, the will of God. To live and die to
maintain law and order in society, thereby remaining a faithful
instrument in the hand of God, is the privilege of a man born in
a kshatriya family.

The Lord's purpose is to convince Arjuna that, from the point
of view of his duty, the only worth-while course is to shake off
his reluctance to fight and face up to the action for which he is
born. Having explained to him in the previous verse that from
the viewpoint of life's eternal existence he need not grieve either
for the living or for the dead, He wants to bring home to Arjuna
that to him, born a kshatriya, fighting is natural; it is his normal
duty in life. To do 'battle in accord with dharma' and establish
righteousness for the good of the world is the most glorious and
justifiable way of fulfilling the life of a kshatriya, who is born to
protect dharma at any cost.

Dharma[11] maintains the stream of evolution in life. The
kshatriya who does not accept a just fight wavers from this
natural stream of evolution.

11. See I, 1, commentary.

VERSE 32

यदृच्छया चोपपन्नं स्वर्गद्वारमपावृतम् ॥
सुखिनः क्षत्रियाः पार्थ लभन्ते युद्धमीदृशम् ॥३२॥

Happy are the kshatriyas, O Partha,
who find, unsought, such a battle —
an open door to heaven.

'Open door to heaven': by following his dharma, a kshatriya
serves to uphold law and order in society and maintains the stream
of his own evolution. If he dies while fighting in this cause, he is
a hero of cosmic life and gains the highest happiness in heaven.

This verse makes a general statement proclaiming the good
fortune of a kshatriya who gains an opportunity for such a battle.
At the same time, by calling him 'Partha', the son of Pritha, Lord
Krishna reminds Arjuna that he is a kshatriya.

When a kshatriya has a chance of battle he feels happy, because he gains whether he wins or loses: [12] victorious, he achieves
glory on earth; dying in battle, he gains heaven.

What will happen if Arjuna does not participate in the battle?

VERSE 33

अथ चेत्त्वमिमं धर्म्यं संग्रामं न करिष्यसि ॥
ततः स्वधर्मं कीर्तिं च हित्वा पापमवाप्स्यसि ॥३३॥

Now, if you do not engage in this
battle, which is in accord with dharma,
then casting away your own dharma and
good fame, you will incur sin.

'Casting away your own dharma' means falling out of the path
of evolution, and that in itself is a positive sin.

12. See verse 37.

'Sin' is that through which a man strays from the path of evolution. It results in suffering.

Having reminded Arjuna of his great good fortune in being given this opportunity for battle, the Lord immediately impresses upon him the danger of not accepting it. To abstain from fighting, and so neglect his dharma, would bring loss of fame and would plainly be sinful.

Dharma and fame are placed together in this verse. The connexion between them is clarified in the commentary on the following verse.

In the 31st verse the Lord began the argument on the basis of duty. Having enlightened Arjuna about his duty, his dharma, which maintains the natural stream of evolution, He now wants to make clear also the nature of duty from the level of social consideration.

It may be mentioned that the moral code of conduct in any society has dharma at its basis, whether or not the people in that society are aware of the inner workings of nature guided by the invincible force of dharma. The fundamentals of social behaviour in every society on earth are based on this principle which governs the laws of evolution. Therefore the Lord wants to analyse the nature of duty in the light of its influence on society. How others think of one's life, how others are affected by one's actions and how others talk about one are here the main concern. The word 'fame' covers all these points.

The following three verses are devoted to this consideration, which will complete the wisdom of Sankhya.

VERSE 34

अकीर्तिंश्चापि भूतानि कथयिष्यन्ति तेऽव्ययाम् ॥
संभावितस्य चाकीर्तिर्मरणादतिरिच्यते ॥३४॥

Moreover men will ever tell of your
disgrace, and to a man of honour ill
fame is worse than death.

Those who are esteemed are they who, living for themselves, live for others and dying, die for others. Their lives are justified in the degree to which others recognize them. Their happiness in life is in proportion to the goodwill accorded to them. Therefore if those who have enjoyed goodwill and fame in society lose it, they suffer shame and misery, which is worse than death. Loss of renown for a once famous man is more than death to him. Arjuna was the most famous archer of his time; that is why Lord Krishna makes this telling point about the nature of a famous man.

The underlying principle of good fame in society is that when a man constantly does good he becomes a centre of harmonious vibrations which, enjoyed by the people around him, naturally create warmth and love in their hearts. That is why he is described in glowing terms by all. In this way the good fame of a man is the criterion of his goodness, and ill fame the criterion of his badness. No one who is good could possibly acquire ill fame. It is the vibrations spreading from a man's actions that induce people to speak well of him or otherwise. The Lord particularly wants to bring home this truth to Arjuna.

The way to uplift a man is first to remind him of the glorious aspects of his character and so gain a sympathetic response. The second step is to point out at once some delicate feature in the situation. The Lord does this in the next verse by saying that the brave will attribute cowardice to Arjuna. A close study of this verse in relation to preceding and subsequent verses will make the point clear.

The Lord lays stress on the importance of fame, not for the sake of fame itself but to call Arjuna's attention to a principle of life : if he behaves in a way that will bring him ill fame, he will become a centre of something unrighteous, and this will impair his personal evolution. It is primarily the principle of personal evolution that is the subject of this consideration of life from the point of view of Sankhya.

VERSE 35

भयाद्रणादुपरतं मंस्यन्ते त्वां महारथाः ॥
येषां च त्वं बहुमतो भूत्वा यास्यसि लाघवम् ॥३५॥

The great warriors will think you fled
from battle out of fear, and they who
held you in esteem will belittle you.

The Lord now speaks to Arjuna of the great humiliation which
awaits him if he does not fight. For a man of honour and repute
this is a very telling point. Arjuna is being reminded of the
different implications of ill fame. Lord Krishna is helping him to
break through the state of suspension by raising points that will
touch his heart and mind and induce him to fight.

VERSE 36

अवाच्यवादांश्च बहून्वदिष्यन्ति तवाहिताः ॥
निन्दन्तस्तव सामर्थ्यं ततो दुःखतरं नु किम् ॥३६॥

Your enemies will speak many ill words
of you and will deride your strength.
What greater pain than this!

The Lord shows Arjuna exactly how he will be put to shame in
the eyes of the world.[13]

Having demonstrated in the previous verses the validity of
fighting from the point of view of its social implications, and
having made it quite clear in the present verse that pain awaits
him if he does not fight, the Lord, in the following verse, shows
Arjuna the rewards that fighting will bring him both in this life
and hereafter.

13. See verse 34, commentary.

VERSE 37

हतो वा प्राप्स्यसि स्वर्गं जित्वा वा भोक्ष्यसे महीम् ॥
तस्मादुत्तिष्ठ कौन्तेय युद्धाय कृतनिश्चयः ॥३७॥

Slain, you will reach heaven;
victorious, you will enjoy the earth.
Therefore, O son of Kunti, stand up,
resolved to fight!

This verse considers the performance of duty from the point of
view of gain.

The Lord says to Arjuna: You should realize that, whether
you die on the battlefield or whether you survive, you stand to
gain,[14] because fighting is in accordance with the natural course
of your evolution. And if you are established on that course, then
you are automatically on the path of increasing fortune in this
life and hereafter. Therefore without losing more time, come,
make up your mind to fight.

This places the teaching of Sankhya on the most practical level
of life. It is not right to associate this teaching with the life of
the recluse only.

VERSE 38

सुखदुःखे समे कृत्वा लाभालाभौ जयाजयौ ॥
ततो युद्धाय युज्यस्व नैवं पापमवाप्स्यसि ॥३८॥

Having gained equanimity in pleasure
and pain, in gain and loss, in victory
and defeat, then come out to fight.
Thus you will not incur sin.

14. See verse 32.

Having made clear to Arjuna in the last verse that he stands to gain whether he dies or wins the battle, the Lord now wishes to convince him that he should waste no more time in the consideration of victory or defeat. Whatever the consequences, he should be prepared to fight, because at least one thing is certain : by fighting he will not incur sin. If, on the other hand, he refuses to fight, he is certain to fall into sin.

Arjuna was convinced that, whether he won or lost the battle, by killing he would in fact incur great sin. That is why, in this verse, bringing to an end the intellectual aspect of His discourse, the Lord says to him : I am not asking you to fight with a view to this or that loss or gain, but because by fighting you will not incur sin.

Unfortunately, for the last few centuries this part of Lord Krishna's teaching has been interpreted as indicating that a mood of equanimity should be cultivated during the experience of either loss or gain. In fact, the Lord means that right or wrong, virtue or sin, should be the primary consideration when deciding upon the validity of an action. It should not be decided on the basis of loss or gain. In judging the validity of an action, the first consideration should be its nature – whether or not it will in any way be sinful.

It is the purpose of the action that creates its need. Once the need for an action is felt, the first step is to make sure that it is not in any way sinful. To consider the loss or gain is only the second step. If it is an action leading to the fulfilment of one's mission in life, or an action which it would be sinful to leave undone, then its performance becomes a necessity. In such a case the consideration of a temporary loss or gain becomes all the more unimportant.

In this verse the Lord is clearly saying to Arjuna : First rise to the wisdom of life given so far (11–37). Established in this wisdom, come out to fight. Thus you will not incur sin.

'You will not incur sin' : this is the guarantee that the Lord offers. One becomes uninvolved in sin as a result of 'having gained equanimity in pleasure and pain, in gain and loss, in victory and defeat'. This state of equanimity is born of the wisdom so far given to Arjuna, starting from verse 11 – the wisdom of Sankhya, as the Lord names it in the verse that follows.

To sum up, this wisdom of Sankhya comprises:

1. Understanding of the perishable and imperishable phases of life (11–30).
2. Understanding of dharma (31–3).
3. Understanding of one's relationship with others (33–6).
4. Understanding of the results of actions (36–7).
5. Understanding of the nature of the doer as uninvolved with action, giving rise to equanimity in loss and gain.

Knowledge of the perishable and imperishable aspects of life broadens the vision and makes a man see beyond the mundane and limited sphere of daily life. This, when supplemented by knowledge of dharma, induces in him a natural tendency to act rightly. His life becomes more useful to himself and to others. Through the understanding of his relationship with others, he rises above selfish ends to more and more universal aspects of life. This growing universal outlook, enriched by the proper understanding of the results of action, helps a man to develop and make progress on all levels of life. And finally, with the understanding of the nature of the doer as uninvolved, he gains equanimity,[15] rises above the influence of dualities, lives a life free from sin and suffering and enjoys eternal freedom.

The following verse begins the teaching of Yoga, whereby the mind will rise above the binding influence of action – the teaching whereby the intellect, cultured by the wisdom of Sankhya, will be eternally established in the oneness of life, in the oneness of absolute Being, the eternal liberation in divine consciousness here and now.

15. See verse 15.

VERSE 39

एषा तेऽभिहिता सांख्ये बुद्धिर्योंगे त्विमां शृणु ॥
बुद्ध्या युक्तो यया पार्थ कर्मबन्धं प्रहास्यसि ॥३६॥

This which has been set before you is
understanding in terms of Sankhya; hear it
now in terms of Yoga. Your intellect
established through it, O Partha, you will
cast away the binding influence of action.

Yoga, the path of Union, is a direct way to experience the
essential nature of Reality. This Reality is described and understood intellectually by a system which the Lord calls Sankhya,
and which has been set forth in the previous verses.

The Sankhya of the Bhagavad-Gita presents the principles of
all the six systems of Indian philosophy, while the Yoga of the
Bhagavad-Gita presents their practical aspects.

This verse illustrates the technique of intelligent teaching. The
subject is introduced and its result made clear in one stroke so
that, seeing both the scale of the subject and the possibility of
achieving the desired goal, the disciple is eager to begin the
practice. For the Lord assures him that he will 'cast away the
binding influence of action'[16] as a result of his intellect becoming
established in Yoga.

Intellectual understanding of Reality convinces a man of the
existence of a nobler and more permanent field of life that lies
beyond and underlies the ordinary level of phenomenal existence.
That has been the purpose of the discourse up to this point. Now
Lord Krishna wishes to introduce Arjuna to the practice whereby
his intellect will become established in Reality. This is to give
him that positive experience of the truth of existence which will
bring him to a state where he is unaffected by the binding influence of action.

The direct experience of transcendental bliss gives a man such

16. See verse 50, commentary.

great contentment that the joys of the relative world fail to make
a deep impression on him, and he rises above the binding influence
of action, just as a contented business man, having achieved great
wealth, is not affected by small losses or gains.

By using the word 'intellect', the Lord makes it clear that the
mind, purified or settled by the wisdom of Sankhya, becomes
established in the Self through the practice of Yoga.

As has already been shown in the commentary on verse 15, no
practice is involved in gaining the understanding of life through
Sankhya. If one wants to practise, one should turn to Yoga. The
use of the words 'intellect established' indicates that it is the intellect that accomplishes Yoga, not the wandering mind. The suggestion is that the mind should be raised to the state of intellect
through the wisdom of Sankhya and then be turned to Yoga to
become established in the Self. This presents Sankhya and Yoga
as complementary, a point which is developed in Chapter V.

It is interesting to note that the essence of the wisdom of
Sankhya was given in four verses (12–15) and that the essence of
Yoga is also given in four verses (45–8). These two groups of four
verses expound the essential wisdom of the Bhagavad-Gita. All
other verses are simply an extension of them.

In the following verse, the Lord conveys to Arjuna the simplicity and effectiveness of the technique which he is about to
give him and which will establish him in complete contentment,
the state of eternal freedom from the bondage of action.

VERSE 40

नेहाभिक्रमनाशोऽस्ति प्रत्यवायो न विद्यते ॥
स्वल्पमप्यस्य धर्मस्य त्रायते महतो भयात् ॥४०॥

In this (Yoga) no effort is lost and
no obstacle exists. Even a little of
this dharma delivers from great fear.

'Obstacle' : the Sanskrit word *pratyavaya* also means any reversal
of progress or any adverse effect.

BHAGAVAD-GITA 118

'Dharma' signifies the path of evolution. The practice of Yoga is a direct way to evolution. Through it, the individual mind gains the state of cosmic intelligence – that unbounded state of universal Being which is the summit of evolution. Dharma is natural to man, and so is this practice of Yoga, for it is in accordance with the very nature of the mind and brings fulfilment to life. That is why this Yoga is the dharma of everyone.

Lord Krishna's wonderful teaching in this verse brings great hope to mankind. On the way to eternal freedom 'no effort is lost'. Any effort on this path results in the goal; the process, having started, cannot stop until it has reached its goal. This is so in the first place because the flow of the mind towards this state is natural, for it is a state of absolute bliss, and the mind is always craving for greater happiness. Therefore as water flows down a slope in a natural way, so the mind flows naturally in the direction of bliss.

Secondly, 'no effort is lost' because, for the mind to become blissful, no effort is needed! If effort were necessary, then the question of effort being lost would arise. When an action is being performed, one stage of the process leads to another, which in turn gives rise to a further stage, so that when one stage has been reached, the previous stage is a thing of the past. In the performance of every action, therefore, some stage is lost, some energy is lost, some effort is lost. When the Lord says here that no effort is lost, it can only be because no effort is required. This means that Lord Krishna's technique of establishing the intellect in the Absolute is based on the very nature of the mind.[17] We must therefore inquire how the mind, motivated by its own nature, succeeds in gaining divine consciousness without effort.

When a man is listening to music and a more beautiful melody begins to come from another source, his whole mind will turn to enjoy it. No effort is needed to shift the attention to the more charming melody; the process is automatic. There is no loss of energy between starting to listen and enjoying the music with rapt attention. This is the Lord's meaning: since the field of eternal freedom is absolute bliss, the process of uniting the mind with it, once having begun, comes to completion without loss of

17. See verse 45, commentary.

energy or effort. It does not stop until the experience is full, for 'no obstacle exists'.

Seen from this angle, the very beginning of the process is its fulfilment, for it is the movement of the mind to bliss. The end is found in the beginning. The very start of the process brings the mind to the goal because, according to the Lord, there is no resistance on the way, there is 'no obstacle' to surmount. It is a path of no resistance, a pathless path, a path whose goal is omnipresent. That is why 'a little of this' 'delivers from great fear'.

Following the path of no resistance means that the technique of establishing the mind in the Absolute has only to be started, and from that point deliverance from suffering follows. The very start in this direction relieves a man 'from great fear' in life.

To establish the mind in the Absolute, says the Lord, very little – if anything – has to be done. This is because not even the natural direction of the mind has to be changed. The mind wanders from object to object, and it wanders, not for the sake of the object itself, but for the possibility of happiness that the object provides. Thus it does not actually wander from object to object but moves from a point of lesser happiness to a point of greater happiness. Since the greatest happiness is its goal, and the flow of the mind is already in the direction of greater happiness, the direction need not be changed. And since there is no need even to change the direction of the mind, it appears that nothing need be done to realize the goal.

But the Lord says 'a little of this' practice. This shows that something has to be done. What is necessary is only to begin to experience the increasing charm on the way to transcendental absolute bliss. As in the case of diving, one has only to take a correct angle and let go – the whole process is accomplished in an automatic manner. This is what the Lord means by 'a little of this'.

Just as the first ray of the sun dispels the darkness of the night, so the first step in this practice dispels the darkness of ignorance and fear. But although the first ray of the rising sun is able to dispel the darkness of the night, the sun still continues to rise, because its nature is not only to remove darkness, leaving the atmosphere dimly lighted, but also to shine forth in splendour and illumine the whole earth. The glory of the sun is its full mid-day light.

The Lord clearly means that the path of divine unfolding is so simple and natural that the process, once having been consciously started, encounters no obstacles. Quickly it produces an effect strong enough to enlighten the mind and release a man from all negativeness in life, from fear of the cycle of birth and death.

This is a noble way of enlightening the aspirant. There is a confident assurance of results from the very beginning of the practical teaching. Arjuna is told the nature of the technique and the results that will follow from its practice so that he may know in advance what it involves. Realization is not something that comes from outside: it is the revelation of the Self, in the Self, by the Self.

This revelation cannot occur unless a man gives himself completely to it, and then it happens by itself. But in order to be able to give himself completely to it, he has to know at least two things: first, that it is within his power to accomplish, and secondly, that its accomplishment will be of use to him. This is why Lord Krishna speaks the words of this verse. Arjuna is being prepared for the direct experience of Reality which wipes out all uncertainties and brings stability to life. The Lord proclaims to him the simplicity of the approach to the Divine and at the same time describes its result.

Why is it that in the modern world this spiritual practice has faded into the background of life? The answer lies in the wrong interpretation of verses such as this and the consequent spread of a misguided view of Reality which has persisted for many centuries.

Having explained the simplicity and effectiveness of the principle of establishing the intellect in the Divine, the Lord, in the following verses, introduces the technique for its accomplishment.

VERSE 41

व्यवसायात्मिका बुद्धिरेकेह कुरुनन्दन ॥
बहुशाखा ह्यनन्ताश्च बुद्धयोऽव्यवसायिनाम् ॥४१॥

In this Yoga, O joy of the Kurus,
the resolute intellect is one-
pointed, but many-branched and
endlessly diverse are the intellects
of the irresolute.

'In this Yoga': in this path to bliss. When the mind moves
towards bliss, it experiences increasing charm at every step; as
when one proceeds towards the light, the intensity increases continuously. When the mind experiences increasing happiness, then
it does not wander; it remains focused in one direction, unwavering and resolute. Such is the state of the mind moving in the
direction of bliss, and when it arrives at the direct experience of
bliss, it loses all contact with the outside and is contented in the
state of transcendental bliss-consciousness. When the mind comes
out of this state into the field of action again, it remains contented and therefore maintains its resolute state to a greater or
lesser degree. Through practice this state becomes established.
This is what the Lord means when He says that 'in this Yoga ...
the resolute intellect is one-pointed'.

The minds of those who do not practise this Yoga are constantly
in the field of sensory experience. This fails to provide the mind
with that great joy which alone can satisfy its thirst for happiness. That is why the minds of such people continue to search
and wander endlessly.

The Lord here further clarifies verse 38. Arjuna is advised to
rise to the state of resolute intellect. For only in this state will he
be able to win that evenness of mind in pleasure and pain, loss
and gain, victory and defeat, which the Lord makes the prerequisite for battle.

It may appear that there is something negative in this approach

to Reality, for although the purpose is to establish Arjuna in the
resolute state of mind, in this verse the characteristics of the
irresolute mind are emphasized. This is significant. If a man on a
mountain peak, wishing to guide another who is only half-way
up, keeps shouting directions about where he himself is standing,
it will not help the other man to arrive at the top. The direct way
of guiding him up is first to tell him where he is and describe his
surroundings, thus making him aware of his own position, and
then to guide him to the peak. Arjuna is in a state of irresolute-
ness, and the Lord's intention is to bring him to the resolute state
by first showing him all about the irresolute state of his mind,
and then guiding him to the resolute state.

Having pointed out these two states of mind, the Lord, in the
following three verses, explains the conditions under which the
mind continues to remain irresolute. After this He will direct
Arjuna to rise from that state and become resolute, so that his
mind may be established in Reality.

VERSE 42

यामिमां पुष्पितां वाचं प्रवदन्त्यविपश्चितः ॥
वेदवादरताः पार्थं नान्यदस्तीतिवादिनः ॥४२॥

*The undiscerning who are engrossed
in the letter of the Veda, O Partha,
and declare that there is nothing
else, speak flowery words.*

The Vedas are authentic expositions of the path of evolution.
They elucidate, step by step, the gradual process of the integration of life and teach the knowledge by which a man may quickly
rise through all levels of evolution and attain final liberation.

To enable a man to profit by this great wisdom of life, the Vedas
advocate a course of disciplined action and thought. The discipline
of action is dealt with in those chapters collectively called Karma
Kanda, which means pertaining to action, while discipline of

mind is set forth in the chapters called Upasana Kanda, which means pertaining to the mind in relation to Reality.

The nature of the supreme Reality and of life's fulfilment forms the subject of the chapters collectively called Gyana Kanda, which means pertaining to knowledge.

The purpose of the Vedic Karma Kanda is to establish a code of action that will bring success and prosperity in this life and hereafter. It deals with the rites and rituals necessary to establish coordination between the different aspects of individual life : coordination between man and other creatures, between man and the different forces in nature, between man and angels, and between man and God in heaven.

It is great practical wisdom of the highest order; it deals with innumerable types of action and the unfathomable nature of their influence. When those who are learned in this field begin to enlighten others, their discourse is both fascinating and positive. Their exposition of the theory and practice of the rites and rituals is so complete in itself and so decisive and precise in its nature as to be completely authoritative.

The Karma Kanda of the Vedas lays down specific conditions for the attainment of specific results. It is a clear, practical exposition of the laws of nature governing cause and effect in creation.

Innumerable are the aspirations of man, innumerable the objects to be attained. Innumerable also are the ways and means of acting to attain these ends. The purpose of the Karma Kanda is to bring about the coordination of the mind with the body and with the forces of nature in such a way that it results in progress to a higher level and an improved quality of life.

The purpose of the Upasana Kanda is to bring about the coordination of the mind with the inner forces of nature and the ultimate transcendental Being in such a way that it results in the integration of life.

In this and the following two verses, the Lord refers to the Karma Kanda, and then in the 45th verse He brings out the glorious practical aspect of the Upasana Kanda – that of bringing the diffused mind to a resolute state, in order that it may be established in Reality and may live It, thereby fulfilling the purpose of the Gyana Kanda of the Vedas. This is what makes the Bhagavad-

Gita the essence of the Vedas and the highway to the fulfilment of the Vedic way of life.

VERSE 43

कामात्मानः स्वर्गपरा जन्मकर्मफलप्रदाम् ॥
क्रियाविशेषबहुलां भोगैश्वर्यगतिं प्रति ॥४३॥

Filled with desires, with heaven as
their goal, (their words) proclaim birth
as the reward of action and prescribe
many special rites for the attainment
of enjoyment and power.

This verse speaks of the tendency of man to resort to Vedic rites for the sake of a better life and greater worldly joys. The result of being engrossed in wordly desires is that one remains in the cycle of birth and death. For the joys of the senses can never satisfy; they involve man more and more and thus keep him in bondage. There being no chance of lasting contentment, the cycle of birth and death continues.

The following verse reveals the loss that occurs when the mind becomes entangled in these joys which enrich life only with material gains.

VERSE 44

भोगैश्वर्यप्रसक्तानां तयापहृतचेतसाम् ॥
व्यवसायात्मिका बुद्धिः समाधौ न विधीयते ॥४४॥

The resolute state of intellect does
not arise in the mind of those who
are deeply attached to enjoyment and
power and whose thought is captivated
by those (flowery words).

It does not necessarily follow that a man who has great knowledge of relativity cannot also have the wisdom of the Absolute.
If even an illiterate man can enjoy the absolute bliss which is his
own Being, why not the man of learning? The verse objects not
to worldly enjoyment and power, not to the Vedic wisdom of
action, which is a way of gaining such enjoyment and power, but
to the mental state of being engrossed in them that is produced
by hearing the glory of Vedic rites proclaimed in flowery words.

It is not surprising that those always occupied in the field of
action should proclaim that every attainment is possible through
action – and specifically through the Vedic way of action, which
undoubtedly provides a direct path to the attainment of anything
whatsoever. This point of view, while quite valid in the relative
field of life, obviously does not concern itself with the Being of
the Absolute. The manifested and the unmanifested fields of life
together comprise the whole of Reality. But those who only
possess the wisdom of the Vedic Karma Kanda aspire within the
manifested field alone. Their wisdom of action does not directly
give them the wisdom of the unmanifested field of Reality.

Owing to lack of knowledge of the unmanifested Absolute,
such people are heard proclaiming in flowery language that there
is nothing beyond the field of Vedic action (verse 42).

In the 43rd verse, the Lord has depicted the mind held fast in
the grip of action. Fascinated by the flowery language which proclaims the glory of action, it becomes involved in vigorous and
manifold activities. Such an ever-active mind naturally remains
outside the realm of the resolute intellect.

Wordly joys, together with a sense of progress through action
and effort, keep the mind engaged in outside activities. It is difficult for such a mind to converge towards the resolute state by
itself; activity engages the mind in diversity and by so doing is
clearly opposed to the process of convergence, which leads to the
resolute state. Only if the intention is there and guidance is
received can the mind gain one-pointedness, and that even in the
midst of 'enjoyment and power'.

In the following verse, the Lord gives the principle of the
technique for bringing such a diffused mind to a resolute state.

VERSE 45

त्रैगुण्यविषया वेदा निस्त्रैगुण्यो भवार्जुन ॥
निर्द्वन्द्वो नित्यसत्त्वस्थो निर्योगक्षेम आत्मवान् ॥४५॥

The Vedas' concern is with the three
gunas. Be without the three gunas,
O Arjuna, freed from duality, ever
firm in purity, independent of possessions,
possessed of the Self.

This is the technique of instantaneous realization. The Lord
shows Arjuna a practical way of converging the many-branched
mind into the one-pointedness of the resolute intellect. Here is an
effective technique for bringing the mind to a state where all
differences dissolve and leave the individual in the state of
fulfilment.

Everything that has so far been said by Lord Krishna is to prepare Arjuna to understand this practice of bringing his mind
from the field of multiplicity to that of eternal Unity. This practice is to brighten all aspects of his life by bringing his mind to
transcendental consciousness, the limitless source of life, energy,
wisdom, peace and happiness. It is to raise him to that cosmic
status which harmonizes all the opposite forces of life.

Modern psychological theories investigate causes in order to
influence effects. They grope in darkness to find the cause of
darkness in order to remove it. In contradistinction, here is the
idea of bringing light to remove darkness. This is 'the principle
of the second element'. If you wish to produce an effect on the
first element, ignore that element, do not seek its cause; influence
it directly by introducing a second element. Remove the darkness
by introducing light. Take the mind to a field of happiness in
order to relieve it of suffering.

However, even if we accept that by investigating the cause it is
easy to influence the effect, we shall find that this verse will serve
our purpose, for it provides a technique by which the ultimate

cause of all human life can be investigated. If knowledge of the cause can help to influence the effect, then knowledge of the ultimate cause of life will effectively put an end to all suffering.

The greatness of Lord Krishna's teaching lies in its direct practical approach and its completeness from every point of view. The idea of introducing a second element and the idea of investigating the cause in order to influence its effect represent two principles distinctly opposed to each other, yet both of them are fulfilled in one technique. It is this completeness of practical wisdom that has made the Bhagavad-Gita immortal.

Lord Krishna commands Arjuna : 'Be without the three gunas'; be without activity, be your Self. This is resolute consciousness, the state of absolute Being, which is the ultimate cause of all causes. This state of consciousness brings harmony to the whole field of cause and effect and glorifies all life.

Arjuna's main problem was to reconcile love of kinsmen with the necessity to root out evil. He was desperately seeking a formula of compromise between righteousness and evil. But on any plane of relative life these are irreconcilable. That is why, having explored all the avenues of his heart and mind, Arjuna could not find any practical solution, could not decide on any line of action. Lord Krishna, however, shows him the field where righteousness and love merge in eternal harmony, the eternal life of absolute Being.

The Lord makes clear to Arjuna that all influences of the outside world, and their consequences as well, will cling to him and affect him so long as he is out of himself, so long as he allows himself to remain in the sphere of relativity and under its influence. Once out of that sphere, he will find fulfilment in his own Self.

It is difficult for a man to improve his business affairs while he himself is constantly immersed in all their details. If he leaves them for a little while, he becomes able to see the business as a whole and can then more easily decide what is needed. Arjuna has a deep belief in dharma; his mind is clear about considerations of right and wrong. But the Lord asks him to abandon the whole field of right and wrong for the field of the Transcendent. There, established in a state beyond all duality, beyond the influence of right and wrong, he will enjoy the absolute wisdom of life, from which springs all knowledge of the relative world. And the Lord says to Arjuna: The field of that absolute wisdom is not outside you. You have not to go out anywhere to acquire it. It is within you. You have only to be within yourself, 'possessed of the Self', ever firm in the purity of your Being.

Here indeed is the skill of bringing light to remove darkness. Arjuna is not asked to come or go anywhere; he is only asked to 'be without the three gunas'. This instruction serves as a direct means to take man to the absolute state of his consciousness. It is enough for the Lord to say: 'Be without the three gunas, O Arjuna, freed from duality.'

The entire creation consists of the interplay of the three gunas – sattva, rajas and tamas – born of prakriti, or Nature. The process of evolution is carried on by these three gunas. Evolution means creation and its progressive development, and at its basis lies activity. Activity needs rajo-guna to create a spur, and it needs sato-guna and tamo-guna to uphold the direction of the movement.

The nature of tamo-guna is to check or retard, but it should not be thought that when the movement is upwards tamo-guna is absent. For any process to continue, there have to be stages in that process, and each stage, however small in time and space, needs a force to maintain it and another force to develop it into a new stage. The force that develops it into a new stage is sato-guna, while tamo-guna is that which checks or retards the process in order to maintain the state already produced so that it may form the basis for the next stage.

This explains why the three gunas have inevitably to be together. No one guna can exist in isolation without the presence of the other two. It is for this reason that the Lord asks Arjuna to be out of all the three gunas, to be entirely out of the influence of the forces that constitute life in the relative field.

While giving him the wisdom of Sankhya, the Lord has told Arjuna that there are two aspects of life, perishable and imperishable. The perishable is relative existence, and the imperishable is absolute Being. All life in the relative field is under the sway of the gunas. Therefore, in order to give Arjuna the direct experience of the absolute state of life, He asks him to 'be without the three gunas'.

There are gross planes of creation, and there are subtle planes. When the Lord says: 'Be without the three gunas', He means that Arjuna should bring his attention from the gross planes of experience, through the subtle planes and thus to the subtlest plane of experience; transcending even that subtlest plane, he will be completely out of the relative field of life, out of the three gunas. So the Lord's words: 'Be without the three gunas', reveal the secret of arriving at the state of pure consciousness.[18]

When you say to someone: 'Come here', you imply by these two words that he must get up and begin to put one foot before the other, and that this walking on both feet will bring him to you. When the Lord says: 'Be without the three gunas', He obviously means that in whichever field of the three gunas you have your stand, from there you are to begin moving towards subtler planes of the gunas and, arriving at the subtlest, come out of it, transcend it, be by yourself, 'possessed of the Self' – 'freed from duality', 'ever firm in purity', 'independent of possessions'.

Lord Krishna, in this verse, has really given the technique of Self-realization. Arjuna was held in suspension between the dictates of his heart and mind. The Lord suggests to him that he should come out of the conflict and he will then see his way clear. That is why, having said: 'Be without the three gunas', He immediately adds: 'freed from duality', freed from the field of conflicts. The relative field of life is full of conflicting elements: heat and cold, pleasure and pain, gain and loss, and all the other pairs of opposites which constitute life. Under their influence life is tossed about as a ship on the rough sea from one wave to another. To be freed from duality is to be in the field of non-duality, the absolute state of Being. This provides smoothness and security to life in the relative field. It is like an anchor to the ship of life in the ocean of the three gunas. One gains steadiness and comfort.

Arjuna was highly sensitive to right and wrong. For this reason the Lord, after saying: 'freed from duality', at once adds: 'ever

18. See Appendix: Transcendental Meditation.

firm in purity'. He wants to assure Arjuna that this state will
always prove right, in accordance with dharma, ever furthering
the process of evolution for the good of all. Nothing wrong can
possibily result from it, because that is the state of fulfilment.

To convey this idea of fulfilment the Lord says : 'independent of
possessions'. The Sanskrit word used in the text is *niryogakshema*,
which carries the meaning that in this state one is not required to
think of gaining what one does not have or of preserving what
one has. Duryodhana's desire to possess and preserve possessions
is the cause of the battle. Even in the ordinary life of man, it is
this tendency to possess that tempts him to go the wrong way.
So the Lord tells Arjuna that he will transcend this cause of
transgression in life. Thereby He also reminds Arjuna that Duryodhana could take the wrong path because he gained kingdom,
pleasure and power but did not gain the wisdom of remaining
'independent of possessions'. That is why possessions kept him
bound to themselves and he lost his sense of proportion.

By using this expression: 'independent of possessions', the
Lord is providing the answer to Arjuna's own words in verse 32
of Chapter I: 'I desire not victory, O Krishna, nor a kingdom
nor pleasures.' Arjuna had seen how pleasure and power may ruin
a man's life by blinding him to the cause of righteousness. Here
Lord Krishna is educating him in the art of independence in the
midst of possessions, for after the battle Arjuna is going to be
placed in a position of great wealth and power.

Having said: 'freed from duality, ever firm in purity, independent of possessions', the Lord then adds: 'possessed of the
Self'. This is to indicate to Arjuna that this blessed state of life is
not far distant from him. It is within himself and therefore always
within his reach. And moreover, it is his own Self, nothing other
than his own Self.

There is great presence of mind, great skill in enlightening the
ignorant, and the height of perfection in the style of this discourse. If you are told by someone: 'I will take you to the field
of great wisdom and abundance of life', without some indication
of where that field lies, you may well be puzzled about many
things – about the distance, the difficulties on the way, your own
ability to get there. That is why the Lord uses the words: 'pos-

sessed of the Self'. Let yourself be possessed by your Self. Once
you are possessed by your Self the purpose of all wisdom has been
achieved. There the Vedas end. That is the end of the journey
of life, that is the state of fulfilment. For this reason, 'possessed
of the Self' stands at the end of the verse.

Here is a technique that enables every man to come to the great
treasure-house within himself and so rise above all sorrows and
uncertainties in life. From this verse onwards, the entire teaching
of the Bhagavad-Gita proclaims the glory of achieving the state
of the Transcendent.

It is this transcendental state of Being which enables a man to
become a karma yogi, one who is successful on the path of action.
It is this that enables a man to become a bhakta, one who is successful on the path of devotion, and it is this that enables a
man to become a gyani, one who is successful on the path of
knowledge. This is the highway to the fulfilment of life's
purpose.

If a man wants to be a true devotee of God, he has to become
his pure Self; he has to free himself from those attributes which
do not belong to him, and then only can he have one-pointed
devotion. If he is enveloped by what he is not, then his devotion
will be covered by that foreign element. His devotion will not
reach God, and the love and blessings of God will not reach him.
For his devotion to reach God, it is necessary that he should
first become purely himself, covered by nothing. Then the process
of devotion will connect him directly with the Lord, thereby
bestowing on him the status of a devotee. Only when he has
become himself can he properly surrender to the Great Self of the
Lord. If he remains in the field of the three gunas, in the many
sheaths of gross and subtle nature, then it is these sheaths that
prevent direct contact with the Lord.

Therefore the first step towards Union through devotion is to
be oneself. This, likewise, is the first step on the path of Gyana
Yoga, the path of Union through knowledge, and also on the
path of Union through action, Karma Yoga; because it is the
state of transcendental consciousness that is the state of gyana,
or knowledge, and that delivers from the bondage of karma. This
state is also the basis of success in any field of life. The field of

the three gunas is enlivened by the light of the absolute Being beyond the gunas.

The following verse shows that the purpose of all activity is fulfilled in this state of Being.

VERSE 46

यावानर्थ उद्पाने सर्वतः संप्लुतोदके ॥
तावान्सर्वेषु वेदेषु ब्राह्मणस्य विजानतः ॥४६॥

To the enlightened brahmin all the
Vedas are of no more use than is a
small well in a place flooded with
water on every side.

'Enlightened brahmin': one who has gone through the study and practice of the Karma Kanda, Upasana Kanda and Gyana Kanda of the Vedas. That is, one who knows the secret of action, dedication and knowledge.

While every action has the aim of happiness, the actions prescribed by the Vedas at the same time help a man to evolve beyond his present level. But a jivan-mukta, a man of cosmic consciousness, finds himself at the ultimate fulfilment of all the duties prescribed for him. He knows Reality with such great fullness that he becomes established in That, in the state of absolute bliss-consciousness. This is how, having gained the final aim of the whole Vedic way of life, such a man rises above the field of Vedic injunctions about right and wrong and also above the need for Vedic rituals; he rises above the need of the Vedic guidance.

The state of realization is like a reservoir full of water, from which people quite naturally draw to satisfy all their needs instead of getting their water from many small ponds. Therefore the Lord asks Arjuna to 'be without the three gunas' and not waste his life in planning and achieving small gains in the ever-changing field of the three gunas, to be a self-contained whole instead of trying to achieve a little here and there.

Not only does the state of realization fulfil the overall purpose of man's craving for greater and greater happiness, it also
brings the mind naturally to the highest degree of mental development. It brings a realized man to a state where, by virtue of a
high development of mental strength and harmony with the laws
of nature, he finds that his thoughts naturally become fulfilled
without much effort on his part. A man in this state has given
such a natural pattern to his existence that he enjoys the full
support of almighty Nature for life. He is in direct attunement
with cosmic law, the field of Being, which forms the basis of
all the laws of nature.[19]

VERSE 47

कर्मण्येवाधिकारस्ते मा फलेषु कदाचन ॥
मा कर्मफलहेतुर्भूर्मा ते सङ्गोऽस्त्वकर्मणि ॥४७॥

You have control over action alone,
never over its fruits. Live not for
the fruits of action, nor attach
yourself to inaction.

There is a marvellous sequence of instruction here. This verse
demonstrates once more the awareness of Lord Krishna and His
clear and deep insight into Arjuna's mind.

As Arjuna was instructed to 'be without the three gunas' in
verse 45 and in the next verse was told that as a result he would
fulfil all his aspirations in the relative field, he might very well
infer that he was not required to do anything more. Therefore
in order that Arjuna might not develop an aversion to action, the
Lord says in this verse: 'You have control over action alone.'
This should bring Arjuna to feel that he is to concern himself
with nothing but action. He should be so completely absorbed
in the action itself as to become oblivious of everything else, even
of its fruits. For this reason the Lord adds: 'never over its fruits'.

19. See Appendix: Cosmic Law.

This does not mean that Arjuna is not to fight for the sake of winning the battle; it does not mean that the action should be done without caring for its result. That would be hypocrisy.

It is the anticipated fruit of an action that induces a man to act. It is desire for a result that makes him begin to act and enables him to persist in the process of action. The Lord wishes to show that the result of the action will be greater if the doer puts all his attention and energy into the action itself, if he does not allow his attention and energy to be distracted by thinking of results. The result will be according to the action, there is no doubt about that.

If a student thinks the whole time about passing an examination, the progress of his study will be hampered, and this will jeopardize the result. It is to ensure the greater success of an action that the doer is asked not to concern himself with results during the course of the action. But this does not imply that he should be indifferent to results. If he becomes consciously indifferent to results, the process of action will certainly become weak, and this will also weaken the results.

It would be absurd to infer from this verse that a man has no right to the fruits of his action. Only the technique for achieving the maximum result from an action is given here. The doer has every right to enjoy the fruits of his action; the Lord says that he has no control over the fruits because the fruits will inevitably be according to the action. Having fixed the objective, having begun to act and having become intimately engrossed in the process of action, he should fulfil the action with such complete devotion and undivided attention that he is oblivious even of its fruits. Only in this way will he achieve the maximum results from what he does.

The teaching of non-anticipation of the fruit of action has an even deeper, cosmic significance in that it is supported by the very process of evolution. If a man is held by the fruit of action, then his sole concern is centred on the horizontal plane of life. Seeing nothing higher than the action and its fruit, he loses sight of the Divine, which pervades the action and is the almighty power at its basis leading it to ultimate fulfilment. He thus loses direct contact with the vertical plane of life, on which the process of evolution is based.

Thus it is clear that the Lord's teaching on the one hand supports activity and on the other upholds evolution and freedom.

The following verse indicates that it is possible for everyone to live the values of the Divine in the world.

VERSE 48

योगस्थः कुरु कर्माणि सङ्गं त्यक्त्वा धनञ्जय ॥
सिद्ध्यसिद्ध्योः समो भूत्वा समत्वं योग उच्यते ॥४८॥

Established in Yoga, O winner of
wealth, perform actions having
abandoned attachment and having
become balanced in success and
failure, for balance of mind is
called Yoga.

'Established in Yoga' means established in cosmic consciousness.[20]

Yoga, or Union of the mind with the divine intelligence, begins when the mind gains transcendental consciousness; Yoga achieves maturity when this transcendental bliss-consciousness, or divine Being, has gained ground in the mind to such an extent that, in whatever state the mind finds itself, whether waking or sleeping, it remains established in the state of Being. It is to this state of perfect enlightenment that the Lord refers in the beginning of the verse when He says: 'Established in Yoga.' Towards the end of the verse He defines 'Yoga' with reference to action as 'balance of mind'. This balanced state of mind is the result of the eternal contentment which comes with bliss-consciousness. It cannot be gained by creating a mood of equanimity in loss and gain, as commentators have generally thought.

Yoga is the basis of an integrated life, a means of bringing into

20. See verse 51, commentary.

harmony the inner creative silence and the outer activity of life, and a way to act with precision and success. Established in Yoga, Arjuna will be established in the ultimate Reality of life, which is the source of eternal wisdom, power and creativity.

Part of the training for one who wishes to become a good swimmer is the art of diving. When one is able to maintain oneself successfully in deep water, then swimming on the surface becomes easy. All action is the result of the play of the conscious mind. If the mind is strong, then action is also strong and successful. The conscious mind becomes powerful when the deeper levels of the ocean of mind are activated during the process of transcendental meditation,[21] which leads the attention from the surface of the conscious mind to the transcendental field of Being. The process of diving within is the way to become established in Yoga.

When the Lord says that having been through this process Arjuna should come out and act, He gives him the mechanics of successful action. To shoot an arrow successfully it is first necessary to draw it back on the bow, thus giving it great potential energy. When it is brought back to the fullest possible extent, then it possesses the greatest dynamic power.

Unfortunately the art of action, which Lord Krishna expounded to Arjuna in this discourse, seems to have disappeared from practical life today. This is because for many centuries, owing to the lack of proper interpretation of these verses, it has been considered difficult to lead the mind to the Self and become established in Yoga. It is, in fact, perfectly easy to lead the attention to the field of Being: one has only to allow the mind to move spontaneously from the gross field of objective experience, through the subtle fields of the thought-process to the ultimate transcendental Reality of existence. As the mind moves in this direction, it begins to experience increasing charm at every step until it reaches the state of transcendental bliss-consciousness.

The reward of bringing the mind to this state is that the small individual mind grows to the status of the cosmic mind, rising above all its individual shortcomings and limitations. It is like a small business man becoming wealthy and reaching the status

21. See Appendix.

of a multimillionaire. The losses and gains of the market, which
before used to influence him, now have no effect upon him and
he rises quite naturally above their influence.

The Lord wants Arjuna to act, but He wants him, before beginning the action, to gain the status of cosmic mind. This is
His kindness. When a wealthy man wants his son to start a
business, he does not usually wish him to begin in a small way,
because he knows that in that way small losses and gains will
influence his dear son and make him miserable or happy over
trivialities. Therefore he gives him the status of a wealthy man
and then asks him to start business from that level. Lord Krishna,
like a kind and able father, advises Arjuna to attain the state of
cosmic intelligence and then to act from that high state of freedom in life.

A man cannot remain balanced in loss and gain unless he is in
a state of lasting contentment. Here the Lord is asking Arjuna
to get to that state of lasting contentment by a direct experience
of transcendental eternal bliss. He is not advising a mere mood
of equanimity.

The state of transcendental bliss in eternal Being is so self-
sufficient that, in its structure, it is absolute. It is fullness of life,
perfection of existence, and therefore completely unattached to
anything in the relative field, completely free from the influence
of action. When the Lord says: 'having abandoned attachment',
He means having gained this state of eternal Being, which is
wholly separated and detached from activity. And when He says:
'having become balanced in success and failure', He means having reached stability in this state of eternal Being.

The regular practice of transcendental meditation is the direct
way of rising to the state of transcendental Being and stabilizing
it in the very nature of the mind, so that irrespective of the mind's
engagements in the conflicts inherent in the diversities of life,
the structure of Unity in eternal freedom is naturally maintained and life is not lost to itself.

Here is the definition of Yoga for which the ground was prepared by the words 'Be without the three gunas' in verse 45:
Yoga is that eternally balanced and never-changing state of transcendental consciousness which, remaining transcendent while

yet grounded in the very nature of the mind, sets the mind free
to participate in activity without becoming involved in it.

The following verses extol the glory of this Yoga, the balanced
state of mind, and make clear its usefulness in raising the dignity
of action and bringing eternal freedom to the doer.

Verse 49

दूरेण ह्यवरं कर्म बुद्धियोगाद्धनञ्जय ॥
बुद्धौ शरणमन्विच्छ कृपणाः फलहेतवः ॥४९॥

Far away, indeed, from the balanced intellect
is the action devoid of greatness, O winner
of wealth. Take refuge in the intellect.
Pitiful are those who live for the fruits
(of action).

'Balanced intellect' (buddhi yoga): the balanced state of mind
as explained in the last verse.

Here the Lord makes clear the distinction between the action
in which the intellect becomes involved and that in which it remains uninvolved. He says that the action performed without
gaining balance of mind, or Yoga, is of an inferior nature – it
is ineffective and weak, 'devoid of greatness'. He asks Arjuna to
rise to the uninvolved state of intellect, so that his action may
acquire greatness and he may be enabled at the same time to gain
the state of freedom.

The Lord derides the fate of those who are unable to rise to this
state of action in non-attachment. He says that they are 'pitiful' who seek only to enjoy the outer field of life, who do not
live the fullness of the inner and outer glories of life by developing the balanced state of mind described in the previous verse.

The Lord says: 'Take refuge in the intellect', thereby asking
Arjuna first to turn within and 'be without the three gunas'
('nistraigunyo bhav-Arjuna', verse 45) and then, remaining established in the state of Yoga, in the Self, to perform actions
('yogastah kuru karmani', verse 48).

The Lord wants Arjuna, before he begins to act, to establish himself in Yoga. He has defined Yoga as 'balance of mind', a state of fullness which is a state of natural equanimity. In this state a man is not affected by success or failure. It is not that he consciously tries to treat loss and gain as the same, but that he is naturally unaffected by them – a really good and desirable state which is reached through the practice of transcendental meditation referred to in the 45th verse. The endeavour to preserve equanimity of mind without gaining this state, merely by trying to view all things as alike, may be called hypocrisy or self-deception.

The Lord is certainly not telling Arjuna to cultivate a mood of equanimity or maintain a conscious indifference towards results during the process of an action. Any such attempt to maintain equanimity on the thinking level can only lead to tension and dullness of mind. The emphasis here, as in the previous verse, is on gaining pure intelligence, or Being. It is the state of Being which cultures the mind to be one-pointed, thus improving its effectiveness during action.

It is unfortunate that, for many centuries past, this and similar verses spoken by Lord Krishna on the Yoga of action have been misinterpreted, for this has caused people to lose their vigour and perseverance in action in the name of non-attachment. The result has been idleness, impotence and the weakening of the very structure of both individual and social life.

Here is a dynamic philosophy which is meant to inspire a disheartened man and strengthen a normal mind. Instead, owing to general misinterpretation, it has become a means to incapacitate man in all fields of activity; it has become a dragging influence on human endeavour.

The whole philosophy of karma, or action, is clearly explained to Arjuna so that he may become an integrated and dynamic person.

The Lord says: 'Pitiful are those who live for the fruits' of action – those who look forward to the results of their actions are to be pitied. This statement in particular has been much misunderstood by commentators. They have advised people to work but not to aim at a result. It is certain, however, that an action must be done to achieve some result. No action can be performed without some clear result in view. The Lord here only means to show Arjuna a principle of raising the value of action by raising the level of the mind and enabling it to rise to the state of unbounded consciousness in eternal freedom.

When an arrow is to be shot, the first step is to pull it back on the bow. If, instead, in the hurry of things, the arrow is shot forward without being pulled back on the bowstring, then the aim will not be achieved, the target will not be reached, the action will be without force and the actor will remain unfulfilled.

The Lord means that pitiable are those who are in such a hurry to achieve the fruit of action that they begin to act without adequate preparation to make the action forceful. They are not pitiable because they aim at the fruit of action, as so many commentators wrongly declare, but because they fail to achieve the full fruit of their action. They are pitiable because they do not know how to make their actions yield the maximum result and bring fulfilment to their aspirations.

They are pitiable because they care nothing for the cause, they care only for the effect. In this way they lose opportunities for improvement and greater gain. The intellect is the source or cause of action. Therefore the Lord says : 'Take refuge in the intellect' and 'far away, indeed, from the balanced intellect is the action devoid of greatness'.

Unless his mind is withdrawn and brought back to the absolute state of intellect, a man's deeds in the world will be weak, and that is why he is called pitiable. Pitiable is he, says the Brihadaranyaka Upanishad, who fails to commune with the inner divine consciousness. He is pitiable because he is neither able to enjoy the full result of his actions nor to overcome their binding influence.

Action is performed on the level of the senses but has its origin at the inception of the thinking process. A thought starts from the deepest level of the mind; it is appreciated on the thinking level, where it takes the form of a desire; desire, in its turn, expresses itself in the form of action. This is why the Lord says that the 'balanced intellect' and the field of action are far apart.

One is on the level of absolute life-energy; the other is on a weak and diffused level of energy because, as the process of manifestation of a thought develops into action, the concentration of energy becomes weaker. For this reason the Lord declares that they are pitiable who tend towards action alone, rather than towards a resolute state of intellect first and then to action later.

He who practises transcendental meditation and becomes acquainted with the inner divine consciousness truly enjoys the greatest fruit of action in the world. At the same time he grows increasingly free from bondage and eventually achieves integration of life.

This is the purpose of Lord Krishna's teaching: 'Take refuge in the intellect.' It introduces the ideal principle for the integration of life and provides a simple technique for its achievement.

The Lord wants Arjuna to have a deep conviction and a clear conception of the relationship between the state of Yoga and action, and also between Yoga and the doer.

VERSE 50

बुद्धियुक्तो जहातीह उभे सुकृतदुष्कृते ॥
तस्माद्योगाय युज्यस्व योगः कर्मसु कौशलम् ॥५०॥

He whose intellect is united (with
the Self) casts off both good and
evil even here. Therefore, devote
yourself to Yoga. Yoga is skill in
action.

Here the Lord contrasts the opposing characteristics of Yoga and karma (action). Yoga is pulling the arrow back; karma is shooting the arrow forward.

One who tries to shoot the arrow without first pulling it back on the bow is said to have a poor sense of action. His shot will not be strong, and his arrow will not go far because it will not be carried forward with force. Wise in the skill of action are those who first pull the arrow back before they proceed to shoot it ahead.

As the mind becomes established in transcendental consciousness, the state of Being becomes infused into the very nature of the mind, which thus gains the status of cosmic intelligence. Coming out of the transcendental state of consciousness, a man regains individuality, by virtue of which he is able to act in the relative field of life, but he now acts infused with Being. Such a person is as naturally above the influence of right and wrong as the wealthy business man is above loss and gain.

In this verse, the Lord emphasizes that the effect of Yoga is to raise a man to his real stature of eternal freedom in divine consciousness, where he will ever remain untouched by the influence of action, be it good or bad. This is not because he should be deprived of the good and bad fruits of his action, but because it is his due that, while enjoying the fruits of his actions, he should enjoy the state of eternal freedom as well.

It is not the action or its fruits that bind a man; rather it is the inability to maintain freedom which becomes a means of bondage. Yoga removes this inability. It is the glory of Yoga that it increases the power of both the action and the actor, bringing dignity to life in all its aspects.

Bondage certainly lies in the field of action, but it is not born of action: it is born of the weakness of the actor. When a small business man incurs a loss, his mind is profoundly affected by it. This creates a deep impression, which comes to the surface again as a desire for gain when favourable conditions present themselves. An impression on the mind is the seed of the desire which leads to action. Action in turn produces an impression on the mind, and thus the cycle of impression, desire and action continues, keeping a man bound to the cycle of cause and effect, the cycle of birth and death. This is commonly called the binding influence of action, the bondage of kharma.

When the Lord says that Arjuna will transcend the binding influence of right and wrong, He immediately makes it clear that this will not be the result of inaction but will be due to 'skill in action'.

What is 'skill in action'? It is the technique of performing an action so that the whole process becomes easy. The action is completed with the least effort, leaving the doer fresh enough to enjoy fully the fruits of his action while at the same time remaining untouched by its binding influence. And not only this; the action is performed quickly so that the doer begins to enjoy the results immediately. 'Skill in action' does not allow any negative influence from outside to hinder the performance of action, nor does it produce any negative influence either upon the doer or upon anyone anywhere; on the contrary, the influence it creates is wholly positive.

The process of action, if carried out with what is here called 'skill in action', produces good results in all directions and enables the doer to derive maximum benefit from it. At the same time, it fails to produce a binding influence on him. This is because it influences the doer in such a way that its fruits do not leave an impression in the mind deep enough to form the seed of future action, the doer being established in the Self, the eternal Being, and ever unattached to the field of activity.

VERSE 51

कर्मजं बुद्धियुक्ता हि फलं त्यक्त्वा मनीषिणः ॥
जन्मबन्धविनिर्मुक्ताः पदं गच्छन्त्यनामयम् ॥५१॥

The wise, their intellect truly united
with the Self, having renounced the
fruits born of their actions and being
liberated from the bonds of birth,
arrive at a state devoid of suffering.

'Liberated from the bonds of birth': birth marks a step on the long road of evolution. Births continue one after the other until the goal of evolution is reached. Individual life reaches its highest state of evolution when it finds itself established on the level of cosmic life, on the level of unbounded and eternal Being.

In this verse, Arjuna is made to realize that by establishing his

BHAGAVAD-GITA 144

mind in transcendental Being he will rise to a state separate from and unattached to the sphere of action. The Lord tells him that because they are established in Being, which is naturally unattached to activity, the wise live in eternal freedom and are not bound by the fruit of action. Fully established in the divine intelligence, they break the shackles of bondage and are free even while remaining in the field of action, for they are ever in the state of the eternal unchanging existence of absolute Being.

It is a wonderful way of enlightenment. The Lord asks Arjuna to come completely out of the field of action: 'Be without the three gunas, O Arjuna' (verse 45). He thereupon bids him act with full force (verse 47). Then, combining these two commands, the Lord tells Arjuna to act while remaining established in Self-consciousness (verses 48–50). And in the present verse, He demonstrates that action of this kind leads to cosmic consciousness – liberation from all suffering and bondage during lifetime here on earth. Arjuna is given a systematic and direct way to the highest state of human evolution.

The first step is to bring the mind to the Transcendent. Through transcendental meditation,[22] the attention is brought from gross experience to subtler fields of experience until the subtlest experience is transcended and the state of transcendental consciousness is gained. The march of the mind in this direction is so simple as to be automatic; as it enters into experience of a subtler nature, the mind feels increased charm because it is proceeding towards absolute bliss. Once the mind reaches transcendental consciousness it no longer remains a conscious mind; it gains the status of absolute Being. This state of transcendental pure consciousness, also known as Self-consciousness, Self-awareness, samadhi, represents the complete infusion of cosmic Being into the individual mind.

When, after this infusion, the mind comes out again into the field of relativity, then, being once more the individual mind, it acts while established in Being. Such action is called Karma Yoga; it is by virtue of Karma Yoga that transcendent Being is lived in the field of activity. And when complete fullness of Being has begun to be lived in the field of activity, the relative
22. See Appendix.

field of life, then one gains all-embracing eternal life in absolute
freedom. That is cosmic consciousness, jivan-mukti. That is the
state of which the Lord says: 'their intellect truly united with
the Self.'

We may say that there is only one step on the path to this
state of cosmic consciousness: a step out of the field of action
into the Transcendent and back to action again. Thus we find
a man reaches his highest evolution on the plane where he is already. He has only to take himself to a field which is outside
action and come back again to his normal field of activity. One
dives into the ocean, reaches the bottom, gathers the pearls and
comes out of the water to enjoy their value – the whole act is
done in one dive. The technique of diving lies only in taking a
correct angle and then letting go; reaching the bottom and coming up with the pearls follows automatically.

What a seeker of Truth has to do is only to learn how to take
a correct angle for the dive within. This will quite naturally
result in Self-consciousness, which in its turn develops into cosmic consciousness in the most natural way; the whole process goes
by itself.

The state of cosmic consciousness is inclusive of transcendental consciousness as well as of consciousness of the relative order;
it brings cosmic status to the individual life. When the individual consciousness achieves the status of cosmic existence then,
in spite of all the obvious limitations of individuality, a man is
ever free, unbounded by any aspect of time, space or causation,
ever out of bondage. This state of eternal freedom, set out here
in principle, is a result of establishing the mind in the state of
transcendental consciousness.

The Lord tells Arjuna that when he becomes established in
the eternal freedom of divine intelligence, his life will become
naturally full of meaning. That is why he need no longer seek
the meaning of all the words of wisdom that he may hear or
may have already heard, as the following verse makes clear.

VERSE 52

यदा ते मोहकलिलं बुद्धिर्व्यतितरिष्यति ॥
तदा गन्तासि निर्वेदं श्रोतव्यस्य श्रुतस्य च ॥५२॥

When your intellect crosses the mire
of delusion, then will you gain
indifference to what has been heard and
what is yet to be heard.

Arjuna is caught up in what he has learnt about right and
wrong. All his knowledge of the scriptures has not prevented
him from falling into a state of suspension, or saved him from
becoming inactive. He is still held in the state of suspension. This
he will overcome only when his intellect rises above duality and
reaches the field of pure transcendental consciousness.

The state of realization is beyond the limitations of thought,
speech and action; having reached it one truly rises above doubt
and delusion.

The Lord is here summarizing all that he has so far told Arjuna.
He has described to him the real state of Yoga, a state which
satisfies both the intellect and the heart because, bringing fulfilment to both, it leaves no room for doubt or discontent in
the domain of either. The emphasis in this verse is on the practice of arriving at transcendental consciousness and allowing the
intellect to gain purity. This will mean the fulfilment of all the
wisdom of life, of what has been heard in the past and what
is worthy of being heard in future. 'What has been heard and
what is yet to be heard' will be superseded by the experience of
Reality, for all hearing about Truth gains fulfilment in Its direct
experience.

This verse takes one to a level of life that is free from problems. It makes clear the state in which one will 'gain indifference', and thereby shows a way to 'abandon attachment', as demanded by verse 48.

VERSE 53

श्रुतिविप्रतिपन्ना ते यदा स्थास्यति निश्चला ।।
समाधावचला बुद्धिस्तदा योगमवाप्स्यसि ।।५३।।

When your intellect, bewildered by
Vedic texts, shall stand unshaken,
steadfast in the Self, then will you
attain to Yoga.

'Vedic texts': this refers to verses 42–4.

The Vedas expound the wisdom of right and wrong at various
levels of evolution. They lay open the whole field of life, leaving
a man to make his choice as to how he wants to proceed on the
path of his evolution. Therefore it is quite possible that the mind
influenced by Vedic learning, finding such a vast range of knowledge at its disposal, may become bewildered. But when once it
has recourse to its own nature, the mind stands 'unshaken'. In
this resolute state, when it transcends the whole field of relative
life, it gains Self-consciousness, or pure awareness; and when
this pure state of consciousness is never lost under any influence,
then Yoga, or skill in action, is achieved.

Vedic wisdom comprises various expressions of Reality, as seen
from different points of view and taught by different schools of
thought. These manifold theories are meant to satisfy the different
levels of human understanding, the purpose of the Vedas being
to enlighten people of all types.

When one sees the different perspectives in Vedic literature,
one may be confused by the differences of opinion about the
path of realization. But when the mind comes to samadhi, or
transcendental consciousness, the goal of all paths is reached.
This resolute state of the mind in attainment stands completely
clear, free from any confusion about the path towards it.

From the centre of Reality the whole circumference of life is
seen to be completely harmonious, for when the centre is found
it becomes clear that the innumerable radii all converge from

the circumference towards a single point. If the centre is not found, then the various radii will be regarded as separate from one another with no common meeting-point. That is why the Lord stresses the importance of the direct experience of samadhi, pure consciousness. This alone can dispel the uncertainties of the mind.

The purpose of the present verse is to strengthen the teaching given by the Lord in the 45th verse; it is in no way to refute the validity of the knowledge contained in the Vedic texts, without which intellectual satisfaction would not be possible. Scriptural knowledge becomes significant once Reality has been directly experienced.

Yoga here means 'skill in action', as defined in verse 50. The Lord makes it very plain to Arjuna that unless his mind first arrives at transcendental consciousness, and unless the intellect is then unshakably established in this state of pure consciousness, that is to say, unless cosmic consciousness is attained, he cannot obtain Yoga, or skill in action.

In order to understand more thoroughly how transcendental consciousness is compatible with action and gives rise to skill in action, Arjuna, in the following verse, asks a very practical question.

VERSE 54

अर्जुन उवाच ।
स्थितप्रज्ञस्य का भापा समाधिस्थस्य केशव ॥
स्थितधीः किं प्रभाषेत किमासीत व्रजेत किम् ॥५४॥

Arjuna said:

*What are the signs of a man whose
intellect is steady, who is absorbed
in the Self, O Keshava? How does the
man of steady intellect speak, how does
he sit, how does he walk?*

Arjuna's question shows that the discourse up to this point has been very clearly understood by him and that his mind is attuned to Lord Krishna's thought.

'Keshava': one with long hair, Lord Krishna. When Arjuna asks for the outward 'sign' of the man of steady intellect, he addresses Lord Krishna by a name which refers to His outward appearance. Arjuna wants to know the distinctive characteristics of a man of steady intellect both when he is deep within himself, withdrawn from activity, and when he is active.

There are two ways of life: that of a householder and that of a recluse. Karma Yoga is the way of the householder, while Sankhya, the way of knowledge, is for the recluse. Both types of men achieve the state of steady intellect and, having attained it, rise above the limitations of life and of society. Their lives present a synthesis of individual and cosmic existence. The freedom that they live and the universal outlook that they hold inspire the society to which they belong. Their lives are an expression of those ultimate values which are the foundation of social values of all time. Wherever they are, busy in the market-place, or silent in a Himalayan cave, they are the guiding light of the human race. Arjuna asks for some signs, some distinguishing marks of such souls. Being a practical man he wants to know the outward signs of a life of inner fulfilment.

The question shows that his mind is clearer at this moment than it was at the beginning of this chapter, when he could not think decisively. It also indicates the power of the teaching of Sankhya and Yoga to clarify a man's mind and raise his consciousness.

Arjuna has been quietly listening to Lord Krishna. A discourse of forty-three verses (11–53) has turned his state of suspension to thoughts of a concrete nature. No longer occupied with thoughts of sorrow, his mind now rises to ask about the practical aspect of the integrated state of life. And this transformation has taken place within five to ten minutes, the time required to speak these verses.

His question is answered in the following eighteen verses, which present the characteristics of realized men who have

gained steady intellect, whether by renouncing action through
the knowledge of Sankhya, or by way of Karma Yoga.

VERSE 55

श्रीभगवानुवाच ।
प्रजहाति यदा कामान्सर्वान्पार्थ मनोगतान् ।।
आत्मन्येवात्मना तुष्टः स्थितप्रज्ञस्तदोच्यते ।।५५।।

The Blessed Lord said:

When a man completely casts off all
desires that have gone (deep) into the mind, O Partha,
when he is satisfied in the Self through
the Self alone, then is he said to be of
steady intellect.

Here Lord Krishna addresses Arjuna as 'Partha'. This is to maintain the tide of love created by the use of the same word when
He spoke to Arjuna for the first time on the battlefield. Now that
the Lord finds Arjuna's mind thinking on a more practical level,
He still wants the qualities of Arjuna's heart to remain at their
height and not be overshadowed by those of the mind.

This verse presents the 'steady intellect' in the state of samadhi, or transcendental consciousness, and also in the state
of nitya-samadhi, or cosmic consciousness; in both cases the mind
gains that state in which it 'completely casts off all desires that
have gone (deep) into the mind'.

When, through the practice of transcendental meditation, the
mind gains transcendental consciousness, it is completely out of
the field of desires. This is the 'steady intellect' in the state of
samadhi.

How then is the 'steady intellect' maintained in nitya-samadhi,
when the mind, established in pure consciousness, is yet engaged
in the field of action? Because in this state the mind has become
transformed into bliss-consciousness, Being is permanently lived
as separate from activity. Then a man realizes that his Self is

different from the mind which is engaged with thoughts and
desires. It is now his experience that the mind, which had been
identified with desires, is mainly identified with the Self. He
experiences the desires of the mind as lying outside himself,
whereas he used to experience himself as completely involved with
desires. On the surface of the mind desires certainly continue,
but deep within the mind they no longer exist, for the depths of
the mind are transformed into the nature of the Self. All the
desires which were present in the mind have been thrown upward, as it were – they have gone to the surface, and within
the mind the finest intellect gains an unshakable, immovable
status. 'Pragya' [23] is anchored to 'Kutastha'.[24] This is the 'steady
intellect' in the state of nitya-samadhi, cosmic consciousness.

Thus the wavering intellect gains a very stable basis, and as
a result the field of activity is managed with great efficiency. It
is quite wrong to think that one who has gained this state remains slumped in inertia and does not engage in action. This
state of life is such that it maintains the freedom of the inner
Being, keeping It uninvolved with activity, and at the same time
deals with all actions most efficiently and successfully.

The word 'when' is very important. It indicates that one is said
to be of 'steady intellect' only when one has gained transcendental consciousness, the state of separation from activity; or when
one has gained cosmic consciousness, the state where one naturally maintains Self-consciousness even together with consciousness of the waking, dreaming or sleeping states, and where the
Self, or Being, remains unshadowed by any experience whatsoever.

It is wrong to conclude that only a recluse, who has given up
all worldly desires, can attain this state of 'steady intellect'. It
can be gained by anyone through the practice of transcendental
meditation.[25]

The recluse way of life does not necessarily produce a condition where 'a man completely casts off all desires that have gone
(deep) into the mind'. The state described by this phrase has

23. 'Pragya' : intellect.
24. 'Kutastha' : the Immovable, the Rocklike. See VI, 8.
25. See Appendix.

nothing to do with any particular way of life. Lord Krishna is clearly referring to a state in which one is free from desires and 'satisfied in the Self'. And this is easily attained by anyone who knows how to meditate and transcend relativity, whether he be recluse or householder, whether he meditate in a palace or a cave.

Shankara, the great exponent of the philosophy of integrated life, says in his commentary on this verse : 'By direct experience of the blissful nectar of the transcendent Reality the steady intellect holds itself absolutely without anything other than itself.' [26] And again he defines the man of steady intellect in the following words : 'He whose intellect, born of realization of the distinction between the ultimate and non-ultimate, is settled; he is a man of steady intellect.' [27] The intellectual understanding gained by the analysis of, and discrimination between, the ultimate and non-ultimate aspects of life does not produce the state of steady intellect. Such practices, remaining as they do on the level of thinking, can at best create moods of the mind; they certainly will not produce the state of mind called 'steady intellect'. This results only from direct experience of pure consciousness to such a degree of clarity that the difference between the 'ultimate' and the 'non-ultimate' is clearly cognized and appreciated on the intellectual level as well.

Thus Shankara plainly holds that this state of steady intellect is produced by the practice of transcending relativity, as expressed in verse 45, and not by merely spinning words about it or merely trying to understand it. The process of experience is very different from that of intellectual discrimination of Reality and non-Reality. [28]

This should be sufficient to remove the misunderstanding created by commentators or translators of the Bhagavad-Gita who hold that the steady intellect can only be gained by recluses, a view which is responsible for spiritual decadence in modern

26. 'Paramārtha-darshana-amrita-rasa-lābhena anyasmāt alam-pratyayavān sthitapragyāh'.
27. 'Stihtā pratishthitā ātmānātma-vivekajā pragyā yasya sah sthita pragyah.'
28. See verse 40, commentary.

society. Unfortunately, Shankara's own view has been misrepresented by commentators who undertook to propagate his philosophy. They seem to have missed the central part of spiritual life – transcendental consciousness and the direct way to its realization. As a result, everything which aimed at clarifying the process of transcending has been held to belong to the path of renunciation and attributed to the recluse way of life. This lack of insight into principle cast the centre of spiritual life on to the recluse order, thus debarring the householder from the gains of spirituality, and throwing the whole of humanity out of joint.

This verse does not record any outer sign of the man whose intellect is steady and who is established in the Self, because there cannot be any outer sign to show that a man is absorbed deep within himself. The inner state of such a man cannot be judged by outer signs. It cannot be said that he sits like this or like that or closes his eyes in any particular manner. No such external signs can serve as criteria of this state.

A man may sit in any style and go deep within himself and be in bliss-consciousness. It may be said that when someone goes into samadhi his face becomes serene and more glowing, but this is not something that can be gauged by any fixed standard. For this reason the Lord does not enter into any such description. The signs recounted here are only subjective. They concern the inner condition of the mind as indicated by 'casts off all desires' and 'is satisfied in the Self'.

This verse brings to light the basis of the steady intellect: the realization of Being in transcendental consciousness or in cosmic consciousness. The next verse presents the nature of the man who has gained steady intellect. Verse 57 describes the nature of the means whereby he acts in the state of steady intellect: non-attachment. Verse 58 explains the nature of his activity in this state: his senses are withdrawn from their objects. Finally, verse 59 points to the influence of the Unseen on the steady intellect.[29] It shows that not merely are the senses withdrawn from their objects, but even their taste for these objects vanishes when the Supreme unfolds Itself to them in Its unbounded grandeur –

29. The basis, the doer, the means, activity and Providence are the five factors for the accomplishment of any action, as given in XVIII, 14.

when the Supreme comes to be lived on the sensory level of existence. These five verses taken together reveal the essentials of the 'steady intellect'.

VERSE 56

दुःखेष्वनुद्विग्नमनाः सुखेषु विगतस्पृहः ॥
वीतरागभयक्रोधः स्थितधीर्मुनिरुच्यते ॥५६॥

He whose mind is unshaken in the midst
of sorrows, who amongst pleasures is
free from longing, from whom attachment,
fear and anger have departed, he is
said to be a sage of steady intellect.

'A sage' (*muni*) is defined in this verse.

The Lord begins to answer Arjuna's question about the man of steady intellect, who quite naturally maintains balance of mind while he continues to act in the field of relative existence. The verse does not provide any signs of an objective nature, but it describes the subjective aspect of a man of steady intellect.

Just as a millionaire who has great wealth remains unaffected by the rise and fall of the market, so the mind which has gained the state of bliss-consciousness through transcendental meditation remains naturally contented on coming out from the transcendental state to the field of activity. This contentment, being grounded in the very nature of the mind, does not allow the mind to waver and be affected in pleasure or pain, nor allow it to become affected by attachment or fear in the world. This natural equanimity of the mind, even while it is actively engaged, is the state of steady intellect.

'Sorrows' arise in the mind through want of understanding. When one understands only so much and no more of life, lacking vision of the whole span of life, then one feels sorrow. But the man who understands both the unchanging eternal phase of life and the unending nature of the ever-changing cycle of life and death will recognize the ephemeral nature of sorrow and not be overwhelmed by it.

The feeling of sorrow in the heart, as distinct from the mind, is due to lack of fulfilment, lack of love, lack of happiness. One who practises transcendental meditation experiences the bliss which fills the heart and brings eternal contentment, wh'ch leaves no room for any negative emotion, for sorrow, depression, fear or the like. Neither does it leave room for waves of joy or other positive emotions because the heart is by nature full and contented. It is like the heart of a grown man remaining unaffected by the toys which create great emotions in the hearts of children.

The experience of transcendental consciousness raises a man's consciousness to a level where he finds his Self completely separate from all activity, and naturally his values will change. The values of life are different at different levels of evolution. This is why, when the normal behaviour of a man of steady intellect, established on the level of divine consciousness, is seen from the ordinary level of human consciousness, it appears different and more than normal – unshaken by pleasure and pain, fear and anger.

The basis of such a detached state of life is explained in the following verse.

VERSE 57

यः सर्वत्रानभिस्नेहस्तत्तत्प्राप्य शुभाशुभम् ॥
नाभिनन्दति न द्वेष्टि तस्य प्रज्ञा प्रतिष्ठिता ॥५७॥

He who has no undue fondness towards
anything, who neither exults nor
recoils on gaining what is good or
bad, his intellect is established.

The man whose mind is established in the Unity of blissconsciousness knows by experience that his Self is separate from all activity. He acts in the field of relativity, but experience cannot make any deep impression. This is why he naturally remains consistent in his outlook and behaviour with others, even while experiencing the diverse nature of the world.

Many a commentator upon these verses has introduced the idea that in order to achieve the state of established intellect one should try to be dispassionate and detached. But in the field of behaviour and experience the strain of attempting to be dispassionate and detached, of trying to make a mood of equanimity in pleasure and pain, only puts unnatural, undue stress on the mind, resulting in the development of an unnatural and warped state of the inner personality. This kind of practice has helped to bring dullness, artificiality and tension to life in the name of spiritual growth; it has spoiled the brilliance of many a genius in every generation for centuries past. As a consequence, there has grown up in intelligent levels of society throughout the world a kind of fear of the spiritual life, which has gone so far that young and energetic people today find even discussion about spiritual practices embarrassing.

In his reply to Arjuna's question, the Lord wants to bring home to him that through the practice of transcendental meditation the mind becomes infused with divine intelligence and bliss. Thereafter, even while one acts in the world, the state of equanimity is naturally maintained.

This verse can never be interpreted in terms of mood-making, or of controlling the mind in an attempt to live evenness intellectually. It brings out that the man of steady intellect is by nature grounded in non-attachment.

Unfortunately some interpreters have gone so far in misrepresenting the truth of this verse as to disapprove even of enjoying a flower in full bloom or rejecting a faded one. And this way of making life cold and devoid of heart has been recommended as a way of gaining established intellect. What cruelty to life!

It is a mistake to copy the behaviour of a realized man while remaining in the unrealized state. If a poor man puts up the sign of a wealthy man and tries to behave like one, this can only result in tension. By superficially copying the behaviour of a rich man, he cannot possibly become rich. Similarly, the behaviour of a man of steady intellect provides no standard for one whose intellect is not steady. If he tries to go that way, his life will become cold, deprived of the qualities of heart and mind. This has been the destiny of many a sincere seeker of Truth down the ages. Misguided interpretations of verses like this, which are found in almost all scriptures, are responsible for the spiritual plight of innumerable generations.

It must not be forgotten that there are two ways of life, that of a householder and that of a recluse. Men from both ways who meditate and arrive at the state of steady intellect will continue in their respective ways of life. The householder, by nature habituated to the field of activity with all the diversity of phenomenal existence, continues to act in the world, while the recluse continues in his detachment from worldly affairs. The state of steady intellect simply brings them fulfilment. They rise above attachment and detachment, finding their life on the level of eternity, unbounded by any limitation of time, space and causation, far above the boundaries of any social bond or obligation. Their life is one of cosmic consciousness. They are above the distinction of day and night: waking or sleeping they are established in the oneness of divine intelligence and bliss. This world of joys and sorrows, of man's great enterprise and ambition, is for them like a world of dolls and toys with which children play and amuse themselves. Toys are a source of great excitement for children, but grown-ups remain untouched by them. The man of established intellect remains even and does not rejoice or recoil 'on gaining what is good or bad'.

'Has no undue fondness' means is not too emotionally attached. But this does not imply that the man of established intellect is cold and without warmth of heart. On the contrary, he alone is a man of full heart. He is an unbounded ocean of love and happiness. His love and his happiness flow and overflow for everyone in like manner; that is why he has no 'undue fondness towards anything'.

It may be stated that the detached and unshakable nature of a man of established intellect, described in the previous verse, is based on the principle of non-attachment, as taught in this verse. Such non-attachment develops naturally with the growth of awareness of the Self as separate from activity. This same natural

state of non-attachment is at the basis of activity in the state of
steady intellect even when the senses remain 'withdrawn' from
their objects, as shown in the following verse.

VERSE 58

यदा संहरते चायं कूर्मोऽङ्गानीव सर्वशः ॥
इन्द्रियाणीन्द्रियार्थेभ्यस्तस्य प्रज्ञा प्रतिष्ठिता ॥५८॥

And when such a man withdraws his
senses from their objects, as a
tortoise draws in its limbs from
all sides, his intellect is
established.

This verse pictures the state of the senses of a man of established
intellect by drawing a comparison with the indrawn limbs of a
tortoise that from the outside seems to have no limbs at all. By
this example the Lord also implies that it is not possible correctly
to express the outward signs or distinguishing marks of a man of
established intellect. But at least one thing is clear – his senses
are drawn in, they are not turned in an outward direction.

It may appear that the man of steady intellect referred to in
this verse is only he who is in the state of transcendental consciousness, for in this state alone are the senses completely withdrawn from their object. But 'withdraws his senses' does not
necessarily mean that the senses do not experience outside objects,
as in the state of transcendental consciousness. The senses can be
involved with outer experiences and yet not be totally engrossed in them to the extent that they transfer to the mind impressions deep enough to become the seed of future desires. It is very
important to understand the verse in this way; otherwise, the
man of steady intellect would have to remain for ever outside
the domain of sensory activity, which is physically impossible.
The established intellect has, in fact, little to do with the activity
or non-activity of the senses; its basis lies in the natural state

of non-attachment described in the previous verse. It is plain, therefore, that the present verse refers not to transcendental consciousness alone but also to cosmic consciousness, where it is possible for the senses to be in a state of non-attachment even while they are active.

The Lord is here emphasizing that in the state of established intellect the senses, being free from attraction towards their objects, remain as though withdrawn from them. When the mind is mainly identified with the inner Being, the senses do not identify themselves with their objects. Moreover the next verse shows that when the senses are exposed to the unbounded grandeur of the Supreme, they lose even the taste for their objects. This makes it clear that when the transcendent Being fills the mind and begins to be lived on the sensory level, then the intellect is established.

This is a very different state from mere non-indulgence of the senses, which is certainly no absolute criterion of the established intellect. A man who, because of some circumstance, does not enjoy the objects of sense may appear to be like an indrawn tortoise, although the mind within may be active, quietly absorbed in the thought of the joys of the senses. Such a state of mind is obviously not the resolute state; it is not established intellect.

The principle here brought out does not depend on whether or not the senses are active. It reveals the inner condition of non-attachment, on the sensory level, in the state of established intellect.

VERSE 59

विषया विनिवर्तन्ते निराहारस्य देहिनः ।।
रसवर्जं रसोऽप्यस्य परं दृष्ट्वा निवर्तते ।।५९।।

The objects of sense turn away from him
who does not feed upon them, but the
taste for them persists. On seeing the
Supreme even this taste ceases.

'Taste for them persists' means that the mind continues to experience objects through the finer levels of the senses. In thus distinguishing between the gross and subtle fields of sensory perception, the Lord means to convey that in the state of steady intellect even the finer faculties of the senses remain unattached to objects.

This verse presents a challenge to the whole philosophy of control of the senses. It shows clearly that the senses cannot be controlled from their own level.

In the field of the senses, the senses predominate. They drag the mind towards their objects, towards the joys of the world. None of the objects of the senses, however, is able to satisfy the longing of the mind for happiness. Therefore the mind is ever found wandering in the field of the senses. Only when the state of established intellect is gained and the mind ceases to wander, can the senses be controlled.

It is wrong to assume that unless the senses are controlled one cannot realize the Truth. As a mater of fact, the converse is true: according to this verse, the senses come under complete control only with the light of realization – only when the transcendent Self, or Being, comes to be appreciated on the level of the senses.

Wrong interpretations of this and other verses have led many genuine seekers of Truth to undertake rigorous and unnatural practices in order to control the senses, thus wasting their lives and benefiting neither themselves nor others. Mastery of the senses is gained only through the state of established intellect, for in this state where man is established in awareness of the Self as separate from activity, his behaviour is quite naturally unaffected by the otherwise overpowering influence of the senses. At the end of this chapter, the Lord concludes that when behaviour in the sensory field does not in any way disturb the state of established intellect, and established intellect behaves as master of the senses, the highest state of human evolution has been reached.

'On seeing the Supreme' : when the intellect goes beyond the field of the three gunas and cognizes the transcendent Reality, that is, gains transcendental consciousness. When this state of transcendental consciousness is maintained even while the senses are active, then a situation is created in which the Transcendent

comes to be lived naturally on the level of sensory perception.
And when the Transcendent comes to be appreciated on the
sensory level, then a man is said to have truly gained established
intellect.

VERSE 60

यततो ह्यपि कौन्तेय पुरुषस्य विपश्चितः ॥
इन्द्रियाणि प्रमाथीनि हरन्ति प्रसभं मनः ॥६०॥

The turbulent senses, O son of Kunti,
forcibly carry away the mind even of
a discerning man who endeavours (to
control them).

Here the Lord describes to Arjuna the nature of the senses. Being
the instruments which enable the mind to enjoy the glory of the
diversity of creation, they are in duty bound to draw it towards
objects of pleasure. Their main purpose is to bring the greatest
possible happiness to the mind. And this they will continue to do
so long as the mind has not become eternally contented in the
bliss of the Absolute.

  How to make best use of the senses in order to come to the
experience of eternal bliss is described in the following verses.

VERSE 61

तानि सर्वाणि संयम्य युक्त आसीत मत्परः ॥
वशे हि यस्येन्द्रियाणि तस्य प्रज्ञा प्रतिष्ठिता ॥६१॥

Having brought them all under control,
let him sit united, looking to Me as Supreme;
for his intellect is established whose
senses are subdued.

The previous verse explained the nature of the senses and their overpowering influence on the mind, while the verses that follow depict the dangers which result from their indulgence when the level of the Transcendent is not maintained. In this verse the Lord holds out hope by showing that it is possible to control the senses and that 'his intellect is established whose senses are subdued'.

The Lord says: 'Having brought them all under control, let him sit united, looking to Me as Supreme.' This opens up a way, for when the attention has been brought to the Transcendent, the activity of the senses ceases and they will be automatically controlled. In this state of life, says the Lord, 'let him sit united, looking to Me as Supreme'.

The technique of bringing them 'all' under control is to engage any one sense in providing increasing happiness for the mind on the path of transcending – that is, to begin the practice of trans-cendental meditation. In this process the mind, using a particular sense for passing through the finer levels of experience and transcending the subtlest experience, also transcends the field of that sense and the fields of all the senses. Gaining bliss-conscious-ness in this way, the mind wins automatic control over all the senses.

'Let him sit united, looking to Me as Supreme': the man who sits united is one whose self is united with the Self, or Being, even though he is engaged in action. Through the repeated prac-tice of transcendental meditation, he has realized Being to such fullness that no activity can overshadow It; that is to say, he has realized Being as separate from activity. Having gained this state, says the Lord, let him maintain it and in that state be devoted to Me, the Lord of all creation, who presides over both the absolute and relative phases of existence.

The teaching is that, having gained cosmic consciousness and having thereby created a situation where mind and senses remain naturally organized, using their full potential to fulfil desires that further the good of the world, a man should devote himself to God and let the heart flow and overflow in love for Him, the great Lord of all. He alone can be someone to whom life in cosmic consciousness can turn; for, being omnipotent and omniscient, He ranks higher than life in cosmic consciousness. The purpose

of this teaching of devotion to God on that high level where man
has reached his full potentiality is to enable him to experience
the great waves of bliss in the ocean of cosmic consciousness —
experience that joyfulness of eternal life which brings complete
fulfilment to his existence.

VERSE 62

ध्यायतो विषयान्पुंसः सङ्गस्तेषूपजायते ।।
सङ्गात् संजायते कामः कामात् क्रोधोऽभिजायते ।।६२।।

Pondering on objects of the senses,
a man develops attachment for them;
from attachment springs up desire,
and desire gives rise to anger.

This verse depicts one who is not turned towards the Divine, but
towards the objects of the senses. The Lord shows how such a
man gradually sinks deeper and deeper into the mire of delusion
until he perishes.

   Thought is a great force in man. It develops into desire, which
in turn translates itself into action, bringing glory or disgrace.
'Anger' arises from weakness or inability to fulfil one's desires,
although it is generally attributed to obstacles in the way of such
fulfilment. And thus desire is said to be the direct cause of anger.[30]

VERSE 63

क्रोधाद्भवति सम्मोहः सम्मोहात्स्मृतिविभ्रमः ।।
स्मृतिभ्रंशाद्बुद्धिनाशो बुद्धिनाशात्प्रणश्यति ।।६३।।

From anger arises delusion; from delusion
unsteadiness of memory; from unsteadiness
of memory destruction of intellect; through
the destruction of the intellect he perishes.

30. See III, 37, commentary.

Anger excites the mind, which loses its balance and power of discrimination; it loses proper vision and foresight and a right sense of values. This state of 'delusion' obscures the track of memory, and thereby one feels as if disconnected from the harmonious rhythm of life. Wisdom fails, and the intellect ceases to function. The boat of life is left with nobody in control; it meets with disaster as a matter of course.

The intellect is the finest aspect of one's subjective nature. As long as the intellect is intact there is every hope of the advancement and fulfilment of life. That is why the Lord says that the destruction of the intellect results in a man's ruin.

VERSE 64

रागद्वेषवियुक्तैस्तु विषयानिन्द्रियैश्चरन् ॥
आत्मवश्यैर्विधेयात्मा प्रसादमधिगच्छति ॥६४॥

But he who is self-disciplined, who
moves among the objects of the senses
with the senses freed from attachment
and aversion and under his own control,
he attains to 'grace'.

'Grace' here means delight and wholeness, resulting from the state of pure consciousness.

This verse contrasts with the two preceding verses. Having explained to Arjuna the plight of those who surrender themselves to the call of desire without possessing control of the senses, the Lord, in this verse, shows him the reward gained by the man who disciplines himself before plunging into worldly life.

The Lord here explains the status of the integrated man. He is established in the Self, and by virtue of this, even when he acts in the field of the senses and experiences their objects, he is not lost in them; maintaining his status in Being, he quite naturally maintains evenness of mind. His sense of values is balanced. Acting in the world, he is not lost in it. He is above attachment and detachment, contented in himself, not bound by anything.

The results of reaching this state of blissful freedom are described in the verses that follow.

VERSE 65

प्रसादे सर्वदुःखानां हानिरस्योपजायते ॥
प्रसन्नचेतसो ह्याशु बुद्धिः पर्यवतिष्ठते ॥६५॥

In 'grace' is born an end to all his
sorrows. Indeed the intellect of the
man of exalted consciousness soon
becomes firmly established.

The experience of pure bliss-consciousness puts an end to all suffering; filling the heart with happiness it brings perfect tranquillity to the mind.

The principle is that if freedom from suffering, lasting peace, health and fulfilment are desired, it is necessary to gain bliss-consciousness.

VERSE 66

नास्ति बुद्धिरयुक्तस्य न चायुक्तस्य भावना ॥
न चाभावयतः शान्तिरशान्तस्य कुतः सुखम् ॥६६॥

He who is not established has no
intellect, nor has he any steady thought.
The man without steady thought has no
peace; for one without peace how can
there be happiness?

The glory of the established intellect is brought out here. When the mind is established in the Self, then it is in tune with cosmic intelligence, and then only has it what the Lord calls 'intellect', the faculty of discrimination. Unless one is in tune with cosmic intelligence there is no wisdom, no steadiness, no peace, no happiness in the real sense.

The verse may also be interpreted as showing the stages through which a worldly mind passes on the way to bliss-consciousness. Confused in the world as the mind is, it has to become peaceful in order to have a steady thought, which then converges into a state of one-pointedness called 'intellect', which then becomes established in Being.

When, during meditation, the mind enters into the experience of subtle levels of thought, it becomes more collected, more steady, with every step and therefore feels itself entering a field of increasing charm. This process ends in the absolute happiness of the Transcendent.

If the mind is more steady, it is in a better position to experience greater happiness. As on a calmer surface of water the sun reflects more clearly, so a calmer mind receives a clearer reflection of the omnipresent bliss of the absolute Being. As the mind fathoms finer fields of thinking during meditation, the metabolism is simultaneously reduced. This establishes the nervous system in degrees of ever-increasing peace. Eventually, when the entire nervous system comes to a completely peaceful state, it reflects Being, and this gives rise to bliss-consciousness.

The state of transcendental consciousness cannot be gained unless the nervous system is completely peaceful. This is the truth revealed by the words 'for one without peace how can there be happiness?'. The bliss is already there; it is only necessary to calm down the wanderings of the mind.

A question arises here. If the wanderings of the mind are due to its search for happiness, could it not be said: unless there is happiness how can there be peace? But no; the expression 'unless there is happiness' is completely wrong; it could not have been framed by Lord Krishna because it is not true. For bliss is omnipresent and eternal, while happiness is the expression of the reflection of the omnipresent bliss on the mind. Absolute bliss being always there, the experience of happiness thus depends upon the degree of steadiness of the mind. If the mind is more collected, more peaceful, it experiences more happiness.

During meditation the mind, entering the subtle phases of a

thought, becomes more collected and more peaceful,[31] that is why
it proceeds that way automatically. This truth is expressed by the
Upanishads when they declare that happiness varies in different
states of creation, at different levels of evolution. As the mind
evolves to higher levels of consciousness during meditation, it
experiences increasing degrees of happiness, until it comes to
absolute bliss in the most highly evolved state of pure transcendental consciousness.

VERSE 67

इन्द्रियाणां हि चरतां यन्मनोऽनुविधीयते ॥
तदस्य हरति प्रज्ञां वायुर्नावमिवाम्भसि ॥६७॥

When a man's mind is governed by any
of the wandering senses, his intellect
is carried away by it as a ship by the
wind on water.

The mind by nature thirsts for greater happiness. Let us suppose
it is enjoying experience through a particular sense. In its eager-
ness to enjoy the utmost which that sense can provide, it becomes
absorbed in the process of enjoying, and in this one-sided absorp-
tion loses the power of discrimination, which is the main faculty
of the intellect. This is what the Lord means when He says the
senses rob a man of intellect.

The mind is prepared to accept anything that can tempt it with
the promise of happiness. Any sensory object which promises
happiness is capable of taking possession of the mind. This is not
to the discredit of the mind, for its nature is to enjoy.

If the senses draw the mind to the joys of their objects, this
similarly is no discredit to the senses. They are the machinery
through which the mind enjoys and, like a ready servant, are
waiting to serve the mind.

As a ship is carried away by the wind, so is the mind com-
31. See verse 70.

pletely carried away by the senses in the outward direction of
gross creation, the direction of the objects of the senses. It loses the
power of concentration, for it travels as if in a diverging beam,
a course naturally opposed to the concentrated state of intellect.

The following verse advises control over the senses for safety's
sake.

VERSE 68

तस्माद्यस्य महाबाहो निगृहीतानि सर्वशः ॥
इन्द्रियाणीन्द्रियार्थेभ्यस्तस्य प्रज्ञा प्रतिष्ठिता ॥६८॥

Therefore he whose senses are all
withdrawn from their objects, O
mighty-armed, his intellect is
established.

This verse, which is almost a repetition of verse 58, presents the
conclusion of the last six verses. It gives the quintessence of the
entire scheme of fulfilment in life, which is to channel the mind
into regions of experience more blissful than the ordinary gross
fields of sensory life.

'Therefore' refers back to the words of verse 66: 'for one
without peace how can there be happiness?' It indicates that if
happiness is sought, peace has to be created, the nervous system
has to be brought to a state of restful alertness. For this to happen,
the activity of the senses must cease. That is why the Lord says:
'whose senses are all withdrawn from their objects.'

The verse establishes that the senses lose their relationship to
their objects when the intellect is resolute, when it is established
in the Self.

The senses function on different levels. On the gross level they
enable the mind to enjoy the external aspects of their objects.
Functioning on subtler levels, they enable it to experience the
more subtle aspects of objects; and joys arising from the experience of the subtler states of objects are greater than those
arising from their gross states.

When, during meditation, the mind begins to experience the subtler aspects of a thought, it experiences increasing charm and thus is naturally attracted to the experience of the subtlest aspect of the thought. The experience of this finest state of thought, which is on the subtlest level of creation, provides the mind with the greatest joy in the field of relativity, but even this joy is not permanent, is not of absolute nature.

Arjuna is being directed to bring his mind to a state beyond the greatest joy of relativity, so that he can free himself from dependence upon the transitory relative joys of life and become established in the bliss of the Absolute. To reach this eternal bliss, the Lord asks him to leave completely the field of sensory perception, both gross and subtle. Thus he will come to established intellect, intellect established in the Transcendent. To live this principle in daily life is simple, for one need only know how to allow the mind to come quite naturally out of the field of the senses and reach the state of established intellect.[32]

Thus in this verse, the principle that has already been explained from the point of view of the mind is illustrated from that of relative sensory perception.

The following verse distinguishes between the fields of life of the enlightened and the ignorant.

VERSE 69

या निशा सर्वभूतानां तस्यां जागर्ति संयमी ॥
यस्यां जाग्रति भूतानि सा निशा पश्यतो मुनेः ॥६९॥

That which is night for all beings,
therein the self-controlled is awake.
That wherein beings are awake is night
for the sage who sees.

'Sage' (*muni*): not necessarily a recluse, but rather a man of calm, far-seeing prudence and wisdom.

    'Sees' means sees the Truth.

32. See II, 45, commentary.

Here the Lord shows Arjuna the difference between the state of
the ignorant man and that of the realized : one exists in darkness,
the other in light. Or the night of the one is the day of the other,
for the realized man is awake in the light of the Self, while the
ignorant is awake in the light of the senses. The realized man is
awake in the light of absolute bliss, the ignorant in the light of
relative joys of perishable nature.

The Lord says that the light in which the established intellect
behaves is not perceived by the ignorant, and the light in which
the ignorant behave is looked upon as darkness by the enlightened.

VERSE 70

आपूर्यमाणमचलप्रतिष्ठं
    समुद्रमापः प्रविशन्ति यद्वत् ॥
तद्वत्कामा यं प्रविशन्ति सर्वे
    स शान्तिमाप्नोति न कामकामी ॥७०॥

He whom all desires enter as
waters enter the ever-full and
unmoved sea attains peace, and
not he who cherishes desires.

When a man has risen to this lasting state of consciousness, the
state where his Self is detached from and not overshadowed by
the relative states of life – waking, dreaming and deep sleep –
then his state is like that of an ever-full and steady ocean. This,
being the state of absolute bliss, is the goal of all desires in life.

Desires arise from a particular want, from a lack of happiness;
the mind is ever seeking a field of greater happiness. Thus desires
are always flowing towards eternal bliss-consciousness, as rivers
to the ocean.

Once bliss-consciousness is permanently attained, desires have
served their purpose and therefore cravings do not arise. This is
a state of true contentment, a state of lasting peace.

The Lord says that lasting peace is never achieved by one who is not complete in himself and still craves worldly things. However, this does not mean that in order to attain peace in life a man should cease to desire and to aspire. It is the desires that lead a man to greater happiness and to fulfilment – not the control and killing of desires, which has been widely advocated through the ages.

This verse too has been wrongly interpreted, with a consequent increase in dullness and inefficiency, particularly in the lives of young people in India. The undue stress laid on fatalism has proved disastrous for their physical well-being and for the material progress of society. Thinking that to desire and to aspire will not lead to peace, people begin to abstain from enterprise and cease to open the gates of progress. This is simply a wrong understanding of the Lord's teaching.

The verse shows Arjuna very clearly that the Self-awareness of the realized is like an ocean, which will accept any stream of desires and will satisfy it without being affected.

The ocean accepts the river as it comes and denies no stream rushing in, yet its status remains unaffected. Such is the state of established intellect, which cannot be affected by anything. It is a state of eternal peace.

The following verse gives the technique of maintaining such a permanent state of peace in the midst of activity.

VERSE 71

विहाय कामान्यः सर्वान्पुमांश्चरति निस्पृहः ।।
निर्ममो निरहङ्कारः स शान्तिमधिगच्छति ।।७१।।

When a man acts without longing,
having relinquished all desires,
free from the sense of 'I' and
'mine', he attains to peace.

'Having relinquished all desires' does not mean that the mind no longer entertains any desires, because this would not be possible for a living being. It means that the Self has been realized as detached from activity, as was made clear in the commentary on verse 55. Because a man in this state acts while remaining 'free from the sense of "I" and "mine" ', it is quite natural that activity does not in any way disturb his state of established intellect. He has gained that eternal freedom in life where the status of one's Being remains unaffected by any activity. The following verse throws more light on this.

To have 'relinquished all desires' means to have gained trans-cendental divine consciousness permanently. This happens through meditation.

When, after meditation, the mind comes out infused with the transcendental divine nature, the individual acts in the world, and this action is quite naturally free from the narrowness of petty individuality, from the shortsightedness of selfish attach-ment, which previously held him imprisoned. Everything moves according to the cosmic plan,[33] and although the individual ego continues to function, the action is that of divine intelligence working through the individual who is living cosmic existence.

Such a life is a very natural expression of cosmic intelligence in the world. It represents the state of eternal freedom here on earth. Nothing in the world is able to overshadow or disturb this state, because it is inclusive of all that lies between two extremes of life – the transcendental divine nature of the Absolute and human nature in relative existence.

VERSE 72

एषा ब्राह्मी स्थिति: पार्थ नैनां प्राप्य विमुह्यति ॥
स्थित्वाऽस्यामन्तकालेऽपि ब्रह्मनिर्वाणमृच्छति ॥७२॥

This is the state of Brahman, O Partha.
Having attained it, a man is not deluded.
Established in that, even at the last
moment, he attains eternal freedom in
divine consciousness.

33. See Appendix: Cosmic Law.

The state of life described in the previous verse, says the Lord, is the state of cosmic consciousness. If a man is to attain to this state, it is necessary for him to gain stability of Self-consciousness in the midst of activity. This entails culturing the nervous system, the seat of consciousness, in such a way that it becomes capable of maintaining Self-consciousness, which in its nature is transcendental, along with the waking, dreaming or sleeping states of consciousness. The process of refining the nervous system is a delicate one and takes its own time, depending upon the various factors of individual life.

When the mind transcends during transcendental meditation, the metabolism reaches its lowest point; so does the process of breathing, and the nervous system gains a state of restful alertness which, on the physical level, corresponds to the state of bliss-consciousness, or transcendent Being. In order that the consciousness of the waking state may be maintained along with transcendental bliss-consciousness, it is essential for the nervous system not to lose this state of restful alertness corresponding to bliss-consciousness. At the same time, the nervous system should maintain a metabolic rate corresponding to the activity taking place in the waking state.

For this to come about, regular and continued practice of such meditation as leads to transcendental consciousness is necessary. This has to be followed by activity, because activity after meditation brings an infusion of transcendental Being into the nature of the mind and through it into all aspects of one's life in the relative field. With the constant practice of meditation, this infusion continues to grow and when it is full-grown cosmic consciousness will have been attained.

Once this state is attained, to fall from it is impossible. It holds transcendental consciousness intact in the field of all the relative states, waking, dreaming and deep sleep. Thus, in 'the state of Brahman', the state of eternal life, the activity or the silence of relative existence belongs to the absolute Being.

Having reached this state, a man's life is really the expression of divine life. The divine life is found in the individual life, the absolute Being on the human level, eternal freedom within the limitations of individuality: time, space and causation. It would

be wrong to estimate the state of cosmic consciousness in a man
by anything he displays in the field of action, because this state
accepts every activity, great or small, and at the same time retains
complete stillness. His state cannot, in principle, be judged by
what he does. There are no outer signs of a man who has risen
to this state of Brahman.

Those seekers of Truth who have accepted a life of renunciation
naturally continue to abstain from all activities of life even when
they attain cosmic consciousness. This is due to their long-
established habit of non-indulgence in activity. In the same way,
when men of the world, actively engaged in many phases of life,
reach the state of cosmic consciousness through Yoga, they continue to act, mainly from force of habit. But whether involved in
activity or leading a quiet life, a soul evolved to this cosmic state
is eternally contented.

This state is ever the same, whether the mind is active in the
waking or dreaming state, or inactive in deep sleep. It is a state
of eternal liberation during life here on earth. The Lord's words
'even at the last moment' provide a firm assurance that the fulfilment of life's purpose will be achieved through the teaching of
this chapter. Arjuna has been given all that he needs to enable
him to rise to 'eternal freedom in divine consciousness'.

*Thus, in the Upanishad of the glorious
Bhagavad-Gita, in the Science of the Absolute,
in the Scripture of Yoga, in the dialogue
between Lord Krishna and Arjuna, ends the
second chapter, entitled: The Yoga of
Knowledge, Sankhya Yoga.*

CHAPTER III

A VISION OF THE TEACHING IN CHAPTER III

Verses 1–4. Equanimity, the basis of all success and salvation in life, is gained and made permanent in two ways: by the path of knowledge and the path of action.

Verses 5–16. Both paths culture the mind and re-orientate the functioning of the senses. By the practice of gaining transcendental consciousness and then engaging in action, the infusion of Being into the nature of the mind enables it to maintain equanimity and sets the senses spontaneously to perform actions which are natural and useful to evolution.

Verses 17–20. When, through practice, transcendental consciousness becomes permanent, the purpose of all action is accomplished. In this state of fulfilment action that is right must be performed, because it brings perfection in life and good to the world.

Verse 21. One should be careful of one's actions, because others follow one's example.

Verses 22–6. The Lord of Creation, Himself remaining uninvolved, is engaged in constant activity. So a man living in the light of God should engage in action, remaining himself uninvolved, inspiring others to perform their natural duty.

Verses 27–9. All actions are performed by the forces of Nature. But, through ignorance, man takes their authorship upon himself and becomes bound by them. The enlightened man knows the truth and enjoys freedom even while engaged in activity.

Verses 30–35. The enlightened man should help to raise the consciousness of the ignorant. The technique for raising consciousness is to surrender all action to God. Control does not accomplish anything, because everything is worked out according to nature. The criterion of right action is not like and dislike, but natural duty.

Verses 36–43. The excitement born of desire and anger is opposed to the practice of gaining equanimity. The seat of desire and anger is in the senses, mind and intellect. By raising awareness above these and becoming established in transcendental consciousness, one becomes capable of spontaneously performing right action in the state of freedom. When transcendental consciousness is developed to co-exist with the waking state of consciousness, then the inner state of no problems co-exists with the outer world of problems. Man lives in freedom while acting in the field of bondage. This is the glory of the path of action.

THE second chapter has presented Brahmaa Vidya – the wisdom of the full life, the wisdom of the Absolute and the relative – in both its aspects, theoretical and practical. The theoretical aspect is called the wisdom of Sankhya; it brings *understanding* of the absolute and the relative fields of life as separate, one from another. The practical aspect is called Yoga, and it brings *direct experience* of these two fields of life in separation.

The nature of this experience gained through the practice of Yoga and its application to life in the world are unfolded in this third chapter. The aim is to make permanent the state of absolute bliss-consciousness, so that it will not be lost even when the mind is engaged in the activity of the relative field. This alone can give full experience of life, for life is relative and absolute simultaneously.

This third chapter presents a practical application of the second. It describes in detail the role of the 'established intellect' in practical life, so as to provide those occupied in the market-place of the world with a direct way of evolution and eternal liberation. Its teaching is applicable to everyone, whatever his vocation.

This chapter develops the seed-thought contained in the first three words of verse 48 of the second chapter: '*Yogastah kuru kármani* – established in Yoga, perform actions'. This doctrine of Karma Yoga, the Yoga of action, forms the chapter's main theme.

Karma is in the field of diversity, and Yoga is Unity. Therefore in order to understand Karma Yoga one must be as familiar with the Unity of life as with the field of diversity; only by being at home in both fields can one understand the link between them. The teaching of the third chapter is designed to bring this about. But it is important for the student of Karma Yoga to remember that an intellectual understanding of the teaching of this chapter, without personal experience of the real nature of Unity, can never bring the fruits of Karma Yoga. The technique of directly contacting the transcendental divine consciousness, as brought out in verse 45 of the second chapter, has to be practised; only on the basis of that personal experience is it possible to attain fulfilment in life through Karma Yoga. The practice of transcendental meditation is essential if the wisdom of this chapter is to be put to practical use.

VERSE 1

अर्जुन उवाच ।
ज्यायसी चेत्कर्मणस्ते मता बुद्धिर्जनार्दन ॥
तत्किं कर्मणि घोरे मां नियोजयसि केशव ॥१॥

Arjuna said:
If Thou considerest knowledge superior
to action, O Janardana, why dost Thou spur
me to this terrible deed, O Keshava?

Arjuna's question, with which this chapter opens, does not indicate that he was confused and had missed the import of the Lord's discourse in the second chapter, as commentaries have often suggested. Such interpretations show the commentators' own inability to follow the sequence of the Lord's words. They have clearly failed to understand the aptness of Arjuna's questions in helping to develop the Lord's theme. His questions represent the glorious links between the teachings which precede and follow them in the ascending order of the Lord's discourse.

A close examination of the context will reveal that Arjuna's questions present themselves in a natural way. This is due not only to the skill of the Lord's teaching and Arjuna's promptness in following it, but also to the nature of the subject under consideration. The teaching about life deals with many points, even points opposed to each other, for it deals with the unlimited fields of the relative and absolute phases of existence. These lie so far apart that in their essential nature there exists no link between

179 CHAPTER THREE

them. The mind, however, can serve as such a link, because it is able to remain in activity and in the state of absolute Being at the same time. Moreover it uses activity as a means to end activity and thus to make possible the state of transcendental consciousness. Karma thus becomes a means to Yoga.

Such are the apparently self-contradictory phases of the teaching about life to which Arjuna's questions draw attention. It is obvious, therefore, that his questions are pertinent and arise out of his right understanding of the discourse. The relevance of the questions asked by the pupil reveals the success of the teaching. The teacher even creates an opportunity for the pupil to ask each question, thus sustaining his interest and making sure that he is properly following the discourse. And when the teaching advances in this manner, by way of question and answer, it unfolds the whole of wisdom for the pupil.

'If Thou considerest knowledge': in order to probe deep into the nature of Arjuna's understanding about 'knowledge', it is necessary to analyse the teaching of the second chapter.

Life has two aspects, relative and absolute.[1] The relative aspect is perishable and the absolute is imperishable. In order to give meaning to life, it is first necessary to bring the perishable aspect into living harmony with the imperishable. This is achieved through action according to one's dharma,[2] which maintains existence in a way that furthers one's own evolution and that of others. In order to set the whole stream of life flowing naturally in the ascending current of dharma, it is necessary to cultivate the resolute intellect.[3] This will ensure that both aspects of man's life, perishable and imperishable, the body and the Self, will naturally maintain their dharma and be in perfect harmony, the Self remaining in Its state of eternal freedom in absolute Being and the mind entertaining activity which will naturally be in tune with the process of evolution.

In order to cultivate the resolute intellect, one has to be 'without the three gunas',[4] completely out of the field of activity, established in the transcendental state of Being. When, through constant practice in gaining the state 'without the three gunas', the mind gains fixity in Being, one becomes aware of the Self, or

1. See II, 11–38.   2. See II, 31.   3. See II, 41.   4. See II, 45.

Being, as separate from activity. In this state one acts in the world while established in the eternal contentment and freedom of divine consciousness.

Therefore although knowledge begins with the intellectual understanding of the two aspects of life, perishable and imperishable, it becomes a living Reality only when, through the practice of transcendental meditation, one becomes directly aware of the Self as separate from activity. This awareness is the state of knowledge, the state of established intellect.[5]

Arjuna has rightly understood all that the Lord has spoken about knowledge. But he demands confirmation that his understanding is correct. The word 'if' brings out this meaning.

'Knowledge superior to action': Arjuna asks his question not because he has failed to grasp the principle of action in the state of knowledge,[6] but because he has thoroughly understood that 'when a man acts without longing, having relinquished all desires, free from the sense of "I" and "mine", he attains to peace'.[7] He has understood that by fighting he will not incur sin.[8] But for that great heart of Arjuna's, merely to escape from sin is not a sufficient reason for plunging into action. He judges the action of fighting at its face-value and finds that to kill his dear ones would be a 'terrible deed'. He raises the question whether, on the strength of knowledge, he could after all avoid the 'terrible deed' of battle. Having reached this high state of established intellect, should not a man have freedom to act or not to act? This is Arjuna's question from his high state of consciousness. Arjuna here silently uses the Lord's teaching about the freedom which knowledge gives, in favour of freedom to choose what actions he wishes to perform. He probes deep into the Lord's teaching and finds that this point has not yet been answered.

This question further indicates that Arjuna has understood not only the relationship between action and knowledge, but also that between action and dharma. He has understood the Lord's teaching about dharma.[9] He has understood that one's own dharma is the best criterion for judging the appropriateness of an action,

5. See II, 55–8, 61.   6. See II, 48.   7. See II, 71.   8. See II, 38.
9. See II, 31–7.

and that, for a kshatriya, a battle such as this is in accord with
dharma.

But the stress that the Lord has put on knowledge gives Arjuna
an opportunity to question Him about the relationship between
knowledge and dharma, which has not yet been made clear and
without which the teaching about action remains incomplete.
Arjuna wants to know whether knowledge can override dharma
to the extent of permitting one to forego a particular 'deed';
whether knowledge gives a man sufficient freedom to enable him
to make his own choice about action. Arjuna implies that if it
does he would like to choose to forego 'this terrible deed'.

The question that Arjuna raises is of deep significance and has
great value in furthering the theme of the Lord's discourse. It is
this question of Arjuna's that brings forth a complete doctrine of
action from the lips of the Lord.

Commentators in general have missed the great depth of understanding from which Arjuna was speaking and asking questions,
because they have misunderstood his position right from the first
chapter.

Arjuna, from his high level of consciousness, is able to distinguish the finest points of the Lord's discourse and to weigh them
up in terms of practical life. His alert mind locates many contradictory statements in the teaching so far, and he makes mention
of these in the verse which follows.

This explains how apt is Arjuna's question and how well it
serves to unfold the wisdom of action in the light of knowledge,
which forms the main subject of this chapter.

VERSE 2

व्यामिश्रेणेव वाक्येन बुद्धिं मोहयसीव मे ॥
तदेकं वद निश्चित्य येन श्रेयोऽहमाप्नुयाम् ॥२॥

With these apparently opposed statements
Thou dost, as it were, bewilder my intelligence.
So, having made Thy decision, tell me the one by
which I may reach the highest good.

The tone of this verse brings to light Arjuna's intimacy with the Lord and his good understanding of the teaching. It also further reveals the alertness of Arjuna's mind in evaluating different aspects of the discourse.

'Apparently opposed' : in verse 38 of the preceding chapter, the Lord enjoined Arjuna to 'come out to fight'. But in verse 45 He said to him, 'Be without the three gunas', which means: come out of the field of activity. Again, in verse 47, He said: 'You have control over action alone', do not 'attach yourself to in-action'. Then, in verse 48, He expressed the synthesis of action and the established intellect in the words: 'Established in Yoga, O winner of wealth, perform actions'. In verse 49, however, he went on to destroy the very principle of this synthesis by declaring: 'Far away, indeed, from the balanced intellect is the action devoid of greatness'.

Arjuna wants to verify whether 'these apparently opposed statements' point to some hidden principle which has not yet been expressed, or whether there exists some hidden link joining them together.

In the seventh verse of Chapter II, Arjuna had surrendered himself to the Lord, saying : 'tell me decisively what is good for me'. Now he finds that he is being provided with two boats, each apparently going in an opposite direction. He is asked simultaneously to come on to this and to get into that. So he stands bewildered and asks : Tell me which boat to take, this or that, for if I start in two boats I am sure to drown. His question is a pertinent one.

The words 'apparently opposed' indicate Arjuna's modesty. Wishing to draw attention to the fact that Lord Krishna is offering him statements that oppose each other, he softens the expression by adding 'apparently'. And again, when he wants to convey that the Lord is bewildering his intelligence, he shows his modesty by adding 'as it were'.

Arjuna needed some intellectual jolt, some means of quickly shaking the intellect to bring him out of the state of suspension. To this end the Lord showered Arjuna with apparently opposed statements of Truth. Thus Lord Krishna succeeded in bringing Arjuna's mind to the level where he could think in a practical

manner. He became so practical as to say : 'Thou dost . . . bewilder
my intelligence.' Now the Lord begins the second course of His
teaching, the most glorious aspect of the wisdom of practical life.

Verse 3

श्रीभगवानुवाच ।

लोकेऽस्मिन्द्विविधा निष्ठा पुरा प्रोक्ता मयाऽनघ ॥
ज्ञानयोगेन सांख्यानां कर्मयोगेन योगिनाम् ॥३॥

The Blessed Lord said:
As expounded by Me of old, O blameless one,
there are in this world two paths: the
Yoga of knowledge for men of contemplation
and the Yoga of action for men of action.

In this verse the word 'Yoga' is common to both Gyana Yoga,
the Yoga of knowledge, and Karma Yoga, the Yoga of action. The
state of transcendental consciousness is the state of Yoga, or
Union, where the mind remains so completely united with the
divine nature that it becomes It. When this Union is naturally
maintained, irrespective of the modes of the mind in the waking,
dreaming and sleeping states, then that state of consciousness is
said to be cosmic consciousness.

When the state of transcendental consciousness, or Yoga, is
supplemented by the process of thinking and discrimination in
order to develop it into cosmic consciousness, the way is called
the Yoga of knowledge, Gyana Yoga; whereas when the state of
transcendental consciousness is supplemented by action on the
sensory level in order to develop it into cosmic consciousness, the
way is called Karma Yoga, the Yoga of action. These two types of
Yoga fulfil the needs of all men, whether contemplative or active.

The experience of the Transcendent during meditation is realization of only one aspect of Reality – the unmanifested, absolute
aspect. For realization of the complete Truth, this experience has
to go hand in hand with the experience of the manifested aspect,
which is the relative phase of existence.

BHAGAVAD-GITA 184

In order that transcendental bliss-consciousness may be lived at all times, it is necessary that it should not be lost when the mind comes out of meditation and engages in activity. For this to be possible the mind has to become so intimately familiar with the state of Being that It remains grounded in the mind at all times, through all the mental activity of thinking, discriminating and deciding, and through all phases of action on the sensory level. For this in turn, it is necessary that the process of gaining transcendental consciousness through meditation and that of engaging in activity should be alternated, so that transcendental consciousness and the waking state of consciousness may come close together and finally merge into one another to give rise to the state of cosmic consciousness, the state in which one lives bliss-consciousness, the inner awareness of Being, through all the activity of the waking and dreaming states and through the silence of the deep sleep state.

As there are two types of people, men of thought and men of action, so there are two ways of life, the way of the recluse for the man of thought and the way of the householder for the man of action. The man of thought, after meditation, engages in the mental activity of contemplation and thereby achieves the integration of the transcendental and waking states of consciousness; whereas a man of action, after meditation, engages in the field of action and thereby accomplishes the same goal.

Thus the Gyana Yoga of the recluse and the Karma Yoga of the householder differ from one another only in the phase of activity. One type of man devotes himself to the mental activity of thinking, discriminating and deciding about the nature of the world and the Divine; the other devotes himself to action without making the process of thinking a means of fulfilment. In this way, both engage in activity after gaining transcendental consciousness.

The Lord says to Arjuna that these two ways of realization have been handed on from generation to generation, from time immemorial. They are two distinct paths for the two distinct types of people who lead two distinct ways of life.

Unfortunately a muddle has been created in the understanding of this principle of realization, the highway of evolution. If the householder adopts the outlook of the Yoga of knowledge, then he falls into the world of thought and becomes less practical. Similarly, if a recluse embraces the outlook of the Yoga of action, he loses the opportunity of impartial discrimination and the constant flow of contemplation. He falls into the field of action, into the market-place of life.

Both paths are equally valid for developing cosmic consciousness. Karma Yoga and Gyana Yoga each presents a direct way to fulfilment, but the path chosen should suit the way of life and the natural tendencies of the aspirant. A householder should not try to realize through Sankhya or Gyana Yoga : let him adopt the path of Karma Yoga and, fulfilling the aspirations of a life in the world, he will gain cosmic consciousness in a natural and harmonious manner. Similarly, a recluse, or sanyasi, should not aspire to adopt the path of Karma Yoga. He should follow the Sankhya teaching, or Gyana Yoga, and fulfilling the aspirations of a recluse way of life, he also will attain cosmic consciousness in a natural and harmonious manner.

Those interested in spiritual progress have for centuries adopted an outlook suited only to the recluse way of life. While perfectly valid for the few who retire from the world, such an outlook has no place in the lives of the vast majority of mankind who lead the householder's way of life. The path of Karma Yoga does not, like the path of knowledge, proceed by way of thinking or intellectual understanding; it is the innocent path of action, supplemented by transcendental meditation. Thinking of the divine Self or of God has no place on the path of Karma Yoga. Those who try to keep their mind on God while they are engaged in action neither succeed in taking the mind to God-consciousness at the level of transcendental Divinity, nor do they properly succeed in the field of action, because action becomes weak when the mind is divided and not fully given to it. This amounts to a loss in both directions. They neither fully become men of God nor succeed as men of the world.

For those who want to be successful both in the field of the Divine and in the world, the path is that of Karma Yoga – a few minutes of meditation in the morning and in the evening and normal activity during the rest of the day. The meditation, however, should be of a kind that takes the mind directly to trans-

cendental consciousness, and the activity during the day should
be undertaken with ease and without strain.

It must be borne in mind that the practice of meditation is
essential for both the recluse and the householder. At the same
time, it is essential for enlightenment that after the practice both
should engage in activity – whether the activity is of the intellect,
as in the case of the recluse, or of the senses, as in the case of
the householder, is immaterial.

A recluse is provided with a particular code of thinking which
serves to keep him fixed to his path of renunciation. The householder likewise is provided with a code of action to keep him
fixed to his path of action. This activity after meditation is important for the integration of the waking and transcendental
states of consciousness, but the actual content of the thinking of
the recluse and the action of the householder does not in any
way help to bring about the integration of the two states of consciousness. It is the activity as such, physical or mental, which
is of value in bringing about integration. The content of thought
and action certainly has its value in the two ways of life but
it does not touch the field of Being.

The purpose of both paths is to establish a man on a level of
consciousness where he will enjoy a meaningful life, established
in the eternal freedom of bliss-consciousness. Such a man becomes
more powerful and successful in his own way of life – the activity
of the householder and the seclusion of the recluse are fully protected and brought to fulfilment.

VERSE 4

न कर्मणामनारम्भान्न ैष्कर्म्यं पुरुषोऽश्नुते ॥
न च संन्यसनादेव सिद्धिं समधिगच्छति ॥४॥

Not by abstaining from action does
a man achieve non-action; nor by
mere renunciation does he attain to
perfection.

'Non-action' is the nearest translation of the Sanskrit word *naish-karmyam*, which expresses a specific quality of the doer, a quality of non-attachment whereby he enjoys freedom from the bondage of action even during activity. It expresses a natural and permanent state of the doer. Whether he is engaged in the activity of the waking or dreaming state or in the inactivity of deep sleep, he retains inner awareness. It is a state of life where Self-consciousness is not overshadowed by any of the three relative states of consciousness – waking, dreaming or sleeping. In this state of 'naishkarmyam', the doer has risen to the fourth state of consciousness, 'turiya'; this, in its essential nature, is Self-consciousness, the pure absolute state of bliss-consciousness – Sat-Chit-Ananda – but yet is inclusive of the three relative states of consciousness.

The Lord began to explain 'non-action', in verse 48 of Chapter II, in terms of abandonment of attachment. In the present verse He explains it without any reference to attachment. In verse 30 He will explain it with reference to Himself – surrender of all actions to God. But in every case the direct experience of Being forms the basis of non-action.

'By abstaining from action' one merely falls into a state of idleness or the inactivity of sleep. This is far removed from the state of non-action, where the mind, deep within itself, remains attuned to absolute Being even when activity is maintained on the surface; where the two fields of Being and activity are cognized as separate from one another.

'Renunciation': a state of non-attachment where the doer remains separate from the field of activity; the state of non-action.

The blessing of the state of renunciation, or non-action, is that the Self finds Itself separate from the field of activity. But the awareness of separation from activity resulting in the total loss of activity for the self, will not bring 'perfection'. Perfection demands not only separation from activity, but positive Union with God. It means that the individual self, detached from activity on the level of individual life, comes to unite itself with cosmic Being, God, who is detached from activity on the level of cosmic life. Cosmic consciousness, the permanent state of Self-consciousness, rises to the state of God-consciousness; the state of non-action rises to the state of God's action.

VERSE 5

न हि कश्चित्क्षणमपि जातु तिष्ठत्यकर्मकृत् ।।
कार्यते ह्यवशः कर्म सर्वः प्रकृतिजैर्गुणैः ।।५।।

No one, indeed, can exist even for an
instant without performing action;
for everyone is helplessly driven to
activity by the gunas born of Nature.

In all the states of waking, dreaming and deep sleep, which constitute relative life, outward and inward physical activity continues. Everything in creation evolves, and the process of evolution is always through activity. This is what the Lord means when he says: 'No one, indeed, can exist even for an instant without performing action.'

'Nature': this is the nearest English rendering of the word 'prakriti'. The ultimate aspect of creation is transcendental un-manifested absolute Being. Its 'nature' consists of the three 'gunas',[10] whose various permutations and combinations consti-tute all phenomenal existence. Their activity continues unceas-ingly in all fields of creation, and that is why the Lord says that 'everyone is helplessly driven to activity by the gunas'. It is only in the transcendental field of existence that no activity is found.

This verse, by establishing activity as universal, demonstrates the impossibility of gaining the state of 'non-action' through non-engagement in activity.

10. See II, 45, commentary.

VERSE 6

कर्मेन्द्रियाणि संयम्य य आस्ते मनसा स्मरन् ॥
इन्द्रियार्थान्विमूढात्मा मिथ्याचारः स उच्यते ॥६॥

*He who sits, restraining the
organs of action, and dwelling
in his mind on the objects of
sense, self-deluded, he is
said to be a hypocrite.*

The previous verse established activity as absolutely necessary
for life in the relative field. The present verse makes it clear that
even thinking belongs to the sphere of activity. This leads to the
conclusion that, if action binds, one becomes subject to its binding influence even if one has entertained only a thought of
action.

The Lord says that it is wrong to sit 'restraining the organs
of action' while the mind is dwelling on the objects of the senses.
Here is a definite negation of the principle of sense-control. It
silently suggests that the technique of controlling the senses does
not lie in direct restraint; it lies, rather, in the field of the
mind, in the sphere of mental activity. The teaching of this
verse is: do not create strain by attempting directly to bridle
the senses. The actual technique is given in the following verse.

'A hypocrite' is he who is neither true to himself nor true to
others. He hides his true nature.

VERSE 7

यस्त्विन्द्रियाणि मनसा नियम्यारभतेऽर्जुन ॥
कर्मेन्द्रियैः कर्मयोगमसक्तः स विशिष्यते ॥७॥

*But he who, controlling the senses by the mind,
without attachment engages the organs of action
in the Yoga of action, he excels, O Arjuna.*

BHAGAVAD-GITA   190

The Yoga of action, or Karma Yoga, is performance of action
with a skill that does not allow the senses of perception to register deep impressions of experiences. The organs of action [11] remain at work during activity; the senses of perception [12] also
continue to experience, but the manner of their activity is such
that, while experiencing fully, they do not register deep impressions of experiences. The man who is able to experience in this
manner is described here as acting 'without attachment'.

Karma Yoga is that state where the senses of perception are
functioning in an organized and controlled manner, while the
organs of action are active. How do the senses remain organized
and controlled? The Lord says that it is by virtue of a particular
state of mind. How the mind arrives at this state is not explained
here, for it has already been made clear to Arjuna in the 45th
verse of the preceding chapter – the mind has to be established
in the absolute bliss of divine consciousness, through transcendental meditation. This is the simple technique by which the
senses of perception are automatically controlled and organized;
to become a karma yogi, nothing need be done save to infuse the
mind with transcendental consciousness. When the senses of perception are active while the mind is in this state of pure consciousness, then this is called Karma Yoga : the senses remain
on their objects and the mind remains established in Being.

The technique of controlling the senses by the mind is elaborated in verses 42 to 43 : one has to transcend the fields of mind
and intellect or, as the Lord puts it in verse 45 of Chapter II,
one has to 'be without the three gunas'.

11. The five organs of action : hands, feet, tongue, organs of repro-
duction and elimination.
12. The five senses of perception : sight, hearing, smell, taste and
touch.

VERSE 8

नियतं कुरु कर्म त्वं कर्म ज्यायो ह्यकर्मणः ॥
शरीरयात्रापि च ते न प्रसिध्येदकर्मणः ॥८॥

*Do your allotted duty. Action is indeed
superior to inaction. Even the survival of your
body would not be possible without action.*

'Allotted duty' is that which it is natural for one to do, that for
which one was born – natural action in accordance with the
laws of nature, action according to one's own dharma, action
which is in line with the natural stream of evolution, action
which is an innocent link between Self-consciousness and cosmic
consciousness, action which serves as a way to achieve God-
consciousness, the fulfilment of life.

An important aspect of natural duty is that it is imperative
for a man; if he does not perform his allotted duty, he will be
engaging in actions which lie outside the path of his own evolution.

Allotted duty comprises all actions which enable a man to
survive and to evolve. The rightness of such actions lies in this:
that in performing them a man feels no strain; they are not a
burden in life; in one stroke they maintain life and lead to
evolution.

It is equally essential to understand that action which is not
natural will inevitably produce strain and tension both in the
doer and in the atmosphere around him. If the process of action
is strained, it interferes with the harmony between the doer and
his work, the subject and the object; this in turn hinders the
infusion of the divine nature into the field of activity, and resistance is created to the development of cosmic consciousness.
That is why the Lord particularly mentions 'allotted duty'.

The question arises of finding out what is one's allotted duty.
In those parts of the world where natural divisions of society
still exist, a man's duty is apparent by virtue of his birth in a

particular family. Thus, Arjuna is born a kshatriya and it is natural for him to fight. But in the complexities of the mixed civilizations and mixture of traditions in the world today, it seems hard to discover one's 'allotted duty'.

If, in the absence of any scriptural authority or tradition, a criterion of natural duty has to be found, it may be said on the basis of common sense that an action which is necessary and does not produce any undue tension or strain in the doer and his surroundings is his natural duty. It is true that there may be many flaws in a criterion based only on common sense. Meditation, however, smooths the flow of life and naturally sets the stream of life in accordance with the laws of nature, upholding it on the way to higher evolution. Therefore in the absence of any other means to discover one's allotted duty, it would be wise to accept transcendental meditation as a means to direct one towards a natural way of life.

It may be recalled that when the Lord began to instruct Arjuna in the art of spontaneous right action, He advised him to come out of the field of relativity and take his stand in the field of the Absolute;[13] he would thereby rise to that state of life – cosmic consciousness – where one becomes capable of performing actions in complete accordance with the laws of nature, thus fulfilling one's dharma and serving the cosmic purpose.

The Lord says: 'Action is indeed superior to inaction', and He then adds: 'Even the survival of your body. ...' These words contain great wisdom about the integration of life and a supreme secret of evolution by way of action. The word 'even' is of deep significance. If survival of the body is the least result that the Lord attributes to action, what then is the greatest? It is the attainment of God-consciousness, the highest state of human evolution. The Lord means that, without action, not only would the body not survive, but the heights of evolution would not be attained. It must therefore be understood how action is necessary for attaining God-consciousness.

When, during transcendental meditation, the mind goes so deep within that it transcends the subtlest state of relativity, it attains the transcendental absolute state of Being. This is the

13. See II, 45.

state of pure awareness, or consciousness of the Self. When the
mind, having been in that state, is subjected to action, the transcendental divine nature of the Self is brought out to be lived in
the field of relativity. First the worldly mind of the waking state
is led to the inner divine nature by the inward stroke of meditation, which is a withdrawal from activity; then, by virtue of
embracing activity through the outward stroke of meditation, the
inner divine nature is brought out into the world.

It should be noted that, in stressing the indispensability of
action for the maintenance of life and the attainment of its purpose, the Lord is careful to qualify the action to which He refers.
He does not say: Do your duty. He says: 'Do your alloted duty',
your natural duty. How this commandment of the Lord's may be
brought to bear on life can be expressed in one word: meditate.

Meditation is the key to the performance of one's alloted duty.
It is a direct way to make glorious every aspect of life, for it
transforms a life of bondage in the world into the divine life of
eternal freedom in cosmic consciousness, where one experiences
the Self as separate from activity.

Cosmic consciousness in turn develops into God-consciousness
through devotion, the most highly refined type of action, which
unites in the light of God the two separate aspects of cosmic
consciousness, the Self and activity. This is the blessing of action,
that it leads one from the waking state of consciousness to transcendental pure consciousness, thence to cosmic consciousness and
finally to God-consciousness, the highest state of human evolution.

VERSE 9

यज्ञार्थात्कर्मणोऽन्यत्र लोकोऽयं कर्मबन्धनः ॥
तदर्थं कर्म कौन्तेय मुक्तसङ्गः समाचर ॥६॥

Excepting actions performed for yagya, this
world is in bondage to action. For the sake
of yagya engage in action free from attachment.

'Engage in action free from attachment': having stabilized the state of bliss-consciousness and thereby clearly realized the Self as separate from activity, engage in action, do your 'allotted duty', as enjoined in the previous verse.

The process of action brings the doer out of himself; action is a direct way to bring the Self out into the field of relativity. This limits the unlimited absolute Self, and the effect is called the binding influence of action. Here the Lord gives Arjuna a technique whereby action itself may be used to take the individual back to his eternal status of absolute Being.

'Yagya' is action which helps evolution. Any action in the world which tends towards absolute Being helps to free man from bondage; actions in any other direction result in bondage.

When the Lord begins, in this chapter, to teach the theory of action, He naturally draws a distinction between those actions which are a means of liberation and those which lead to bondage.

The word 'yagya' commonly means a religious performance or a holy ritual, a sacrificial ceremony in which gifts are offered to the presiding deity and are consumed in fire. But here the Lord means the act of going to the transcendental Being – bringing the attention from the gross external experience of the world to the state of the Transcendent, allowing all thoughts and desires to converge upon the Transcendent, as objects of oblation consumed in the sacrificial fire.

In the light of this verse, yagya is not confined to the narrow limits of particular ceremonies. It is a way of life which furthers evolution.

The interpretation of yagya in terms of transcendental conciousness does not in any way undermine the validity of the Vedic rites performed to please different gods. Whatever a man does by way of activity after the practice of transcendental meditation, it helps him to integrate transcendental consciousness with the waking state of consciousness and thereby to develop cosmic consciousness. If, during such activity, he cherishes the act of pleasing the higher powers in nature, the gods, this in no way hinders his progress; on the contrary, it brings him greater accomplishment through the support he receives from these powers in nature.

Yagya is the subject of the Vedas. The Vedas are divided into various branches, called shakhas. Each shakha expounds its yagya, covering the whole range of life, relative and absolute, and aiming at glorifying life in all its aspects, gross, subtle and transcendent. Every shakha has three sections. One section, called 'Karma Kanda' (Chapter of Action), deals with the gross aspect of yagya, which is designed to improve the gross aspect of life, the body and all that relates to it in the world. The gross aspect of yagya establishes the duties of men belonging to different levels of evolution, living in different times, in different places and under different circumstances, so that they do not act against the laws of nature. This helps a man to evolve by virtue of whatever he does or experiences on the gross levels of life.

The second section of the shakha is called 'Upasana Kanda' (Chapter of Worship) and deals with the subtler aspects of yagya, which win the blessings of the higher powers of nature, the Vedic gods. This section has its own gross and subtle aspects. The gross aspect deals with ritualistic performances to please different Vedic gods and win their blessings, while the subtle aspect deals with training the mind to contact higher powers and receive their blessings upon all achievements in life.

The main purpose of this section is to connect man with the more evolved beings in creation so that he may receive their good-will, their blessings and their help in improving every aspect of his life.

The third section of each shakha is called 'Gyana Kanda' (Chapter of Knowledge), and it contains the wisdom of eternal life. The Upanishads belong to this section. Each shakha has its own Upanishad to show the way of contacting Brahman, the ultimate Reality, for all those people to whom traditionally the teaching of that shakha applies. The wisdom of the Absolute and the way to transcend the relative fields of life and thereby infuse the divine nature into all spheres of human existence are dealt with in this section of each shakha.

In this way, each Vedic shakha contains wisdom to shape the entire field of human life in such a way that all its aspects, physical, mental and spiritual, are perfectly coordinated with each other on every level and at the same time are in perfect har-

mony with the entire scheme of evolution. The aim is to lead
every soul to the state of perfection, the highest and most exalted
state of existence, God-consciousness. Such is the comprehensive
scope of yagya.

VERSE 10

सहयज्ञाः प्रजाः सृष्ट्वा पुरोवाच प्रजापतिः ॥
अनेन प्रसविष्यध्वमेष वोऽस्तिबष्टकामधुक्॥१०॥

In the beginning, having created
men along with yagya, the Lord of
Creation said: By this yagya shall
ye prosper and this shall bring
forth the fulfilment of desires.

Yagya has been defined as action which helps evolution. It follows, therefore, that yagya ultimately leads man to the highest
state of evolution, to realization of God. Every step of evolution
is connected with yagya. Yagya thus upholds life from its beginning to its ultimate goal. This is what the Lord means when he
says 'having created men along with yagya'.

God is the source of all creation, and man's link with Him is
through pure transcendental consciousness. Creation came out of
this absolute level of Life, and the Creator proclaimed that It
would be forever the source of all prosperity and advancement
in life. By attuning the mind with It, one finds great intelligence,
energy, happiness and harmony and, possessed of these, no limit
to the fulfiment of desires.

In this verse the Lord points to the prosperity of the individual as one result of yagya; in the following verse He goes on to
show another of its advantages.

VERSE 11

देवान् भावयतानेन ते देवा भावयन्तु वः ॥
परस्परं भावयन्तः श्रेयः परमवाप्स्यथ ॥११॥

Through yagya you sustain
the gods and those gods
will sustain you. By
sustaining one another, you
will attain the highest good.

The various types of yagya expounded by the Vedas connect
the individual with the entire process of cosmic evolution. Yagya
thus has various levels of influence, ranging from the grossest
to the subtlest states of creation, but always pointing towards
the ultimate goal of God-consciousness.

This verse explains the mechanics of the vast influence which
one's actions create throughout the universe – all the laws of
nature on the level of the doer react to every action.

Yagya is regarded as the means to that complete success in life
which consists of all possible achievements in the world together
with freedom from bondage. Yagya, in fact, is a means to accomplish perfection of life. It brings the blessings of the powers
which control and direct the evolution of the entire creation, wins
the favour of almighty Nature and ultimately brings fulfilment
in God-consciousness.

Yagya is a process of bringing the individual into harmony with
the stream of evolution, which enjoys the favour of all the forces
of nature engaged in the advancement of life, individual and
cosmic.

The 'gods' mentioned here are the deities presiding over the
innumerable laws of nature, which are present everywhere
throughout relative life. They are the powers governing different
impulses of intelligence and energy, working out the evolution
of everything in creation. The existence of gods may be understood by an analogy : each of the myriad cells in the human

body has its own level of life, energy and intelligence; together, these innumerable lives produce human life. A human being is like a god to all these small impulses of energy and intelligence, each with its own form, tendencies, sphere of activity and influence, working for the purpose of evolution.

The Lord wishes that by way of yagya, the act of coming to the Transcendent, men should simultaneously please the world of gods. This is possible only if the means of gaining transcendental consciousness is such that the influence produced by it supports the stream of evolution and wins the favour of the deities presiding over the laws of nature, the gods. We take a word which produces such an influence of harmony in creation and experience its subtle states until the mind transcends even the subtlest and gains the state of transcendental consciousness. This is how the Lord wants us to create and maintain a mutual harmony with the higher powers of nature on the way to becoming one with the transcendental eternal Divine.

When, through the practice of transcendental meditation, activity is realized as separate from the Self, then all of life's activity is said to have been given over as an offering to the gods. This means that activity continues in its sphere of relative life, over which the gods preside, while the Self remains in the freedom of the Absolute. This is the way to please all the gods through every activity at all times. A situation is created in which every activity automatically becomes a yagya.

This manner of offering actions to the gods does not imply surrender to them or coming under their subjugation. The Self in this state becomes completely free from all the influences of relative life, including the gods.

'Highest good' : the ritualistic aspect of yagya produces effects in the relative field of life; its highest attainment is heaven, the summit of the relative world, where life is free from suffering. The technique of transcending through the process of yagya, on the other hand, leads the individual to transcendental bliss-consciousness, the state of eternal freedom in life, and thence to God-consciousness, which is the 'highest good' of all – higher than the highest in the relative sphere of life.

Verse 12

इष्टान्भोगान्हि वो देवा दास्यन्ते यज्ञभाविताः ॥
तैर्दत्तानप्रदायैभ्यो यो भुङ्क्ते स्तेन एव सः ॥१२॥

Satisfied by the yagya, the gods
will certainly bestow the enjoyments
you desire. But he who enjoys their
gifts without offering to them is
merely a thief.

'Without offering to them': without forgoing possession in their
favour, without performing the act of transferring ownership to
them. The fruit of every action is the response of nature to that
action and is therefore nothing but the gift of the powers of
nature, the gods. How is it possible to forgo possession of everything that we gain in life? It is possible only by putting into
effect the teaching of verse 48 of Chapter II and realizing the
Self as separate from the field of activity. When a man has become established in the state where he is aware that all things
are separated from the Self, he has, in effect, given over all things
completely to nature, or to the powers of nature, the gods. In
this way, he has risen above the charge of theft made by this
verse and is able to enjoy the advantage shown in the following
verse.

To create a mood of offering is to make a mockery of 'offering'.
The teaching of this discourse is a teaching of practical life – it
is a discourse of Yoga Shastra, the Scripture of Yoga, the science
of Divine Union. Its truth is far removed from imagination or
mood-making. Unfortunately, owing to superficial interpretations
current for many centuries, the essential teaching of this whole
discourse has been greatly distorted, and society stands today
surrounded by superstitions and lacking a proper sense of the
values of life.

The prosperity and happiness that arise from the blessings of
the gods, gained by means of yagya, should not cause a man to

become engrossed in enjoyment to the extent of forgetting the
source of his prosperity. The Lord says that he who undermines
the higher forces in nature by possessing himself of the field of
action, which actually belongs to them, acts like a thief. This is
because he has not realized his Self as detached from activity.
Anyone who has not gained fixity in Being automatically remains
involved with activity; he assumes authorship of action and
obtains ownership of its fruit, which in reality belong to nature
or to the gods, the powers of nature. That is why such a man is
called a 'thief', a usurper of possessions belonging to others.

A thief commonly enjoys the wealth of other men but makes
no attempt to grow wealthier by his own efforts. Here is the warning that the Lord gives: one should not be satisfied only with
the growth of material prosperity, wisdom and creativity in the
relative field of life, but should aspire to go beyond this and
achieve oneness with the eternal life of absolute Being in God-
consciousness. This is how one becomes established at the level
of life underlying all creation and automatically produces life-
supporting influences for all the powers of nature and, indeed,
for everything that exists throughout all the gross and subtle
strata of creation. Thus one begins to live the basic teaching of
this verse.

VERSE 13

यज्ञशिष्टाशिनः सन्तो मुच्यन्ते सर्वकिल्बिषैः ॥
भुञ्जते ते त्वघं पापा ये पचन्त्यात्मकारणात् ॥१३॥

The righteous, who eat the
remains of the yagya, are
freed from all sins. But
the unrighteous, who prepare
food for themselves alone,
truly, they eat sin.

'Remains of the yagya': that which is left over after the performance of a yagya has come to an end.

Yagya is action which furthers evolution, from the waking
state of consciousness to transcendental consciousness, from transcendental consciousness to cosmic consciousness, from cosmic
consciousness to God-consciousness. These are the different states
which develop through different types of practices. Each practice
in itself is a performance of yagya. Evolution finds ultimate fulfilment in God-consciousness, and once this is gained the goal of
yagya has been attained. That is why 'the remains of the yagya'
in its highest sense refers to the state of God-consciousness.

The state of cosmic consciousness, which forms the basis of
God-consciousness, may also be said to be the remains of a yagya.
So may the state of transcendental consciousness, which forms
the basis of cosmic consciousness.

That which is left over after the performance of the yagya of
transcendental meditation is bliss-consciousness. This is the remains of the first and fundamental yagya on the path to God-
consciousness and forms the basis of cosmic consciousness and
God-consciousness; he who partakes of it is 'righteous', says the
Lord, because in this state his life is transformed into a life without wrong, a life that is wholly righteous. It is in this state that
through every thought, word and action, he creates life-supporting influences for himself and for the whole creation, because he
is established in eternal Being, the basis of all life in creation.

Transcendental consciousness being the remains of the fundamental yagya, transcendental meditation is the most important of
the yagyas.

The wise man, established in bliss-consciousness, is free from
any sinful attitude because of the inner contentment which he
experiences in the state of absolute consciousness. In contrast, the
Lord describes those who concern themselves only with the affairs
of their petty individuality and do not attempt to gain the unbounded status of the Absolute. Moved by their selfish thought,
they forgo the chance of higher evolution; blinded by selfishness,
their joys are only in the field of the senses. The Lord says they
commit sin who do not work for their connexion with the higher
powers of nature or for their own evolution.

Here is the technique for rising above the influence of all sin.
It is, as Lord Krishna put it, to 'eat the remains of the yagya'.

This is a metaphor explaining that the states of transcendental consciousness, cosmic consciousness and God-consciousness should be made use of in daily life, so that actions may be free from sin. The Lord means that if the mind has not completed the course of yagya – if it has not taken a dive into the Self and has not become connected with absolute Being, if it has not realized the Self as separate from activity, if it has not attained God-consciousness – then it is not attuned to cosmic Being and its activity is not attuned to the cosmic purpose. Therefore actions are not wholly in harmony with the process of evolution. Under the circumstances there is no certainty that a man's activity will be wholly right; there is always the possibility of an element of sin.

Even in the state of cosmic consciousness, before God-consciousness has been attained, every action fulfils the cosmic purpose and serves as a yagya. But if one has not yet attained cosmic consciousness and created a situation where the Self is lived as separate from activity, then one's activity will not be graceful; it will be gripped by individuality, it will not have been set free to become universal. Such activity does not belong to the dignity of cosmic life. When those who have not realized Being as separate from activity engage in action, they appropriate the action to themselves and in so doing are taking something which does not belong to them, something which belongs to a realm outside the self, belongs to cosmic life. They fall within the category of thieves (verse 12) and partake of what, in the present verse, is called 'sin'.

The self, then, has no right to usurp activity, because activity belongs to cosmic life. There is also a further consideration. Activity thus usurped will actually damage the self by overshadowing its nature. The overshadowing of the true nature of the self, bliss-consciousness, is the basis of all suffering, and that which causes suffering is called sin. For this reason the present verse also speaks of the association of the self with activity as 'sin' – ignorance is sin.

Only when a man has become permanently established in the eternal freedom of absolute Being is he 'freed from all sins'. Such a man alone is a 'righteous' man, a man who is always right. Through all his activity he produces life-supporting influences in nature because, having gained freedom from activity, his actions belong to the dignity of cosmic life. They fulfil the cosmic purpose of evolution; that is why they never fall into the realm of sin. This is what the Lord means when he uses the word 'righteous'.

If a man has not become 'righteous', if he has not placed his life in tune with the cosmic life of absolute Being, then he may be committing sin in everything he does. The only way out of the field of sin, or the binding influence of karma, is to come under the influence of the eternal freedom of absolute Being. This is the subtlest level of the message of this verse. At its more obvious levels it refers to the gross fields of life, which demand ritualistic performances of yagya for their development.

The quality of the mind depends upon the qualities of various factors, such as food and environment and the experiences, past and present, which have an effect upon it. The quality of food directly affects the quality of the mind. It depends on many factors, such as the materials themselves and the manner in which they were earned, whether this was legal or illegal, and also the manner of cooking and its purpose. Here the Lord lays emphasis on the purpose of cooking the food. He says that if the food is cooked to be offered to God and eaten by a man after the offering has been performed, then the man enjoys the blessings of God by means of that food; and thus the mind produced by such food will be pious, progressive and graceful. Such a mind will certainly be quite naturally outside the sphere of sin. The contrary will be true, however, if the food is prepared without the purpose of making the offering, but with the sole intention of satisfying the man's own hunger.

In the following verse the Lord gives a graded sequence of creation.

VERSE 14

अन्नाद्भवन्ति भूतानि पर्जन्यादन्नसम्भवः ।।
यज्ञाद्भवति पर्जन्यो यज्ञः कर्मसमुद्भवः ।।१४।।

From food creatures come into being;
from rain is produced food; from
yagya comes forth rain and yagya
is born of action.

'From food creatures come into being': the Lord says that individual life is born of food, implying that it has little to do with
divine Being, which is the Self of all; it is born of food, of nourishment that does not belong to the field of Being. Ego, intellect,
mind, senses and body belong to the relative field of existence.

'Food' likewise is born of rain, which again has little to do
with divine Being.

'Yagya' has been considered in the previous verses as the process whereby the Self comes to be experienced as separate from
activity. In this state of realization, activity is completely natural
and perfectly attuned to the cosmic purpose of creation and evolution. As such, it produces a life-supporting influence in every
field of creation and as a result the whole of nature remains harmonious. The sun shines in due time, rain falls in due time, and
all the seasons remain regular. This is how yagya comes to be regarded as a cause of rain which, in turn, is responsible for the
production of food.

'Yagya is born of action': it is through action that a yagya is
performed. Yagya is a performance or an activity of a specific
nature whereby one becomes united with cosmic Being. This is
the true meaning of yagya in the present context of a discourse on
Yoga. But this interpretation should not be understood as de-
tracting from the truth of Vedic action, the performance of the
Vedic rites, known as yagya. The Vedas prescribe certain ritualistic performances by certain competent people to produce certain
life-supporting influences in nature. This also results in gaining

the sympathy of the laws of nature by creating an influence of harmony in the atmosphere and maintaining the rhythm of nature, so that rain comes in due time for the production of food. Naturally this type of yagya too 'is born of action' – has action for its basis.

The more gross aspect of yagya, that is, performance of rites and rituals to please the higher forces of nature for the sake of material well-being, needs action in the gross field of life for its accomplishment. Likewise, the more subtle aspect of yagya, which is the process of contacting the transcendental divine Absolute, needs action in the subtle fields. This action in the subtle aspect of life is the process of transcendental meditation, whereby the mind travels through all the subtler levels of existence and transcends the subtlest level of manifested life to reach the state of absolute Being.

This explains why the glory of action [14] is emphasized here.

VERSE 15

कर्म ब्रह्मोद्भवं विद्धि ब्रह्माक्षरसमुद्भवम् ॥
तस्मात्सर्वगतं ब्रह्म नित्यं यज्ञे प्रतिष्ठितम् ॥१५॥

*Know action to be born of Brahma
(the Veda). Brahma springs from
the Imperishable. Therefore the
all-pervading Brahma is ever
established in yagya.*

It has been said in the previous verse that 'yagya is born of action'. Here the Lord says that action (karma) and all knowledge of it is contained in the Vedas, and that the Vedas are an expression of eternal life.

The Vedas expound the theory of action and everything pertaining to it, its causes and its effects. This is the first reason why the Lord says that action arises out of the Veda. The second is

14. See verse 19, commentary.

understood when we discover the origin of the Veda in the un-manifested transcendental divine Being.

The first manifestation of creation is the self-illuminant effulgence of life. This is the field of established intellect, or the individual ego in its own established state. This self-illuminant effulgence of life is called the Veda. The second step in the process of manifestation is the rise of what we call vibration, which brings out the attributes of prakriti, or Nature – the three gunas. This point marks the beginning of the *functioning* of the ego. Here experience begins in a very subtle form: the trinity of the experiencer, the experienced, and the process of experience comes into existence. This is the beginning of action in the process of creation. Just before the beginning of action, just before the beginning of the subtlest vibration, in that self-illuminant state of existence, lies the source of creation, the storehouse of limitless energy. This source of creation is the Veda, the field of almost absolute intelligence which underlies and pervades all activity responsible for the creation and evolution of life. This, being the source of all creation, is said to be Brahma, the Creator. Brahma, or the Veda, is naturally the source of all activity. That is why the verse says: 'Know action to be born of Brahma.'

Yagya is that which helps evolution. It is a way to all accomplishment in life. Extending the meaning of yagya to the fields of common life, it could be said that any action that helps evolution can be called yagya. Thus we find that every yagya is permeated with, and gives rise to, some degree of divine consciousness. In its higher aspect, yagya is the way to cosmic consciousness and ultimately to fulfilment of life in God-consciousness; in its lower, it is the performance of rites and rituals to win the favour of the gods. This is the complete conception of yagya.

Certainly the Divine is omnipresent and is therefore present in a latent form even in those things which are opposed to evolution. But the Lord says here that divine consciousness, the Brahma, is present in yagya. He does not say that divine consciousness is present in actions other than yagya.

Every orange is meant to contain juice, but a shrivelled orange does not yield any. So it is said that juice is present in a fresh orange. Even a shrivelled orange has juice, but because this

cannot be extracted, such an orange is not considered when juice
is wanted. Likewise divine consciousness can be developed through
those types of action which help evolution. It cannot be developed
through sinful or impious actions, which tend to make the mind
coarse and lead to inertia. This robs the mind of its ability to
transcend relativity and attain divine consciousness.

That is why the Lord says that actions which fall into the category of yagya carry divine consciousness in them.

VERSE 16

एवं प्रवर्तितं चक्रं नानुवर्तयतीह य ॥
अघायुरिन्द्रियारामो मोघं पार्थ स जीवति ॥१६॥

He who in this life does not follow
the wheel thus set revolving, whose
life is sinful, whose contentment lies
in the senses, he lives in vain, O Partha.

'The wheel thus set revolving': life passes through different
spheres of existence, gross and subtle, and by this means the process of evolution is carried out. The beginning of life is in the
unmanifested pure consciousness, 'the Imperishable' of the previous verse. If a man remains always in the field of the senses
and fails to reach the source of his being, if his mind does not
travel from gross to subtle in order to realize that Imperishable,
the ultimate source of all creation, 'he lives in vain'. He has not
made use of the opportunity of enjoying that great happiness
which lies beyond the range of the senses; he has not traversed
the whole field of life; he has not gone from origin back to origin;
he 'does not follow the wheel thus set revolving'. He has com-
mitted sin against himself and sin against God, because he has
failed to rise to fulfilment. Therefore the Lord says that his 'life
is sinful'.

One who has realized life through all the subtle and gross layers
of existence and lives the ultimate Being through all actions, who
lives fulfilment in God-consciousness, can be said to have fol-

lowed the 'wheel' of creation – he has gone to That whence he came.

In the following verses, the Lord brings out in detail the state of one who is enjoying this full life.

VERSE 17

यस्त्वात्मरतिरेव स्यादात्मतृप्तश्च मानवः ॥
आत्मन्येव च सन्तुष्टस्तस्य कार्यं न विद्यते ॥१७॥

But the man whose delight is in
the Self alone, who is content in the
Self, who rejoices only in the Self,
for him there is no action that he
need do.

'The man': one who is firmly established in the Self, the eternal Being, and is not involved with anything else; who has realized Being as separate from the field of activity and is always detached from everything other than his own Self; who, despite any activity on the surface of life, eternally remains in the awareness of the Self; who, living through the relative states of consciousness, waking, dreaming and sleeping, is ever established in the absolute state of consciousness, the state of Being, the awareness of Self.

All actions that a man performs are prompted by the desire to accomplish something and to enjoy it. When he reaches the field of absolute bliss-consciousness, that state which is the fulfilment of all desires, he becomes filled with lasting contentment, for the purpose of all desires and actions is achieved. This is why the Lord says that 'for him there is no action that he need do'.

Does he then cease to act? The Lord answers in the following verse.

VERSE 18

नैव तस्य कृतेनार्थो नाकृतेनेह कश्चन ॥
न चास्य सर्वभूतेषु कश्चिदर्थव्यपाश्रयः ॥१८॥

Neither has he any profit to gain in
this life from the actions he has done
or from the actions he has not done; nor
is there any living creature on whom
he need rely for any purpose.

The man who is thus contented in himself certainly continues to
act in the world, but his behaviour has become natural behaviour.
It is no longer motivated by selfish desires, nor is its effectiveness disturbed by any shortcomings that might arise from dullness on his part.

   This comes about because he has fulfilled the purpose of all
possible desires and all possible actions in his life. He now engages
himself in actions motivated not by selfish individuality but by
cosmic purpose. Through him works the divine intelligence, for
he has become a fitting instrument to carry out the divine plan
in the world. Such a life is a natural life. It is the result of the
established intellect.

   This verse has generally been thought to advocate desireless
action arrived at by creating a mental sense of disinterestedness
in action but this interpretation is wrong. Such a sense of disinterestedness has no bearing on the realization of either Self-
consciousness, cosmic consciousness, or God-consciousness, nor
does it in any way add to effectiveness in life. It can only weaken
all phases of life, material, mental and spiritual. In the next verse
the Lord emphasizes the validity of action for the integration of
life.

VERSE 19

तस्मादसक्तः सततं कार्यं कर्म समाचर ॥
असक्तो ह्याचरन् कर्म परमाप्नोति पूरुषः ॥१९॥

Therefore, remaining unattached,
always do the action worthy of
performance. Engaging in action
truly unattached, man attains to
the Supreme.

Therefore, says the Lord, uninvolved as you are, detached as you
are, forever separated as you naturally are from the field of action,
perform 'action worthy of performance'.

The Lord demands action in the state of freedom and proclaims that freedom is there, natural to man – man's life is already
in liberation. No effort is needed for the attainment of freedom;
it is already there.

The doctrine of Karma Yoga, then, only asks man to be in his
natural and normal state of Self-consciousness, to be in his own
nature. The Lord, indeed, advises him to act, and this advice is in
order to cultivate liberation in God-consciousness.

The mind, moved by its own nature to enjoy more, flows towards the subtler fields of experience during transcendental meditation and most spontaneously attains the state of Being. Activity
after this state of Being is gained is likewise spontaneously carried out by nature. Therefore the development of cosmic consciousness, which forms the basis of the supreme attainment of
God-consciousness, is a natural process, free from effort.

'The Supreme': God, presiding over the relative and the Absolute in the fullness of both. This verse reminds us of the 47th
verse of the second chapter. The Lord reveals the significance of
unrestricted natural action on the way to the realization of God-
consciousness. The previous verses brought out man's ability to
act in a natural manner by virtue of possessing cosmic consciousness. The present verse shows that performance of action

in an unstrained, natural manner is a means of realizing 'the Supreme'. In the state of cosmic consciousness the validity of action is accepted for the sake of developing God-consciousness. This verse should be studied very carefully in order to understand the means by which God-consciousness may be attained. The means should not be confused with the end. Cosmic consciousness, in which the Self is experienced as separate from activity, is not the end, not the final state of development; it is a means to God-consciousness.

When, through meditation, the mind has reached transcendental Self-consciousness and then returns from the field of absolute Being, it becomes necessary for it to engage in activity. In this way the nature of transcendental Being, infused into the mind, has an opportunity of maintaining itself even when the mind is engaged in experiencing the relative field of life through the senses. This is how one remains permanently established in Self-consciousness and thereby enjoys life in cosmic consciousness.

This is how, by virtue of action, the transcendental divine nature is infused into practical life, making a man fully integrated, so that he acts in the relative field of existence while remaining established in absolute Being. In this state of contentment his actions are natural and normal, 'worthy of performance'.

When, in the state of cosmic consciousness, the Self has been realized as separate from all activity, 'the action worthy of performance' is action in devotion to God.[15] The activity of devotion is the highest and most refined type of activity, for it directly raises the awareness of separateness of Being from activity, as experienced in the state of cosmic consciousness, to a unified state of awareness of God alone. The awareness of Self and of activity, the awareness of the two, gives way to oneness in the awareness of God, in God-consciousness. The duality of the Self and activity finds itself pervaded by God. He alone remains, He alone dominates life, and in the light of Him, permeated by Him, the Self stands in Unity with Him and with the whole field of action dominated by Him. In Him are found united forever both the Self and the activity of cosmic consciousness.

15. See II, 61, commentary.

This is the state of life in the oneness of God-consciousness expressed by the words 'attains to the Supreme' in this verse which
extols action in the state of cosmic consciousness.

Action worthy of performance may be considered on five
different levels of life: one, during the ordinary waking state of
consciousness; two, when Self-consciousness has been gained and
is developing into cosmic consciousness; three, action in the state
of cosmic consciousness; four, action which helps cosmic consciousness to develop into God-consciousness; and five, action in
the state of God-consciousness. This verse is concerned with the
last three levels of action. The expression 'worthy of performance' lays emphasis upon the quality of the action which is
helpful for gaining the higher states of consciousness.

One who has realized the Self in transcendental consciousness,
who has realized the Self as completely separate from activity in
cosmic consciousness, and who has gained fulfilment by realizing
the Self in Union with God in God-consciousness, has reached the
state where the purpose of all [16] activity has been fulfilled. Because his self is fixed in the universal Self, there is nothing that
he could gain from another. His Self is uninvolved in every way –
it is uninvolved with activity (verse 17) and it is uninvolved with
the *selves* of individual beings (verse 18). His own Self is the
Self of all beings.

VERSE 20

कर्मणैव हि संसिद्धिमास्थिता जनकादयः ॥
लोकसंग्रहमेवापि संपश्यन् कर्तुमर्हसि ॥२०॥

By action alone, indeed, Janaka and
others gained perfection. Moreover,
even looking to the welfare of the
world, you should perform action.

16. See IV, 23.

This verse extols action for its value to the world and as a means to eternal liberation from bondage. At the same time it illustrates with concrete examples the abstract principles of Karma Yoga and their effects.

It was the glory of action that brought integration of life in God-consciousness to 'Janaka and others' and enabled them to do good to the world.

Integration of life depends upon the mind passing in a cycle between the field of the Absolute and the field of activity. The mind goes to the unmanifest and comes back to the manifest, thus experiencing both fields of life, absolute and relative. This is the state of the integrated man in cosmic consciousness.

When King Janaka and others like him were found to be established in Reality while fully active in the world, the secret did not lie in their continuous outward activity. It lay in the fact that such activity was supplemented by their experience of the Transcendent through the inward activity of meditation. If we consider the march of the mind from gross outward activity to the Transcendent, we can say that it is activity in the direction of putting an end to activity that gives the mind the status of the Absolute. Meditation itself is an activity. In view of this, it can certainly be held that it is 'action[17] alone' that brings perfection.

The Self is omnipresent and eternal. It does not need anything to realize Itself. Man loses It by remaining in the field of activity. Therefore in order to realize It, he has simply to come out[18] of activity, to engage himself in subtler fields of activity until he is completely out of the field of activity, in the field of the Transcendent. This explains the principle of enlightenment through action.

As a direct result of this inward activity of meditation, outward activity in the world becomes more successful, more perfect. This is what the Lord means when He says: 'By action alone, indeed, Janaka and others gained perfection.'

Every action starts from the subtlest stratum of relative life, which is almost one with the level of the Absolute, with pure Being. It starts as a thought. The thought itself passes through many stages from the subtle to the gross. At a certain stage it reaches that level of the mind where it is consciously appreciated

17. See verse 19, commentary.   18. See II, 45.

as a thought, and it may then be translated into speech or action.

Through the practice of transcendental meditation, the thought begins to be appreciated at a subtler level. Here it is more powerful and results in more successful action. Thus, by direct experience of transcendental Being through the inward stroke of action during meditation, a man not only gains spiritual freedom but also greater success in the world.

The contentment and serenity gained through this action of meditation produce harmonious and life-supporting influences for the whole world. By raising man's consciousness, they fill his heart with universal love, which induces him to work for 'the welfare of the world' in a most natural way.

It should be remembered that it does not need a long time of silent meditation to reach transcendental Being: just a dive within the Self for a few minutes and the mind is infused with the nature of pure consciousness, which keeps it enriched through all the activities of the day. This is the way to live the spiritual life, which makes glorious even the physical and material aspects of life in the world.

VERSE 21

यद्यदाचरति श्रेष्ठस्तत्तदेवेतरो जनः ॥
स यत्प्रमाणं कुरुते लोकस्तदनुवर्तते ॥२१॥

Whatsoever a great man does, the very
same is also done by other men.
Whatever the standard he sets, the
world follows it.

A great man is he who lives the awareness of Being in his daily life and has gained a state in which he naturally maintains his high status of eternal Being even when engaged in activity and in doing good to others.

This verse describes the tendency of the masses to follow the example of evolved men. At the same time, it touches Arjuna's pride. In this lies the great skill of the discourse. Although indirectly stated, the idea is conveyed to Arjuna that he is venerated in society, and that people will follow his example. Therefore he has a responsibility which extends beyond the limits of his own interest.

For the evolution of his own soul, Arjuna is expected to stand up and engage in activity. And even should he not care about his own evolution, it behoves him to embrace activity for the sake of others.

The following verses throw more light on this.

VERSE 22

न मे पार्थास्ति कर्तव्यं त्रिषु लोकेषु किंचन ॥
नानवाप्तमवाप्तव्यं वर्त एव च कर्मणि ॥२२॥

In the three worlds there is no
action which I need do, O Partha;
nor is there for Me anything worth
attaining unattained; even so I
am engaged in action.

Having mentioned 'Janaka and others' in verse 20, the Lord here points to Himself as an example to illustrate the principle affirmed in verse 21. He speaks from His absolute state of eternal contentment.

Having brought to light the importance of action in man's evolution, and having shown the authenticity of this principle by citing the example of men who lived perfection in life through action, the Lord now reveals the validity of action in the pure field of the Divine, which is completely free from activity in the relative field. It may be explained that whereas man in the state of enlightenment lives fully both activity and divine consciousness because his life has two aspects, relative and absolute, there is no trace of relativity in the pure transcendent divine field of the Lord. Nevertheless, the Lord says that He is 'engaged in

action'. The supreme Lord of creation, presiding over the absolute
and the relative fields of life and the refuge of both, is 'engaged
in action' – the divine activity that underlies the continuity of
ever-changing creation.

When the Lord speaks about Himself and the three worlds, He
addresses Arjuna as 'Partha' to maintain the fine bond of love
between Himself and Arjuna. This is skill in teaching. Arjuna
should see Lord Krishna as close to himself and not far off as a
high ideal beyond his reach.

By 'the three worlds' is meant the entire field of relative
existence.

VERSE 23

यदि ह्यहं न वर्तेयं जातु कर्मण्यतन्द्रितः ॥
मम वर्त्मानुवर्तन्ते मनुष्याः पार्थ सर्वशः ॥२३॥

*What if I did not continue unwearyingly
in activity, O Partha? Men in every
way follow My example.*

The Lord means to convince Arjuna of the truth of the great
principle that there can be no escape from duty without setting a
sinful example in which the whole of society will be involved.

Moreover, the Lord points out that His own incessant activity
lies at the root of all life. The entire creation is the manifested
aspect of His unmanifested Being. Remaining unmanifested, He
manifests Himself, and this action of manifestation expresses
itself as creation. His continued activity is responsible for the
maintenance and evolution of everything that exists; without it
the entire creation would be reduced to nothingness.

This is how the Lord explains His perpetual activity, quoting
it as an example to be followed by others.

VERSE 24

उत्सीदेयुरिमे लोका न कुर्यां कर्म चेदहम् ॥
सङ्करस्य च कर्त्ता स्यामुपहन्यामिमाः प्रजाः ॥२४॥

If I did not engage in action, these
worlds would perish and I would be the
cause of confusion and of the destruction
of these people.

The principle elaborated in the previous three verses is again
emphasized, and a point is brought out similar to that raised by
Arjuna in the 39th to the 45th verses of the first chapter. In these
verses Arjuna had said that by fighting he would be causing the
disruption of society.

In this verse, the Lord, by referring to Himself, turns the tables
on Arjuna. He brings home clearly to him by His own example
that if he does not engage in action he will corrupt the whole of
society, and that his bad example will be responsible for allowing
its values to be destroyed.

The conclusion is that even if a man has gained fulfilment in
his own life, it behoves him to act for others. This idea is brought
out very clearly in the following verse.

VERSE 25

सक्ताः कर्मण्यविद्वांसो यथा कुर्वन्ति भारत ॥
कुर्याद्विद्वांस्तथाऽसक्तश्चिकीर्षुर्लोकसंग्रहम् ॥२५॥

As the unwise act out of their
attachment to action, O Bharata,
so should the wise act, but without
any attachment, desiring the welfare
of the world.

The Lord shows Arjuna that there is absolutely no difference
between the action of an ignorant man and that of one who is
enlightened; action is action whether performed by the ignorant
or the enlightened. The difference is found only in the result.

The result of an ignorant man's action is enjoyed by himself
and concerns mainly himself, because he is attached to it; when
the doer is attached to the action, the result of the action is
naturally attached to the doer. But when the doer is not attached
to the action, the results are not attached to him.

The ignorant man acts and benefits from the results of his
actions; since he is attached to these results, they make a deep
impression on him. The effects of the enlightened man's actions
spread out in the world and everything benefits from them; the
impression of the result passes him by, leaving him free from the
bondage of action because he has realized the Self as separate
from activity and acts from the basis of eternal contentment. His
actions are in response to the needs of the time; they fulfil the
demands of their surroundings. The wise are tools in the hands
of the Divine; they innocently carry out the divine plan. Their
actions arise from their desire for 'the welfare of the world'.

VERSE 26

न बुद्धिभेदं जनयेदज्ञानां कर्मसङ्गिनाम् ॥
योजयेत्सर्वकर्माणि विद्वान्युक्तः समाचरन् ॥२६॥

*Let not the wise man create a division
in the minds of the ignorant, who are
attached to action. Established in
Being, he should direct them to perform
all actions, duly engaging in them
himself.*

'Let not the wise man create a division in the minds of the
ignorant': the state of a realized man is the result of many years
of inner development founded on right values in life. This causes

his life to flow naturally in right channels of conduct. Although his Being is above the realms of right and wrong, his actions are quite naturally right actions. He is advised in this verse to allow the ignorant man to do his duty. He should refrain from telling him that the state of enlightenment is free from both good and evil, and that the whole field of relativity is just the play of the three gunas, which do not belong to his Being.

It is perhaps even more important that the wise man should not confuse the ignorant by telling him about the uninvolved nature of the Self. The intellect of the man who is not realized is wholly involved with activity. The realized should not create a division in such a man's mind. He should not talk to him of the separateness of the Self from activity, otherwise the ignorant man may lose interest in practical life, and if this happens he will never be able to gain realization. It is not the intellectual under-standing of the separateness of the Divine and of activity, but rather the experience of this state which brings a man enlighten-ment. In order that one may gain this experience and become established in it, conscious activity both in the gross and subtle fields of life is necessary. The Lord exhorts the wise : Teach transcendental meditation to the ignorant man so that he may engage himself in subtler phases of activity and thereby realize the transcendent Being, the Self, in Its true nature as devoid of any activity. Teach him that, having gained this realization, he should continue to act in daily life so that it may become firmly established in the very nature of his mind. And then set him an example by 'duly engaging' in actions yourself.

'All actions' : every type of activity is necessary for life in the world, activity of the ego, intellect, mind and body. All activity, gross and subtle, in every field of life, has its place in the scheme of one's evolution.

Activity at more subtle levels is the activity of the thought-process. During meditation, the process of experience becomes at every moment more and more refined, and eventually the mind transcends the finest level of activity. The Lord implies that this finer activity also should not be ignored in the midst of the gross activity of thinking, speaking and acting. It is given to the wise to see that all activity, gross and subtle, is undertaken by every man in society in due proportion – the activity of daily life should be supplemented by morning and evening meditations.

'All actions' should not be taken to include wrong actions. This has been shown in verses 8 and 9.

The following verses present Lord Krishna's justification for the performance of all right activity by the ignorant.

VERSE 27

प्रकृतेः क्रियमाणानि गुणैः कर्माणि सर्वशः ॥
अहङ्कारविमूढात्मा कर्ताहमिति मन्यते ॥२७॥

Actions are in every case performed
by the gunas of Nature. He whose
mind is deluded by the sense of 'I'
holds 'I am the doer'.

This verse reveals the doer of all actions and provides a graceful answer to the question which naturally presents itself when, through the practice of transcendental meditation, one begins to live in bliss-consciousness, begins to feel self-contained. How can action, which is always motivated by some desire, be possible in the state of complete contentment? The answer to this question is : 'Actions are in every case performed by the gunas.'

Sattva, rajas and tamas are the three gunas of Nature (*prakriti*). Prakriti is the primal motive force. It is the essential constituent of manifested creation and is at the basis of all activity. This is what the Lord means when He says that all actions and all happenings in creation arise out of the three gunas and their permutations and combinations.

How the gunas interact may be made clear by an example. It is a natural law that when a vacuum is created somewhere in the atmosphere, at once a flow begins from an area of greater pressure. But while the flow starts from the area of greater pressure, the cause lies in the vacuum. It is the vacuum that creates the situation. Similarly, the currents of the three gunas flow in order to keep a balance among themselves. They continually flow from one field of existence to another and in this way create and maintain various activities in a natural way. The entire phenomenal world is nothing but the interplay of the three gunas.

The gunas find an expression, for instance, in the metabolic processes of the body, and on their basis feelings of hunger and thirst arise. The need for food and water is in the physiological sphere, but the ego feels 'I am hungry', 'I am thirsty'. The gunas are responsible in a similar way for all experience. They are the basis of all events and activities, but the ego takes these upon itself and feels 'I am acting'.

As long as the Self has not been experienced as separate from activity, the mind remains 'deluded' about its own status and its relationship with activity; associating itself with the nature of the gunas, it assumes the authorship of action, which actually belongs to the gunas. This is how, through ignorance of his own Self, man falls into the bondage of action.

VERSE 28

तत्त्वविन्तु महाबाहो गुणकर्मविभागयोः ॥
गुणा गुणेषु वर्तन्त इति मत्वा न सज्जते ॥२८॥

But he who knows the truth about
the divisions of the gunas and their
actions, O mighty-armed, knowing that
it is the gunas which act upon the
gunas, remains unattached.

This verse, in contrast to the preceding verse, shows the state of mind of the man who is realized, and at the same time provides insight into the process of realization through knowledge of the three gunas.

There are three gunas which constitute prakriti. Prakriti is eight-fold.[19] This gives rise to the twenty-four basic divisions in

19. See VII, 4.

the field of the gunas. Knowledge of these twenty-four divisions
and their actions liberates man from the bondage of action by
showing how both the subjective and objective aspects of our life
emanate from the gunas, and how the Self is eternally uninvolved
with anything in the manifested field of life.

The path of liberation from bondage here laid out has the
following significant features :

1. The knowledge has to be thorough and comprehensive, for
the Lord says : 'he who knows the truth'.

2. The knowledge has to be about
   (a) 'the gunas',
   (b) their 'divisions',
   (c) their 'actions'.

3. The knowledge has also to be about the interplay of the
gunas; one has to know that the gunas are themselves the subject,
are themselves the object and are themselves the subject-object
relationship; and that they constitute the entirety of phenomenal
existence. For the Lord says : 'It is the gunas which act upon
the gunas.'

Having, in the previous verse, attributed the authorship of
action to the three gunas, the Lord, in this verse, says that he
who knows the truth about the gunas and their actions 'remains
unattached'.

The question may be asked : Is intellectual understanding of
the gunas sufficient to bring freedom? If intellectual understanding could fulfil the conditions of knowledge given above,
then, according to this verse, it could certainly make a man sufficiently 'unattached' to become completely free. But it is doubtful
if the 'truth' about the three gunas and their interplay can be
known only on the level of intellectual understanding, without
directly comprehending the nature of the gunas at the subtlest
level of creation.

The question then arises : What is the way to such direct comprehension? The answer is simple. The gunas are the finest aspect
of creation. Therefore if a man could take his attention to the
subtlest level of creation, it would be possible for him to know
what the gunas are, their divisions, and all details concerning

their actions. In fact, all this knowledge is gained during transcendental meditation when the mind is about to transcend the subtlest state of the object of attention. Consequently, the Lord's saying: 'he who knows the truth about ... the gunas' may be said to include in its scope the teaching: 'Be without the three gunas', for this is the way of knowing 'the truth' at the subtlest level of creation.

Once established in transcendental consciousness, the state without the three gunas, the knower of Reality knows by experience that the realm of action lies at the surface of his life and is separate from his real existence. Thus 'he who knows the truth' does not mean only he who knows 'the divisions of the gunas and their actions', but also he who has realized the Self as separate from activity. This natural state of separation from action, gained through the practice of transcendental meditation, is the basis of his remaining 'unattached'. When the state of Being, or pure consciousness, is firmly established in the very nature of the mind, one lives quite naturally this state of pure existence separated from the field of activity, even while ego, intellect, mind and senses are engaged in action. One finds that the field of activity remains in the province of the three gunas and is no longer intimately connected with one's existence. This is how one naturally 'remains unattached' in the midst of activity. This state of knowledge fills the whole field of one's understanding. That is why the Lord says: 'knowing that it is the gunas which act upon the gunas, remains unattached.'

The present verse speaks of action in terms of freedom through the knowledge of Sankhya, but as this knowledge gains completeness only through the process of direct experience, it is inclusive of the technique and philosophy of Yoga. Therefore the Lord, in this verse, brings together the philosophies of Sankhya and Yoga, described separately in the second chapter, and initiates a principle of liberation from the bondage of karma resulting from the combined effect of the two teachings. This provides the basis of Karma Yoga and the essentials for its fulfilment.

The whole purpose of this verse, even though it speaks in terms of the gunas, is to throw light on the state of fullness of life in absolute bliss-consciousness – jivan-mukti.

VERSE 29

प्रकृतेर्गुणसंमूढाः सज्जन्ते गुणकर्मसु ॥
तानकृत्स्नविदो मन्दान् कृत्स्नविन्न विचालयेत् ॥२९॥

Those deluded by the gunas of Nature
are attached to the actions of the gunas.
Let not him who knows the whole disturb
the ignorant who know only the part.

Again the Lord warns the enlightened man not to thrust his
understanding of life upon the unenlightened. The reason for this
is that the enlightened man, established in Being, has a permanent ground on which to stand; from this he sees the world as the
interplay of the three gunas and knows by experience that the
effects of sattva, rajas and tamas have no bearing on him. But if
an ignorant man tries to copy the state of the enlightened in his
own life, then he will create confusion in his behaviour, and his
action may fall into a pattern in which the validity of good and
evil in the field of practical life is undermined. Such a man will
prove useful neither to himself nor to others. After committing a
theft, the unenlightened man might say that it was only the three
gunas reacting among themselves, while his Self was uninvolved,
so that he is not responsible. He has not done anything! This is
why the Lord warns the enlightened not to reveal the inner state
of their mind to the ignorant.

The inference is that if the enlightened man wants to bless
one who is ignorant, he should meet him on the level[20] of his
ignorance and try to lift him up from there by giving him the
key to transcending, so that he may gain bliss-consciousness and
experience the Reality of life. He should not tell him about the
level of the realized, because it would only confuse him.

20. See verse 35, commentary.

VERSE 30

मयि सर्वाणि कर्माणिसंन्य स्याध्यात्मचेतसा ॥
निराशीर्निर्ममो भूत्वा युध्यस्व विगतज्वरः ॥३०॥

Surrendering all actions to Me by
maintaining your consciousness in
the Self, freed from longing and the
sense of 'mine', fight, delivered from
the fever (of delusion).

As the whole of creation is the play of the three gunas, the Lord
tells Arjuna to contact the source of the three gunas. By bringing
the attention to transcendental consciousness and becoming established in that field of Being, He says, you will be freed from
all activities and their influence. In that state of freedom and
contentment, stand up and fight.

This verse is complementary to verse 28 because the knowledge
of relativity gains fulfilment in the realization of the Supreme.
Furthermore, even for the complete knowledge of the three gunas,
which form the basis of the whole creation, a thorough intimacy
with the Creator is essential.

'Fever (of delusion)': the Lord reminds Arjuna of the bewilder-
ment which he expressed in verse 2.

'Freed from longing': because one has gained fulfilment in life
(verses 17 and 18).

'Freed from ... the sense of "mine"': when one has gained
Union with Being and disunion from the field of activity (verses
27 and 28), the 'I' ceases to assume authorship of actions and
therefore ceases to be bound by their fruits. All action is automatically passed on to the Lord of creation.

During the inward stroke of meditation, one gains a clear
experience of transcendent Being. With repeated practice of
transcending, one experiences one's Self as aloof from activity
and recognizes It as non-doer, even though one is engaged in
action. In this state one attributes all activity to the power of
the Almighty underlying the gunas, their divisions and their

actions (verse 28). One remains fixed in the Self, while the Lord is recognized as the author of all actions, carrying them out through the agency of the gunas.

The steps by which this state is attained are as follows: through the practice of transcendental meditation one first experiences the Self, or Being, and then, as a result of this experience becoming deeper and clearer, one experiences the separateness of Being from activity. Again, as this experience of separateness becomes deeper and clearer, one is enlightened by knowledge about the mechanics of activity (verses 23, 24, 27, 28). This knowledge reveals one's own true position in the scheme of things and one's relationship with activity and with the Lord of all creation. This provides one with a sound basis for eternal life in God-consciousness. The glory of the present discourse is this: direct connexion with God is established for ever by virtue of one's having gained proficiency in the art of action.

Surrender of all actions to God is the living Reality of one's life. It is not a fanciful thought or a mood of surrender. It is the Truth of one's life in activity.

The range of surrender is not restricted to any one aspect of life: it comprehends all spheres of one's existence, physical, mental and spiritual. Therefore it certainly includes the mind and the intellect. But to regard this state of surrender of action to God as merely an act of the mind, a thought or feeling, will be to do injustice to the principle brought to light by this verse.

'Maintaining your consciousness in the Self' means maintaining Self-consciousness while performing action. Maintenance of transcendental Self-consciousness along with activity in the waking state of consciousness requires co-existence of the two states of consciousness. The ability of man's nervous system, which is the physical machinery through which consciousness expresses itself, has to be developed to express these two states simultaneously. This is brought about by regularly interrupting the constant activity of the waking state of consciousness with periods of silence in transcendental consciousness. When, through this practice, the nervous system has been permanently conditioned to maintain these two states together, then the consciousness remains always centred in the Self. The Lord explains that this centring

of consciousness in the Self is the way of 'surrendering all actions
to Me'.

VERSE 31

ये मे मतमिदं नित्यमनुतिष्ठन्ति मानवाः ॥
श्रद्धावन्तोऽनसूयन्तो मुच्यन्ते तेऽपि कर्मभिः ॥३१॥

*Those men who are possessed of
faith, who do not find fault and
always follow this teaching of Mine,
they too are liberated from action.*

The teaching of the previous verse was directed to Arjuna himself, for the Lord said to him: 'fight'. The present verse extends
the teaching to all men at all times.

'Possessed of faith' means that faith is unwavering, that it is
permanent. When a man has become fixed in faith, he is freed
from doubt and therefore ceases to find fault.

Not finding fault and not speaking ill of others is counted an
essential prerequisite to the realization of God and freedom from
bondage. When a man speaks ill of others, he partakes of the sins
of those of whom he speaks. Such a man thus draws more and
more bad influence to himself; that is, he falls deeper into impurity. Here the Lord means: Those who are devoted and who
feel full in themselves do not find fault with Me or My teaching;
they are released from bondage.

The benefits of the teaching are gained only when one begins
to practise it. The teaching of the Lord in the previous three
verses is so complete that its practice can result in nothing less
than the fulfilment of life. It may be that one is not able to grasp
the scope and significance of the teaching intellectually, but those
who practise it faithfully, even without understanding it, 'they
too are liberated from action' – they too realize that eternal contentment in bliss-consciousness which establishes the Self as
separate from activity and thereby brings fulfilment in God-
consciousness.

VERSE 32

ये त्वेतदभ्यसूयन्तो नानुतिष्ठन्ति मे मतम् ॥
सर्वज्ञानविमूढांस्तान्विद्धि नष्टानचेतसः ॥३२॥

But those who find fault and
do not follow My teaching: know
them to be deluded about all
knowledge, doomed and senseless.

The Lord's words are plain and effective.

'Those who find fault' do so because, failing to understand, they begin to misunderstand.

They 'do not follow My teaching' means that they do not understand it and do not put it into practice; they do not investigate the nature of the three gunas or the Reality which lies beyond.

'Deluded about all knowledge' means confused about the knowledge of relative existence and about the nature of absolute Reality.

'All knowledge': knowledge about the divisions of the gunas and their actions (verses 27 and 28), knowledge about the Self as separate from the field of action (verses 17 and 18), knowledge about the great Lord of all creation presiding over the absolute field of the Self, or Being, and over the relative field of the gunas (verses 30 and 31) and knowledge about the activity of the Lord (verses 22 and 23).

'Doomed': the purpose of their life is lost. They cannot find worldly fulfilment and they are lost to the Divine. They fail to live bliss-consciousness and so remain in suffering.

'Senseless': without proper values in life and devoid of pure consciousness. They have not attained the state of Being. They have not experienced the Self as separate from activity; their self is involved in activity, it is not in its own nature. For this reason the Lord says that they are 'senseless', as if without life, without consciousness.

In this verse the Lord declares that realization of the state of all

knowledge is the only way to salvation and success in life; there is
no other way.

VERSE 33

सदृशं चेष्टते स्वस्याः प्रकृतेर्ज्ञानवानपि ॥
प्रकृतिं यान्ति भूतानि निग्रहः किं करिष्यति ॥३३॥

Creatures follow their own nature.
Even the enlightened man acts
according to his own nature.
What can restraint accomplish?

This verse brings out the truth that freedom from bondage is
gained in a natural manner. The Lord denies the validity of control on the path of enlightenment. He means to introduce a
natural way of life for fulfilment. In the field of activity, it is not
desirable to create stress and strain by attempting control either
from within or from without. Let everyone proceed naturally,
complementing the state of transcendental consciousness gained
during meditation with the activity of daily routine, and so be
sure to win fulfilment.

Because the natural tendency of the mind is towards greater
happiness, it will inevitably find contentment in the supreme
happiness that is transcendental bliss-consciousness and will rise
above 'attachment' (verse 34), which is the basis of bondage. In
condemning 'restraint', the Lord, in this verse, advises Arjuna to
take things easily [21] and not strain even to follow the teaching.[22]
Restraint, being unnatural, cannot bring about that natural state
of life where the Self stands by Itself in the state of non-attachment, uninvolved with activity.

Having said in the previous verse: 'know them to be deluded
about all knowledge', the Lord, in this verse, gives the clue to all
knowledge: in order to be 'liberated from action' (verse 31) it is
not necessary to use 'restraint'; it is only necessary to raise the

21. See II, 40.   22. See verse 29, commentary.

level of one's consciousness by the experience of Being, it is only
necessary to become 'enlightened'. 'Restraint' offered to activity
does not 'accomplish' the goal because, as the next verse explains,
the natural seat of bondage does not lie with the mind or the
senses, which alone could be influenced by restraint. Attachment, the seat of bondage, does not lie within; it is located outside, in the region of the object of experience. Therefore non-
attachment cannot be gained by restraining the mind or senses;
keeping them away from activity does not create a state of non-
attachment; non-attachment cannot be gained by non-activity
(verse 4) or by any kind of restraint. It can only be gained by
realizing the Self (verse 17) and by realizing Its separateness
from activity (verse 28). There is no other way, because creatures
must 'follow their own nature'. They must be engaged in activity
according to their own level of consciousness, and therefore enlightenment, if it is to be of universal application, must be
possible irrespective of the kind of activity in which one is
engaged. That is why the state of enlightenment, the state of
knowledge, cannot be gained through restraint, which discrimi-
nates between different kinds of activity. It must be on the level
of absolute Being, on the level of realization of the Self and
completely regardless of the activity that a man undertakes
'according to his own nature'.

The next verse throws more light on this.

Verse 34

इन्द्रियस्येन्द्रियस्यार्थे रागद्वेषौ व्यवस्थितौ ॥
तयोर्न वशमागच्छेत्तौ ह्यस्य परिपन्थिनौ ॥३४॥

The attachment and aversion of
each sense are located in the
object of that sense; let no man
come under their sway, for both
indeed are enemies besetting his
path.

The Lord means to point out that all is well and wisely set: let everything remain in its place. The attachment and aversion of each sense are located in 'the object of that sense'. Let them remain in that field and let the field of the Self remain free from them.

This verse supplements the previous verse, for even the idea of restraint engages the mind in the objects of the senses: in order to forget them, the mind continues to think of them. And the moment the mind comes in contact with the object through the senses, it is influenced by attachment or aversion, which is present in the object. Therefore it is wrong to think in terms of abstinence from the activity of experience as the means of gaining a state of permanent freedom from attachment and aversion, because it is not physically possible to remain without activity at all times.

The teaching is: realize Being in Its fullness, realize It as separate from activity; and this will automatically maintain the Self as aloof from attachment or aversion in the midst of all activity and in the presence of all objects of the senses.

In the previous verse, the Lord asked Arjuna not to follow the way of 'restraint'. In this verse, he puts attraction and aversion on one level: 'both indeed are enemies besetting his path.'

This leads to a remarkable conclusion in the following verse.

VERSE 35

श्रेयान् स्वधर्मो विगुणः परधर्मात् स्वनुष्ठितात् ॥
स्वधर्मे निधनं श्रेयः परधर्मो भयावहः ॥३५॥

Because one can perform it, one's
own dharma, (though) lesser in merit,
is better than the dharma of another.
Better is death in one's own dharma:
the dharma of another brings danger.

Life has different stages of evolution. For the process of evolution to advance, it is necessary that one stage should give rise to the next, and in this process each successive stage is of vital importance. The Lord gives expression to this truth by laying down a principle which has its significance at every level of evolution: 'Because one can perform it, one's own dharma, (though) lesser in merit, is better than the dharma of another.'

There are people at various levels of evolution, and each level has a guiding principle, a standard of its own. The guiding principle, or dharma, of a higher level will be suitable and practical for that level, but will not be so for men of lesser development. The Lord emphasizes that a person should go by his own level of consciousness, because only by following that will he make sure of reaching the next stage of evolution. So far as the process of evolution of life is concerned, one's own dharma is the most suitable even though it may appear 'lesser in merit' when compared with the dharma of another. The true merit of dharma lies in its usefulness in promoting evolution in the most effective manner.

Life at one stage, when promoted by the dharma of that stage to a higher stage, begins to be governed by the dharma of that higher stage. This is how, stage by stage, life evolves through the dharma of different stages of evolution. The comparative merit of the dharma of one's present state may be less than the dharma of a higher state, but its merit in its own place is greater by far. The First English Reader is certainly inferior to Milton's Paradise, but it is more valuable for the student of the first grade because it is more suited to him.

If a man were to try to follow a dharma suitable for one of higher development, he would not be able to put it into practice successfuly and thus would waste his time and energy. This may go so far as to entail loss of the path of his evolution. Following his own dharma, should he die, he would naturally rise to a higher state of life; but if he were to die while trying to practise the dharma of another, he would die dislocated from his own level of development, in utter confusion about the path of his evolution.

The Lord says: 'Better is death in one's own dharma', and the reason which He gives is that 'the dharma of another brings danger'. It is evident from this that there is a yet greater danger to life than the phenomenon of death.

Death as such only causes a temporary pause in the process of evolution. A pause like this is no real danger to life because, with a new body taken after the pause, more rapid progress of life's evolution becomes possible. A greater danger will be something that actually retards the process of evolution.

In following the dharma of another, one certainly produces some effect in one's life, but it will not have any bearing on one's present level of evolution, for this is solely concerned with one's own dharma. The dharma of another belongs to a level of evolution different from one's own. Because man has freedom of action, he is certainly capable of trying to assume the role of action belonging to different levels of evolution. This means that he is capable of attempting to perform actions suitable to the dharma of another. But if he performs such actions, he loses the continuity of progress on the level from which he could evolve. This is the greatest danger to life: that one lives life, time goes by, without any progress on the path of evolution.

The Lord teaches that everyone should live according to the level of his own dharma, for this will ensure steady progress on the path of evolution. Certainly there are ways to enhance one's progress, but each of them starts by raising the present level and not by abruptly abandoning it.

The present teaching being a discourse on Yoga Shastra, it is necessary to consider dharma not only on the level of relative life, the level of the three gunas and their activity, but also on the level of Being, which is devoid of activity. The dharma of the Self is eternal, while dharma in the relative field has its different values at different levels of activity. Life is inclusive of both these types of dharma – the eternal dharma of the unchanging Self and the changing states of dharma on different levels of life in the relative field.

The teaching of this verse on its highest level is this: it is better to remain established in the dharma of the Self, which is absolute bliss-consciousness, than to partake of the dharma of the three gunas and come under the sway of attachment and aversion. For when a man is established in his own dharma, the dharma of the Self, his activity is carried on under the direct influence of almighty Nature and enjoys Its full support; whereas

if he partakes of the dharma of another, the dharma of the three
gunas, he loses the support and patronage of almighty Nature in
cosmic life, and his activity becomes limited by the limitations
of individual life.

As this principle is true for the dharma of the Self, it is equally
true for the dharma of the three gunas. Let not the field of activity
usurp the field of the Self. Only thus can a man naturally live
both the dharma of the Self and dharma in the field of activity
at every level of evolution. The field of the Self and the field of
activity will be forever maintained in their full stature. Man
will live eternal freedom in the midst of all success in the different spheres of life's activity, individual and social.

When the body of a realized man meets with death and the
nervous system finally ceases to function, the Self remains estab-
lised in Its own dharma, the eternal dharma of Being, while the
sphere of the three gunas continues in its dharma of continuous
change, transforming the dead body into its different component
elements. In such a case, death only amounts to the cessation of
individual activity, leaving the Self in Its unbounded state of
eternal freedom. Such a death is just a silent declaration of no
return – no return to the cycle of birth and death. When the
Lord says: 'Better is death in one's own dharma', He is not
extolling death; He is only establishing a principle of gaining
that state of eternal Being in which death loses its miserable
significance.

This, then, is the Lord's answer to all the concern that Arjuna
has shown regarding dharma in verses 40–5 of the first chapter.
Whereas Arjuna considered dharma mainly on the level of
behaviour, on the level of the gross aspect of relative life, the
Lord's consideration of dharma comes from the very basis of life,
from the level of Being, the basis of the three gunas. Considered
from this fundamental level of life, dharma will provide a solution to any problem at any stage of life's evolution.

VERSE 36

अर्जुन उवाच ।
अथ केन प्रयुक्तोऽयं पापं चरति पूरुषः ॥
अनिच्छन्नपि वार्ष्णेय बलादिव नियोजितः ॥३६॥

Arjuna said:

*What is it that impels a man to
commit sin, even involuntarily,
as if driven by force, O Varshneya?*

'Varshneya': Lord Krishna, a member of the Vrishni family
belonging to the Yadava clan.

It is an essential and practical question that Arjuna asks; he
wants to know what force it is that is driving on Duryodhana
and his supporters and may cause him personally to commit the
great sin of killing his kinsmen.

A thief knows that he is committing a sin and that this will
result in punishment. Yet he is not able to resist. Why is this?

Having heard the deep philosophy of the separateness of the
inner divine Self from the field of activity, and having clearly
understood from the previous verse that it is dangerous for the
Self to fall from Its dharma of eternal existence into the sphere
of dharma in the ever-changing nature of the three gunas, it
amazes Arjuna to see that this truth of the separateness of the
Self and activity, which is the natural state of life, is not manifest in the daily lives of the people. It is this which makes him
ask the question in the present verse. He wants to understand
the force that robs man of the Reality of his existence.

VERSE 37

श्रीभगवानुवाच ।
काम एष क्रोध एष रजोगुणसमुद्भवः ॥
महाशनो महापाप्मा विद्ध्येनमिह वैरिणम् ॥३७॥

The Blessed Lord said:
It is desire, it is anger, born of
rajo-guna, all-consuming and most evil.
Know this to be the enemy here on earth.

'Rajo-guna': rajas, one of the three gunas of Nature. It is responsible for motion and energy.

It is desire that establishes contact of the senses with their objects and thereby influences the Self by way of attachment or aversion (verse 34), which in turn create a spur to activity involving the self.

Self-consciousness, unmanifested pure consciousness, manifests as vibration – consciousness vibrates and becomes conscious mind, and a thought arises. The process of manifestation continues, and the thought develops into a desire. Desire is vibrating consciousness set in motion and channelled in a particular direction. It is all motion superimposed on ever-motionless pure consciousness; and this is by virtue of rajo-guna.

When the flow of a particular desire is obstructed by another flow, energy is produced at the point of collision, and this flares up as anger, which disturbs, confuses and destroys the harmony and smooth flow of the desire. Thus confusion is created in the manifested field of Reality, and the purpose of manifestation, which is the expansion of happiness, is marred; the very purpose of creation is thwarted.

That is why anger is called 'the enemy' by the Lord. It is like a whirlpool in a river which threatens to upset the smooth flow of everything passing along it. It is like fire which burns up everything in its path. Anger is said to be the great evil, mutilating the very purpose of creation.

Here desire and anger both stand accused. Whereas anger destroys the purpose of creation, desire keeps the mind floating in the field of sensory experience and is therefore responsible for the mind's involving the Self with action unless the self has gained stability in its own nature. And thus the natural eternal freedom of the Self is overshadowed. Desire in the state of ignorance overshadows the pure nature of the self, which is absolute bliss-consciousness, and this keeps the life in bondage and suffering.

'All-consuming': this expression is preceded by 'born of rajo-guna'. This implies that since rajo-guna is responsible for the functioning of sattva and tamas,[23] since rajo-guna lies at the basis of all the constructive and destructive forces of nature, desire, having its source in rajo-guna, also has the natural capacity of either supporting the whole field of the three gunas or overthrowing their entire purpose. The Lord here does not discuss the upholding and supporting aspect of desire, because in the present context he is analysing its very nature as bringing the Self out of Itself. As such, it is 'all-consuming and most evil', for it overshadows the real nature of the Self and so obscures absolute bliss-consciousness, the true nature of life eternal.

The nature of desire, as brought to light here by the Lord, applies only so long as one has not gained enlightenment. It is only true of a seeker, an ignorant man, and not of a realized man. When one gains realization of the Self as separate from activity, desire ceases to be 'the enemy here on earth', because it is then upheld only by the three gunas, while the Self remains completely free from its influence.

In the remainder of this chapter the Lord continues to reflect upon the nature of anger and desire, and eventually shows a way to conquer these enemies of life.

23. See II, 45, commentary.

VERSE 38

धूमेनाव्रियते वह्निर्यथाऽदर्शो मलेन च ।
यथोल्बेनावृतो गर्भस्तथा तेनेदमावृतम् ॥३८॥

As fire is covered by smoke, as a
mirror by dust, as an embryo is covered
by the amnion, so is This covered by
that.

'This covered by that': pure consciousness is overlaid by desires.

There are three metaphors in this verse, each with its own significance.

Smoke arises from fire and covers it: desire arises from pure consciousness and veils it.

The mirror is covered by dust, which comes from outside it. The source of desire lies outside the field of Being in the field of the gunas. This outer stimulus creates a desire and covers pure Being. So it can be said that the desire coming from outside covers Being as dust covers a mirror.

As the amnion covering the embryo supports it and keeps it alive, so does the desire overshadowing Being support and give life to beings, nourish them and keep them alive.

Therefore it is desire which in every way veils the uninvolved nature of the Self and leaves It involved, as it were, and as if bound by activity.

VERSE 39

आवृतं ज्ञानमेतेन ज्ञानिनो नित्यवैरिणा ॥
कामरूपेण कौन्तेय दुष्पूरेणानलेन च ॥३९॥

Wisdom is veiled by this insatiable
flame of desire which is the constant
enemy of the wise, O son of Kunti.

'Wisdom': see verse 32.

Desire, as defined in the 37th verse, is like an unquenchable fire, because the flow of desire in a particular direction, kept moving by the experience of happiness or the search for it, continues to flow from point to point, there being no point in the field of relativity to satisfy finally its craving for greater happiness.

This is how the ceaseless activity of desire continues to maintain a close tie of association between the self and the outside world, thus keeping the self bound, as it were, to the field of action. Desire does not allow the self to remain uninvolved with the field of action, even though all activity is in reality carried on by the three gunas.

'The wise' in this context are they who know 'the truth about the divisions of the gunas and their actions' and who know 'that it is the gunas which act upon the gunas', as explained in verse 28. The wise are they who, established in the knowledge of the three gunas, remain uninvolved with the field of action. When the Lord says in this verse that desire 'is the constant enemy of the wise', He is warning students of Sankhya that mere intellectual understanding of the three gunas is not sufficient to establish the Self as uninvolved with action and its fruits. It is necessary to rise above the influence of desire. But as long as life continues, it has to be in the field of desires. No practical man could ever be without desires. When the Lord says: 'wisdom is veiled by this insatiable flame of desire which is the constant enemy of the wise', He does not intend to lay down the principle that desire has to be eradicated, because this is not physically possible. Any attempt in that direction will only make life dull, useless or tense.

The Lord's purpose is to lay the facts before Arjuna, and then to give him a technique by which he can rise with ease above the binding influence of desire and make his life brighter, more successful and fulfilled on every level. The Lord explains clearly the mechanics of bondage, so that Arjuna may be better able to realize that to rise above this bondage and live a life of eternal freedom is not difficult but easy. The great emphasis in this verse upon the enmity of desires implicitly shows that the Lord is going to lead Arjuna to a way that will transform the influence of

desire from enmity to usefulness. Desires will cease to be the
'enemy of the wise'; they will prove to be supporters of the wise
and will bring them fulfilment on every side.

The Lord, out of His great kindness, is going to give Arjuna a
simple technique of transforming the whole machinery that gives
rise to desire, of transforming the mind and heart so that the
rising up of desires and all their activities will serve as tidal waves
of love and bliss in the unbounded ocean of the oneness of God-
consciousness. This involves giving a pattern to the machinery
that creates desire – senses, mind, and intellect – so that even
while remaining in the field of desire, it remains free from the
impact of desire. This allows the Self to remain uninvolved,
leaving the desires to be taken care of by the three gunas, by
virtue of which they arise, grow and have their play.

The following verse analyses the machinery which gives rise
to desires, and the remaining verses of this chapter are devoted to
bringing out the basic and at the same time most highly advanced
teaching of the technique whereby one passes out of the binding
influence of desires.

VERSE 40

इन्द्रियाणि मनो बुद्धिरस्याधिष्ठानमुच्यते ॥
एतैर्विमोहयत्येष ज्ञानमावृत्य देहिनम् ॥४०॥

The senses, the mind and the intellect
are said to be its seat. Overshadowing
wisdom by means of these, it deludes the
dweller in the body.

Having thus far explained that the loss of wisdom is due mainly
to the mind's incessant engagement in the field of activity, to
desire, the Lord now begins to describe a way whereby the subjective aspect of one's life, which is responsible for all desire and
activity, can be influenced in such a manner that, on the one
hand, it does not permit desires to overshadow Being and, on the

other, it brings fulfilment to them, thus bringing both success and salvation to life.

The Lord first describes the subjective machinery responsible for making concrete the abstract essence of desire. Through the intellect, mind and senses, abstract desire in the form of a thought takes on a concrete shape. As a result, the Self becomes as if involved with the field of activity. This is how the uninvolved nature of the Self is deluded, as it were. The wisdom that holds the Self to be uninvolved and out of bondage is overshadowed by the senses, mind and intellect coming into action under the sway of desire.

Having shown the senses to be the direct means through which desires function, the Lord, in the following verse, stresses the necessity of conditioning the senses to become free from the over-shadowing nature of desires.

VERSE 41

तस्मात्त्वमिन्द्रियाण्यादौ नियम्य भरतर्षभ ॥
पाप्मानं प्रजहि ह्येनं ज्ञानविज्ञाननाशनम् ॥४१॥

*Therefore, having first organized the
senses, O best of Bharatas, shake
off this evil, the destroyer of
knowledge and realization.*

'Organized': the Sanskrit word used in the text is *niyamya*, which means literally having introduced law and order, having organized something to function in an orderly manner. Even the word 'organize' is inadequate to convey the accurate meaning, but it has been chosen to avoid the sense of control and restraint which has generally been implied by commentators and which has only resulted in mutilating the whole meaning and purpose of the teaching.

This verse brings out a fundamental principle showing how to make life free from 'this evil' of desire, leaving it in fullness of wisdom and freedom in divine consciousness.

The previous verse has declared the senses, mind and intellect to be the 'seat' of desire. In teaching Arjuna how to regulate and organize the flow of desire so that it may cease to overshadow the essential nature of the Self, the Lord begins with a consideration of the field of the senses; for the senses are the fountainhead from which all the streams of desire flow.

In a mountain, various underground currents of water flow from all directions and all of them find a common outlet in a spring. The only way to organize all these underground currents is to organize the outlet. Desires in the fields of intellect and mind are like currents underground. The field of the senses is like the outlet from which the currents emerge into the open air. By controlling the outlet, it is quite possible to use the whole outflow of water to advantage. According to this verse, organizing the outlet, organizing the senses, is the way to make the best use of the underground currents of desire.

The advice here is not to abandon or kill desires, not to control desires as such, but to control the outlet of desires by organizing the senses. The purpose is to give a pattern to the functioning of the senses so that their activity will always, as a matter of course, be in accordance with the laws of nature conducting the process of evolution. This is the simple and effective means to 'shake off this evil, the destroyer of knowledge and realization'.

Organizing the senses lies at the root of all real accomplishments in life. The verses which follow expound the technique.

VERSE 42

इन्द्रियाणि पराण्याहुरिन्द्रियेभ्यः परं मनः ॥
मनसस्तु परा बुद्धियों बुद्धेः परतस्तु सः ॥४२॥

The senses, they say, are subtle;
more subtle than the senses is mind;
yet finer than mind is intellect;
that which is beyond even the intellect
is he.

After emphasizing in the previous verse the necessity of organizing the senses, the Lord now indicates the sequence of the subtler aspects of subjective life which lie beyond the senses. This is to find the key to organizing the senses.

If one has difficulty in dealing with an officer, one should seek out his superior in rank. In the field of inner life, the Lord says, he who is beyond the intellect is the highest authority of all.

The next verse makes clear that, by contacting him, the senses are naturally subdued.

VERSE 43

एवं बुद्धेः परं बुद्ध्वा संस्तभ्यात्मानमात्मना ॥
जहि शत्रुं महाबाहो कामरूपं दुरासदम् ॥४३॥

Thus, having known him who is
beyond the intellect, having stilled
the self by the Self, O mighty-armed,
slay the enemy in the form of desire,
difficult to subdue.

'Having known him': this means having known the indweller of the body in his true nature as Being, separate from the whole field of activity of the body,[24] senses, mind and intellect. The expression implies that this is the way to 'slay the enemy in the form of desire'.

'Difficult to subdue': subduing of desires will be difficult by any attempt that aims directly to subdue them. Desires are the impulses of the mind. Unless the mind turns to Being it is naturally engaged in desire. As this is the natural relation of the mind to desires, and as the mind is the basis of the existence of desires, the only way to subdue them is to turn the mind to Being.

This is the great wisdom of life, the essence of the doctrine of Karma Yoga. The Lord makes a fundamental statement about cause and effect: influence the cause to modify the effect, go to

24. See II, 18–26, 29, 30.

the realm of Being in order to modify the nature of the intellect, mind and senses. Go to the absolute ultimate Reality, and all levels of relativity will cease to be a burden. Be illumined, and life will ever be in freedom and fullness, away from the darkness of ignorance.

The Lord says: Realization of the Ultimate is within your easy reach. You have the power to realize the Supreme, provided you do not undermine that power. It only amounts to being what you are. Being what you are, you will find the whole field of existence set in eternal harmony. Intellect, mind and senses, all will function in accord, none will overpower the others, and no side of life will be impaired. Life will be lived in fullness.

This is a reaffirmation of the Lord's words in the 45th and 46th verses of the second chapter. It is an approach which does away with the need for controlling the senses by any unnatural or strenuous austerity. It makes unnecessary any practice of detachment or renunciation for the sake of cultivating the state of enlightenment.

A very practical method of realization is provided, whether one is on the path of Gyana Yoga, the way of knowledge, or of Karma Yoga, the way of action. Irrespective of one's way of life, that of a householder or that of a recluse, this is a direct approach to fulfilment.

Unfortunately it is commonly held that desires should be subdued in order to attain enlightenment. This is completely wrong. The misunderstanding has grown during the last few hundred years, and in consequence the task of those who seek the Truth has become more difficult than ever before. Here the Lord says: Go to the state of enlightenment in order to come out of the bondage of karma, bring the light in order to remove the darkness. It is this which is the underlying principle of the verse; not that one should try to remove the darkness in order to come into the light.

So that Arjuna may be released from the bondage of karma, the Lord wishes him to leave the whole field of karma. He wants him to know the transcendental Reality and thereby build up his mind to such a degree that it will rise above the binding influence of desires and actions. This is a direct way of realizing

the state of integration and of eternal freedom during one's lifetime here on earth.

This, being the last verse of the chapter, sums up the Lord's
answer to Arjuna's questions in verses 1, 2 and 36.

This chapter, which expounds the science of action, advocates
transcending desire as a technique of subduing desires and also
of bringing fulfilment to them; useless desires will be subdued
while useful ones will find their fulfilment. The principle of maintaining the life of a tree is to go beyond the tree. If one attends
to the area surrounding the root, to the transcendental field of
the tree, it is easy to bring nourishment to all its parts. If one
attends to the field of the Transcendent one can make the whole
tree of life healthy and fruitful.

The blessing of this chapter is the principle of transcending
the field of action in order to bring fulfilment to action. It upholds
and supports both the life of a householder and the life of a recluse.

Thus, in the Upanishad of the glorious
Bhagavad-Gita, in the Science of the Absolute,
in the Scripture of Yoga, in the dialogue
between Lord Krishna and Arjuna, ends the
third chapter, entitled: The Yoga of
Action, Karma Yoga.

CHAPTER IV

A VISION OF THE TEACHING IN CHAPTER IV

Verses 1–8. This path of action for gaining success in the world and freedom in divine consciousness has a long tradition. In its content it is eternal. Even if in time its purity is lost and it is forgotten by man, each time it is restored in the world by a wave of revival that comes from God.

Verses 9, 10. Knowledge of the Divine as separate from activity, and knowledge of the Lord's birth and actions as divine, raise man's consciousness to that purity which places him on the divine level.

Verses 11, 12. Divine reaction to man depends upon man's action towards the Divine. Success is born of action in the world of men.

Verses 13–15. Having known the Divine as Creator and yet as unattached to activity, the seekers of liberation follow this example and engage in action.

Verses 16–22. The course of action being unfathomable, performance of proper action is only possible with knowledge of the divine nature. This knowledge is fully gained in divine consciousness, in which inner freedom and outer activity are simultaneously maintained.

Verses 23–33. Gaining divine consciousness, man rises to oneness of life, and in this state all activity is in the light of God. All actions culminate in the knowledge of God.

Verses 34–8. Established in this knowledge, a man sees all beings in himself and finds himself in God. This supreme state of purity in God-consciousness puts an end to ignorance and all bondage of action.

Verses 39–42. The light of this knowledge is kindled in one who is full of faith, intent of purpose and has his senses subdued. It brings abiding peace without delay.

Gain the state of non-attachment and freedom from doubts; be established in the Self and actions will not bind.

THIS chapter springs from the same breath of the Lord as Chapter III. Verse 48 of Chapter II contains the seed-thoughts which give rise to both chapters: 'Established in Yoga ... perform actions' to Chapter III, and 'having abandoned attachment and having become balanced in success and failure' to Chapter IV. These two chapters together are therefore sufficient to bring enlightenment to a seeker. They give him, in so far as words can, the desired experience and full understanding of it.

The second chapter presented the doctrine of liberation. It analysed life in its relative and absolute aspects and promised liberation through knowledge of these.

Knowledge in its entirety comprises both understanding and experience. Therefore in order to gain fulfilment a man must necessarily acquire both understanding and experience of the relative and the Absolute, irrespective of whether his path is that of a householder or a recluse. It follows that the wisdom of Sankhya, which brings liberation through *understanding* of the relative and the Absolute, and the practice of Yoga, which brings liberation by providing direct *experience* of these two spheres of existence, are both paths to enlightenment. All this teaching is contained in the second chapter.

The third chapter presented a doctrine of action designed to make permanent the experience of the Absolute first mentioned in the 45th verse of the second chapter.

When this experience of the Absolute has become permanent, Self-awareness is naturally maintained through all the waking, dreaming and deep sleep states of consciousness. One experiences oneself as separate from activity. As one lives this life of non-involvement, of natural non-attachment, one's intellect begins to inquire: 'Is this the truth of life? Has this sense of separateness or non-attachment anything to do with real life, or is it an escape from life? Is the reality of life a duality – the duality of Being and activity?' Such doubts are removed by the knowledge given in the fourth chapter.

This chapter, dedicated to the knowledge of renunciation, analyses the nature of action and the nature of the actor on both the individual and cosmic levels – on the level of man and on the level of God – and then proclaims the result of this systematic and rational analysis: action and actor are independent of one another; there exists a natural state of separation between them at every level. This state of non-attachment, or renunciation, provides on the one hand a solid foundation of eternal freedom for the actor, and on the other the maximum possible success in action with most glorious fruits. It is this state of renunciation that provides the eternal playground for the Divine and for man. Ignorance of this natural basis of life is the cause of bondage and all suffering. Knowledge of it results in eternal freedom. To unfold this knowledge is the purpose of the fourth chapter.

The most fascinating aspect of this chapter is that, in bringing out knowledge of the renunciation of action, it explains the whole field of action, showing how the stream of life advances towards the higher spheres of existence (verse 10) and towards the higher forces in nature (verse 12), until it merges with the ocean of eternal freedom in God-consciousness (verse 9).

This chapter of knowledge is of the utmost importance to a seeker, for it explains the most valuable experience on the path to enlightenment, the experience of the separateness of the Self and activity. As his practice advances, every seeker must necessarily reach this experience; and if he is to proceed smoothly on his path, unhindered by doubts, he must possess this knowledge.

In order to bring out the complete knowledge of the separation, or the state of renunciation, that exists between the Self and activity, this chapter explains the two spheres of life, relative and absolute. In so doing, it proclaims the philosophy of two fullnesses found in the Upanishads: this is full and That is full, 'purnamadah purnamidam' – That transcendental unmanifested absolute eternal Being is full, and this manifested relative ever-

changing world of phenomenal existence is full. The Absolute is
eternal in its never-changing nature, and the relative is eternal
in its ever-changing nature.

This living Reality of two fullnesses in cosmic consciousness
finds its consummation in the grand Unity of God-consciousness.
In expounding this unified philosophy of the two fullnesses, this
chapter presents the core of the wisdom contained in this Scripture of Yoga, and for this reason the Lord begins by giving Arjuna
an account of the tradition of this Yoga.

VERSE 1

श्रीभगवानुवाच ।

इमं विवस्वते योगं प्रोक्तवानहमव्ययम् ॥
विवस्वान्मनवे प्राह मनुरिक्ष्वाकवेऽब्रवीत् ॥१॥

The Blessed Lord said:

I proclaimed this imperishable Yoga
to Vivasvat, Vivasvat declared it to
Manu and Manu told it to Ikshvaku.

'This imperishable Yoga': the preceding chapters have been
devoted to Yoga – Sankhya Yoga and Karma Yoga. By saying:
'this ... Yoga', the Lord speaks of them both as one. This is to
bring home to Arjuna that, although they have been declared to
be different, they have the same basis and yield the same results.
The basis is: 'Be without the three gunas', which brings fulfilment both to the wisdom of Sankhya and to the practice of Karma
Yoga.[1] Thus the word 'Yoga' in this verse stands for both Sankhya
and Karma Yoga.

The Yoga expounded by Lord Krishna is imperishable because
it brings to light the wisdom of the Absolute and the wisdom of
the relative. The relative and the Absolute, both these are eternal;
and so is Yoga, which expounds the truth of both, the truth of life
in its fullness. It is eternal because it serves the cosmic purpose
and is natural to the mind of man.

1. See III, 28, commentary.

The Lord says that He taught this eternal Yoga to Vivasvat in the beginning of creation in order to infuse strength into the kshatriyas [2] and to enable them to maintain law and order and preserve the path of righteousness for the well-being of society. Vivasvat revealed it to the son Manu,[3] the law-giver to the world. And Manu gave it to his son Ikshvaku, who ruled at Ayodhya as the first king of the Solar dynasty.

The Bhagavad-Gita is the highest expression of divine intelligence understandable by man. Dealing with the unseen aspects of life, it also touches on the past and present of the world of our daily life. Furthermore, the Bhagavad-Gita, while expounding universal Truth, is itself a historical record and relates incidents that took place five thousand years ago.

In order to understand the historical significance of the Bhagavad-Gita, one must be familiar with the Indian conception of history and time.

The study of history has a definite purpose and a place in the life of the individual. Its aim is to educate the mind of the present with information from the past in order to ensure a better present and a better future. In this way each generation takes advantage of the achievements of the past and advances towards greater wisdom in life.

But it is not knowledge of the chronological order of events that educates students of history; it is the value of events that is important, and this is the aspect of history on which Indian historians have concentrated. They have put on record, for all generations to read, only such instances in the great span of time as can help to integrate men's lives. Their purpose is to inspire men both as individuals and as members of society.

The sage of enlightened vision, Veda Vyasa, who is regarded as the greatest historian of the Aryan culture of India, had before him a vast span of time to take into account. As a conscientious and fully integrated man, he could not write the history of

2. It is interesting to note that the ancient wisdom was given to the kshatriyas, the warriors.
3. Manu: the seventh Manu, being the son of Vivasvat, is called Vaivasvat Manu. He is said to be the progenitor of the present human race.

this immeasurable period as a sequence of days and years. He could only select particular happenings and record them in such a way as to inspire and guide people of all times on the path of evolution and educate them in the integration of their life. This is why no chronological order is to be found in Indian histories. Vyasa thought it absurd to pin every event down chronologically just for the sake of establishing each link on the long road of time.

Moreover, it is not physically possible to write the history of millions of years in chronological sequence. In the case of small countries with a few thousand years of civilization, it is quite practicable for historians, with a vision of that small area and that small span of time, to maintain chronological order. But Vyasa had a clear vision of the whole span of time beginning from the day of creation. Such a mind would not and could not assign any value to chronology.

The Indian conception of time, as set out below, will clearly show the situation that confronted Vyasa and other writers of Indian history.

Time is a conception to measure eternity. Indian historians base their conception of time on eternal Being; for them eternity is the basic field of time.

To arrive at some conception of the eternal, the best measure will be the life-span of something that has the greatest longevity in the relative field of creation. This, according to the enlightened vision of Vyasa, is the Divine Mother, the Universal Mother, who is ultimately responsible for all that is, was and will be in the entire cosmos.

The eternity of the eternal life of absolute Being is conceived in terms of innumerable lives of the Divine Mother, a single one of whose lives encompasses a thousand life-spans of Lord Shiva. One life of Lord Shiva covers the time of a thousand life-spans of Lord Vishnu. One life of Lord Vishnu equals the duration of a thousand life-spans of Brahma, the Creator. A single life-span of Brahma is conceived in terms of one hundred years of Brahma; each year of Brahma comprises 12 months of Brahma, and each month comprises thirty days of Brahma. One day of Brahma is called a Kalpa. One Kalpa is equal to the time of four-

teen Manus. The time of one Manu is called a Manvantara. One
Manvantara equals seventy-one Chaturyugis. One Chaturyugi
comprises the total span of four Yugas i.e. Sat-yuga, Treta-Yuga,
Dvapara-yuga and Kali-yuga. The span of the Yugas is conceived
in terms of the duration of Sat-yuga. Thus the span of Treta-yuga
is equal to three quarters of that of Sat-yuga; the span of Dvapara-
yuga is half that of Sat-yuga, and the span of Kali-yuga one quar-
ter that of Sat-yuga. The span of Kali-yuga equals 432,000 years
of man's life.[4]

Now consider the time of creation : for how many billion tril-
lion years the world has been ! Even if the account of one year
were to occupy a page or even a single line, how could anyone
possibly read such a history and apply its lesson to his life? This
is why chronological order was not maintained by Indian historians. Apart from being impracticable, it was considered to be unnecessary, useless and damaging to the very purpose of history.

All this should be borne in mind by those modern historians
who tend to reject as non-history any series of events for which
they fail to find a proper chronological order. It is deplorable that
such precious accounts of life on the highest human level as are
to be found in the historical material of ancient India should
have been regarded as myth. They should, on the contrary, be
recognized as a most useful history of the highest civilization
that has ever existed on earth.

The Bhagavad-Gita forms the central core of the most authentic record of Indian history, the Mahabharata. This cannot be
dismissed as mythology just because the narrow vision of modern
historians, tied to rigid chronology, fails to understand it as a historical record and puts it in the compartment of imaginative literature.

It is regrettable that some modern commentators on the Bhagavad-Gita have followed in the footsteps of modern historians
and refused to admit its historic authenticity. It is to be hoped
that the light will dawn and truth will be recognized as truth.

When Lord Krishna recalls for Arjuna that the great wisdom
of the Bhagavad-Gita was given to Vivasvat in the beginning of

4. This elaboration of the conception of time also serves as a commentary to verse 17 of Chapter VIII.

this Kalpa, He does not enumerate in detail all the custodians of this supreme knowledge. To satisfy Arjuna about the original source of the teaching, it is sufficient to give him the idea of this eternal wisdom being handed on from generation to generation.

VERSE 2

एवं परम्पराप्राप्तमिमं राजर्षयो विदुः ॥
स कालेनेह महता योगो नष्टः परन्तप ॥२॥

Thus having received it one from another,
the royal sages knew it. With the long
lapse of time, O scorcher of enemies, this
Yoga has been lost to the world.

The Lord says that this technique of integration of life was handed on to the philosopher-kings, men who led active lives and had great responsibilities in the world. In those days the rulers were held responsible for every aspect of the development of their people, physical, mental and spiritual. They gave this wisdom of Yoga to the people in general. In the modern democratic world each man has to look after his own affairs. Thus it is in keeping with our times that each man should feel responsible for his own development.

As spiritual development is the basis of all other forms of de-velopment, it is necessary that this great science and art of suc-cessful living should now be handed on to every man everywhere in the world.

The Lord says: 'having received it one from another'. By this, He brings an unquestionable authenticity to this system of Yoga. It has been since the beginning of history. Again He says: 'the royal sages knew it', showing it to be a precious doctrine fol-lowed by those in positions of great responsibility.

The reason for its loss, the Lord says, is 'the long lapse of time'. But in the first verse He has spoken of this Yoga as 'imperish-able'. This implies that while its principle is imperishable its prac-tice needs periodic revival, according to the changed conditions of living from age to age. Because it awakens man's consciousness to extreme purity, this system of Yoga is equally suitable for people in every age. Sometimes, however, it is not followed in its pure form; then the desired results are not achieved and this eventually leads to indifference towards its practice. Thus this great principle of life becomes lost from time to time. But it cannot be lost for ever because, as the Truth of existence, it must be brought to light again and again. Nature helps to restore it. From time to time great teachers come with the proper inspiration to reveal the path once more. They renew the tradition which maintains the teaching. The renewed tradition remains dominant so long as it continues to inspire the people. But when it fails to respond to the need of the age new teachers arise. This cycle is repeated again and again.

Some who come to revive the tradition honour the ancient line of teachers; others, failing to relate the traditional solutions to their present need, break away from the established tradition. Their teachings form new branches of the old trunk.

The custodians of the ancient tradition of Vedic wisdom act as the guardians of the main trunk, from which different branches have sprung from time to time in the form of different religions, faiths, philosophies and cultures in different parts of the world.

Today the most cherished tradition of Vedic wisdom is the Shankaracharya tradition which, in its present shape, began about 2,500 years ago [5] with the teaching of the first Shankaracharya. He revived the forgotten Truth. By his faithful interpretation of the essence of Vedic literature, he re-established the principle of the Unity of all-pervading Being in the midst of the diversities of life. He established the unified philosophy of the two fullnesses as the essential teaching of the Vedanta. His commentaries on the Brahmasutra, the Upanishads and the Bhagavad-Gita are extolled for their depth of wisdom and magnificent exposition of the Reality of life.

5. According to the records kept by the 'maths' or monasteries of the Shankaracharya tradition, though some modern scholars assign the life of Shankara to the ninth century A.D. They have perhaps confused an illustrious successor with Shankara himself, because all his successors are known as Shankaracharyas; the name has become a title.

Strange how the truth of a teaching becomes distorted with the passage of time! The truth of Shankara's teaching has been so misrepresented by his interpreters that modern writing about his thought retains little of his spirit. The sanyasi, or recluse orders, of Shankara's tradition have been interpreting Shankara-Vedanta as being completely closed to the householders, who form the main section of society, and open only to themselves. This has resulted in spiritual decadence and in the moral downfall of Indian society.

Such decay is nothing new. It happens, says Lord Krishna, 'with the long lapse of time'. The Truth is overshadowed, and distorted interpretations take its place. But when these depart so far from the Truth that the principle itself is in danger of extinction, then a revival comes to save it.

The holy tradition of great masters,[6] which is responsible for reviving the teaching after every lapse, has captured the minds and heart of lovers of Truth in every age. It is not merely held in high regard, but has come to be actually worshipped by seekers of Truth and knowers of Reality. A verse [7] recording the names of the greatest and most highly revered masters has not only inspired seekers, but has been a joy even to the fulfilled hearts of realized souls passing through the long corridor of time.

'Scorcher of enemies': by using this expression, the Lord indicates to Arjuna that this Yoga has been lost through falling into the hands of the weak, and that now, by finding its way into the strong hands of Arjuna, it will prove its worth and help the world to restore and maintain the path of righteousness.

The Lord's expression also indicates to Arjuna that he will not prove unworthy of this great blessing.

In the following verse He gives further reasons for teaching this wisdom to Arjuna.

6. See Appendix.   7. See Appendix.

VERSE 3

स एवायं मया तेऽद्य योगः प्रोक्तः पुरातनः ॥
भक्तोऽसि मे सखा चेति रहस्यं ह्येतदुत्तमम् ॥३॥

This same age-old Yoga, which is
indeed the supreme secret, I have
today declared to you because you
are my devotee and friend.

'Age-old Yoga' indicates that the teaching has withstood the test of time, and that it cannot but prove useful. The Lord is not trying out any new method; He is only restoring the old tradition. Such has been the declaration of all the great masters from time immemorial; they never claimed that their teaching was new, but rather that they were bringing out the forgotten wisdom of life. They spoke only of restoration because the truth of any useful principle continues to exist in time.

The Lord here mentions two qualities of Arjuna's which entitle him to receive this great secret wisdom: 'friend' and 'devotee'. And also two qualities of the system of Yoga: 'supreme' and 'secret'. That which is secret can be passed on to a friend, but that which is supreme can be passed on only to a devotee. A devotee never questions his master. In order to allow Arjuna the freedom to question, Lord Krishna calls him His friend.

Arjuna makes use of this freedom in the following verse.

VERSE 4

अर्जुन उवाच ।
अपरं भवतो जन्म परं जन्म विवस्वतः ॥
कथमेतद्विजानीयां त्वमादौ प्रोक्तवानिति ॥४॥

Arjuna said:
Later was Thy birth and earlier
the birth of Vivasvat: how am I
to understand this saying that Thou
didst proclaim it in the beginning?

This question shows Arjuna's alertness to every word that the Lord speaks to him, his vigilance and careful scrutiny of every point. Such is the mind of a good seeker of Truth. A good master is only encouraged by such questions.

In the previous verse, Lord Krishna, through Himself, has connected the far distant past with the present. Now Arjuna isolates Him in time and states his difficulty in understanding the eternity of time in Him.

Lord Krishna's answer is plain and simple.

VERSE 5

श्रीभगवानुवाच ।
बहूनि मे व्यतीतानि जन्मानि तव चार्जुन ॥
तान्यहं वेद सर्वाणि न त्वं वेत्थ परन्तप ॥५॥

The Blessed Lord said:

Many births have passed for Me and
for you also, O Arjuna. I know them
all but you know them not, O scorcher
of enemies.

This verse may be said to exemplify what verses 12 and 22 of the second chapter spoke of in principle : bodies change in time, but time changes in the Self, in Being, which continues to be, regardless of past, present or future. As the embodied self re-mains unchanged when the body passes into the changing states of childhood, youth and old age,[8] so does the Self continue un-changed in the eternity of time.

The Lord says : 'I know them all but you know them not.' This points to a difference between the life of man and the Incarnation of God. Man is born as a result of his past actions, good and bad, so that his vision remains coloured or obstructed by those in-fluences. The nature of the divine Incarnation is ever pure eternal unbounded intelligence. His vision is absolutely clear;

8. See II, 13.

that is why for Him the eternity of knowing is maintained and the factor of time fails to obstruct it.

The Lord's Being is the playground of the time which He creates. It comes and goes, but He, steadfast in His eternal Being, for ever and ever continues to be. He is the ocean of life, while time rises and falls as the tide on the surface of the ocean. Though the tidal waves draw on the depths they can never fathom the unfathomable abyss.

The life of man is like a wave which rises up to see – it can see so far and no more; but Lord Krishna's stature is like that of an ocean on which the whole of space is reflected. Thus the Lord knows 'them all' and Arjuna knows 'them not'.

Arjuna had challenged Lord Krishna's words, and the expression 'you know them not' shows that the Lord is obliged to use His authority. But at the same time He addresses Arjuna as 'scorcher of enemies', so as to prevent his morale from sinking. Lord Krishna uses His authority with love.

The next verse further explains the Lord's nature.

Verse 6

अजोऽपि सन्नव्ययात्मा भूतानामीश्वरोऽपि सन् ॥
प्रकृतिं स्वामधिष्ठाय सम्भवाम्यात्ममायया ॥६॥

Though I am unborn and of imperishable
nature, though Lord of all beings, yet
remaining in My own nature I take birth
through My own power of creation.

At this point there is an illustration of an important psychological technique. As the Lord has earlier affirmed the authenticity of this system of Yoga, declaring that it is ancient and has a great tradition, He must also make clear to Arjuna that He who is giving out this eternal wisdom is great in Himself, is one whose word alone can be taken as authoritative.

The direction of the discourse is such that it makes Arjuna question the Lord on the very point about which He wants to speak next. Had the Lord spoken the words of this and the preceding verse in a different context and not in reply to Arjuna's question (verse 4), then they would not have been so effective and convincing. It is the greatness of the teacher that brings out the right question from the pupil. In answering it, the teacher freely develops his own theme and at the same time keeps the interest of the pupil more actively engaged than it would be if only the teacher spoke.

Although manifest creation, which includes men and other creatures, springs from the unmanifest, its manifestation is by virtue of prakriti. But the divine manifestation of the unmanifest Being, which comes to re-establish the forgotten wisdom of life, is by virtue of 'Lila-shakti', which is the very power of the Absolute, an integral part of Its transcendent divine nature.

Surgery is the inseparable power of the surgeon. Sometimes it is active, as when the surgeon works at the operating table, but at other times it is latent, as when he is resting at home. Lila-shakti (the play-power of Brahman) functions in an analogous way, and by virtue of this the unmanifest, ever remaining in its absolute state, manifests into creation. The almighty nature of the eternal Being thus maintains Reality in both Its aspects, absolute and relative.

The Lord says: 'remaining in My own nature I take birth'. Just as the sap in a tree appears as a leaf and a flower without losing its quality as sap, so the unmanifest Being, remaining unmanifest, imperishable and eternal, takes birth. Nothing happens to the Absolute, and yet the Incarnation of the Absolute springs up, by virtue of Its own nature.

Here the Lord is saying: While remaining in My own nature I take birth through My power of creation, and through that I function; that is how I remain unbound and at the same time am able to restore law and order in creation.

This principle is developed in the following verse.

VERSE 7

यदा यदा हि धर्मस्य ग्लानिर्भवति भारत ।
अभ्युत्थानमधर्मस्य तदात्मानं सृजाम्यहम् ॥७॥

Whenever dharma is in decay and
adharma flourishes, O Bharata, then
I create Myself.

'Adharma': the opposite to dharma.

'Dharma' is derived from the root *dhri*, meaning 'that which upholds'. Dharma is that which upholds or sustains all that is. What is this that sustains creation? Charaka and Sushruta, the ancient Indian exponents of Ayurveda, the doctrine of health, hold that it is the equilibrium of the three gunas – sattva, rajas and tamas – that sustains all things. Creation gains in integrity with the rise of sattva and disintegrates with the rise of tamas. The equilibrium of the three gunas is maintained automatically, just as law and order are automatically maintained by a government. But whenever a crisis arises, the head of state has to exercise his special power. Whenever dharma is in decay, the balance of the three gunas is disturbed, the equilibrium in nature is lost, the path of evolution is distorted and chaos prevails. At such special times the Lord incarnates. The Incarnation of Lord Krishna is such a special manifestation of Brahman, the eternal immutable Being.

Life has two phases, relative and absolute. Both are full: the Absolute is full in its eternal never-changing nature, and the relative is full in its eternally ever-changing nature. This eternally ever-changing nature of relative life is maintained in all its aspects of creation and evolution by virtue of the enormous power of nature called dharma, which is at the basis of the smooth functioning of the three gunas. It is like a powerful current which forcibly carries with it all that comes in its path.

Dharma upholds evolution; but when, as a result of the wrong-doing of a large majority of people on earth, the power of dharma

becomes greatly overshadowed, the natural force of evolution in
nature becomes weak. A situation is created whereby the ever-
changing world of relative existence begins to lose its natural
pattern. This endangers the fullness of the relative aspect of life.
The almighty power that holds intact the fullness of the Absolute together with the fullness of the relative phase of life is
stirred. And that almighty power incarnates.

The decay of dharma – the distortion of the path of evolution,
the decline of righteousness in society – brings about a need for
the restoration of the true principles of life; the Incarnation
comes, the whole of nature rejoices in that coming, dharma is
restored and evil is brought to an end.

The righteous, therefore, feel obliged to the wicked because, as
wickedness increases and dominates the world, the need is created
for the Almighty to take form and be enjoyed by the righteous.

The full purpose of Incarnation is made clear in the following
verse.

VERSE 8

परित्राणाय साधूनां विनाशाय च दुष्कृताम् ॥
धर्मसंस्थापनार्थाय संभवामि युगे युगे ॥८॥

To protect the righteous and destroy
the wicked, to establish dharma firmly,
I take birth age after age.

The Lord says that He has a twofold purpose: to protect the
righteous and destroy the wicked. The protection of the righteous
is implied in the destruction of the wicked; but when the Lord
here speaks of protecting the righteous, He means something
more than merely removing the thorns from their path.

The righteous continue to uphold dharma and they succeed in
this, even in times when unrighteousness dominates society, by
virtue of the great strength that they receive when, during their
daily meditations, they come into communion with the Divine.
As their minds grow in divine consciousness, the purity of their
lives increases until they eventually begin to feel a strong need

for the abstract bliss of God-consciousness to be materialized, to be brought to the level of the senses, where it will become the object of all the senses and be enjoyed by them. Their hearts are more and more filled with love, and the need for divine revelation in some form becomes increasingly intense. When nature can no longer resist it, then the Lord takes birth and fulfils the desire of the righteous. This is how the righteous are protected by the Lord.

The Lord says: 'I take birth age after age.' This shows that in every age there are those ardent, loving devotees of God for whose sake He takes form; and when He comes to satisfy them, He also purifies the earth by destroying the negative forces which contaminate the atmosphere by opposing righteousness.

Destruction of the wicked, although a reason for the Lord's Incarnation, is not His main purpose. He comes to satisfy and protect the righteous. He comes on earth moved by the righteous, for the love of the righteous, for the fulfilment of the righteous; and to come on earth in order to give His love to His devotees is a joy for Almighty God. He comes on earth, and the light comes; it brings extinction to the darkness of ignorance and destruction to the wicked. Equilibrium in nature is restored, and the forces of evolution become stronger. Dharma becomes firmly established in the world.

The establishment of dharma in God's creation is His own work. He does it. He does it again and again, either through the automatic arrangement of His government, He Himself remaining behind the scenes, or by taking a body and coming to be active in the affairs of the world.

VERSE 9

जन्म कर्म च मे दिव्यमेवं यो वेत्ति तत्त्वतः ॥
त्यक्त्वा देहं पुनर्जन्म नैति मामेति सोऽर्जुन ॥६॥

My birth and My activity are divine.
He who knows this in very essence, on
leaving the body is not reborn. He
comes to Me, O Arjuna.

'My birth': the birth of the Lord is not the same as the birth of man. It is divine in the sense that He, the Divine, ever remaining in His cosmic state of transcendental Being, takes a body and comes on earth. The divine birth needs no period of transition and involves no process of physical birth: the divine Being does not become non-divine and non-Being; remaining divine and remaining Being, He appears as man to save human life on earth and re-establish the path of righteousness.

'My activity': the unmanifest transcendental Divine, assuming human form, remains in His divine nature and He acts. The divine nature is all Being, eternal, unchanging and non-active, even though it is the infinite source of life-energy. Because the Lord acts while remaining in His divine nature, His actions also are divine.

In order to understand the divine birth and the activity of the divine Incarnation, man has to rise to the state of Divinity. Having risen to this state, having become established in the eternal Being of the Absolute, he rises above the bondage of time, space and causation. For him there is no question of birth or death. He has life eternally, and he has it in the timeless unbounded omnipresence of the Lord; his life is in His life. 'He comes to Me,' says the Lord. There is no question of his rebirth in the world.

VERSE 10

वीतरागभयक्रोधा मन्मया मामुपाश्रिताः ॥
बहवो ज्ञानतपसा पूता मद्भावमागताः ॥१०॥

Freed from attachment, fear and anger,
absorbed in Me, taking refuge in Me,
purified by the austerity of wisdom,
many have come to My Being.

The sequence of expressions is highly significant: 'Freed from attachment, fear and anger' is a prerequisite to 'absorbed in Me'.

'Freed from attachment, fear and anger': attachment,[9] fear and

9. See III, 7, 28, 31.

anger [10] find fertile ground in the soil of ignorance, where the self
has not discovered its meaning in the Self. Transcendental meditation, as explained in Chapter II, verse 45, takes the mind to
the field of bliss-consciousness, supreme contentment and infinite
energy, leaving no room for any kind of weakness. It brings the
mind to the state of Being, which forms the basis of God-consciousness, expressed in the words 'absorbed in Me' and 'taking
refuge in Me'.

'Purified by the austerity of wisdom': austerity means denial
of the pleasures of the senses, or coming out of the field of sensory
activity and enjoyment. The purpose of austerity is to purify by
freeing the mind from the impact of the objects of sense. Likewise knowledge separates the Self from the whole field of activity.
This is the significance of the expression: 'austerity of wisdom'.
It should not be understood to mean that, as the practice of
austerity involves hardship, so does the path of knowledge. On
the contrary, gaining knowledge is joyful from beginning to
end: from the state of transcendental consciousness, through cosmic consciousness to God-consciousness. As the mind proceeds
towards the Transcendent, it becomes more and more free from
the gross fields of experience and this brings it nearer and nearer
to a state of purity. Eventually, when the mind transcends the
subtlest state of experience, it is left to itself, and then it reaches
the state of absolute purity.

This state of absolute purity, gained during transcendental consciousness, becomes permanent in cosmic consciousness and finds
its purpose and consummation [11] in the state of purity born of
knowledge of the ultimate oneness of life in God-consciousness.
In this state of knowledge man finds that Union with God of
which the Lord says: 'many have come to My Being.'

By the use of the word 'many', the Lord extends the hope of
Union with God to any man.

Having now described the direct way of attaining the ultimate
knowledge in God-consciousness, the Lord, in the following verse,
speaks about His reaction to the method of approach adopted by
the seeker.

10. See III, 41, 43.   11. See verse 38.

VERSE 11

ये यथा मां प्रपद्यन्ते तांस्तथैव भजाम्यहम् ॥
मम वर्त्मानुवर्तन्ते मनुष्याः पार्थ सर्वशः ॥११॥

As men approach Me, so do I favour them;
in all ways, O Partha, men follow My path.

'As men approach Me, so do I favour them': it is an established
natural law that action and reaction are equal to one another. In
the fullness of Divinity, God is ever full, and like the water of a
great lake, so does this fullness remain. The water has a tendency
neither to flow away nor to resist flowing; it just remains as it is.
If a farmer wants to take water to his field, he brings a pipe up
to the level of the water. The water does not refuse to flow
once the pipe is raised to its level.

Furthermore, the Lord says: 'in all ways, O Partha, men follow My path.' This has different meanings at different levels. First,
the nature of man is like the nature of God in that man behaves
to others as others behave to him.

Secondly, learning that the nature of the Lord is such that He
Himself does not take any initiative, that He only responds, people
try to derive the maximum benefit from surrendering themselves
completely to Him through meditation, which is the direct way to
God-consciousness. One who reaches this state, truly losing his
limited identity, gains the status of unbounded eternal Being in
God-consciousness. The Lord's purpose in disclosing this essential
characteristic of His nature is that thereby all men should reach
this state of divine existence. Here is the exposition of a technique
by which the limited personality of man is enabled to rise to the
unlimited status of eternal existence in God-consciousness. It is
open to all.

Thirdly, the natural tendency of every man is to turn towards
greater happiness, and therefore to proceed towards the eternal
happiness of God-consciousness. This is another reason why the
Lord says: 'in all ways, O Partha, men follow My path.'

Finally, 'in all ways, O Partha, men follow My path' indicates that God's own consciousness is the sole guiding factor of man's consciousness. It underlies all life in the cosmos and is the basic motivating intelligence of all beings. Cosmic intelligence upholds man's intelligence.

VERSE 12

काङ्क्षन्तः कर्मणां सिद्धिं यजन्त इह देवताः ॥
क्षिप्रं हि मानुषे लोके सिद्धिर्भवति कर्मजा ॥१२॥

Those who desire fulfilment of actions
here on earth make offerings to the gods,
for success born of action comes quickly in
the world of men.

Success is certainly gained by effort. Those who know how to contact the Vedic gods do so through specific sacrificial ceremonies and, having contacted these higher powers in nature, receive their goodwill and achieve greater success in life. When the Lord says here: 'success born of action comes quickly in the world of men', He means to bring home to Arjuna that whereas in the lower species the evolution of the soul depends upon the upward moving currents of evolution in nature, in the human species the soul has freedom of action, and that therefore the development of man depends upon how he acts and what he does.

This verse establishes the necessity of action as such for success in the world and at the same time shows the direction in which the activity must proceed.

VERSE 13

धातुवर्ण्यं मया सृष्टं गुणकर्मविभागशः ॥
तस्य कर्तारमपि मां विद्ध्यकर्तारमव्ययम् ॥१३॥

The fourfold order was created by Me
according to the division of gunas and
actions. Though I am its author, know Me
to be the non-doer, immutable.

The entire creation is the interplay of the three gunas. When the
primal equilibrium of sattva, rajas and tamas is disturbed, they
begin to interact and creation begins. All three must be present
in every aspect of creation because, with creation, the process of
evolution begins and this needs two forces opposed to each other
and one that is complementary to both.

Sattva and tamas are opposed to each other, while rajas is the
force complementary to both. Tamas destroys the created state;
sattva creates a new state while the first is being destroyed. In
this way, through the simultaneous processes of creation and
destruction the process of evolution is carried on. The force of
rajas plays a necessary but neutral part in creation and destruction; it maintains a bond between the forces of sattva and tamas.
Thus all three gunas are necessary for any state of manifested life.

'The fourfold order': mathematically, the three gunas may
combine with each other in six possible ways:

1. Sattva dominates, rajas is secondary
2. Sattva dominates, tamas is secondary
3. Rajas dominates, sattva is secondary
4. Rajas dominates, tamas is secondary
5. Tamas dominates, sattva is secondary
6. Tamas dominates, rajas is secondary.

Combinations 2 and 5 are not possible because of the contrast
in the nature of sattva and tamas. Thus the three gunas have only
four possible combinations.

This is the fourfold order in creation. Every species, whether vegetable, animal or human, is divided into four categories according to the four divisions of the gunas, which determine the natural mode of activity of each category.

'Non-doer': activity in all fields of life is caused by the three gunas.[12] The ultimate universal Being is the basis of the gunas; therefore it is said that the 'I' of the unmanifested omnipresent immutable Being is the Creator. He is the Creator and at the same time, ever remaining established in His own Being, is uninvolved, 'the non-doer'.[13]

This may be further clarified by an example. Oxygen and hydrogen ions combine to give rise to the properties of water. The water freezes, giving rise to the properties of ice. In these different states of gas, liquid and solid, the basic elements – oxygen and hydrogen – remain the same. In as much as they are the fundamental material from which gas, water and ice are formed, oxygen and hydrogen could be said to have created these different substances. But because they remain oxygen and hydrogen through their various stages, they could be said to be non-doing. Such is the state of ultimate Being. Lying at the base of all creation, it is the 'author' and, remaining unchanged, it is the 'non-doer' and 'immutable'.

When the Lord says: 'know Me to be the non-doer', He is asking Arjuna to take his mind to the transcendental state of consciousness, beyond the field of the three gunas, and gain first-hand knowledge of the source of creation; to see for himself that absolute silence is the creative energy and intelligence of eternal Being, the fountain-head of all creative energy and intelligence in the relative field.

In this verse, the Lord takes upon Himself the authorship of creation, at the same time declaring His absolute immutable nature. Being almighty, He is able to maintain His non-involved status even while giving rise to creation. The next verse further clarifies this idea.

12. See III, 27.   13. See verse 6.

VERSE 14

न मां कर्माणि लिम्पन्ति न मे कर्मफले स्पृहा ॥
इति मां योऽभिजानाति कर्मभिर्न स बध्यते ॥१४॥

Actions do not involve Me, nor have
I any longing for the fruit of action.
He who truly knows Me thus is not
bound by actions.

Anyone who has God-consciousness, constant awareness of the
source of creation, will know by his own experience that it is
transcendental in nature. That is why the Lord says: 'He who
truly knows Me thus is not bound by actions.' 'Truly knows Me
thus' means knows Me completely. Complete knowledge means
knowledge on the basis of experience as well as understanding.[14]

'Actions do not involve Me': it will be recalled from verse 28
of Chapter III that 'it is the gunas which act upon the gunas'
while Being remains uninvolved. Again, it will be recalled from
verse 9 of the present chapter that the activity of the Lord is not
worldly, not within the field of the gunas; it is divine and takes
place in His eternal freedom. The nature of the Lord as absolute
has been brought out in verse 6. The uninvolved nature of the
Lord is therefore perfectly clear.

'Nor have I any longing for the fruit of action': the Lord has
already expressed His eternal state of contentment in Chapter III,
verse 22.

'He who truly knows Me thus' means he who has thoroughly
known My nature as absolutely uninvolved with actions as well
as with their fruits. The word 'truly' is highly important. It means
knowing by participation, indicating that a man has gained God-
consciousness.

The expression: 'nor have I any longing for the fruit of action'
brings out by implication a feature common to the manifested
and unmanifested spheres of life. Both eternally continue to be

14. See verse 38, commentary.

by virtue of the eternal nature of the almighty and supreme Lord. Precise knowledge of the non-involvement of the Supreme in the midst of the vast activity of unlimited creation can only dawn on the basis of one's own experience of the Self as uninvolved with the field of activity.

Here is the sequence of realization of the true nature of the Lord : first, one realizes one's own Self as separate from activity and thus, gaining knowledge of the true nature of one's Self, surrenders all activity to the Lord and takes refuge in Him (verse 10). Then, in Unity with Him, one knows Him in His true nature as uninvolved with activity and without any longing for the fruits of action. This knowledge of the true nature of God results in eternal freedom from the binding influence of action. That is why the Lord says : 'He who truly knows Me thus is not bound by actions.'

This verse presents one of the most important teachings of Sankhya. It reveals the non-involved nature of the Lord and, simply through the knowledge of this fact, promises liberation from bondage. This is the strength of Sankhya, which offers liberation through the path of knowledge.

A similar teaching was contained in verse 28 of Chapter III. But there the argument was in terms of the knowledge of the three gunas, the knowledge of the relative field of activity; whereas in this verse it springs from the knowledge of the essential nature of the divine Being, personified by Lord Krishna, who is beyond the relative and the Absolute, beyond the Unity of Being and the diversity of creation, but holds within Himself the fullness of both.

VERSE 15

एवं ज्ञात्वा कृतं कर्म पूर्वैरपि मुमुक्षुभिः ॥
कुरु कर्मैव तस्मात्त्वं पूर्वैः पूर्वतरं कृतम् ॥१५॥

Having known this, even the ancient
seekers of liberation performed action;
therefore, do you perform action as did
the ancients in olden days.

'Having known this' refers to the teaching of the two previous verses.

In order to bring home to Arjuna that there could be a state of life in which the greatest activity would not disturb the eternal status of absolute Being, the Lord, in the two previous verses, gave an example of this state by referring to His own case. Seeing thus before him a living embodiment of the ideas which were being taught to him, Arjuna might then become convinced that he also could rise to this state in his own life.

'Ancient seekers of liberation' : this expression refers to 'Janaka and others' (III, 20). The use of the phrase 'seekers of liberation' makes it clear that action is necessary even for those who have devoted their lives to the pursuit of Truth and are not interested in anything other than liberation. But, as the expression 'Having known this' shows, knowledge about the real nature of the Lord is a prerequisite for the activity of 'seekers of liberation'.

When the seeker of liberation has attained cosmic consciousness and realized himself as separate from activity, he has reached his goal. He will be liberated from the bondage of action and, if he has no greater ideal before him, he will feel fulfilled. But if one feels fulfilled in the state of cosmic consciousness and does not aspire to God-consciousness, then one has missed the chance of the supreme attainment that is Union with God. For this reason, knowledge about the real nature of the Lord is essential even for the seekers of liberation. There is no doubt as to its necessity for the seekers of God.

In this verse, the Lord wants to make clear that knowledge of the three gunas and their interplay[15] should be supplemented by knowledge of the essential nature of the supreme Lord[16] in order that it may bring fulfilment to the state of liberation.

'Ancients in olden days': by this expression the Lord gives authority to His statement. The teaching is that the path of evolution that has withstood the test of time should not be doubted, because only that which is in accordance with the laws of evolution can last. Anything that does not conform to these laws is thrown off by nature.

15. See III, 28; IV, 13.   16. See verse 14.

In the following verses the argument turns to a close analysis of action.

VERSE 16

किं कर्म किमकर्मेति कवयोऽप्यत्र मोहिताः ॥
तत्ते कर्म प्रवक्ष्यामि यज्ज्ञात्वा मोक्ष्यसेऽशुभात् ॥१६॥

What is action, what inaction?
Even the wise are bewildered here.
I shall expound to you that action,
knowing which you will be freed from
evil.

In the previous verse the Lord gave Arjuna reasons for action; so it is natural that in this verse He should bring out the gravity and far-reaching influence of action in order to prepare Arjuna's mind for the details of that action which will be useful to him and deliver him from all 'evil'.

Ignorance of one's own blissful divine nature as non-involved and independent of activity keeps one under the binding influence of action, causing the complications and sufferings of life.

The Lord says that 'even the wise are bewildered' over the issue of action and inaction. The wise man is he who has understood that action is by virtue of the three gunas and that he himself remains uninvolved because his true nature is transcendental. But such understanding, says the Lord, is not sufficient, for even the wise continue to be bewildered.

The 'wise' have known the Self as separate from activity and thereby they have attained liberation. The Lord says that even the wise are bewildered over action and inaction. Gaining freedom from action is one thing; gaining full knowledge about action and inaction is quite another. The Lord says in the next verse: 'Unfathomable is the course of action.' It is impossible to know the full range of action on the level of intellectual understanding. That is why the Lord says: 'Even the wise are bewildered'.

It may be recalled that while enlightening Arjuna with the

wisdom of Sankhya in verse 38 of Chapter II the Lord said:
'Having gained equanimity ... you will not incur sin'; in the
present verse He says : 'I shall expound to you that action, knowing which you will be freed from evil.' A careful study of these
expressions unfolds the ascending order of the Lord's teaching; as
the capacity for understanding increases, the teaching is imparted
in subtler yet simpler forms. In the earlier verse it is implied that
something has to be done to gain the equanimity which will result
in freedom from sin. In the present verse, the Lord shows that
nothing has to be done, that simply by the knowledge of activity
Arjuna will be freed from evil. The teaching has shifted from
the level of doing to the level of knowing. It may well be that, as
the teaching advances, even knowing will be replaced by a simpler process on the common sensory level of hearing or seeing.
This is the technique of teaching Sankhya – a series of arguments
will eventually culminate in some simple spoken word which will
revolutionize the whole understanding of life and will once and
for all raise a man to the state of eternal freedom from bondage.

It is also of interest to note that the two preceding verses proclaimed liberation from bondage through knowledge of the non-
involved nature of the transcendent Lord; whereas this verse
promises freedom through knowledge even of the relative field,
the knowledge of activity and non-activity. This knowledge is
given in the following five verses.

VERSE 17

कर्मणो ह्यपि बोद्धव्यं बोद्धव्यञ्च विकर्मणः ॥
अकर्मणश्च बोद्धव्यं गहना कर्मणो गतिः ॥१७॥

Action, indeed, should be understood,
wrong action should also be understood
and inaction should be understood as
well. Unfathomable is the course of
action.

'Action': to understand action it is necessary to know the differ-ent states of consciousness of the actor, because the value of action depends mainly upon the level of consciousness of the one who acts. The possible states of consciousness are: waking, dreaming, sleeping, transcendental consciousness, cosmic consciousness and God-consciousness.

Action is here used to mean right action, which produces life-supporting effects for the doer and for the entire creation, action which helps the evolution of the individual and simultaneously serves the cosmic purpose. Such action is possible only when man's mind is in complete harmony with the transcendent Being, which underlies all creation and is the basis of all life and all the laws of nature. This is the case in cosmic consciousness. God-consciousness is another state where such action is automatically carried out. In cosmic consciousness, a man established in cosmic life performs action as an individual; in the state of God-con-sciousness, the individual's activity, set in the light of God, is on a level which corresponds to the level of cosmic activity. He lives the eternal Unity of life through all activity.

'Unfathomable is the course of action': one's natural activities in the three relative states of consciousness – waking, dreaming and sleeping – are governed by the dharma of one's level of evolu-tion. Dharma differs at different levels of evolution. Moreover, even on the same level dharma differs in different circumstances and in different spheres of life. In all these differences there is the additional complexity that in each case dharma refers not only to activity as it affects the individual, but also as it affects the family, society, the nation and the world. Every thought, word or act sets up waves of influence in the atmosphere. These waves travel through space and strike against everything in creation. Wherever they strike they have some effect. The effect of a par-ticular thought on any particular object cannot be known because of the diversity and vast extent of creation. This complexity goes beyond the possibility of comprehension. That is why the Lord says: 'Unfathomable is the course of action.'

'Wrong action' can be of many kinds: actions that harm the doer in the present or the future; those that do not succeed; those that hinder evolution; those that lead to dissolution; those that bind the doer to the cycle of birth and death; those that produce life-damaging influences upon the surroundings and upon others; those that are against the laws of nature. Even the field of wrong action is thus found to be 'unfathomable'.

Such wrong actions are possible so long as the doer is in a state of ignorance about his own dharma, so long as he is unaware of the essential nature of his own self, the nature of activity and the nature of God, and so long as his waking state of consciousness is not supported by transcendental pure consciousness.

'Inaction' : absence of activity. Deep sleep is a state of inaction, but it is not the only such state. The state of inaction is also found in transcendental consciousness. Furthermore, inaction is an essential constituent of cosmic consciousness and also of God-consciousness, the highest state of human evolution. On the one hand inaction is the inertia of sleep, while on the other it becomes the basis of the living Reality of the whole cosmos. This is what the Lord means when He says : 'inaction should be understood as well.' This shows not only action but also inaction to be unfathomable.

'Indeed' : by this word the Lord emphasizes the need for knowledge of action. Life means action – no one can escape activity. This being so, it is wise to know not only what one is going to do, but where, as a result, one is going to end up.

It will be interesting to observe closely how the Lord, having admitted that the course of action is unfathomable and having emphasized that it has to be understood, manages to steer a fine course between these opposing facts. To justify His expression 'unfathomable', wisdom demanded that He did not enter upon an examination of the course of action. But the word 'indeed' demands that whatever way He adopts, whether He enters into detail or not, knowledge of action must be conveyed. The Lord adopts a mode of instruction whereby, without knowledge of the whole field of action, one can acquire every benefit that such knowledge could bestow. He brings to light the art of action whereby, without having to gain knowledge of action, one can enjoy the blessings which such knowledge would give. This art of action is like the art of a gardener who, by watering the root,

makes the sap rise to every part of the tree without having to
know anything about the mechanics of rising sap.

Such is the marvel of perfection of this discourse. The Lord has
said that knowledge of action is necessary and yet, the course of
action being unfathomable, knowledge of it must remain incomplete. He therefore brings to light a technique by which the
effects of knowledge will be gained without the necessity for
gaining the knowledge. This is because the Lord's teaching is not
for the sake of knowledge as such; it is solely to produce a specific
effect in practical life. What is important is the effect, not the
knowledge. This is the discourse of Yoga Shastra, the most practical philosophy of Divine Union. Its purpose is to give the
practical wisdom whereby any man may naturally gain the
highest good through his activity.

The following verses clarify this teaching.

VERSE 18

कर्मण्यकर्म यः पश्येदकर्मणि च कर्म यः ॥
स बुद्धिमान्मनुष्येषु स युक्तः कृत्स्नकर्मकृत् ॥१८॥

He who in action sees inaction
and in inaction sees action is
wise among men. He is united, he
has accomplished all action.

'In action sees inaction': this means that while the mind is engaged with the senses and through them in the process of action,
it is anchored to the silence of the inner Being. This anchorage
provides the experience of silence in the midst of all activity.

For the man who 'in action sees inaction', the permeation of the
whole field of action by the non-active ever-silent Being is a living
reality. Action for him does not overshadow the state of inaction,
or Being, that underlies it. He lives the ever-silent Being that
permeates all activities of senses, mind and body; he sees silence
in activity and activity in silence.

Here is a teaching which enables a man to enrich the liberation attained by the knowledge that 'it is the gunas which act upon the gunas'.[17] It connects the active world of the three gunas with the silence of Being and thus, on the level of silence, establishes the co-existence of the ephemeral and the eternal. It confirms the ultimate teaching of the Upanishads: 'purnamadah, purnamidam' – this manifested world of activity is full (purna), That life of absolute Being is full.

Realization of this truth comes in the state of cosmic consciousness, but the teaching of this verse extends even to God-consciousness.

The realization of complete Reality establishes a state of life lying beyond the Unity of the Absolute and the multiplicity of the relative and produces the wholeness of vision that holds this and That both together in the light of God, in God-consciousness. One who has achieved it is 'wise among men'. According to this phrase, 'men' are those who have realized either the truth of activity[18] or the truth of silence.[19] But 'wise' is he who has realized the truth of both, either in the state of their separation in cosmic consciousness or in the state of their Union in God-consciousness.

The definition of man given in this verse points to the conclusion that one who has not realized the truth of activity or the truth of silence does not deserve to be called a man. It is therefore an essential feature of man's life that he should be established either on the path of knowledge or on the path of action. And if he wants to be 'wise', then he must also rise to embrace the goal of both.

'He has accomplished all action' means that in his individual life he has performed the whole range of activity, gross and subtle. Moreover, he has performed activity on the level of cosmic life as well. Activity on the individual level includes not only ordinary mental and physical activity but also the subtlest activity of transcending and gaining Union with divine Being. Activity on the cosmic level is of two types: first, activity in cosmic consciousness, which is fully in accordance with the pro-

17. See III, 28.   18. See III, 28.   19. See II, 45.

cess of evolution, and secondly, activity in God-consciousness, which is on the level of the ultimate Unity of life.

'He has accomplished all action' also means that he has attained perfection. Action is a way of fulfilling one's desires. To have 'accomplished all action' means to have accomplished all desires, indicating that one has gained fulfilment. It should be noted that the accomplishment of an action does not lie in gaining the fruit of action alone. It lies in gaining the fruit of action along with freedom from the binding influence of action and its results. The cognition of inaction in action and of action in inaction is the result of the fulfilment gained through the direct experience of absolute bliss, and of the eternal freedom from bondage that lies in the state of cosmic consciousness, where the Self is experienced as separate from activity.

In this verse the sequence of expressions is highly important. In order to convey that 'he who in action sees inaction and in inaction sees action' is not insane, the Lord adds that such a man has better understanding than other people: he is 'wise among men'. Further, in order to indicate that this wise man is not just a theorizing man engaged in mere idealistic thinking, the Lord says: 'He is united', implying that he is a practical man, who has gained fulfilment in life.

There are four expressions in this verse, each containing distinct and independent ideas:

1. In action sees inaction
2. In inaction sees action
3. Wise among men he is united
4. He has accomplished all action.

It is interesting to observe that each of these thoughts is developed successively in the next five verses. The first thought of this verse is developed in the first thought of each of the other verses. The second, third and fourth thoughts of this verse likewise find their development in the corresponding second, third and fourth thoughts of the other five verses.

The comparative study of these five verses presenting the science of action has been summarized at the end of the commentary on verse 23.

The Lord gave Arjuna a vision of activity in inactivity and of inactivity in activity when, in verses 13 and 14, He referred to Himself as an example. That is why it is sufficient for this verse to make a statement of fact without entering into details and explanations.

The following verses, however, discuss this point from the more concrete considerations of practical life.

VERSE 19

यस्य सर्वे समारम्भाः कामसङ्कल्पवर्जिताः ॥
ज्ञानाग्निदग्धकर्माणं तमाहुः पण्डितं बुधाः ॥१९॥

He whose every undertaking is free
from desire and the incentive thereof,
whose action is burnt up in the fire
of knowledge, him the knowers of
Reality call wise.

This verse presents the thought of the previous verse in a more developed form. In order to see inaction in action it is necessary to undertake action and yet to remain free from desire within oneself. A man's inner state 'free from desire' is a field of 'in-action'. This is how he 'whose every undertaking is free from desire' 'in action sees inaction' (verse 18).

The Lord mentions the special qualities of the action of an enlightened man. The action must certainly have impetus and an effective start, but the 'wise' man is not motivated by personal attachment in beginning the action any more than during its process or at its completion. Nor does he depend upon its fruits. Thus through the whole range of action he is involved yet not involved. That is why the Lord says : 'whose action is burnt up in the fire of knowledge, him the knowers of Reality call wise.'

The realized man does undertake activity but, by virtue of the knowledge that the Self is separate from activity, he remains free from the binding influence of action. This knowledge is com-

BHAGAVAD-GITA 282

pared here to a blazing fire which burns up all his action, in the sense that the action is set completely free from the binding influence of action or its fruits.

'Undertaking is free from desire': commonly a man begins an action only when he has become aware of the desire for it. The level at which a desire is appreciated differs according to the level of the conscious mind of the individual. Men of purer mind appreciate thought and desire at a much subtler level during the process of thinking.[20] It should be understood that a thought starts from the deepest level of consciousness and develops into a desire when it reaches the conscious level of the mind. A man for whom the level of transcendental consciousness has become the level of the conscious mind appreciates the thought at its very start before it actually develops into a desire. His thought becomes transformed into action without expressing itself as a desire.[21] This explains how, when a man succeeds in harmonizing his mind with transcendental consciousness, his 'every undertaking is free from desire'.

This state of non-attachment is more advanced than that described in the previous verse, in which one sees inaction in action and action in inaction. As the practice of transcendental meditation advances, Being begins to become established in the nature of the mind and one begins to feel oneself as separate from activity. Activity is then found on the quiet level of inner awareness. This is how one naturally begins to appreciate silence and activity simultaneously.

As the practice of meditation advances further, the silence of Being becomes appreciable even at the start of activity, so that a natural situation arises for every action to be 'free from desire and the incentive thereof'. It should be noted that the start of action engages the mind more deeply than action in progress. This is why the Self is first experienced as uninvolved during the process of action, and only when the practice is fairly well advanced does It begin to be appreciated as uninvolved at the start of action. Thus, with the growth of Being in the nature of the mind, a natural situation arises in which 'every undertaking'

20. See Appendix: Transcendental Meditation.
21. See III, 7.

is on the level of the silence of Being, which in Its essential nature is bliss-consciousness. This bliss-consciousness provides a level of eternal contentment on the basis of which 'every undertaking is free from desire and the incentive thereof'.

At this stage of the growth of Being into the nature of the mind, one feels unattached to the action both at its start and during its progress. But because every action is begun to accomplish some end, the purpose of an action engages the mind more deeply than does its start and progress; therefore non-attachment to the fruit of action demands a much fuller infusion of Being into the nature of the mind. By the time cosmic consciousness is gained, one has completely 'cast off attachment to the fruit of action' (verse 20). This, the most advanced state of non-attachment,[22] eventually finds its fulfilment in God-consciousness, in which 'you will see all beings in your Self and also in Me' (verse 35).

Every action depends upon the state of consciousness of the actor. Therefore if it is desired that all actions shall have a particular quality, it is necessary to produce a state of consciousness which will allow that quality of action to arise.

The word 'every' is very important in this context. It includes the whole range of sensory and mental activity. It suggests that the state of man's consciousness should be such that any action undertaken by him at any time is naturally free from desire and its incentive. Such a state of consciousness is found in cosmic consciousness and God-consciousness.

A man for whom the level of transcendental consciousness has become the level of the conscious mind has gained cosmic consciousness, and in this state he experiences Being as separate from action. This experience creates a natural condition in which there is action on the surface and a state of inaction within. Desire is a link between the doer and the action. But when a natural state of separation is established between the doer and action, there exists no link between them. In such a situation between the doer and his actions, desire has no place. This is how it is possible for 'every' undertaking to be free from desire.

'Free from ... the incentive thereof': in order to understand 22. This is dealt with in the commentary on the following verse.

the incentive of desire, we must analyse the process of the forma-
tion of a desire. Experience results when the senses come in
contact with their objects and an impression is left on the mind.
The impulse of this new impression resonates with an impression
of a similar past experience already present in the mind and
associates itself with that impression. The coming together of the
two gives rise to an impulse at the deepest level of consciousness,
where the impressions of all experiences are stored. This impulse
develops and, rising to the conscious level of the mind, becomes
appreciated as a thought. This thought, gaining the sympathy of
the senses, creates a desire and stimulates the senses to action. In
principle, the incentive of desire is due to the feeling of want.
In the state of cosmic consciousness, where one finds eternal
contentment within oneself and the field of activity is naturally
separate from oneself, the Self is self-sufficient – It can have no
want. In this state, therefore, every undertaking is free from the
incentive of desire.

The question may then be asked: What is responsible for
initiating action in such a man?

The answer is the almighty power of Nature,[23] which is the
cause of the vast and incessant activity of creation and evolution
throughout the cosmos.

Being forms the basis of nature. When the mind comes into full
unison with Being, it gains the very status of Being and thus
itself becomes the basis of all activity in nature. Natural laws
begin to support the impulses of such a mind: it becomes as if
one with all the laws of nature. The desire of such a mind is then
the need of nature, or, to put it in another way, the needs of
nature are the motive of such activity. The Self has nothing to
do with 'desire and the incentive thereof'. This is how it becomes
possible for 'every undertaking' to be naturally 'free from desire
and the incentive thereof'.

We must remember that the development of such a state of
consciousness comes about through the presence of Being on the
level of the conscious mind, the surface mind. There is no way
to develop it through any process of thinking or understanding.
The purpose of this verse is to give an explanation of this state;

23. See III, 27, 28.

it does not describe the way to accomplish it. It would be quite wrong to imagine that, by trying to eliminate desire and to reduce one's wants in order to lessen the incentive of desire, one could gain this natural state of non-attachment, which makes a man 'wise' in the eyes of the knowers of Reality.

'Fire of knowledge': awareness of Being as separate from the field of action.

The actions of such an enlightened man are, therefore, not his actions; they are the actions of the three gunas (III, 28). He remains unattached, contented (IV, 20), his heart and mind disciplined (21), beyond the pairs of opposites (22) and liberated (23).

VERSE 20

त्यक्त्वा कर्मफलासङ्गं नित्यतृप्तो निराश्रयः ॥
कर्मण्यभिप्रवृत्तोऽपि नैव किञ्चित्करोति सः ॥२०॥

Having cast off attachment to the
fruit of action, ever contented,
depending on nothing, even though
fully engaged in action he does
not act at all.

In the commentary on the previous verse it was explained how, with the growth of cosmic consciousness, non-attachment becomes so profound that a man casts off even 'attachment to the fruit of action'.

The present verse can be considered from another angle. When pure honey comes on the tongue, the taste of great sweetness surpasses in degree all the sweet tastes experienced up to then. If the tongue continues to cherish the taste of honey, then there will be no chance for a previous sweet taste to recur. This is what happens when the mind lives permanently in the experience of transcendental bliss in the state of cosmic consciousness; there then remains no chance for impressions of past experiences to capture it. This is how the enlightened man has 'cast off attachment to the fruit of action' performed in the past.

If one has the taste of concentrated sweetness on the tongue

and then tastes other sweets, these tastes do not leave any significant impression. When a man, established in the bliss of the
absolute Being, acts in the relative field of life, his experiences
will not leave on the mind any deep impression which could give
rise to future desires. In this way the cycle of action-impression-
desire-action is broken. It is thus that, in an enlightened man,
activity and experience in the world are debarred from sowing
the seed of future action. This will be further clarified in the
following verse.

'Even though fully engaged': his organs of action[24] continue
to perform their duties motivated by nature, and his senses of
experience likewise remain engaged; in this way he is found
acting.

'He does not act at all': his mind, established in the fullness of
Being, remains uninvolved in activity. This is his state of life –
outwardly engaged in activity, inwardly established in eternal
silence.[25]

VERSE 21

निराशीर्यतचित्तात्मा त्यक्तसर्वपरिग्रहः ॥
शारीरं केवलं कर्म कुर्वन्नाप्नोति किल्बिषम् ॥२१॥

Expecting nothing, his heart
and mind disciplined, having
relinquished all possessions,
performing action by the body
alone, he incurs no sin.

'Expecting nothing': the cause of anxiety and expectation is
desire. The actions of the enlightened man have been declared to
be 'free from desire and the incentive thereof' (verse 19). That is
why he acts 'expecting nothing'.

'His heart and mind disciplined': see Chapter III, verse 43.

'Having relinquished all possessions': this expression runs
parallel with 'depending on nothing' (verse 20). The word 'possessions' indicates all that one has gathered around oneself, every-

24. See III, 7.   25. See III, 7, 27; IV, 14.

thing other than one's own Self; relinquishing everything that is outside one's own Self means abandoning the whole field of relative existence, being 'without the three gunas'.[26]

'Performing action by the body alone': it has been explained in the commentary on verse 19 how the mind of the enlightened man remains unattached, even when he is performing actions on the level of the senses,[27] so that 'every undertaking is free from desire and the incentive thereof'. The mind of an enlightened man does not register deeply any impressions of actions performed by the body on the level of the senses; through all activities his mind remains ever fixed in Being. Established in the absolute purity of Being, he is out of the field of ignorance, out of the field of 'sin'.

VERSE 22

यदृच्छालाभसन्तुष्टो द्वन्द्वातीतो विमत्सरः ॥
समः सिद्धावसिद्धौ च कृत्वापि न निबध्यते ॥२२॥

*Satisfied with whatever comes
unasked, beyond the pairs of
opposites, free from envy, balanced
in success and failure, even
acting he is not bound.*

This verse presents the picture of one who is liberated.

'Satisfied with whatever comes unasked': the enlightened man lives a life of fulfilment. His actions, being free from desire, serve only the need of the time. He has no personal interest to gain. He is engaged in fulfilling the cosmic purpose and therefore his actions are guided by nature. This is why he does not have to worry about his needs. His needs are the needs of nature,[28] which takes care of their fulfilment, he being the instrument of the Divine.

'Beyond the pairs of opposites': beyond the three gunas.[29] This

26. See II, 45.   27. See III, 7.   28. See verse 19, commentary.
29. See II, 45, 50, 56, 57.

expression applies equally to transcendental consciousness, cosmic consciousness and God-consciousness. Transcendental consciousness is absolute in nature, without any trace of duality. Cosmic consciousness accepts 'the pairs of opposites', but as completely separate from the Self. God-consciousness also accepts 'the pairs of opposites', but as inseparable from the Self, which in Its turn is inseparable from God.

'Free from envy': envy is a quality which disturbs one's equilibrium and allows one to be invaded by the dharma of a level of consciousness different from one's own.[30] This is a great danger, for it is apt to throw a man off the path of his own evolution. One who is free from envy is free from this danger. Such a man is not tempted by anything, because he has risen to absolute freedom. To what more could he aspire? Having risen to the state of cosmic consciousness he could aspire to God-consciousness, and this might be thought to leave open a possibility for envy. But if a man of cosmic consciousness were to see a man of God-consciousness, he would be filled with love and devotion for him rather than envy his state.

'Balanced in success and failure': see Chapter II, verses 38, 48, 50.

'Even acting he is not bound': see Chapter III, verse 28.

When the mind, through meditation, has become contented in the bliss of the Self, there is no possibility of discontent. Then there is evenness of mind both in pleasure and in pain. Such is the state of a liberated man.[31]

VERSE 23

गतसङ्गस्य मुक्तस्य ज्ञानावस्थितचेतसः ॥
यज्ञायाचरतः कर्म समग्रं प्रविलीयते ॥२३॥

He who is freed from attachment,
liberated, whose mind is established
in wisdom, who acts for the sake of
yagya, his action is entirely dissolved.

30. See III, 35, commentary.   31. See II, 71; III, 17, 28.

CHAPTER FOUR

This verse demonstrates that when, through constant practice of meditation, a man has gained cosmic consciousness, when pure transcendental consciousness is grounded in the very nature of his mind, he becomes 'liberated' from the field of action and 'freed from attachment'. In this state, every action produces life-supporting influences in creation and thus helps cosmic evolution; therefore every action is 'for the sake of yagya'.

Thus the actions of one who practises transcendental meditation are worthy of being ranked as yagya.

The four expressions of this verse conclude the development of the four expressions contained in each of the previous five verses.[32] To illustrate this development, they are set out below:

I. 'He who in action sees inaction' (18)
   'He whose every undertaking is free from desire' (19)
   'Having cast off attachment to the fruit of action' (20)
   'Expecting nothing' (21)
   'Satisfied with whatever comes unasked' (22)
   'He who is freed from attachment' (23).

II. 'In inaction sees action' (18)
   (He whose every undertaking is free from) 'the incentive thereof' (19)
   'Ever contented' (20)
   'His heart and mind disciplined' (21)
   'Beyond the pairs of opposites, free from envy' (22)
   'Liberated' (23).

III. 'Is wise among men he is united' (18)
   'Whose action is burnt up in the fire of knowledge' (19)
   'Depending on nothing' (20)
   'Having relinquished all possessions' (21)
   'Balanced in success and failure' (22)
   'Whose mind is established in wisdom' (23).

IV. 'He has accomplished all action' (18)
   'Him the knowers of Reality call wise' (19)
   'Even though fully engaged in action he does not act at all' (20)

32. See verse 18, commentary.

'Performing action by the body alone, he incurs no sin' (21)
'Even acting he is not bound' (22)
'Who acts for the sake of yagya, his action is entirely dis-
solved' (23).

It is by reason of the teaching contained in these six verses
that this fourth chapter is the chapter of wisdom – the wisdom of
Karma Yoga and Sankhya at the same time. It reveals the state
of a realized man on the level of action and behaviour, thus presenting the practical aspect of the abstract metaphysical quest
which confronts man on the path of his evolution.

VERSE 24

ब्रह्मार्पणं ब्रह्म हविर्ब्रह्माग्नौ ब्रह्मणा हुतम् ॥
ब्रह्मैव तेन गन्तव्यं ब्रह्मकर्मसमाधिना ॥२४॥

Brahman is the act of offering.
Brahman the oblation poured by
Brahman into fire that is Brahman.
To Brahman alone must he go who is
fixed in Brahman through action.

This verse does not teach that during the performance of ritualistic yagya, or any other type of action, one should hold in the
mind the idea that everything is Brahman. The teaching here
concerns far deeper levels of life than the surface level of thinking
and making moods.

In the preceding verse it was said: 'who acts for the sake of
yagya, his action is entirely dissolved'. These words are further
explained in the present verse, which considers different aspects
of action performed by the enlightened man. It speaks of that
state of consciousness which realizes oneness of existence in all
the diversity of action.

In this verse and those following the Lord enumerates different
aspects of the action of yagya and says that all aspects are
Brahman. Certainly offering is offering, oblation is oblation, fire

is fire and the performer is the performer – on the level of relative life duality prevails. Everything is Brahman only on the level of consciousness of the performer who is established in cosmic consciousness.[33] What has been said in verses 19 to 23 leads to the conclusion that the enlightened man, established in bliss-consciousness at all times, irrespective of the engagement of the mind and senses in action, is intent on Brahman, while at the same time everything that action entails proceeds naturally at the level of the senses,[34] through the agency of the gunas.[35]

When the mind becomes infused with Being, then no thought, word or act can take the mind out of Being. This is the state of cosmic consciousness.[36] The purpose of the present verse is to describe clearly the relationship of action to cosmic consciousness in which all actions form an integral part of that consciousness and are therefore appreciated as none other than that consciousness, none other than Brahman.

The verse also implies that fixity in Brahman constitutes mastery over action and is at the same time the fulfilment of action.

The Lord speaks of yagya in order to explain that the different parts of an action and the various modes of their performance do not leave any trace of bondage for the enlightened man. Ever established in the state of pure consciousness, or eternal Being, he is simply a silent and innocent witness of what is happening through him; he is a means through which nature fulfils its purpose of evolution. His actions are a response to the needs of the time. Quite naturally he performs actions which result in every kind of good.

'To Brahman alone must he go': Brahman is the Reality which embraces both the relative and absolute fields of life. Having gained the state of Brahman, a man has risen to the ultimate Reality of existence. In this state of enlightenment he has accomplished eternal liberation, and once a man has risen to this state there is no falling away from it. That is why the Lord says: 'To Brahman alone must he go who is fixed in Brahman through action.'

The expression 'must he go' does not mean that on leaving the

33. See II, 71, 72.   35. See III, 28.
34. See III, 7.   36. See II, 72.

body he departs to some other place. The word 'go' here finds its
meaning in the fact that, with the destruction of the body, the
realized man is no longer found as an individual, and when
someone is not to be found he is said to have gone. Where then
has he gone? In order to explain his position in terms of going,
it must be said that he has gone to Brahman; but in fact there is
no question of going for him who is already 'fixed in Brahman',
who has risen to the omnipresent Reality. He remains what he
was – Brahman – but without the individual body.

'Who is fixed in Brahman through action': one rises to the
state of Brahman in cosmic consciousness, where no activity,
however vigorous, can take one out of Being. This state of fixity
in Brahman is reached by the performance of activity after gaining the state of Being through the activity of meditation – the
inward activity of meditation followed by the outward activity
of daily life. Thus it is clear that it is 'through action' that one
'is fixed in Brahman'. This verse therefore not only describes the
state of Brahman but also shows a direct way to its realization.

VERSE 25

देवमेवापरे यज्ञं योगिनः पर्युपासते ॥
ब्रह्माग्नावपरे यज्ञं यज्ञेनैवोपजुह्वति ॥२५॥

Some yogis perform yagya merely
by worshipping the gods, others by
offering the yagya itself into the
fire that is Brahman.

'Worshipping the gods' is said to be the performance of yagya.
The Lord says that when this worship of the gods is offered to
Brahman, such an offering is also performance of yagya.

An analysis of how 'worshipping the gods' is offered to Brahman
and how the offering to Brahman is the performance of yagya may
make this clear.

Cosmic consciousness is the state of Brahman.[37] Since it is

37. See II, 72.

transcendental Self-consciousness that develops into cosmic consciousness, in order to achieve cosmic consciousness through
worshipping, one has to transcend through worshipping. This
necessitates entering into the subtle phases of the act of worship.
And this is most successfully done in a systematic manner by
taking the name or form of the god and experiencing it in its
subtler states until the mind transcends the subtlest state and
attains transcendental consciousness. Those who are highly emotional, however, may even transcend through an increasing feeling of love for the god during the process of making offerings.

Transcending the act of worship is said to be the offering of the
worship to Brahman. It has the advantage of receiving the
blessings of the god and at the same time of helping to develop
cosmic consciousness.

By transcending, a worshipper arrives at the ultimate fulfilment
of yagya and thereby develops cosmic consciousness, the state
where his every action will prove to be yagya. All that concerns
him will be helpful to evolution and, established in his Being,
he will fulfil the purpose of life. That is why transcending the
field of yagya to arrive at the state of Brahman also ranks as
yagya. When a man has gained cosmic consciousness, all his
actions assume the status of yagya. Because such action is performed in the state of Brahman, it is already on the level of
Brahman. This is offering the yagya itself into the fire that is
Brahman.

VERSE 26

श्रोत्रादीनीन्द्रियाण्यन्ये संयमाग्निषु जुह्वति ॥
शब्दादीन्विषयानन्य इन्द्रियाग्निषु जुह्वति ॥२६॥

Some offer hearing and other senses
in the fires of control; some offer
sound and other objects of the senses
in the fires of the senses.

'Fires': the plural is to indicate that there are different methods for controlling different senses.

There are two types of people: those who keep their senses active, enjoying objects in the world, and those who practise different methods of control. The Lord refers to the second when He says the senses are offered in 'the fires of control'.

The word 'control' has been interpreted by most commentators as implying restraint, and consequently they advocate forcible subjugation of the senses. But it is certainly not possible to put an end to the activities of the senses through the practice of refraining from feeding them. This has already been made clear by the Lord in verse 59 of the second chapter. Therefore it is obvious that the word 'control' means something other than restraint, something which will indeed have the strength to calm the senses. This is explained in two ways: first, as the proper use of the senses, which is the interpretation given in this verse; secondly, as the process of allowing all the senses to converge naturally upon one point and to remain there in the state of contentment. This second path [38] is described in the next verse.

'Some offer sound and other objects of the senses in the fires of the senses': some people have their senses active in the outside world. This is using the senses rightly, for the experience of objects, excepting only those that are forbidden, is also considered to be the performance of yagya.

Thus the meaning of this verse is clear. Some turn their senses inwards through the practice of transcendental meditation and thus create a situation in which their senses automatically converge to Being, thereby naturally fulfilling the very purpose of control. Others do not meditate but keep their senses controlled by righteous action; by not allowing their senses to experience forbidden things, they too follow the path of yagya and evolve to reach the Supreme. This is a slow and difficult process; difficult because the basis of right action is pure consciousness. Right action without a proper basis is very hard, if not impossible. By transcendental meditation, however, it is easy to gain pure consciousness [39] and thereby automatically to perform right action.

38. See also III, 43.   39. See II, 40.

VERSE 27

सर्वाणीन्द्रियकर्माणि प्राणकर्माणि चापरे ॥
आत्मसंयमयोगाग्नौ जुह्वति ज्ञानदीपिते ॥२७॥

Others offer all the activities of
the senses and of the life-breath
in the fire of Yoga, which is self-
control kindled by enlightenment.

It is generally understood that the practice of self-control is
necessary to bring enlightenment; this is clearly contrary to the
Lord's teaching, which states specifically that 'self-control' is the
result of the state of enlightenment.[40]

During the process of transcendental meditation, when the
mind enters the subtler levels of experience, the activity of all
the senses decreases and finally stops; the breath also becomes
more refined and eventually comes to a standstill. This is the
offering of 'all the activities of the senses and of the life-breath
in the fire of Yoga'.

'Self-control kindled by enlightenment': self-control means
the self remaining within itself without any deviation into the
outer world. Control of the mind in its perfect state means the
mind remaining within itself without any deviation into the outer
world. A lesser degree of control of the mind would be deviation
into the outer world in a desired direction. Similarly, control of
the senses in its perfect state means the senses remaining in
themselves without any deviation into the outer world. A lesser
degree of sense-control would be deviation into the outer world
in a desired direction.

'Self-control kindled by enlightenment' means a perfect state
of control of the self, the mind and the senses. It means that in
the state of enlightenment, or pure consciousness, in the state of
Being, the mind and senses are set within themselves without
any deviation into the outer world. This takes place in the tran-

40. See II, 59.

scendental state devoid of any activity. When, however, this transcendental state of consciousness becomes permanent and is transformed into cosmic consciousness, then the mind remains anchored to the state of Being and entertains activity in the outer world in the desired direction.

This is how the mind, even while active, remains within the range of self-control. The senses always follow the pattern of the mind, so when the mind is in this state of self-control, the activity of the senses also remains quite spontaneously within the boundaries of self-control. This means that the senses automatically function in the right direction.

This is how, by means of gaining the state of enlightenment, the 'activities of the senses and of the life-breath' are offered 'in the fire of Yoga'. It is clear therefore that the 'fire of Yoga' has to be lit first, and only then the control follows.

It should be noted that by virtue of this state of self-control on the cosmic level, the activity of the creation and evolution of cosmic life is spontaneously carried out by the nature of the three gunas, while cosmic Being, God, remains uninvolved with activity. This is a picture of the inner functioning of cosmic life; it shows with what spontaneity and precision, based on self-control, the activity of cosmic life is carried on.

Here Yoga has been defined as the state of self-control spontaneously created by enlightenment, by the realization of the Self in transcendental consciousness, and therefore in the state of cosmic consciousness as well.

God-consciousness is the supreme state of enlightenment. As this state is gained, self-control on the level of the individual life rises to self-control on the level of cosmic life.

VERSE 28

द्रव्ययज्ञास्तपोयज्ञा योगयज्ञास्तथापरे ॥
स्वाध्यायज्ञानयज्ञाश्च यतयः संशितव्रताः ॥२८॥

Some likewise perform yagya by means of
material possessions, by austerity and by
the practice of Yoga; while other aspirants
of rigid vows offer as yagya their scriptural
learning and knowledge.

Here the Lord describes material, bodily and mental methods of
purification for the sake of evolution, for the sake of gaining
freedom in cosmic consciousness and its fulfilment in God-consciousness.

'Yagya by means of material possessions' denotes giving away
wealth to the deserving. It also means the performance of Vedic
rituals by offering sacrificial fires.[41]

To perform yagya 'by austerity' means subjecting the body to
heat, cold and other such sufferings for the sake of purification.

'By the practice of Yoga': see II, 45, 50; III, 7.

'Offer as yagya their scriptural learning and knowledge': sit
and meditate and transcend the field of learning; experience the
transcendent Being, which is the goal of all learning.[42]

VERSE 29

अपाने जुह्वति प्राणं प्राणेऽपानं तथापरे ॥
प्राणापानगती रुद्ध्वा प्राणायामपरायणाः ॥२९॥

Others again, who are devoted to
breathing exercises, pour the
inward into the outward breath
and the outward into the inward,
having restrained the course of
inhalation and exhalation.

41. See III, 12, 13; IV, 25.   42. See II, 52, 53.

Here the Lord explains to Arjuna that there is a class of seekers of Truth who try to realize through the process of breathing exercises. They induce 'the inward into the outward breath and the outward into the inward', thus restraining 'the course of inhalation and exhalation'. This results in the suspension of breathing, which brings the mind to stillness in the silence of bliss-consciousness, simultaneously culturing the nervous system [43] to maintain this state of consciousness. That is why the practice of breathing exercises is included here as yagya.

Transcendental meditation also fulfils the requirements of this verse, for during its practice the outgoing and ingoing breaths quite spontaneously begin to become more shallow. The flow of the outgoing breath becomes less, and the flow of the ingoing breath becomes less. This phenomenon of the simultaneous diminution of both has been described as the pouring of one into the other. This is how, through the practice of transcendental meditation, in a very easy manner, one pours 'the inward into the outward breath and the outward into the inward'.

VERSE 30

अपरे नियताहाराः प्राणान्प्राणेषु जुह्वति ॥
सर्वेऽप्येते यज्ञविदो यज्ञक्षयितकल्मषाः ॥३०॥

Yet others, restricting their food,
offer breaths into breaths. All
these indeed are knowers of yagya,
and through yagya their sins are
cast away.

When a man restricts his food, less oxygen is needed for metabolism, and therefore his breathing becomes more shallow.

'Restricting their food' means not feeding the senses with their objects, not engaging in the activity of action or even thought.

43. See verse 38, commentary.

This non-engagement in activity requires a reduction in meta-
bolism, which in turn requires a reduction of respiratory activity.
This, as has been explained in the previous verse, is what the
Lord means by 'offer breaths into breaths'.

All these are different ways of purifying [44] oneself; that is why
they are called yagya. Through their practice 'sins are cast away'.
The Brahmabindu Upanishad declares that a huge mountain of
sins extending for miles is destroyed by Union brought about
through transcendental meditation, without which there is no
way out.[45]

VERSE 31

यज्ञशिष्टामृतभुजो यान्ति ब्रह्म सनातनम् ॥
नायं लोकोऽस्त्ययज्ञस्य कुतोऽन्यः कुरुसत्तम ॥३१॥

Eating the remains of the yagya,
which is nectar, they reach the
eternal Brahman. This world, O
best of Kurus, is not for him
who offers no yagya, much less
the world hereafter.

Having described the various types of yagya in the previous
verses (24–30), the Lord, in this verse, explains their result. Yagya
is the process of purification. Every such process leaves the mind
finer and thus more capable of transcending. When yagya is
over,[46] the mind is purified and gains a higher level of consciousness. This eventually results in bliss-consciousness, which the
Lord calls 'nectar'. The bliss remains,[47] as it were, when the yagya
is over. Those who enjoy this bliss, says the Lord, 'reach the

44. See verse 38, commentary.
45. Yadi shaila samam pāpam
    Vistīrnam bahu yojanam
    Bhidyate dhyāna yogena
    Nānyo bhedah kadāchana
46. See verse 33.   47. See III, 13, commentary.

eternal Brahman', because it is this transcendental bliss-consciousness that, through continued practice, develops into cosmic consciousness and eventually into God-consciousness.

The Lord says further that if a man does not perform yagya he will be successful neither in this world nor hereafter. Unless the arrow is fully drawn back on the bow, it does not gain sufficient energy to shoot forward with great force; unless the mind is drawn inwards and brought to the extreme limit of its inward march, it does not become dynamic. And unless the mind becomes active and powerful, it certainly will not achieve success in the world. The Lord shows that the process of purification, or yagya, is necessary both for success in this world and to gain strength for success in the world hereafter.

Of all the yagyas, the yagya of transcendental meditation [48] is the most [49] effective, for it is a direct means of bringing the mind to absolute purity and enabling it to contact the source of limitless life-energy and intelligence.

VERSE 32

एवं बहुविधा यज्ञा वितता ब्रह्मणो मुखे ॥
कर्मजान्विद्धि तान्सर्वानेवं ज्ञात्वा विमोक्ष्यसे ॥३२॥

In this way yagyas of many kinds are
set forth in the words of the Veda.
Know them all as born of action.
Thus knowing you will find release.

The Vedas speak of various kinds of yagya which help the process of the evolution of man at different levels of life. The Lord means that the knowledge of the various yagyas, as found in the Vedas, is complete in itself; it has only to be adopted. To convey this, He says: 'Know them all as born of action.' Action is necessary to perform yagya: unless they are performed, yagyas will not yield any result. Theoretical knowledge of them has its

48. See Appendix. 49. See verse 33.

value but does not in itself carry the fruits of yagya. The importance of action is emphasized here.

The phrase 'Know them all as born of action' suggests another point. The Lord wants to make it very clear to Arjuna that the knowledge of yagya, which He has been teaching in the previous verses and which has the authority of the Vedas, is essential for success in this world and hereafter. But at the same time He indicates that this is not the final knowledge which will free him from bondage; something more has to be known. While continuing in the activity of yagya, Arjuna should bear in mind that it is all in the field of activity and that Reality is transcendental. So one has not to remain permanently in the field of the activity of yagya. The knowledge that yagya is activity and that Reality is transcendental will certainly free a man.

Here is an important point for the practice of transcendental meditation. The medium of attention must enable the mind to reach the Transcendent and realize the absolute state of Being. If the aspirant is not aware of this fact then, during his practice of meditation (yagya) when he finds that the medium of attention has disappeared, he will feel confused. To save him from such confusion, the Lord says that all the practices which bring enlightenment (yagyas) are in the field of activity, and that the goal is to transcend that field, to arrive at transcendental consciousness, gain cosmic consciousness and ultimately rise to the consummation of all action in the state of Unity in God-consciousness.

The following verse throws more light on this point.

VERSE 33

श्रेयान्द्रव्यमयाद्यज्ञाज्ज्ञानयज्ञः परन्तप ॥
सर्वं कर्माखिलं पार्थ ज्ञाने परिसमाप्यते ॥३३॥

Better than the yagya through material
means is the yagya of knowledge, O scorcher
of enemies. All action without exception,
O Partha, culminates in knowledge.

'Yagya through material means': see verse 28.

'Yagya of knowledge' means action that leads to knowledge.[50] Yagya of 'material means' is performed through material offerings, whereas yagya of knowledge is performed through mental activity — mental activity leading to the state of transcendental consciousness, and also the mental activity of understanding of the Transcendent. Knowledge [51] in its content is God-consciousness, which develops from the state of cosmic consciousness, which in its turn develops from the knowledge (understanding and experience) of transcendental consciousness.

Action is a means of evolution, and evolution gains its highest peak when man has attained Unity with God, God-consciousness. In this state of fulfilment there is nothing that he need do.[52] He has arrived at the goal of all actions.

All means come to an end as a matter of course when the goal is reached. Any form of yagya aims at a certain degree of purification. When pure consciousness has been permanently achieved, when the Self has been realized as separate from activity, and when God-consciousness has been gained, then the extreme limit of purification has been achieved. Having achieved it, a man naturally feels fulfilled in eternal freedom. This state of fulfilment is the goal of all action, the goal of all yagya. That is why the Lord says that knowledge is a field towards which all actions converge and in which they finally become merged: 'All action without exception, O Partha, culminates in knowledge.'

The Lord's discourse is an example of great psychological skill. Gradually (from verse 23 to this verse) He builds up the importance of yagya, the path to enlightenment. When He has established the greatness of it, He suddenly says that this is all in the field of action,[53] thereby implying first that it is within the reach of every man, and secondly that no man should remain held up within the field of action, or yagya, for it is not the final goal of life. Having pointed this out, the Lord, in this verse, immediately concludes His account with the statement that knowledge is the goal of all actions. Yagya through material means can at best raise the level of consciousness in the relative field

50. See verse 38, commentary.   52. See III, 17.
51. See verse 38.   53. See verse 32.

of life. Yagya of knowledge transforms the entire human mechanism into a means by which the Divine expresses [54] Itself in the
world. Because there could be no state of evolution greater than
this, 'the yagya of knowledge', leading as it does to this state, is
better than 'yagya through material means'.

When the Lord lays stress on knowledge as against action, He
addresses Arjuna as 'scorcher of enemies', as one engaged in
vigorous activity. This is to show him that it is through knowledge that life can be made most dynamic. In the verse which
follows, the Lord indicates a direct way to search for this 'knowledge'.

VERSE 34

तद्विद्धि प्रणिपातेन परिप्रश्नेन सेवया ॥
उपदेक्ष्यन्ति ते ज्ञानं ज्ञानिनस्तत्त्वदर्शिनः ॥३४॥

Know this: through homage,
repeated inquiry and service,
the men of knowledge
who have experienced Reality
will teach you knowledge.

Here is the process of gaining enlightenment from the enlightened. By 'homage' is meant submission or surrender. This
serves to produce a state of receptivity. In the state of submission, the heart and mind set aside their own ways of feeling and
thinking; they become free from all that overshadows their potentiality and become fully receptive to the enlightened man, the
embodiment of knowledge.

Submission is a means of depriving the seeker quite naturally of
his limited individuality and overcoming in him any resistance
that prevents him from opening himself to the cosmic Being. In
this verse the seeker of Truth is advised to submit to the enlightened man and not merely to have a sense of submission to

54. See verse 38, commentary.

cosmic Being. This is because submission to omnipresent Being, having no concrete point of focus, remains abstract and indefinite and does not crystallize into concrete results. Direct submission of the individual intellect to the cosmic intelligence takes place only in the state of transcendence. In the field of relativity, submission on the level of thinking and understanding demands a specific point of focus if it is to be valid and productive of results.

The second point in the process of reaching enlightenment is that the intellect should be alert, so that discrimination, or the ability to understand different aspects of Reality, is sharp. This is necessary because the state of full enlightenment includes a clear understanding of Reality, and this again can only be accomplished by an intellect which is alert and sharp, discriminating and decisive. The state of intellectual alertness conflicts with the state of submission. This conflict is resolved by what the Lord calls 'service'.

'Service' means action in accordance with the desire of the master. A sense of service has little to do with the nature of the work itself, but is primarily concerned with the fulfilment of the master's desires; if the master is pleased, service is successful. If he is pleased by the accomplishment of the work, then the service is done and the work has accomplished its purpose. If, in the middle of the work, the master wants it undone, then the success of the service will demand obedience. This art of service covers those states of submission and alertness of intellect which are necessary for enlightenment.

A right sense of service trains the mind of the seeker to adjust itself to the status of the integrated mind of the enlightened man. In order to be successful in the art of service, one has to adjust one's mind, one's likes and dislikes, to bring them into accord with the mind of the master. One does something and then closely watches to see whether he is pleased or displeased. Then one adjusts one's actions accordingly. This does more than merely hold together submission and alertness of intellect. By adjusting itself to the likes and dislikes of the enlightened cosmic mind of the master, the ignorant mind of the seeker gradually gains that same status. Thus we find submission, questioning and service, all these three, are complementary and create a situation favourable to enlightenment.

Commenting on this verse, Shankara says: 'Know by what means it is gained. Having approached the teachers humbly, fall down and prostrate yourself before them, paying them prolonged homage. Ask them what is bondage and what liberation, what is wisdom and what ignorance. Perform service for the master. Pleased by these and other signs of reverence, the teachers, who know the Truth from the scriptures and have also realized It through direct personal experience, will declare to you this knowledge.'

The result of this knowledge is shown in the next verse.

VERSE 35

यज्ज्ञात्वा न पुनर्मोहमेवं यास्यसि पाण्डव ॥
येन भूतान्यशेषेण द्रक्ष्यस्यात्मन्यथो मयि ॥३५॥

Knowing this, O son of Pandu,
you will no more
fall into such delusion;
for through this you
will see all beings
in your Self and also in Me.

'Knowing this': having gained the knowledge given in the preceding verses.

'You will no more fall into such delusion': here the Lord gives Arjuna the technique of rising above the possibility of delusion. The field of the duality of life alone can be the field of delusion. When, in the state of cosmic consciousness, one has realized the Self as separate from activity, and when this state has developed to the eternal Unity of God-consciousness, then you see 'all beings in your Self and also in Me'. In this state of oneness of life, oneness of God-consciousness, there is no trace of duality and therefore there is no possibility of any delusion. The teaching is:

cultivate the state of Unity in God-consciousness; cultivate this
state of knowledge so that you will no more fall into such delusion.

The word 'such' is highly significant. It indicates a special state
of delusion – Arjuna's delusion in particular – delusion in the
state of sattva. Thereby the Lord silently educates Arjuna in the
philosophy of delusion : any delusion experienced in the state of
tamas can be overcome with the increase of rajas; likewise, delusion experienced in the state of rajas can be overcome with the
rise of sattva; but a delusion in the state of sattva, as in Arjuna's
case, cannot be overcome unless one transcends the field of sattva
and gains transcendental consciousness. Here the qualities of
the heart and mind find a common goal, thereby dissolving the
duality of their separate existences and rising above the possibility
of delusion.

It is not physically possible, however, to remain in the Transcendent at all times. Therefore it is necessary to make this transcendental consciousness permanent and to rise to the state of
cosmic consciousness. In this state of cosmic consciousnes one
experiences one's Self as separate from activity. It might appear
that in this state one was living a duality, the duality of Being
and activity; but this type of duality, in which the Self remains
detached from everything, is free from the possibility of delusion.
But the Lord wishes Arjuna to rise above duality even of this
nature. In order that he may do so, He emphasizes the importance
of gaining knowledge of Unity in God-consciousness which results
from devotion in the state of cosmic consciousness.

By the practice of the teaching in the previous verse the heart
and mind of the seeker are automatically refined to become
capable of devotion; this devotion develops God-consciousness, in
which Unity becomes a living reality of life, and the possibility
of any kind of duality is completely eliminated.

'You will see all beings in your Self and also in Me' : when
one sees through green spectacles, then everything looks green.
When, through knowledge, the Self is realized as separate from
activity and Self-consciousness becomes permanent in the state of
cosmic consciousness, then everything is naturally experienced in
the awareness of the Self; and when this permanent state of Self-

consciousness, or cosmic consciousness, has been transformed through devotion into God-consciousness, then everything is naturally experienced in the awareness of God, every experience is through God-consciousness, everything is experienced and understood in the light of God, in terms of God, in God.

Seeing 'all beings' includes knowledge of the whole field of the universe constituted by the three gunas; and seeing 'Me' means seeing the Lord presiding over both the Absolute and the relative. Thus seeing 'all beings in your Self and also in Me' implies having a complete knowledge of both the absolute and relative fields, of the relationship between them and of God presiding over them both.

Seeing all beings in the Self is the start of the transformation of cosmic consciousness into God-consciousness, and this transformation comes to completion when all beings are seen in God. First, all beings are seen in the Self, and then the Self is seen in God. That is why the Lord says : 'you will see all beings in your Self and also in Me.' The two ideas in one phrase not only describe the two states but also the sequence in which they develop.

In the state of cosmic consciousness, the Self is experienced as separate from activity. This state of life in perfect non-attachment is based on bliss-consciousness, by virtue of which the qualities of the heart have gained their most complete development. Universal love then dominates the heart, which begins to overflow with the love of God; the silent ocean of bliss, the silent ocean of love, begins to rise in waves of devotion. The heart in its state of eternal contentment begins to move, and this begins to draw everything together and eliminate the gulf of separation between the Self and activity. The Union of all diversity in the Self begins to grow. The intensity of this Union cultures man's consciousness, which begins to find everything inseparable from the Self; and this is how, in the most natural manner, the Self, which held Its identity as separate from all activity in the state of cosmic consciousness, finds everything in Itself. This happens on the way to God-consciousness, which in its completeness absorbs even the Self, containing all things.

Beings separate themselves from the supreme Being by means of prakriti, but this veil is removed when life is dominated by the light of knowledge, the light of the awareness of life's Unity in God-consciousness, which establishes eternity in the ephemeral world.

This seeing of everything in God is not restricted to the limitations of vision; it is on the level of life as a whole; it is on that high level of life which corresponds to the Life of God Himself. Fortunate is man that he can rise to the Life of God.

Verse 36

अपि चेदसि पापेभ्यः सर्वेभ्यः पापकृत्तमः ॥
सर्वं ज्ञानप्लवेनैव वृजिनं सन्तरिष्यसि ॥३६॥

Even if you were the most sinful of all
sinners, you would cross over all evil
by the raft of knowledge alone.

Having, in the preceding verse, extolled knowledge for its effectiveness in destroying delusion, the Lord now speaks of its effectiveness in destroying sin. The special value of this knowledge lies in the fact that it eliminates the necessity [55] for gaining knowledge about wrong action. The silent teaching here is that knowledge of the Divine is necessary and not knowledge of action, wrong action and inaction as referred to in verse 17. This becomes all the more apparent in the light of the following verse, where the Lord explains that all actions are burned to ashes by the fire of knowledge.

'You would cross over all evil by the raft of knowledge alone': the word 'alone' indicates that nothing other than knowledge is necessary for a man to 'cross over all evil'. How one goes beyond evil in the state of enlightenment should be properly understood.

It has been said in verse 35 that knowledge takes a man beyond delusion and moulds his life in the oneness of God-consciousness. In this state one's life is on the supreme level of existence, being united with the Lord of all. All the laws of nature respond favourably to such a life, for it is in tune with the almighty invincible

55. See verse 17.

force of Nature, which is working out the evolution of everything in creation. In such a state a man's every thought, word
and action produce a life-supporting influence for himself and
for the whole universe. This is a state of life where no wrong
action is possible. In this state one has crossed over all evil by
the raft of knowledge.

'Knowledge' is irresistible, for no one can resist himself. The
state of knowledge at one level is the state of one's own Self,
transcendental consciousness. At another, it is the state of the
Self in the midst of activity, cosmic consciousness. At yet another,
it is the state of God-consciousness. Enlightenment is irrespective
of anything in the relative field; nothing can be an obstacle [56]
to enlightenment. However dense the darkness and however long
it may have existed, one ray of the rising sun is enough to dispel
the darkness, though it takes time to reach the brightness of
the mid-day sun. Even a momentary flash of transcendental consciousness is enough to dispel the delusion of ignorance, though
it takes time to gain full enlightenment in God-consciousness,
where one has crossed over all evil by the raft of knowledge.
This brings hope even to a man whose life may be full of wrong-
doing.

Sin produces coarseness in the nervous system, preventing it
from functioning normally and obstructing its ability to give rise
to pure consciousness. Such an impaired state of the nervous
system prevents Being from directly influencing the field of
activity.

This is how, by attacking the physical structure of the nervous
system and thus preventing pure consciousness from being lived
in daily life, sin causes sorrow and suffering. Knowledge, in eliminating this possibility, at the same time roots out all possibility
of sorrow and suffering. This verse recommends taking refuge in
knowledge in order to rise above the possibility of any sin in life
and promises redemption even to the worst sinner in the world.

While in this verse the Lord promises release from the bondage
of any wrong action through knowledge, in the following verse
He promises the actual annihilation of all action in the fire of
knowledge.

56. See II, 40.

VERSE 37

अथैधांसि समिद्धोऽग्निर्भस्मसात्कुरुतेऽर्जुन ॥
ज्ञानाग्निः सर्वकर्माणि भस्मसात्कुरुते तथा ॥३७॥

As a blazing fire turns fuel to ashes, so does
the fire of knowledge turn all actions into
ashes.

'Knowledge': that by which all 'sins are cast away' (verse 30),
and that by which 'you will see all beings in your Self and also
in Me' (verse 35). Knowledge means awareness, which in its
nature is pure consciousness; this state of knowledge is devoid
of any activity. That is why the Lord says that 'the fire of knowledge' turns 'all actions into ashes'. When this state [57] has become permanently established in the nature of the mind, the Self
is experienced as separate from activity and its fruits (verse 19).
This is how the fire of knowledge, the fire of cosmic consciousness, turns 'all actions into ashes'. When this state of consciousness, the state of knowledge, reaches its consummation in God-
consciousness, the separation of the Self from activity dissolves
into oneness of the Self and activity. Thus in its supreme state
also the fire of knowledge turns 'all actions into ashes'.

When the Lord said in verse 33 that 'all action. . . . culminates
in knowledge', He explained that once knowledge has been gained
actions have come to an end – they have fulfilled their final purpose. In this situation man has risen to a state of consciousness
above the reach of activity; all activity, mental and physical, is
carried out under the direct influence of the forces of nature,
which are unconcerned with the consciousness of the doer. The
doer finds himself established on a level of life which has nothing
in common with the field of action. In this state, the action that
is performed ceases to be, ceases to engage the consciousness of
the actor. This is what the Lord means when He says that 'the
fire of knowledge' turns 'all actions into ashes'.

57. See verse 36, commentary.

'All actions': this expression has both a qualitative and a quantitative meaning and also includes the range of time, past, present and future. The impressions of past actions, which serve as the seed for future actions, become like roasted seeds, losing their potency. This is how the actions of the past are burnt in 'the fire of knowledge'. Actions performed in the present remain on the level of the mind and senses; they do not touch the depths of the mind anchored to Being, and therefore no deep impressions are created to be stored as the seed for future actions. This is how actions performed in the present are burnt in 'the fire of knowledge', completely eliminating the basis of future actions. This puts an end to the cycle of cause and effect in the field of action; and this in turn puts an end to the cycle of birth and death, bringing eternal freedom to life.

Verse 38

न हि ज्ञानेन सदृशं पवित्रमिह विद्यते ॥
तत्स्वयं योगसंसिद्धः कालेनात्मनि विन्दति ॥३८॥

Truly there is in this world nothing so purifying
as knowledge; he who is perfected in Yoga, of
himself in time finds this within himself.

'Nothing so purifying as knowledge': the work of a purifier is first to purify the different ingredients or components and then, having freed the components from impurities, to present the whole compound in its pure state.

Knowledge is the purifier of life. It purifies life in the sense that it analyses the different aspects of existence and distinguishes and separates the eternal aspects from the transient. It acts like a filter to clear the mud from muddy water. The real nature of life is absolute bliss-consciousness; this crystal water of life has been polluted by becoming mixed with the activities of the three gunas. This has resulted in masking the eternity of life behind its transient and ever-changing aspects.

The pure state of Being is realized by knowing the relative and the absolute components of life. This knowing comes to perfection when the knower gains perfect intimacy with Being and becomes fully aware of the basic activity of life, the activity of the three gunas as separate from Being. Perfect intimacy with Being is gained when the mind gains the transcendental state of consciousness. This is the absolute state of knowledge, which can be described as the state of knowingness. When knowledge becomes perfect, it arrives at the state of knowingness and brings life to perfect purity. In this way knowledge removes ignorance, which is the greatest impurity of life, and takes life out of the cycle of birth, death and suffering.

The superficial aspect of knowledge is knowing and understanding; the real nature of knowledge is the state of knowingness, the state of pure consciousness, or Being. Considering knowledge in this way, we find that transcendental consciousness represents the real nature of knowledge. Another phase of knowledge is where transcendental consciousness co-exists with the activity of the waking state of consciousness. In this state, when transcendental consciousness becomes permanently established in the very nature of the mind, the absolute and relative phases of life begin to be appreciated simultaneously : the Self is experienced as separate from activity. There is yet another state of knowledge in which the separateness of the Self and activity dissolves into the Unity of God-consciousness, which is the most purified state of life, free from any stain of impurity. Such a life in absolute purity represents the supreme state of knowledge, about which the Lord says : 'he who is perfected in Yoga, of himself in time finds this within himself.'

It may be added that only through transcendental meditation, which is the direct way to gain pure consciousness and rise finally to God-consciousness, can absolute purity be lived in daily life.

When the state of Yoga, the state of transcendental consciousness, becomes permanent so that it maintains itself throughout all activity, one has reached the state of cosmic consciousness. Such perfect infusion of the Absolute into relativity takes place by degrees, through the regular practice of going to the Transcendent and coming back to the field of action in daily life. A balanced alternation of meditation and activity results in full realization. One analogy will make this clear : we dip a white cloth in a yellow dye and let it remain in the dye to be coloured for a few minutes. Then we take it out and expose it to the sun till the colour begins to fade. We repeat the same process, again putting the cloth into the sunlight till the colour fades. Similarly, we meditate for about half an hour and follow this by coming out to act in practical life for about ten hours, by which time we begin to feel that we are out of the influence of the morning meditation. We meditate again in the same way and again let the influence fade by coming out into practical life; we keep repeating the process of gaining the state of universal Being in transcendence (samadhi) during meditation and of coming out to regain individuality in the field of relative existence. This allows more and more infusion of Being into the nature of the mind even when it is engaged in activity through the senses.

When the full infusion of Being has been accomplished, then the state of cosmic consciousness has been gained.

The state of cosmic consciousness provides the basis for the development of the state of perfected Yoga in God-consciousness. The development of cosmic consciousness into God-consciousness requires that the separation found to exist between the Self and activity be transformed into a fusion of these two separate identities, resulting in the eternal Unity of God-consciousness.

This transformation of the state of separation takes place by virtue of the most refined activity of all, the activity of devotion to God.

In order to analyse the way in which the act of devotion effects this transformation and produces the state of eternal Unity in God-consciousness, it is necessary to examine closely how, in the state of cosmic consciousness, the Self is experienced as separate from activity; how the eternal silence of transcendental Self-consciousness becomes compatible with the incessant activity of the waking state of consciousness. Those practising transcendental meditation experience a slowing down of the metabolism during the inward stroke of meditation; they experience that the nervous system comes to a state of restful alertness when the mind transcends thought and gains transcendental consciousness. Again, they experience that the nervous system becomes active when it engages itself in the activity of thought or action.

Any state of consciousness is the expression of a corresponding state of the nervous system. Transcendental consciousness corresponds to a certain specific state of the nervous system which transcends any activity and is therefore completely different from that state of the nervous system which corresponds to the waking state of consciousness.

Now, for transcendental consciousness to become permanent and to co-exist with the waking state of consciousness, it is necessary that the two states of the nervous system corresponding to these two states of consciousness should co-exist. This is brought about by the mind gaining alternately transcendental consciousness and the waking state of consciousness, passing from one to the other. This gradual and systematic culture of the physical nervous system creates a physiological situation in which the two states of consciousness exist together simultaneously. It is well known that there exist in the nervous system many autonomous levels of function, between which a system of coordination also exists. In the state of cosmic consciousness, two different levels of organization in the nervous system function simultaneously while maintaining their separate identities. By virtue of this anatomical separation of function, it becomes possible for transcendental consciousness to co-exist with the waking state of consciousness and with the dreaming and sleeping states of consciousness.

In the early stages of the practice of transcendental meditation, these two levels of function in the nervous system are unable to occur at the same time; the function of the one inhibits the function of the other. That is why, at this stage, either transcendental consciousness or the waking state of consciousness is experienced. The practice of the mind in passing from one to another gradually overcomes this physiological inhibition, and the two levels begin to function perfectly at the same time, without inhibiting each other and still maintaining their separate identities. The function of each is independent of the other, and that is why this state of the nervous system corresponds to cosmic consciousness, in which Self-awareness exists as separate from activity. Silence is experienced with activity and yet as separate from it.

In order to develop cosmic consciousness to God-consciousness, the nervous system needs to be cultured further so that these two levels, which function independently, come to function in an integrated manner. This will give rise to a state of consciousness in which the sense of separation between the Self and activity is dissolved, and this duality constituting cosmic consciousness is subsumed into the Unity of God-consciousness.

This integration of functions on the physiological level is brought about by a mental activity of ultimate refinement. In order to define activity of this quality, we must analyse the whole range of activity. The activity of the organs of action is the most gross, the activity of the senses of perception is more refined, the mental activity of thought is finer still, and the activity of feeling and emotion is the finest of all. One could further classify different levels of quality in emotional activity, such as anger, fear, despair, happiness, reverence, service and love.

The activity of devotion comprises the feelings of service, reverence and love, which are the most refined qualities of feeling. It is through the activity of devotion that cosmic consciousness develops into God-consciousness.

When the nervous system is constantly exposed to this most refined activity of devotion, the physiological integration of functions that has been described takes place. And it is the permanent state of this condition of the nervous system that enables a man to live God-consciousness in his daily life; acting in the midst of all sorts of circumstances, fulfilling the purpose of cosmic life, he carries the totality of existence within himself and moves in the Unity of God.

From this it is clear that to develop God-consciousness, which represents the supreme state of knowledge, it is necessary to culture the physical nervous system. This requires regular and sustained practice, which obviously needs time. That is why the Lord says 'in time finds'.

'Within himself': by this expression the Lord wishes it to be clearly understood that the supreme state of knowledge is not gained from outside. It is gained within oneself, when one has lived for some time the perfected state of Yoga in God-consciousness. The element of time indicates here that during the early stages of God-consciousness life is full of such overwhelming experience of Unity in diversity that one lives deeply lost in it. Gradually as time passes one begins to appreciate this Unity in terms of other things and activities in the world. It is then that one has realized God, that one has the knowledge of God. Thus it becomes clear why the Lord speaks of the necessity for time in gaining supreme knowledge.

VERSE 39

श्रद्धावांल्लभते ज्ञानं तत्परः संयतेन्द्रियः ॥
ज्ञानं लब्ध्वा परां शान्तिमचिरेणाधिगच्छति ॥३६॥

He gains knowledge who is possessed of
faith, is active of purpose and has subdued
the senses. Having gained knowledge,
swiftly he comes to the supreme peace.

'Knowledge': awareness of Unity in the midst of the diversity of life. When this awareness has become complete, it is said to be God-consciousness.

To rise from the waking state of consciousness to God-consciousness, one has to pass through the states of transcendental consciousness and cosmic consciousness. In the sequence of development, one state leads to another in the order of waking, transcendental, cosmic and God-consciousness. They are as different one from another as spectacles of different colours through which the same view looks different. When the same object is cognized in different states of consciousness, its values are differently appreciated. Life is appreciated differently at each different level of consciousness.

As the mind passes through all these states, it has to undergo various new experiences which, in the absence of faith, can easily be misunderstood at any step. That is why the Lord names faith as a prerequisite to knowledge.

There are three fields of faith: faith in oneself, faith in the teacher and faith in God. Faith in oneself is necessary so that one does not begin to doubt one's own experience. Faith in the teacher enables one to accept the fundamentals of the teaching; if in the absence of faith the basic principles of the teaching are rejected, one can neither derive any benefit from it nor verify its truth, since the truth of the teaching can be verified only by personal experience which arises from the practice given by the teacher. Faith in God protects man's heart and mind and ensures that steady progress which is so important in the life of a seeker.

Faith provides an anchor in life, not only for the seeker of Truth but for any man. It is needed for any accomplishment in life; for greater accomplishment it is needed in greater measure; for ultimate fulfilment in God-consciousness the greatest faith is needed.

Meditation is a process which provides increasing charm at every step on the way to the Transcendent. The experience of this charm causes faith to grow. Moreover, the regular practice of meditation brings the great blessings of harmony and joy to life; this too helps the heart and mind to grow in faith and keeps a man 'active of purpose' on the path to enlightenment, and thus stability is gained on the way. The activity of the senses also becomes balanced and natural. Thus, when a man begins the practice of transcendental meditation, he fulfils the conditions necessary for enlightenment.

The first ray of the rising sun is enough to dispel the darkness of the night, and yet it takes some time for the sun to become fully risen. Through meditation, the mind reaches transcendental consciousness quickly and is enlightened by the first ray of the Divine; yet to allow this transcendental divine consciousness to shine forth through all circumstances, through waking, dreaming and dreamless sleep, regular practice of meditation is absolutely essential.

Meditation takes the mind to transcendental Self-consciousness, and a natural and balanced activity infuses the transcendental divine nature into the mind, where it is not lost even when the mind is engaged in the field of activity. In this way, Self-consciousness grows to cosmic consciousness – Atmananda to Brahmananda, savikalpa samadhi to nirvikalpa – and eventually this state of Yoga, cosmic consciousness, attains its fulfilment in

God-consciousness; the first ray of enlightenment reaches its full glory.

This verse emphasizes the need for a man to be 'active of purpose' and to have a natural balanced activity of the senses and the mind in addition to faith. All these, combining harmoniously, help to produce devotion, that highest quality in a seeker by which he accomplishes the final stage of his evolution. These taken together create a situation for the unfolding of the supreme Reality in its all-embracing nature, raising the limited status of the individual to the unbounded status of cosmic consciousness and eventually to that Unity of life in God-consciousness which eternally satisfies the mind and heart. Having gained this, a man in time gains knowledge,[58] through which he becomes free from any doubt or delusion.[59] This is that state of 'supreme peace' where the heart rests in eternal contentment and the mind is filled with the Unity of life, where there is no trace of duality and therefore peace is abiding.

VERSE 40

अज्ञश्चाश्रद्दधानश्च संशयात्मा विनश्यति ।
नायं लोकोऽस्ति न परो न सुखं संशयात्मनः ॥४०॥

But the man who is without knowledge,
without faith and of a doubting
nature perishes. For the doubting
mind there is neither this world
nor another nor any happiness.

The sequence of expressions is highly important in giving insight into the teaching. Lack of knowledge is the basis of lack of faith, which in turn is the basis of 'a doubting nature'. Therefore it is lack of knowledge, or the state of ignorance, which is at the root of all failure in material advancement and spiritual development. Ignorance is the source of all weakness and suffering in life. The teaching is that one must cast off ignorance and rise to the state

58. See verse 38.   59. See verse 35.

of knowledge in order to win all happiness and progress in this
world and hereafter.

In view of what has been said about the preceding verse, the
significance of this verse is obvious. Yet one must remember that
it is the ignorant who become enlightened, for meditation is a
process which reveals Reality to the ignorant. One thing may be
added here : no man could ever be completely devoid of faith and
completely full of doubt, and no man could be completely ignorant of Reality. Moreover, the practice of transcendental meditation
is such that it can be started from whatever level of faith a man
may have, for it brings faith to the faithless and dispels the doubts
in the mind of the sceptic by providing direct experience of
Reality.

The previous verse demanded faith for the sake of gaining
knowledge. This verse says that lack of faith results from ignorance. This apparent contradiction establishes the principle that
faith and knowledge are interdependent from the most elementary
to the most advanced stage, each deriving inspiration from the
other while at the same time helping the other's growth.

VERSE 41

योगसंन्यस्तकर्माणं ज्ञानसंछिन्नसंशयम् ।।
आत्मवन्तं न कर्माणि निबध्नन्ति धनञ्जय ।।४१।।

He who has renounced action by virtue of Yoga,
O winner of wealth, whose doubts are rent asunder
by knowledge, who is possessed of the Self, him
actions do not bind.

'He who has renounced action by virtue of Yoga': 'he who in
action sees inaction' (18); 'whose every undertaking is free from
desire' (19); 'having cast off attachment to the fruit of action'
(20); 'Expecting nothing' (21); 'satisfied with whatever comes
unasked' (22); 'freed from attachment, liberated ... his action is
entirely dissolved' (23).

Here Yoga means Karma Yoga. When, by the practice of Karma

Yoga – the practice of transcendental meditation[60] supplemented by activity – one begins to live Being together with activity, one experiences It as separate from activity, and this experience of separation of one's Self from activity is called renunciation. Renunciation is thus gained automatically through the practice of Yoga. It may be noted that this state of renunciation is not limited to the mental level of thinking or the intellectual level of understanding: it is on the level of Being, on the level of life itself. It is a living reality for the realized man in cosmic consciousness.

'Whose doubts are rent asunder by knowledge': 'he ... is wise among men ... he is united' (18); 'whose action is burnt up in the fire of knowledge' (19); 'ever contented' (20); 'his heart and mind disciplined' (21); 'balanced in success and failure' (22); 'whose mind is established in wisdom' (23); 'so does the fire of knowledge turn all actions into ashes' (37).

Having stated that renunciation is achieved through the practice of Karma Yoga, the Lord here clarifies a very practical point on the path of enlightenment. As the practice of Karma Yoga advances, one begins to feel one's Self as separate from activity. This experience brings with it a feeling of confusion. One finds oneself active and yet inwardly one feels somewhat aloof from activity. Doubts begin to arise in the mind, and the intellect seeks for some explanation of the situation. Right understanding about the ultimate Reality is provided by the teaching of the preceding forty verses; when a man attains cosmic consciousness, the knowledge that Being is independent and separate from activity confirms that his experience is valid. It is this knowledge that removes all doubt about the nature of Reality. Without proper understanding, even the direct experience of eternal freedom may be found to create confusion and fear. The glory of knowledge is extolled here.

'Possessed of the Self': this is said of him 'who has renounced action by virtue of Yoga' and 'whose doubts are rent asunder by knowledge'. Someone who experiences himself as uninvolved with activity but has no clear understanding of this experience remains confused by it; in this state he fails to live Being fully, fails to

60. See II, 45.

possess the Self in Its full glory and grace. 'Possessed of the Self'
indicates fixity in the Self for all time, the state of cosmic consciousness. Of such a man the Lord says: 'him actions do not
bind'; because he is no more involved with actions, he ceases to
identify himself with his activity. He has identified himself with
eternal Being, he is 'possessed of the Self'.

Various implications of the expression 'possessed of the Self'
have been explained in previous verses of this chapter: 'he has
accomplished all action' (18); 'him the knowers of Reality call
wise' (19); 'depending on nothing' (20); 'performing action by
the body alone' (21); 'balanced in success and failure' (22); 'who
acts for the sake of yagya' (23).

VERSE 42

तस्माद्ज्ञानसंभूतं हृत्स्थं ज्ञानासिनात्मनः ॥
छित्त्वैनं संशयं योगमातिष्ठोत्तिष्ठ भारत ॥४२॥

Therefore, having cut asunder with the sword
of knowledge this doubt of yours born of
ignorance and rooted in the heart, resort
to Yoga. Stand up, O Bharata!

The state of Union is full even in transcendental consciousness.
But it is not considered to be the mature state of Union unless
transcendental consciousness has become permanent in the state
of cosmic consciousness. Thus we find that the Union gained in
the state of transcendental consciousness reaches maturity in cosmic consciousness, which in turn finds fulfilment in God-consciousness.

'Yoga' here again means Karma Yoga, which requires a man to
gain transcendental consciousness and engage in activity. When
samadhi, the state of Yoga, begins to be experienced, nothing
more need be done for full enlightenment – for cosmic consciousness, or jivan-mukti – except regular practice of samadhi, alternating with normal activity in practical life. For this reason the
Lord urges Arjuna to 'resort to Yoga', to gain transcendental
consciousness and be engaged in action. This, He says, will free

Arjuna from all doubts. The Lord brings home to him that all misery is due to ignorance of the state of separation of Being from activity.

'Sword of knowledge': as the sharp edge of a sword is capable of cutting whatever it meets, so the state of knowledge, the awareness of Being as separate from activity, cuts asunder all doubts about the true nature of life and activity. Until this knowledge dawns, doubts are certain to remain. All doubts are due to 'ignorance' of this Reality, says the Lord.

'Born of ignorance and rooted in the heart': the doubt born of ignorance should belong to the mind, but the Lord says: 'rooted in the heart'. The heart is concerned with experience and the mind with understanding. When the Lord speaks of doubt as 'rooted in the heart', He means that even though the doubt is in the mind, it has its roots in the heart, which is devoid of the experience of Being and of the experience of Being as separate from activity.

The teaching is that it is necessary to experience Being and to understand clearly the separateness of Being from activity; thus enlightened, one should perform one's duty.

It should be stressed that the state of renunciation is not exclusive to either Karma Yoga or Sankhya. It is a state that develops on both these paths. Whether one is following Karma Yoga, the practice of transcendental meditation supplemented by physical activity, or the path of Sankhya, the practice of transcendental meditation supplemented by the mental activity of contemplation, one is sure to arrive at the experience of the state of renunciation.

Here is the essence of the teaching of this chapter: remove all doubts about Reality by means of the knowledge of Sankhya, and engage yourself in the practice of Karma Yoga.

Thus, in the Upanishad of the glorious
Bhagavad-Gita, in the Science of the Absolute,
in the Scripture of Yoga, in the dialogue
between Lord Krishna and Arjuna, ends the
fourth chapter, entitled: The Yoga of
Knowledge of Renunciation of Action.

CHAPTER V

A Vision of the Teaching in Chapter V

Verses 1–3. Liberation is gained both through action and renunciation; but the path of action is superior, even though renunciation easily brings liberation from bondage.

Verses 4–10. The two paths are not considered separate by the wise. The seer of Truth sees them both as one; for renunciation is difficult to attain without Union with the Divine, which also brings freedom from the bondage of action.

Verses 11–13. Man established in Divine Union performs actions on the levels of the senses, mind and intellect for the purification of his soul. Remaining in bliss within himself, he is uninvolved with action and its fruits.

Verses 14–16. In reality, authorship of action does not belong to the doer. All action is performed by the force of nature. Under the spell of ignorance, the doer assumes authorship of action and becomes bound to its fruits. Knowledge brings the light of Truth and dispels the darkness of ignorance.

Verses 17–21. Established in that knowledge, wholly purified, in that state of profound equanimity, a man lives eternal freedom in the perpetual bliss of Divine Union.

Verses 22, 23. The joys of the senses are sources of sorrow; the enlightened man does not delight in them. The ability to resist the excitement of desire and anger is the criterion of a man in Union.

Verse 24. Delighted in the Self, freed from desire and anger, man finds abiding freedom in cosmic consciousness and rises to eternal peace in God-consciousness.

Verses 25–9. The principle of renunciation comprehends the same height of human perfection as is achieved by the path of action.

In the second chapter Lord Krishna enlightened Arjuna on the understanding of Sankhya and Yoga so that he might be clear about the perishable and imperishable aspects of life and thereby, casting off his ignorance about the nature of life and its relationship with the field of action, realize his true divine nature in eternal freedom.

The Lord's inspiring words created in Arjuna's mind an urge to follow them. The third chapter brought to light the practice of Karma Yoga, action in the state of Union with the Divine, or action in order to make this Divine Union permanent, thus raising the dignity of both the doer and the action.

Continuing the teaching in the fourth chapter, Lord Krishna gave Arjuna a deeper understanding of the relationship of one's self with the field of action, making clear to him the state of separation that exists naturally between the inner Being and the outer phase of life in activity. This gave him insight into the reality of life and activity, and revealed to him that the inner Being is completely independent of action. Arjuna then perceived that activity does not belong to what life essentially is – Being in eternal freedom.

The fourth chapter has been called 'The Yoga of Knowledge of Renunciation of Action'. The title is significant. It tells us that according to this teaching Yoga, or Union, is gained through the knowledge of renunciation, through the knowledge of the Self as completely detached from activity. It establishes that the state of renunciation is natural on the levels both of cosmic and of individual life: on the cosmic level God remains uninvolved with the activities of creation and evolution; on the level of individual life the Self remains uninvolved with activity. A natural state of renunciation is the true basis of all life, and proper knowledge of it brings freedom from bondage. This is the essential teaching of the fourth chapter.

It might seem that the fourth chapter was challenging the doctrine of Karma Yoga taught in the third. But in fact this is not so. If the chapter had proclaimed enlightenment through renunciation of action, then it would have been contrary to the principle of Karma Yoga. But it proclaims enlightenment through the *knowledge* of renunciation of action. This makes it clear that the principle of renunciation is only to be understood; it is not to be practised. The state of renunciation is produced through Karma Yoga (IV, 41); there is no way of *practising* renunciation. Knowledge of renunciation is extolled here, not the practice of renunciation.

When we state that renunciation is not to be practised we are aware of the recluse way of life. But the renunciation of the recluse is renunciation of external things and is relevant only to a particular way of living; it is not in itself a way to God. It is not the practice of renunciation but the knowledge of it that helps on the way to God.

The knowledge of renunciation expounded in the fourth chapter is necessary for those on the path of Karma Yoga as well as for those on the path of Sankhya. The state of renunciation is experienced on both paths, and unless the intellect is clear about the significance of this experience, doubts will remain and will impede further progress.

Karma Yoga and Sankhya each start on the common ground of transcendental meditation. This leads directly to transcendental Self-consciousness, where even the most refined field of thought has been renounced and the Self stands alone in Its pure state of Being (verse 2). This is a state of complete renunciation, but it is reached only during meditation; it is not permanent. Through the regular and continued practice of meditation, alternating with activity – mental activity on the path of Sankhya and physical activity on the path of Karma Yoga – transcendental Self-consciousness develops into cosmic consciousness, wherein one experiences the Self as separate from activity and lives the natural state of renunciation in daily life. The state of renunciation has become permanent. This state of cosmic consciousness develops further so that the separation between the Self and activity, which already presented the complete state of renunciation, dissolves into the ultimate Unity of God-consciousness. The state in which this separation has been resolved would seem to be beyond the range of renunciation, but it is, in fact, renunciation in its full perfection. Nothing now remains except pure life. The fourth chapter brings out the principle of renunciation in each of these states: transcendental consciousness, cosmic consciousness and God-consciousness.

The knowledge given in that chapter has enriched the teachings about the paths of Sankhya and Karma Yoga given in the second and third chapters. It has silently established the state of renunciation as common ground, a common milestone and the common goal on both paths. The fifth chapter, taking advantage of the knowledge given in the fourth, explicitly places Sankhya and Karma Yoga together, presenting them as equally useful in bringing eternal liberation in the midst of every activity.

It establishes a philosophy of Yoga, or Divine Union, through renunciation of action. This might be expected to contradict the philosophy of Yoga through action, Karma Yoga. But the Lord's theme is so marvellous that, far from offering any sense of contradiction with Karma Yoga, it succeeds in drawing together Karma Yoga and Sankhya. Gloriously, it places them both on the same level of renunciation and, by showing the principles of these two paths to be in close proximity, it uses them both together to evolve a new philosophy of Yoga: the Yoga of renunciation.

Renunciation as such is plainly a state of loss. Yoga of renunciation thus means Yoga of loss: Union through loss. It is the glory of the Lord's discourse that loss becomes a means to perfection – renunciation comes forward to save life and bring fulfilment to it.

Without the philosophy of renunciation, the philosophy of action will always remain incomplete, because the renunciation of action lies at the opposite extreme to the performance of action. Just as separation contrasts with Union, so renunciation of action contrasts with the Yoga of action. Unless these two extremes, Union and renunciation, are taken into account the philosophy will be incomplete.

The philosophy of renunciation is not merely complementary to the philosophy of action, nor just an essential part of that philosophy. Indeed, it can be considered as a complete philosophy of action in itself. The philosophy of renunciation is so complete that by remaining strictly within the boundaries of renunciation, and without having to consider the field of action at all, it is capable of upholding the philosophy of action. The whole philosophy of Karma Yoga can be explained through this philosophy of renunciation, because the basis of Karma Yoga is transcendental consciousness. And as the way to transcendental consciousness is through the withdrawal of the mind from the field of outside experience, it does not matter whether we consider the process of gaining transcendental consciousness in terms of activity towards the Transcendent or in terms of activity away from the field of outside experience. The first would express the principle in terms of Karma Yoga, the second in terms of renunciation. But one should not lose sight of the fact that renunciation does not offer any practice. The practical aspect of the philosophy of renunciation is to be found in the techniques of Sankhya and Karma Yoga. The doctrine of renunciation does not provide an independent practice, and renunciation is therefore not a path in itself – it presents a theory based on the practices of other paths.

The principle of action having been brought out in Chapter III, and knowledge of renunciation in Chapter IV, Chapter V now expounds the compatibility of these two. The marvel is that it does so from the standpoint of renunciation, which is abstract, rather than from that of action, which is concrete. While combining the two extremes of action and renunciation, it combines the two different paths of Yoga and Sankhya, and thus it gives expression to a complete philosophy of the integrated life. Here is a call to every man: Come by any path, and liberation will be yours.

This is what makes the Bhagavad-Gita the Scripture of Divine Union. With ease it proclaims both the Yoga of action and the Yoga of renunciation of action. This is the perfection of the discourse from the lips of the Yogishvara, Krishna, the Lord of the Yogis of all time.

The most extreme contradictions are harmonized and unified

in this chapter. It presents the state of eternal freedom in divine consciousness on the level of action based on renunciation. Moreover, it establishes the necessity of gaining divine consciousness for the sake of successful activity in daily life, and at the same time emphazises the need for activity to gain divine consciousness. By bringing into harmony the material and spiritual aspects of life, it opens a way both to success and to salvation for man, whether householder or recluse, in any age. It enables any man to glorify his world by the light of the Divine – and also to attain divine freedom in a most natural way through the daily activity of life.

Inexhaustible wisdom is contained in the twenty-nine verses of this chapter. It stands as a beacon not only for those who are miserable and confused, but also for seekers, and even for those who are well advanced on the path.

VERSE 1

अर्जुन उवाच ।

संन्यासं कर्मणां कृष्ण पुनर्योगं च शंससि ॥
यच्छ्रेय एतयोरेकं तन्मे ब्रूहि सुनिश्चितम् ॥१॥

Arjuna said:
Thou praisest, O Krishna, renunciation
of action and Yoga (of action) at the
same time. Tell me decisively which is the
better of these two.

Here is the proof of what the Lord has said: 'Even the wise are bewildered' [1] about the problem of action and inaction. Through all his utterances so far, Arjuna has shown himself to be wise, to have great foresight and to have knowledge of dharma.[2] He will not act until he is sure of all the implications of his action.

This is the third question,[3] in the same spirit, that Arjuna has asked about the best course of action to follow for his own

1. See IV, 16.   2. See I, 23, 31, 36, 39–45.   3. See II, 7; III, 2.

good and that of others. These repeated questions arise from his sincere desire to know the Truth; they are in keeping with a character that is without blemish and spring naturally from the state of one who seeks the Truth[4] and has surrendered himself to his master.[5]

If it had not been for these questions of Arjuna's, the great wisdom of this chapter and the next would not have been revealed, and the discourse of the Lord would not have been complete. For this reason those who seek the Truth will always be indebted to Arjuna. Commentators who have portrayed him as confused have missed the depth of his understanding. Arjuna asks profound questions again and again because, being a practical man of great intelligence, he does not wish to take anything for granted. He wants every detail of the plan to come from the Lord, because he knows that any small mistake on his part will prejudice the destinies of many generations to come.

The Lord has said: 'unfathomable is the course of action.'[6] When such is the nature of action, there can be numberless flaws in any exposition of it, there can be an unlimited number of viewpoints about any one situation. That is why, to resolve the riddle of action for all time, the Lord told Arjuna: 'I shall expound to you that action knowing which you will be freed from evil.'[7] He then went on to expound that eternal wisdom[8] which presents the solution to all problems of action and behaviour for all men of every age.

The Lord advocates the performance of action from that level of life where the mind is established in a state of freedom. This state can be lived without difficulty, but to describe it adequately in words is difficult. That is why the Lord asked Arjuna to 'be without the three gunas'.[9] He would then actually come to experience the state of non-attachment described to him by the teaching of Sankhya.[10] The aspirant can be shown the path to follow, but it is hard to give him a definite picture of that state because it lies in the field which transcends all speech.

Because the very nature of action in freedom includes the

4. See IV, 34.   5. See II, 7.   6. See IV, 17.
7. See IV, 16.   8. See IV, 17–42.   9. See II, 45.
10. See II, 11–38.

states of action, inaction and renunciation of action simultaneously, the Lord, in His exposition, has to speak sometimes in terms
of action and sometimes in terms of inaction – sometimes of the
Yoga of action and sometimes of the renunciation of action. It
is the need to clarify these opposing statements that has given
rise to Arjuna's present question. It does not spring from any
inadequacy of his understanding.

The immediate reason for the question can be found in two
expressions at the end of the fourth chapter : 'renounced action
by virtue of Yoga' (verse 41) and 'resort to Yoga' (verse 42). The
first presents Yoga as a means to renunciation, the second emphasizes the practice of Yoga after knowledge of renunciation has
been gained. In one statement Yoga is the means and renunciation
the goal; in the other renunciation is the means and Yoga the
goal. Arjuna, noticing this apparent contradiction, raises the
question which opens this chapter. His question is responsible
for the flow of great wisdom from the Lord and not only presents
the essence of the Lord's teaching so far, but also gives added
momentum to the theme of the Lord's discourse.

VERSE 2

श्रीभगवानुवाच
संन्यासः कर्मयोगश्च निःश्रेयसकरावुभौ ।।
तयोस्तु कर्मसंन्यासात्कर्मयोगो विशिष्यते ।।२।।

The Blessed Lord said:
Both renunciation and the Yoga of action
lead to the supreme good. But of the two,
the Yoga of action is superior to the
renunciation of action.

'The renunciation of action' (Sanyasa) may be interpreted in four
ways. According to the first and more common understanding, a
man detaches himself from all the activity of worldly life. According to the second, he takes to the practice of transcendental medi-

tation [11] in order to renounce even the most refined state of thought and thus reach Self-consciousness. This is the whole concern of Sanyasa – the renunciation of everything in the field of relativity and detachment from all aspects of life, gross and subtle. According to the third, entertaining activity after gaining transcendental consciousness, he rises to cosmic consciousness, in which he experiences the Self as completely separate from activity. Thus he attains a state of life in perfect renunciation. According to the fourth, entertaining the activity of the finest quality, devotion, he rises to God-consciousness, where the state of renunciation experienced in cosmic consciousness as separation of the Self from activity is transformed into a living link to unite the Self and activity. The two merge in the Unity of God-consciousness.[12]

'The Yoga of action' has been defined in the third chapter.[13] When the mind has retired from the field of activity and has reached the state of transcendental Self-consciousness, it comes back again into the field of activity. As the mind returns, the Self-consciousness infused into its nature enables the transcendental absolute Being to become harmonized with the field of activity. This bringing of the Divine into the world is the purpose of Karma Yoga. It reaches maturity in the state of cosmic consciousness and finds its fulfilment in God-consciousness.

In the state of cosmic consciousness the Self is realized as separate from activity, and this makes renunciation a living reality of daily life, bringing the blessings of eternal freedom. Thus we find that Sanyasa and Karma Yoga run parallel. The Lord says: 'of the two, the Yoga of action is superior to the renunciation of action', because the process of renunciation is one of losing and the process of Yoga, or Union, is one of gaining; and gain is more acceptable to the mind than loss, all the more so when, in the process of Union, the mind experiences increasing charm at every moment. Thus it is clear that to engage in the process of gaining Divine Union is easier for the mind than to engage in the process of renunciation of the world. This is what makes Karma Yoga superior to Sanyasa. Moreover, the process of Karma Yoga automatically gives rise to the state of renunciation. When the mind proceeds towards the Transcendent, the state of Divine

11. See II, 45.   12. See IV, 38.   13. See III, 3, 7, commentaries.

Union, it automatically recedes from the world, simultaneously producing the state of renunciation. Considered from this point of view, Karma Yoga is found to be the cause of renunciation. This in itself is a sufficient reason for the Lord to say that 'the Yoga of action is superior to the renunciation of action' even though both, running parallel and simultaneously, 'lead to the supreme good'.

The following verse considers the real sanyasi, the man who is established in the state of renunciation.

VERSE 3

ज्ञेयः स नित्यसंन्यासी यो न द्वेष्टि न कांक्षति ॥
निर्द्वन्द्वो हि महाबाहो सुखं बन्धात्प्रमुच्यते ॥३॥

*Know him to be ever a man of renunciation who
neither hates nor desires; free from the pairs
of opposites, he is easily released from
bondage, O mighty-armed.*

In this verse, the Lord brings out the essential qualities of 'a man of renunciation', a sanyasi. He is free from desire while at the same time he rejects nothing; he takes life easily as it comes, creating no tensions. His life flows freely in harmony with the laws of nature governed by the Cosmic Law.[14]

Such a carefree state of life in freedom is only possible when a man is contented. And contentment is possible only when the mind is established in bliss-consciousness, the state of the transcendental Absolute, because in the relative field there is no happiness so intense that it could finally satisfy the thirst of the mind for joy.

Having gained this state of transcendental consciousness permanently, a man is freed from bondage and lives a life in the eternal freedom of cosmic consciousness. In this state he lives eternal Being as completely separated from the field of activity.

14. See Appendix.

This is the state of perfect detachment, or Sanyasa, described by the Lord as freedom 'from the pairs of opposites'. Such freedom prevails in transcendental consciousness, cosmic consciousness and God-consciousness.

The word 'easily' is of great significance. Freedom from bondage is 'easily' gained by rising above 'the pairs of opposites' to the state of Being, by rising to that state of Sanyasa, that state of separation which naturally exists between Being and activity.

The state of freedom from bondage can be reached either through the wisdom of Sankhya or the practice of Yoga, as shown in the following verse.

VERSE 4

सांख्ययोगौ पृथग्बालाः प्रवदन्ति न पण्डिताः ।।
एकमप्यास्थितः सम्यगुभयोर्विन्दते फलम् ।।४।।

*The ignorant, and not the wise, speak of the
path of knowledge (Sankhya) and the path of
action (Yoga) as different. He who is properly
established even in one gains the fruit of both.*

The teaching of Sankhya brings to light the separation that exists between the imperishable and perishable aspects of life, between Being and activity. The practice of Yoga, by bringing Being into direct experience, also brings to light the separation that exists between Being and activity. This is how Sankhya and Yoga both lead to freedom from bondage.

The phrase 'properly established' is of importance for a true understanding of the teaching of this verse. In order to be 'properly established' in the teaching of Sankhya or Yoga, both understanding and experience are of vital importance. Sankhya and Yoga are each sufficient in themselves to bring liberation. Therefore it does not matter whether the one or the other is given first importance.

'The wise' are those who have risen to the state of freedom.

They do not see Sankhya and Yoga as different, not only because both lead to the same goal, but also because the main feature of both is the same practice of transcendental meditation. The only difference is that on the path of Karma Yoga transcendental meditation alternates with activity on the level of the senses and on the path of Sankhya with mental activity. But for this small difference Sankhya and Yoga are the same. That is why the wise do not look upon them as different.[15]

This verse and the next present the whole purpose of the fifth chapter, which is to place Yoga and Sankhya on the same footing as far as their results are concerned.

VERSE 5

यत्सांख्यैः प्राप्यते स्थानं तद्योगैरपि गम्यते ॥
एकं सांख्यं च योगं च यः पश्यति स पश्यति ॥५॥

The state attained by men on the path of
knowledge is also reached by those on the
path of action. He who sees Sankhya and Yoga to
be one, verily he sees.

This is the verse that promises liberation for both the ways of life, that of a householder and that of a recluse. It establishes the basic unity of Sankhya and Yoga. Eternal liberation is their common goal, and the seer of Truth sees it to be so.

It is evident that the path of Sankhya does not apply to the life of the householder and that Karma Yoga does. But Lord Krishna says here that the difference between the two paths is resolved when the goal is reached. Only an undeveloped intellect dwells on the differences between them. The wise man sets out upon one or the other and reaches the goal. He does not waste his time and energy in a scrutiny of distinctions.

The verse shows that Sankhya and Yoga are designed to satisfy different kinds of people. But so far as their goal is concerned, they are the same.

15. See verse 5 and VI, 2.

This understanding of the matter finds further justification in verses 24 and 25, which describe the attainment of eternal liberation through Yoga and Sankhya respectively, and in verse 21, which speaks of the attainment of immeasurable happiness through both paths.

Furthermore, by studying the details of the path of knowledge and that of action one finds that even the paths themselves are basically the same. The single process of transcendental meditation brings fulfilment to both.[16] That is why 'he who sees Sankhya and Yoga to be one, verily he sees'.

The two paths start from and proceed on the common ground of transcendental meditation, and as they advance both give rise to the same experience of renunciation in cosmic consciousness. But having reached a common milestone in this direct realization of the separateness of Being from activity, they still have not attained their final goal. For complete fulfilment they must proceed further to merge in one goal, in the great Unity in God-consciousness.

Chapter V dwells mainly on the experience of renunciation common to both paths, Chapter VI will give details of their common practice of transcendental meditation, and Chapters VII to XII will unfold the nature of their ultimate goal – God-consciousness – as well as the path to it.

VERSE 6

संन्यासस्तु महाबाहो दुःखमाप्तुमयोगतः ॥
योगयुक्तो मुनिर्ब्रह्म न चिरेणाधिगच्छति ॥६॥

*Renunciation is indeed hard to attain
without Yoga, O mighty-armed. The sage
who is intent on Yoga comes to Brahman
without long delay.*

This verse makes it quite clear that the state of renunciation 'is indeed hard to attain', that the separateness of Being from activity

16. See III, 28, commentary.

is hard to realize, unless the mind is firmly established in Being.

Here the word Yoga does not mean either Karma Yoga or the practice of gaining transcendental consciousness;[17] it means the state of Union itself, transcendental consciousness.

The state of Brahman, which is the fullness of the relative and the Absolute both together, is best appreciated on the level of Union made permanent, transcendental consciousness made permanent. This state of cosmic consciousness gives the experience of Sanyasa, the separateness of the Self from activity; the separateness of the relative and the Absolute here becomes a living reality.

The Lord is referring to this process of making the Union permanent when He says: 'without long delay'. This is because the state of Union, or transcendental consciousness, being blissful in its nature, is always inviting to the mind. The mind arrives at it drawn by its own nature, which is always to want to enjoy more. Thus the attainment of Union becomes easy, without resistance.[18]

The natural process of gaining this state need only be alternated with the natural activity of daily life to bring it to permanency. Thus it is clear that the whole process is a natural one; that is why it does not take a long time.

A man who has attained cosmic consciousness is always established in the Self, even while engaged in activity. This state of consciousness is the mature state of Sanyasa, a state of complete non-attachment of the Self with activity, even while activity continues in the relative field of life. Such complete non-attachment is not possible unless the mind is established in eternal contentment. The constant practice of gaining Yoga, or Union with divine consciousness, brings the mind to the state which gives eternal contentment, thereby establishing a natural state of Sanyasa or renunciation.

With growth towards cosmic consciousness, contentment grows, and with the growth of inner contentment, appreciation of the separation between Being and activity increases until the mind becomes rooted in the nature of Being. It has then achieved cosmic consciousness. By showing the difficulty of attaining renunciation without Yoga, the Lord indicates the simplicity of rising

17. See II, 40, 45.   18. See II, 40.

to a state where Yoga and Sanyasa will become the daily habit of life.

This verse sings the glory of Union. It is the basis of true renunciation and gives rise to the state of Brahman in man's daily life.

The next verse shows how, by means of this Union, a man rises above the binding influence of action and lives a life of eternal freedom.

VERSE 7

योगयुक्तो विशुद्धात्मा विजितात्मा जितेन्द्रियः ॥
सर्वभूतात्मभूतात्मा कुर्वन्नपि न लिप्यते ॥७॥

Intent on Yoga, pure of spirit,
he who has fully mastered himself
and has conquered the senses, whose
self has become the Self of all beings,
he is not involved even while he acts.

Here, as in the previous verse, the word Yoga does not mean either Karma Yoga or the practice of transcending; it is used in the sense of Unity of the mind with Being.

'Intent on Yoga': one who is never out of the Self, whether waking, dreaming or in the state of deep sleep. Such a man is established in himself, and no experience of relativity is able to overshadow his status of absolute Being.

'Pure of spirit': one who has reached the state of Being, absolute consciousness, which is ever the same in its eternal purity, and who has established that state in the very nature of his mind. Action is a veil which hides this essential nature of the Self. Meditation is a process of diving through all the subtle levels of activity; when the subtlest level is transcended, the mind gains the state of pure Being. When the mind, being That, comes out into the field of activity, then the Self is said to shine forth in Its purity. When, through constant practice, complete integration of the Self with the mind is achieved, the pure status of Being gained by the mind is not in any way overshadowed even though the mind occupies itself with activity in the relative field. This is the state of cosmic consciousness, where the Self has separated Itself completely from the field of activity. In this state, where absolute Being and the relative world of activity are lived simultaneously, the self is said to have been permanently freed from all stain; it has achieved absolute purity.

'He who has fully mastered himself.' Self has two connotations : lower self and higher Self. The lower self is that aspect of the personality which deals only with the relative aspect of existence. It comprises the mind that thinks, the intellect that decides, the ego that experiences. This lower self functions only in the relative states of existence – waking, dreaming and deep sleep. Remaining always within the field of relativity, it has no chance of experiencing the real freedom of absolute Being. That is why it is in the sphere of bondage. The higher Self is that aspect of the personality which never changes, absolute Being, which is the very basis of the entire field of relativity, including the lower self.

A man who wants to master himself has to master the lower self first and then the higher Self. Mastering the lower self means taking the mind (mind, intellect, ego) from the gross fields of existence to the subtler fields, until the subtlest field of relative existence is transcended and transcendental absolute unmanifested Being is reached in divine consciousness. This robs the lower self of its individuality bound by time, space and causation and sets it free in the state of universal existence.

When the lower self has been mastered by the higher Self in this way and the higher Self has accepted it completely, then the two become one. And then a state develops in which each is found intimately within the realm of the other in complete cohesion of existence. When the divine consciousness of transcendental absolute Being is found in co-existence with the mind in relative existence, in the field of time, space and causation, then the mastery of the higher Self is accomplished. The Absolute has been as it were brought out from the transcendental field of existence to serve and support the field of relativity. The never-changing is brought into the life of the ever-changing. The relative states of existence – waking, dreaming and sleeping – are infused with the absolute state of Being. Eternal freedom has become infused into the field of bondage. The Unity of the divine nature is lived in the multiplicity of diversified creation. This enables a man to live a life of eternal freedom in a world of transitory existence. Thus the master of the Self, enjoying the whole field of relativity, lives the life of absolute Being in divine consciousness.

It is interesting to discover how the process of transcendental meditation succeeds in mastering both the self and the Self. The inward stroke of meditation takes one to a state where the mind, freed from individuality, surrenders itself to the higher Self. This is the mastery of the lower self. The outward stroke of meditation brings the mind out infused with Being. As a result of constant practice, the mind then lives absolute Being in all fields of relative life. This is mastery of the higher Self.

Thus mastery of the self and of the Self is accomplished by means of the inward and outward strokes of a single technique of transcendental meditation.

'Has conquered the senses': has mastery over them. In actual fact the senses are always under the command of the mind. Everyone knows that the eyes will see only if and when a man wishes to see. If he does not wish to see, he will not do so even with open eyes. Therefore victory over the senses seems to have no obvious meaning. The inner meaning of this expression is that, when Being first begins to be infused into the nature of the mind, the mind becomes as if intoxicated with a feeling of self-sufficiency. When the mind in this state acts through the senses, it behaves in a rather carefree manner, which may be thought of as akin to indifference.

In a more advanced state of enlightenment this peculiar sense of indifference diminishes, and the behaviour of the mind becomes more natural. Activity in the outer sphere of life becomes harmonized with the natural state of inner silence. Activity goes on as a result of the coordination between the mind and the organs of action. At the same time, coordination between the mind and the senses of perception enables the senses to register experience. With the infusion of Being into the mind, the senses of perception, while engaged in the process of experiencing, do not register deep impressions of experiences. The impressions they receive are just sufficient to enable them to experience, but are not deep enough to form the seed of future desires. This happens more and more effectively as the mind becomes more established in Being. Such, then, are the inner mechanics of mastering the senses.

A real conquest is that where the enemy ceases to be an enemy; he is left free to do as he likes, but is not in a position to attack or do any harm. The conquest of the senses is so fully accomplished through the mastery of the Self that the senses are left free to function and, notwithstanding all the experiences of the relative field, life is firmly established in the eternal freedom of divine consciousness.

Once the Self is experienced as separate from the senses and their activity, in the state of cosmic consciousness, a man sees within himself the state of unbounded Being on one side and involvement in the world of forms and phenomena on the other. He sees every living being as supported by that Being which is his own Self.

Thus he naturally experiences his Self as 'the Self of all beings', and in this state 'he is not involved even while he acts'.

This non-involvement can also be understood from another point of view. The light of a lamp is invisible in the light of the sun. The glory of the drop has no effect on the glory of the ocean. The joy of an action leaves no lasting impression upon the bliss of cosmic consciousness. Therefore once a man is established in this state, he naturally enjoys so great a fullness of Being that he never feels he is out of It. For him action does not involve coming out of the Self; there is, indeed, never any chance of his doing so. That is why the Lord says that 'he is not involved even while he acts'. He is firmly secured in cosmic existence which, though the very basis of all action, is without activity. For him it is as if everything were going by itself. This state is further described in the next two verses.

VERSES 8, 9

नैव किंश्चित्करोमीति युक्तो मन्येत तत्त्ववित् ॥
पश्यञ्छृण्वन्स्पृशञ्जिघ्रन्नश्नन्गच्छन्स्वपञ्श्वसन् ॥८॥

प्रलपन्विसृजन्गृह्णन् न्निमिषन्निमिषन्नपि ॥
इन्द्रियाणीन्द्रियार्थेषु वर्तन्त इति धारयन् ॥९॥

*One who is in Union with the Divine
and who knows the Truth will maintain
'I do not act at all'. In seeing,
hearing, touching, smelling, eating,
walking, sleeping, breathing, speaking,
letting go, seizing and even in opening
and closing the eyes, he holds simply
that the senses act among the objects
of sense.*

'One who is in Union with the Divine': the divine nature is
completely separate from the field of activity. When this has
been realized, the Self is experienced as independent of activity.
Then the teaching of this verse becomes a living reality of daily
life.

'One ... who knows the Truth' is one who knows that life has
two aspects, relative and absolute, and that the field of relative
life is governed by the three gunas.[19] He knows through understanding and experience that the Self is separate from the field of
activity.

This basic knowledge about the Self and the nature of activity
creates a situation in the mind where the realized man is automatically established in the truth of the expression: 'I do not
act at all.' It is not that he holds on to this thought artificially
but that the very structure of his mind is based on this natural
non-attachment. He lives this state. To him non-attachment is a
living reality in daily life. He acts and experiences, making use

19. See III, 28.

of his senses, but within himself he is fixed in Being. He lives fullness of Being while fully engaged in the field of the senses. He lives twofold: the stability of changeless Being constitutes the inner core of his life, and on the periphery is found the activity of the sensory level – the senses engaged in the experience of their objects.[20] This is what the Lord means when He says: 'the senses act among the objects of sense.'

These two verses develop the idea expressed in the previous one. When, through the practice of transcendental meditation, cosmic consciousness has been gained, and the individual ego has expanded to cosmic status, the mind automatically functions from the level of its full potentiality and the senses, having reached their maximum development, function at their highest capacity. The objects of sense, however, remain in their unchanged state. That is why the senses, acting from their raised level, experience objects more completely, resulting in an even greater appreciation of the objects and thus providing experience of greater happiness on the sensory level. This creates a situation in which the objects of sense are enjoyed more thoroughly than before, but because Being is more fully grounded in the very nature of the mind, the impressions of sensory experience fail to capture the mind. The enlightened man thus naturally remains in a state where the senses continue to experience their objects while he remains free.

This is merely a comparative statement; it does not in any way imply that such a man becomes incapable of experience. It only means that, whereas before enlightenment experience in the world used to overshadow his Being, now his Being shines forth through all experience. Before enlightenment, if he saw a flower, the flower overwhelmed the mind so completely that only the flower remained and the experiencer was lost in the experience. The subject was as if annihilated by the object.

Life in which objects predominate, where matter alone is found and the values of the spirit or soul are overshadowed, is called material life. After enlightenment, the flower is still seen, but the experience of the flower does not overshadow Being, because Being has been realized as separate from the field of activity, and thus

20. See III, 7.

the subject and the object are both separately maintained; both, so
to speak, alive in their fullness. The flower fails to overshadow
Being and at the same time the light of Being does not diminish
the validity of the flower. Through the light of Being the flower
is appreciated infinitely more, and this brings about the integration of spirit and matter. This is the glory of transcendental meditation : it brings enlightenment that integrates all the material
values of life with the Divine.

VERSE 10

ब्रह्मण्याधाय कर्माणि सङ्गं त्यक्त्वा करोति यः ॥
लिप्यते न स पापेन पद्मपत्रमिवाम्भसा । १०॥

He who acts giving over all actions
to the universal Being, abandoning
attachment, is untouched by sin as a
lotus leaf by water.

'Universal Being' : Brahman, the ultimate Reality, the Absolute
and the relative together at the same time.

The inward stroke of meditation leads the mind to Self-consciousness and infuses the state of Self-consciousness, Being, into
the nature of the mind. The outward stroke of meditation brings
such a mind into the field of action, where it acts with a certain
degree of Being. This practice of meditation and the activity that
follows it – morning and evening meditation and activity during
the day – develop a state in which the nature of the mind becomes transformed into the state of Being, while the ability to act
in all fields of practical life is fully maintained. Only when the
mind, thus established in the Self, acts from that state of universal Being, is it possible to act 'giving over all actions to the
universal Being'; in that state one has gained cosmic consciousness, which is the level of universal Being.

These words do not mean that a man should act while holding
in his mind the thought of the universal Being. This verse does
not teach an intellectually conceived surrender to the universal

Being, or cherishing the thought of It, or making a mood of the
Divine, or remembering God while working. It does not teach
that any such attempts on the level of the mind or intellect can
lead a man to a sinless state. All actions are given over naturally
to the divine Being and all attachments are abandoned [21] naturally
when, through the practice of transcendental meditation, the
mind rises to the level of divine consciousness and maintains it
permanently. When the self has completely separated itself from
activity, then a situation is created in which the authorship of
action becomes automatically transferred to the universal Being.

'Untouched by sin' means free from any wrong;[22] a life that is
completely harmless, being in accordance with the laws of
nature.[23] This state is gained in cosmic consciousness, in which
the Self is completely separate from activity. It is in this state
that actions are motivated by the power of Nature responsible
for all creation and evolution. That is why they all produce life-
supporting effects and no wrong is possible.

VERSE 11

कायेन मनसा बुद्ध्या केवलैरिन्द्रियैरपि ॥
योगिनः कर्म कुर्वन्ति सङ्गं त्यक्त्वात्मशुद्धये ॥११॥

By means of the body, by the mind,
by the intellect and even by the senses
alone, yogis, abandoning attachment,
perform action for self-purification.

Here the Lord makes clear the necessity of action for self-purification. Towards what state of self-purification does a yogi aim
when he performs action? Through the practice of samadhi,[24]
does not a yogi already have a pure state of consciousness? Is not
the practice of samadhi sufficient to purify the soul? It seems not,
for here the Lord is clearly expressing the need for performance

21. See IV, 20; III, 30.   22. See II, 38.
23. See Appendix: Cosmic Law.   24. See II, 53.

of action for that degree of self-purification which is not gained by samadhi alone.

'Yogis' : they who are united with the Divine in transcendental consciousness, cosmic consciousness or God-consciousness.

When a yogi has attained cosmic consciousness and has realized the Self as separate from the field of activity, he is able, by virtue of this realization, to entertain activity [25] while yet remaining in the eternal freedom of the Self. Because performance of action in this state of realization does not involve the Self, it naturally remains on the level of the 'body', 'mind', 'intellect' and 'senses'.[26]

The word 'alone' in this context is highly significant. It establishes without doubt and with all possible emphasis the separateness of the Self from the field of activity in the life of a realized man. Moreover, it also means that in this state of realization the body, the mind, the intellect and the senses are capable of acting quite independently.[27]

During the practice of transcendental meditation, as the mind gains transcendental consciousness, the metabolism of the body is reduced to a minimum and the entire nervous system gains a state of restful alertness.[28] This is the physical condition corresponding to the state of Being. In this state, the mental and physical levels of the individual life come to the level of the cosmic life of omnipresent Being – the individual mind is held by cosmic intelligence and individual physical existence sustained by cosmic existence – they become Its instrument and begin to respond to the cosmic need.

When cosmic consciousness has been gained, this situation is made permanent. 'Body', 'mind', 'intellect' and 'senses' remain the instrument of the divine will, irrespective of their mode of activity. In this state the main motivating force of their activity is the divine will, the almighty cosmic intelligence, responsible for the creation and evolution of the entire cosmos. Just as everything in nature responds to the need of cosmic purpose, so man's body, mind, intellect and senses, brought to the level of cosmic intelligence, respond to the need of cosmic life. This is what the

25. See VI, 1.   26. See III, 7.
27. See III, 7.   28. See IV, 38, commentary.

Lord means when He says: 'By means of the body, by the mind, by the intellect and even by the senses alone, yogis, abandoning attachment, perform action.'

The significance of the expression 'abandoning attachment' in this context is that, in coming under the direct influence of the divine intelligence, the whole field of activity leaves the realm of the individual self, which then gains freedom from the binding influence of action. Because a man has risen to the level of divine Being, 'abandoning attachment' automatically becomes a living reality of his daily life, without the need to cultivate non-attachment at any time.

'Self-purification': pure consciousness is the pure state of the Self; it is of transcendental nature. The mind arrives at it by transcending even the subtlest experience of the relative field. When this state is alternated with activity, the mind gains pure consciousness permanently. Pure consciousness is then naturally maintained in spite of engagement in activity. In this state, the duality of life becomes a living reality – the two aspects of life, Self and non-Self, absolute and relative, become separated, and the Self is lived as pure Being unallied with anything.

This experience of the complete separateness of the Self and activity should mean the culmination of the process of 'self-purification'. But still the process continues, finally to give rise to that state of Unity which does not accept activity even as separate from the Self. Here the separateness responsible for giving rise to a sense of duality in the state of cosmic consciousness is transformed into the light of God, allowing the duality of the Self and activity to merge into the homogeneity of divine existence in the oneness of God-consciousness. This state of the eternal Unity of life is the real culmination of the process of 'self-purification'.

The process of purification of the Self thus has three stages. First, from the waking state of consciousness to transcendental consciousness; second, from transcendental consciousness to cosmic consciousness; third, from cosmic consciousness to God-consciousness. In all three stages it is necessary to 'perform action for self-purification'. Performance of action on the subtler levels of life enables one to transcend the field of activity and gain transcendental consciousness. By the alternation of transcendental consciousness with the normal, natural activity of daily life – the mental activity of discrimination in the life of a recluse and physical activity in the life of a householder – transcendental consciousness becomes permanent and gains the status of cosmic consciousness. Again, cosmic consciousness develops into God-consciousness by virtue of the most highly refined type of activity, the activity of devotion.

This is how the process of purification is carried on to its ultimate conclusion through the performance of action.

This verse brings out a technique for the performance of action in the state of cosmic consciousness; for it says : 'By means of the body, by the mind, by the intellect and even by the senses alone, yogis ... perform action.' It has already been shown, in explaining the significance of the word 'alone', that action on this level is action in the state of cosmic consciousness, and this helps to transform cosmic consciousness into God-consciousness.

VERSE 12

युक्तः कर्मफलं त्यक्त्वा शान्तिमाप्नोति नैष्ठिकीम् ॥
अयुक्तः कामकारेण फले सक्तो निबध्यते ॥१२॥

He who is united with the Divine, having
abandoned the fruit of action, attains to
lasting peace. He who is not united with
the Divine, who is spurred by desire,
being attached to the fruit of action,
is firmly bound.

Gaining Unity with the Divine is the key to gaining freedom[29] from the bondage of the fruits of action, and this in turn is the key to gaining lasting peace. Unity with the Divine is found in three states: in Self-consciousness, which is of transcendental nature; in cosmic consciousness, which includes both the absolute and relative states of consciousness simultaneously – transcen-

29. See IV, 20.

dental Self-consciousness together with the consciousness of the waking, dreaming or sleeping state; and in God-consciousness, which holds together as one both the Self and the field of activity.

'Having abandoned the fruit of action': this expression runs parallel to the expression 'giving over all actions to the universal Being, abandoning attachment'.[30]

In the state of lasting peace, the inner and outer phases of life both grow so strong that ultimately they become completely independent of each other. Inner Being is experienced as wholly separate from activity, while activity grows so strong as to become completely independent of Being. Being and activity both rise to their full stature.

This is the state in which one lives in the Divine and in the world simultaneously, in which activity is carried on spurred by nature and without a spur of desire in the self, in which one enjoys freedom from the bondage of action. This is the ideal of Sanyasa – life in complete detachment from the world of action.

'Who is spurred by desire': who is not firmly established in the Self, or the Divine. Because he lacks such firmness, he remains attached to the fruits of action and, because of this, 'firmly bound' to the whole process of action from beginning to end.[31]

The present verse not only describes the state of one who is united with the Divine, but also of one who is not so united. It points out the mechanics of bondage: when a man is not united with the Self, or the Divine, the attachment to the fruits of action caused by desire is responsible for binding together the self and activity. It should not be lost to sight that this bondage is not real; for the self in its essential nature being eternally free, can never be bound. Only so long as he has not[32] realized this eternally free status of the self, does a man feel attached to activity and therefore remain in bondage. How he can come out of the bondage of desire is explained in the following verse.

30. See verse 10.   31. See IV, 18–20.   32. See verse 16.

VERSE 13

सर्वकर्माणि मनसा संन्यस्यास्ते सुखं वशी ॥
नवद्वारे पुरे देही नैव कुर्वन्न कारयन् ॥१३॥

Having renounced all action by the mind,
the dweller in the body rests in happiness,
in the city of nine gates, neither acting
nor causing action to be done.

Mind is the link between the action and the actor, the self. As
long as the mind is one-sided, subjected only to activity and
without the direct influence of Being, it fails to be a successful
mediator. It fails to safeguard the freedom of the self from the influence of action, and at the same time fails to safeguard action
from the limitations of individuality, so that activity remains
without the direct support of the almighty power of Nature.

This verse explains how the mind can become a successful
mediator and bring strength, grace and glory to action and freedom to life. The mind has to become as familiar with Being as it
is with activity, and for this to happen it has first to come out of
the field of activity and enter the sphere of Being. The present
verse describes how, once out of the field of action,[33] the mind
finds itself as the Self, completely unattached to activity, ever
remaining in the absolute state, 'in happiness', a silent witness
(*sakshi-kutastha*) of all events, 'neither acting nor causing action
to be done'.[34]

'In happiness': happiness lies beyond the range of activity,
where the 'self is untouched by external contacts'.[35] Once it has
reached this state, the mind knows the truth of the relationship
of the doer with his actions and with their fruits, which is proclaimed in the next verse.

33. See II, 55.   34. See verse 14.   35. See verse 21.

VERSE 14

न कर्तृत्व न कर्माणि लोकस्य सृजति प्रभुः ॥
न कर्मफलसंयोगं स्वभावस्तु प्रवर्तते ॥१४॥

The Lord creates neither the authorship
of action nor the action of beings; nor
does He create the link between (the doer),
the action and its fruits. Nature carries
this out.

'Nor the action of beings': this makes it clear that beings create
their own actions.

'Nor does He create the link between the doer, the action and its
fruit': the teaching is that the doer himself creates the link
between himself and his action, while the link between the fruit
of action and the doer is created by nature.

'Nature carries this out': the nature of the doer creates action,
and the nature of action creates the quality of the fruit. The fruit
of an action is linked with the doer by the nature of the doer
and his action.

This verse establishes emphatically the complete separateness
of the inner divine Being and the outer field of action. It enlightens us about the state of perfect renunciation that naturally
subsists between the inner and outer phases of life; for life is composed of activity on the outer surface together with the stability
of Being within. In their essential nature there exists no[36] link
between them. Just as a coconut has two different aspects, the
outer hard cover and the inner milk within, one solid, the other
liquid, without any link between them, so life has two aspects,
one unchanging and eternal, the other ever-changing and relative,
without any link between them.

The previous verse explained how the dweller in the body is
unaffected by action. In the present verse, the Lord intends to
convince Arjuna of the truth that action and the relation

36. See IV, 18-20.

'between the doer, the action and its fruit' belong solely to the relative field of life, they belong to Nature; they have no bearing on the absolute status of Being.[37]

The purpose of creation is the expansion of happiness. The three gunas, born of Nature, are responsible for creation and its evolution; they are responsible for all the various divisions – the doer, the action and the fruits. They alone underlie and are responsible for the creation, the maintenance and the dissolution of everything in the universe, the subjective aspects of the inner life and the objective aspect of the outer world.

The authorship of action does not in reality belong to the 'I'. It is a mistake to understand that 'I' do this, 'I' experience this and 'I' know this. All this is basically untrue. The 'I', in its essential nature, is uncreated; it belongs to the field of the Absolute. Whereas action, its fruits and the relationship between the doer and his action belong to the relative field, to the field of the three gunas.[38] Therefore all action is performed by the three gunas born of Nature. The attribution of authorship to the 'I' is only due to ignorance of the real nature of the 'I' and of action.

The theme of the Lord's teaching about the knowledge of action is developed in a remarkable way. In Chapter II, verse 48, the teaching was to abandon attachment, and the glory of such abandonment was sung in verses 64 and 71. The idea of abandoning attachment led to the teaching of non-attachment in Chapter III, verse 7. In the same chapter, verses 17 and 18 explained that non-attachment is attained by realizing the Self. Verse 19 established the dignity of action in this state of non-attachment gained through realization of the Self. Verse 25 gave a new turn to this theme by introducing the element of natural action. Verse 26 extolled natural action according to a man's level of evolution. Verse 27 explained that in reality all actions are performed by nature, and that only the deluded assume the authorship of action; the enlightened man knows that the gunas interact amongst themselves, that the whole field of activity belongs to the field of the gunas and that the Self remains uninvolved in their activity. Verse 30 introduced the element of God, to whom all actions of the three gunas may be surrendered as a means of

37. See IV, 18–20.   38. See III, 27, 28.

separating the field of activity from the Self. Verse 33 refuted the need for control in bringing about such surrender of action to God and again extolled action according to a man's nature, free from any control. Verse 39 introduced the idea that ignorance of the Self is responsible for bondage. Verse 43 raised the sword of knowledge to cut asunder this ignorance.

The development of the teaching thus far led to the principle that action is necessary for coming out of the field of bondage. The fourth chapter began to expound the nature of the Lord as separate from the incessant activity of the universe. This introduced the exposition of the knowledge of the renunciation of action, which is developed throughout the fourth chapter and in the earlier verses of this chapter until the present verse proclaims that there exists absolutely no relationship 'between the doer, the action and its fruit'. This is true on both levels of life – the level of cosmic life and the level of individual life. The present verse puts the point clearly when it says that 'the Lord creates neither the authorship of action nor the action of beings', meaning that He does not create anything; He remains completely aloof from the incessant activity of creating.

This is the situation on the cosmic level. The same situation is found on the level of individual life, because there exists no real link 'betwen the doer, the action and its fruit'. This eliminates all need for any doing, for any attempt at Self-realization. Abandoning all attempts at realization and living in the state of fulfilment is that high state, renunciation, which finds its consummation in the state of knowledge,[39] in God-consciousness. This is the glory of renunciation.

The most evolved state of life in eternal freedom is readily available in a most natural way to everyone. The sufferings and the joys of life come to man through the ignorance of this, says the next verse, and the glory of knowledge is extolled in the verse that follows it.

39. See IV, 38.

VERSE 15

नादत्ते कृस्यचित् पापं न चैव सुकृतं विभुः ॥
अज्ञानेनावृतं ज्ञानं तेन मुह्यन्ति जन्तवः ॥१५॥

The all-pervading Intelligence does not
accept the sin or even the merit of anyone.
Wisdom is veiled by ignorance. Thereby
creatures are deluded.

'The all-pervading Intelligence' is the absolute Being. Because It
is all-pervading, It is of transcendental nature, and because It is
transcendent, It lies out of the influence of action. It is the silent
witness of the whole of relative life.

The previous verse made it clear that the authorship of action
truly belongs to the three gunas. Therefore no agency other than
that of the three gunas is involved in creating good or bad results.

The state of enlightenment is obscured by ignorance, and
'thereby creatures are deluded'. The knowledge of the Divine as
uninvolved with the field of action, and the knowledge of one's
own Self as divine Being, bring freedom to life; whereas ignorance
of this truth is responsible for the delusion that it is the Divine
which bestows the fruits of one's actions. Here the Lord intends
to show that the unrealized state is the cause of the bondage of
action and involvement in sin and virtue.

Reality is known in two ways : with reference to the Absolute[40]
and with reference to the relative.[41] The gunas are responsible
for action and for everything in the field of relative existence,
and the Lord, 'the all-pervading Intelligence', remains completely
uninvolved.[42] This is how It, the divine Intelligence, or He, the
Lord, remains in eternal freedom. Those who rise to this supreme
knowledge[43] gain eternal freedom, others remain in bondage.

The following two verses throw more light on this.

40. See II, 45.   41. See III, 27, 28.   42. See verse 14.   43. See IV, 38.

VERSE 16

ज्ञानेन तु तदज्ञानं येषां नाशितमात्मनः ॥
तेषामादित्यवज्ज्ञानं प्रकाशयति तत्परम् ॥१६॥

But in those in whom that ignorance is
destroyed by wisdom, wisdom, like the
sun, illumines That which is transcendent.

'Ignorance': about the separateness of the inner and outer aspects of life, about Being as uninvolved with activity, about the real nature of the 'I' and the world, about the permanent and the ever-changing aspects of life, about the nature of freedom and bondage.

'That ignorance': the use of the word 'that', and not 'this', conveys the idea that ignorance is away from oneself. In its nature it is foreign to the Self.

In depicting wisdom as destroying ignorance, this verse shows that the destruction of ignorance and the illumination of the transcendent Being by wisdom go hand in hand. The sun removes the darkness and spreads the light at the same time. This indicates that when ignorance has been destroyed by wisdom, nothing more need be done to realize the Transcendent. It is omnipresent, veiled only by ignorance, and when this veil has been destroyed by knowledge, It shines forth in Its own light. That is why wisdom is attributed to the nature of the Absolute, the transcendent Being – wisdom is the Absolute; as the Upanishads have proclaimed: 'pragyanam brahma'.

This verse makes it clear that ignorance is destroyed by gaining knowledge, and not that knowledge is gained by destroying ignorance. Therefore the seeker has not to try to come out of ignorance; rather, he should try to gain knowledge through direct experience.[44]

It may be interesting to mention here that life, held as one by ignorance, is torn apart by the analysis of Sankhya into two

44. See IV, 38.

different components, the changing and the unchanging.[45] These are cognized as two different fields of life by direct experience through Yoga.[46] The understanding gained through Sankhya is confirmed by Yoga : when, in cosmic consciousness, one begins to live life in a state where the Self remains uninvolved with activity[47] then the truth of the teaching of Sankhya becomes significant in practical life. This enables man to live in the awareness that the two phases of life, relative and absolute, are separate from one another, and that even in the relative field, sin and virtue, which result in suffering and joy, each arise from attachment of the self to activity, which in turn arises from lack of knowledge.

VERSE 17

तद्बुद्धयस्तदात्मानस्तन्निष्ठास्तत्परायणाः ॥
गच्छन्त्यपुनरावृत्तिं ज्ञाननिर्धूतकल्मषाः ॥१७॥

Their intellect rooted in That, their
being established in That, intent on That,
wholly devoted to That, cleansed of all
impurities by wisdom, they attain to a
state from which there is no return.

This verse unites Yoga and Sankhya in their common goal of absolute purity and eternal liberation. It supports the truth of verses 4 and 5, which proclaim the theme of this chapter.

The words 'intellect' and 'being' are of great significance, and so is the sequence in which they are used. It teaches that when the intellect is rooted in That, the whole of one's being also becomes 'established in That'. Moreover, when, during meditation, the intellect becomes 'rooted in That', on coming out of the Transcendent it remains 'intent on That'. When the intellect becomes 'intent on That', one's being becomes 'wholly devoted to That'.

45. See II, 11–38.   46. See II, 45.   47. See II, 48.

The word 'being' has been chosen here to translate the Sanskrit word *atman*, which is variously used to mean the Self, the intellect, the mind, the breath and the body. Therefore the expression 'being' becomes 'wholly devoted to That' means that the mind, the breath and the body all become orientated[48] towards 'That'.

The Lord shows that unless the intellect and the whole of one's being are established in the transcendent Reality, they are not pure; they remain in the realm of temporary existence, unconnected with the state of eternal freedom whence 'there is no return'. Unless the transcendent absolute phase of life is realized, the scope of the individual phase of life remains insignificant and its purpose is not fulfilled; bondage continues and the cycle of birth and death meets no end.

This verse makes it clear that purity of life, which is the basis of all success in the world and at the same time the basis of eternal freedom, is gained by wisdom – realization of the Transcendent. It also states the principle that, unless a man has stabilized this absolute state of purity in his life by rising to the state of cosmic consciousness, there may always be the possibility of his stepping down to a lower level of life. This means that as long as transcendental consciousness has not become permanent, the effect of morning meditation does not persist in its full intensity throughout the day. As the hours go by, the intensity of the effect diminishes, and with this the level of purity in life falls, until the evening meditation restores it.

'Be without the three gunas', as explained by the Lord in the 45th verse of the second chapter, is the key to realizing the teaching of this verse in daily life.

Life finds its goal in the state of the eternal freedom of the Transcendent, spoken of here as 'That'; Knowledge Itself.[49] The use of the word 'That' makes it clear that the goal of life does not lie in the sphere of phenomenal existence; it lies beyond it. The real life is not this which is commonly referred to as life; beyond this is That Reality of life. This is a teaching of life from the standpoint of renunciation.

The Upanishads declare: 'Tat tvam asi – That thou art', implying that this obvious phase of phenomenal existence, which you

48. See IV, 38.   49. See IV, 38.

take as your self, is not your real nature – you, in fact, are That transcendent Reality.

'Cleansed of all impurities by wisdom': refer to verses 35–8 of Chapter IV.

'From which there is no return': as long as the self is not embedded in the eternity of life, as long as the mind has not permanently gained absolute purity in transcendental consciousness, life remains within the relative field of existence. In this situation the cycle of birth and death continues within the various strata of the evolution of life.[50] When one has gained cosmic consciousness, life goes beyond the sphere of birth and death. For being eternal it is changeless; it cannot partake of change. It should be clearly noted that this situation can only be created during man's life on earth. It is as a man that one rises to that 'state from which there is no return'. The way to it lies in the principle described in the 45th verse of Chapter II.

The following verse also is concerned with transcending the diversity of form in creation, and it portrays the oneness of life everywhere. It continues the teaching of the renunciation of this to find That.

VERSE 18

विद्याविनयसंपन्ने ब्राह्मणे गवि हस्तिनि ॥
शुनि चैव श्वपाके च पण्डिताः समदर्शिनः ॥१८॥

In a brahmin endowed with learning and
humility, in a cow, in an elephant, in
a dog and even in one who has lost his
caste, the enlightened perceive the
same.

This verse provides a criterion of vision in the state of enlightenment. Those who have realized the Reality of life 'perceive the same' oneness through all the diversity of experience.

50. See VI, 41.

'Brahmin': a man born in a brahmin family, whose life is dedicated to the study of the Veda and spiritual learning. The use of
this word in conjunction with cow, elephant and dog indicates
that the Lord wants to emphasize that the Being of an evolved
man and that of the animals is the same; and that, established
in the oneness of Being, and having realized the Unity of the
Transcendent underlying all diversity, he gains evenness of vision.

'Learning and humility': wisdom brings humility. Just as the
wise man sees the distinctions and differences in creation as only
temporary, with one ultimate Reality underlying them all, so he
does not insist that things should happen in any particular way.
He takes things lightly, for he knows they all have their common
end. This natural quality of Being in the wise is interpreted as
humility. Indeed, humility is the criterion of wisdom, arising as
it does out of the increased sense of the oneness of life, of the
basic Unity of all beings.

Humility is commonly understood to be the honest recognition
of one's personal limitations, one's ignorance and insignificance;
but true humility lies in the quality of Being and not in any attitude of mind.

The mind of the realized man is fully infused with the state of
Being – the oneness of life – and such a mind naturally has oneness of vision irrespective of what it sees. The apparent distinctions of relative existence fail to create division in its view.

This does not mean that such a man fails to see a cow or is
unable to distinguish it from a dog. Certainly he sees a cow as a
cow and a dog as a dog, but the form of the cow and the form of
the dog fail to blind him to the oneness of the Self, which is the
same in both. Although he sees a cow and a dog, his Self is established in the Being of the cow and the Being of the dog, which is
his own Being. The Lord stresses that the enlightened man, while
beholding and acting in the whole of diversified creation, does
not fall from his steadfast Unity of life, with which his mind is
saturated and which remains indelibly infused into his vision.

'A brahmin endowed with learning and humility' represents all
that is dominated by the influence of sattva. 'A cow' represents
all that is dominated by the mixed influence of rajas and sattva.
'A dog' represents all that is dominated by rajas and tamas. 'An

elephant' represents all that is dominated by the influence of tamas. 'One who has lost his caste' represents the lowest in human life, a man living in complete ignorance, who has lost the path of his evolution. The meaning is that one who has realized the Self as separate from the field of relative existence is steadfast in himself and quite untouched by the influence of sattva, rajas or tamas and tendencies that arise from them. He has evenness of vision everywhere.

The following verse shows the primary importance of such oneness of vision.

VERSE 19

इहैव तैर्जितः सर्गो येषां साम्ये स्थितं मनः ॥
निर्दोषं हि समं ब्रह्म तस्माद्ब्रह्मणि ते स्थिताः ॥१९॥

Even here, in this life, the universe
is conquered by those whose mind is
established in equanimity. Flawless,
indeed, and equally present everywhere
is Brahman. Therefore they are
established in Brahman.

When the mind, through the practice of transcendental medita-tion, rises to the state of cosmic consciousness, absolute Being becomes permanently established in the nature of the mind, and it attains the state of Brahman, the universal Being. Then the mind finds itself on a level of life from which all the gross and subtle levels of creation can be stimulated, controlled and com-manded. It is like a gardener who knows how to work at the level of the sap and can influence the whole tree in any way he likes. Someone who is acquainted with the atomic or sub-atomic level of an object, by working on that level could easily bring about a desired change in any stratum of the object's existence. This is what the Lord means when He says: 'Even here, in this life, the universe is conquered by those whose mind is established in equanimity', in the serenity, the calmness,[51] which is the ultimate level of life.

This verse reveals the status of the established intellect, described here as the state in which 'the universe is conquered'. Contentment, power, wisdom and the ability to support all things are obvious qualities of a conqueror of the world. These qualities, and many more besides, are found in the nature of a man who, while living in the world, has gained equanimity of mind. That stable state of evenness of mind in the eternal oneness of Reality belongs to the field of pure consciousness, or omnipresent Being, which is the very source of life-energy, the reservoir of eternal wisdom, the origin of all power in nature and the fountain-head of all success in the world.

As long as the mind has not risen permanently to the state of Being and cognized the field of activity as separate from itself, so long does it continue to be involved with activity. Indeed, it is like a slave to activity, a slave to the universe. But when it gains stability in Being and acquires a natural state of equanimity, then it finds the universe as separate from itself, responding quite automatically, like a servant, to its every need. This state of separateness of Being from activity, which is the basis of equanimity of mind, is gained through both Yoga[52] and Sankhya.[53]

VERSE 20

न प्रहृष्येत् प्रियं प्राप्य नोद्विजेत्प्राप्य चाप्रियम् ॥
स्थिरबुद्धिरसंमूढो ब्रह्मविद्ब्रह्मणि स्थितः ॥२०॥

He who neither greatly rejoices on
obtaining what is dear to him, nor
grieves much on obtaining what is
unpleasant, whose intellect is steady,
who is free from delusion, he is a
knower of Brahman, established in
Brahman.

51. See VI, 3.   52. See II, 48.   53. See II, 38.

This verse describes the nature of the enlightened man's mind. He stands for full Reality, the relative and the Absolute together. Such a man certainly has his own likes and dislikes, he has his own joys and sorrows in the relative field, but they do not take him out of himself; this meaning is clear from the words 'greatly', qualifying 'rejoices', and 'much', qualifying 'grieves'. It shows that a realized man, even though established in divine consciousness, keeps his feet on the ground. Remaining on the human level, he is divine.

When the mind is deeply rooted in the bliss-consciousness of the Self, it naturally remains unaffected by the attachment or aversion present[54] in the objects of the senses. This is the reason why the enlightened man neither 'rejoices' nor 'grieves'. It is a common experience even in worldly life that when the mind is deeply rooted in one thing it fails to register deeply experiences of other matters. If the idea of catching an aeroplane on time engages the mind fully, none of the many objects that are seen and sounds that are heard while one is driving through the streets will deflect the mind from the air terminal. In such circumstances the experience of the other things remains on the surface level of sensory perception and makes only a very faint impression on the mind. If this can happen within the waking state of consciousness, how much more so when another state of consciousness overtakes the mind.

The mind of an enlightened man is active in the manifested world, but fails to register deeply the experience of that world. His intellect is steady in its own inner light, the light of the Self. He is awake in himself and yet is awake in the outer world. He lives the Divine in the world; he lives the Absolute and the relative together. Therefore 'he is a knower of Brahman, established in Brahman'.

Consider a man in the waking state of consciousness, engaged in the experience of the outside world, while at the same time he carries the experience of the dreaming state of consciousness in his mind. For him the experiences of the waking state are certainly more concrete than those of the dreaming state, but the two types of experience co-exist. This makes it clear that it is

54. See III, 34.

possible for a man to be in one state of consciousness and yet
accept the experience of another state of consciousness at the
same time. When, through meditation, one gains transcendental
consciousness, its self-sufficiency is so overwhelming that even in
the waking state of consciousness one maintains within oneself
the influence of Being. Moreover, when the maintenance of Being
in the active mind becomes full and permanent, the entire activity
of the waking state is found only on the very surface of the mind.
This is the state of cosmic consciousness, in which activity is
experienced as separate from Being.

It will be noticed that the Lord describes two conditions that
have to be fulfilled if a man is to become realized. The first is that
he should be a 'knower of Brahman', that is, he should have a
clear intellectual understanding of Reality. This condition belongs
to the sphere of Sankhya. The second condition is that he should
be 'established in Brahman', that is, he should have direct experience of divine nature so that his daily life becomes its expression.
This condition belongs to the field of Yoga.

Therefore this verse too upholds the teaching of verses 4 and 5
of the present chapter and also that of the last verse of Chapter IV
in that it satisfies both Sankhya and Yoga on the level of renunciation. It describes the inner state of renunciation of a realized
man, whether he has realized through Yoga or through Sankhya.

Because he has realized the independent nature of the Self, such
a man is without delusion about his own identity; this makes the
intellect steady. This steadiness of intellect is the state of life in
which he 'neither greatly rejoices on obtaining what is dear to
him, nor grieves much on obtaining what is unpleasant'.

The present verse brings to light the natural state of renunciation in the life of a realized man, who does not rejoice in anything
external. The following verse explains the reason for his renunciation : he is fixed in the bliss of his own Being.

VERSE 21

बाह्यस्पर्शेष्वसक्तात्मा विन्दत्यात्मनि यत्सुखम् ॥
स ब्रह्मयोगयुक्तात्मा सुखमक्षयमश्नुते ॥२१॥

He whose self is untouched by external contacts
knows that happiness which is in the Self. His
self joined in Union with Brahman, he enjoys
eternal happiness.

'Self is untouched by external contacts': in order to gain the
experience of the inner Self in the transcendental state of consciousness, the experience of outside objects has to be eliminated.
Through constant experience, the Self becomes so familiar to the
mind that the very nature of the mind is transformed into the
nature of the Self. Then transcendental consciousness is maintained together with the waking state of consciousness, which
continues to support all activity as it did before. By virtue of the
permanent maintenance of transcendental consciousness, the Self
is always experienced as Self. And simultaneously, by virtue of
the waking state of consciousness, activity continues to be experienced. This is how the Self is experienced as separate from
activity. In this state the self is lost for ever; it has become the
Self.

With the loss of the self, the contact of the self with objects
through the agency of the mind and senses, which was responsible
for giving rise to experience, becomes non-existent. What remains
is the Self in Its pure nature of bliss-consciousness, devoid of any
contact with the objects that were held by the self. This is what
the Lord means when He says: 'He whose self is untouched by
external contacts'. Now that the Self is for ever established in Its
own essential nature, bliss-consciousness has become permanent.
When this bliss-consciousness comes in contact with objects, it
produces a state described by the expression 'self joined in Union
with Brahman'. This is because Brahman is the state of cosmic
consciousness, which embraces activity and bliss-consciousness.

'Joined in Union with Brahman': this expression, together with 'self is untouched by external contacts', presents a criterion whereby a seeker can know when he has gained 'Brahmi-sthiti',[55] or the state of Brahman – cosmic consciousness. While the mind is experiencing objects through the senses, he is awake in the awareness of his self as separate from the field of experience and action. This then is the state of cosmic consciousness, in which he is awake in the world and awake in himself.

Many commentators have done great injustice to the teaching of this verse by suggesting that it describes a technique of enjoying the bliss of the Self by means of constructing a mood of remaining unaffected while experiencing joy through the objects of the senses. Many translations have treated the original text in a way which, while consistent with the grammar of the verse, presents a false picture of its teaching and is contrary to the essential principle of action and of renunciation.

It is the permanency of bliss-consciousness gained through the Yoga of action, and again it is the state of renunciation gained through the Yoga of renunciation based on bliss-consciousness that keep the Self unaffected during the experience of joy; it is not the intellectual practice of trying to hold the mind back and keep it unaffected during the process of experience that brings one to bliss-consciousness and to the state of renunciation, where the Self is experienced as separate from activity. It is because the Self is joined in Union with Brahman that a man enjoys eternal happiness.

The reason why the joys of the senses cannot make a deep impression on the enlightened man is that his self has become Self, which is wholly blissful in nature. Being wide awake in cosmic intelligence, his natural stand is at the fountain-head of all the joys of all the senses. Being permanently established in absolute bliss, the temporary joys of relative existence fail to fascinate his self. Even when sensory objects come into contact with his senses, the joys of such contacts are not so powerful as to distract the self from its natural state of bliss-consciousness. This is why his self remains unaffected while his senses are fully in contact with their objects.

55. See II, 72.

The expressions 'self is untouched by external contacts', 'knows that happiness which is in the Self' and 'his self joined in Union with Brahman' place Sankhya and Yoga on a common basis, thus upholding verses 4 and 5, which contain the essence of the teaching of this chapter.

VERSE 22

ये हि संस्पर्शजा भोगा दुःखयोनय एव ते ॥
आद्यन्तवन्तः कौन्तेय न तेषु रमते बुधः ॥२२॥

All pleasures born of contact are only sources
of sorrow; they have a beginning and an end,
O son of Kunti. The enlightened man does not
rejoice in them.

This verse contrasts with the previous one in that it explains the principle of the unattached state of the Self, and at the same time complements it by clarifying the principle of happiness and suffering.

'Contact': as in the previous verse, this means contact of the self with the field of activity or experience. It depicts the state in which the self does not remain untouched, the state in which the self remains involved with the field of experience and joys of the senses. Such joys are 'sources of sorrow' by virtue of the self being involved with them. If, however, the Self remains untouched, then the joys of the senses are not sources of sorrow, for in that state the Self is established in eternal happiness.

When the mind begins to take delight in the objects of the senses, this shows that its delight is not within; the mind is not anchored to the bliss of the Self, it is absorbed in the outer direction away from bliss. If the mind no longer faces in the direction of bliss, and if it is not neutral, then it is obviously turned towards sorrow. Therefore when the mind is absorbed in outer joys, then it is absorbed in the field of sorrow. Anything that leads the mind in an outward direction becomes a source of sorrow.

This truth about the enjoyments of the world is valid when considered from the level of cosmic consciousness and from that of God-consciousness, the ultimate Reality of life. Seen from the ordinary level of the consciousness of man, to say that the 'pleasures born of contact are only sources of sorrow' seems absurd. Yet even on this level of consciousness the same principle applies: they 'are only sources of sorrow', the reason being that 'they have a beginning and an end'.

'The enlightened man does not rejoice in them': established in the state of eternal happiness, in Brahmi-sthiti, and experiencing the Self as separate from activity, he has by nature risen above the phenomenal phase of life, above the fleeting joys of the relative field, and so he is not in a state where he can rejoice in temporary joys. When a retailer becomes a wholesale merchant he no longer deals in the retail field, which requires more effort and produces less profit.

The experience of the objects of the senses in the waking state differs from that in the state of cosmic consciousness. It may be likened to the experience of objects through glasses of different colours, whereby the same object is experienced differently. The enlightened man is simply not in a position to 'rejoice in them' as he did before realization, because of the difference in his state of consciousness.

'Sources of sorrow': the intensity of happiness that one can enjoy depends on the level of one's consciousness. At every level of consciousness there is a corresponding intensity of happiness. This principle applies also to intelligence and power.

The difference between the consciousness of the enlightened man and that of the unenlightened is as great as that between the Absolute and the relative, between light and darkness. For this reason the joys of the senses, which delight the ignorant, are looked upon as sources of sorrow by the wise. In comparison with the eternal bliss of the Absolute, in which the enlightened are naturally established, the fleeting joys of the world 'are only sources of sorrow'. When the Lord uses these words, it is to express the truth and at the same time strike hard at the minds of those who are engrossed in such joys and whose vision is thus blinded.

If the self delights in the experience of objects, since the objects are changing, the delight will soon be lost. This loss of pleasure will give rise to suffering. That is why the Lord says: 'they have a beginning and an end. . . . The enlightened man does not rejoice in them.' He who lacks contact with inner Being becomes engrossed in external pleasures.

'They have a beginning and an end': this expression presents a contrast with 'eternal happiness' in the previous verse. When one joy comes to an end, the self is subjected to a state without joy which, in contrast with the experience of joy, is suffering. But if the Self has gained a state of perpetual happiness, then It is left with no possibility of suffering. Absence of bliss-consciousness is the source of sorrow.

VERSE 23

शक्नोतीहैव यः सोढुं प्राक्शरीरविमोक्षणात् ॥
कामक्रोधोद्भवं वेगं स युक्तः स सुखी नरः ॥२३॥

He who is able, even here, before
liberation from the body, to resist
the excitement born of desire and
anger, is united with the Divine.
He is a happy man.

'Even here': remaining within the limitations of the relative field of daily life in the world. The ability 'to resist the excitement born of desire and anger' has its basis in the state of supreme contentment which results from Union with the Divine and from the knowledge of the Self as separate from the field of activity in the state of cosmic consciousness, which is the result of such Union.[56] In this state of lasting contentment there is no possibility of any excitement. Excitement can only arise in a discontented mind ever seeking something more.

56. This principle was presented in verse 66 of Chapter II; verses 50 and 51 of that chapter described the advantages of the established intellect.

'Desire and anger' belong to the realm of the mind. For any mental activity to take place there must of necessity be a corresponding activity in the physical structure of the nervous system. The mental activity of desire and anger produces very powerful 'excitement' in the nervous system. It is this physical excitement that stirs the nervous system to activity. In the case of a non-realized man this excitement is immediately expressed as speech and action; but in the case of a realized man, it is anchored to eternal silence as a ship is anchored to the sea-bed. His nervous system permanently maintains that state of restful alertness which corresponds to pure awareness of the Self, and this state of restful alertness prevents the stir of desire and anger in the nervous system. This is how the state of his nervous system does not allow excitement to arise in a realized man.

Self-awareness acts as a shock-absorber on the mental level, while the state of restful alertness of the nervous system acts as a shock-absorber on the physical level. This is the natural state of life in cosmic consciousness.

Life flows through desire. As long as desire is present, the possibility of anger will always exist, and therefore the stir produced by desire and anger is an essential feature of life. This is why the Lord does not advocate the elimination of desire, but only says that it is necessary to create a situation in which 'the excitement born of desire and anger' is automatically resisted, in the sense that it does not overpower life.

This situation is created by culturing both the mental and physical aspects of life through the practice of transcendental meditation, which produces the necessary refinement in the mind and the nervous system simultaneously.[57] In the state of cosmic consciousness, which is the state described by 'united with the Divine', this refinement is such that it does not allow the excitement of desire and anger to arise. But the Lord says: 'before liberation', before gaining cosmic consciousness. This is because the knowledge that the Self is divine in Its nature and is completely unattached to the field of activity grows as the practice of gaining transcendental consciousness advances, so that long before a man has actually gained cosmic consciousness the infusion

57. See IV, 38, commentary.

of Being into the nature of the mind becomes intense enough to give him the ability to resist 'the excitement born of desire and anger'. The need for resisting this excitement arises only when there is a chance for the excitement to arise. This happens only before cosmic consciousness is actually gained.

Nevertheless, it is clear from this teaching that the ability to resist excitement should be considered as one criterion of being united with the Divine. This is because there is no direct way of measuring the degree of infusion of Being into the mind and ascertaining whether or not full and final infusion of Being has taken place. The second criterion that the Lord gives is: 'He is a happy man'; he is free from the 'sources of sorrow', as shown in the previous verse.

'Before liberation from the body': this expression shows that the present teaching is for an aspirant engaged in the practice of gaining the state of Unity with the Divine. It means before having gained release from the binding influence of action, before having gained the state of cosmic consciousness, in which the Self is permanently experienced as separate from activity, before identification of the self with the body is dissolved, before the state of renunciation has been achieved.

This verse has been generally misunderstood to mean that resisting desire is a way to Union with the Divine, and this has given rise to all sorts of ascetic practices and exhortations to abandon desire for the sake of coming to Union. It is wrong to suppose that this verse offers a path to Union through attempting to resist desire. It merely places Union with the Divine parallel to the natural ability to resist desire. This ability in the relative field is the expression of the Union in the absolute field. Of the two, Union with the Divine is easier to attain.[58] It forms the basis of the ability to resist.

Having declared in this verse that the mind of a yogi remains unshakable in the field of activity, the Lord, in the following verse, goes on to describe the inner state of such a mind.

58. See II, 40, 45; VI, 28.

VERSE 24

योऽन्तःसुखोऽन्तरारामस्तथाऽन्तज्योतिरेव यः ॥
स योगी ब्रह्मनिर्वाणं ब्रह्मभूतोऽधिगच्छति ॥२४॥

He whose happiness is within, whose
contentment is within, whose light is
all within, that yogi, being one with
Brahman, attains eternal freedom in
divine consciousness.

This verse is the crest of the teaching of this chapter on renunciation. It presents a state in which life is wholly converged upon its
innermost aspect, and declares that state to be eternal freedom.
Furthermore, it brings to light the sequence of stages on the way
to realization: as the practice of transcendental meditation advances inner happiness grows; with this, contentment grows, and
at the same time the experience of Being becomes clearer – the
inner light grows. With this, inner awareness grows, and with it
the ability spontaneously to maintain Being during activity.
When one naturally begins to maintain the state of Being in all
states of waking, dreaming and deep sleep, then one has attained
eternal freedom in divine consciousness.

   'He whose happiness is within': this expression is a development of the argument in the two preceding verses. First, 'All
pleasures born of contact are only sources of sorrow. . . . The enlightened man does not rejoice in them' (verse 22). This implies
that the outside world is not the field of happiness for a realized
man. Second, 'He is a happy man' (verse 23). If his happiness does
not lie in the outside world and yet he is happy, his happiness
can only be within himself. The mind wanders in search of happiness but when, through Union with the Divine,[59] the mind is
transformed into bliss-consciousness, it finds the goal of its search
within itself.

   By virtue of bliss-consciousness, even the relative aspect of

59. See verse 21.

man's existence is wholly permeated by bliss. So, experiencing the relative field of happiness outside and absolute bliss within, his whole life is naturally anchored to inner happiness, and therefore to 'contentment' also.

'Whose light is all within': who dwells in the light of the Self, whose inner being is illumined by the light of the inner Divine. The word 'all' is important: it means that he is totally absorbed in the inner light, that his whole life is permeated by the light of inner Being. He is awake within himself and remains so in spite of any activity in the outside world. He is established on that absolute level of existence which is deep within everything, that field of unbounded bliss-consciousness which is self-sufficient and self-illuminating.

This does not mean that he is not active in outer life. It simply means that even though his mind, intellect, ego, senses and body are functioning on their respective levels, and he has the whole phenomenal world around him, his Self remains completely un-attached. It is only superficially affected by this outer field of life. This is that integrated state of existence in which every level of life is self-sufficient and all the different levels progressively function together in harmony.

'Eternal freedom in divine consciousness': this translates the Sanskrit, *Brahmanirvana*, the freedom born of the state of Brahman.

The present verse speaks of 'that yogi' who does not require anything in the outside world to make him happy. Nothing in the outside world attracts him. He does not need an external light, for he is awake in his own light. Established in the freedom of cosmic consciousness, he is always free. The experience of variety in the world in no way takes him out of his liberation; no external light, or knowledge of the relative world, can in any way deprive him of his state. Once Self-consciousness is estab-lished in the nature of the mind, the mind cherishes it in all conditions.

The Lord is saying that nothing in the world will be able to overshadow the perpetual freedom of a yogi in this resolute state. While he acts in the relative field of life, he is yet established in his own Self. Divine consciousness is not opposed to life in the

world, nor is consciousness of the relative world opposed to the
divine consciousness of absolute existence.

The following verse brings out other features of the state of
enlightenment.

VERSE 25

लभन्ते ब्रह्मनिर्वाणमृषयः क्षीणकल्मषाः ॥
छिन्नद्वैधा यतात्मानः सर्वभूतहिते रताः ॥२५॥

The seers, whose sins are destroyed,
whose doubts are dispelled, who are
self-controlled and take delight in
doing good to all creatures, attain
eternal freedom in divine consciousness.

It should be noted that when the Lord presents the state of eternal
freedom through the principle of renunciation, as He does in the
previous verse, He does not lose a moment before adding that in
such a state a man takes 'delight in doing good to all creatures'. In
the state of renunciation a man becomes devoted to all creatures
and capable of doing good not only to himself but to all other
beings. It is this teaching that places the philosophy of renunciation parallel to that of the Yoga of action.

'Seers': the knowers of Reality, established in the realization
of the Self as separate from activity, who see life as the drama of
the Divine while themselves remaining uninvolved.

'Whose sins are destroyed': sins are destroyed by both Yoga[60]
and Sankhya.[61]

'Doubts are dispelled' by both Yoga[62] and Sankhya.[63]

'Self-controlled': this state is gained by both Yoga[64] and
Sankhya.[65]

60. See II, 65; III, 13, 41.   61. See II, 38; IV, 21, 30, 36.
62. See II, 72; V, 20.   63. See IV, 35, 40, 41.
64. See II, 61; III, 7.   65. See IV, 18, 20, 21, 23, 28, 41.

'Delight in doing good to all creatures': this state is reached by both Yoga[66] and Sankhya.[67]

The Lord here describes certain prerequisites for one who is to 'attain eternal freedom in divine consciousness'. It is fortunate for aspirants that all these conditions are fulfilled quite naturally and automatically through the teaching of Sankhya, which is inclusive of the method described by the Lord in the 45th verse of the second chapter: 'Be without the three gunas.' The simple technique of achieving this state 'without the three gunas' is the practice of transcendental meditation, for it readily[68] brings the mind from the field of gross experience to the state of transcendental consciousness.

When the mind transcends during meditation, it reaches the state of pure consciousness, free from all diversity. Once it becomes permanently established in Being, knowledge becomes complete and all its doubts,[69] whatever they may be, quite naturally disappear. Having risen above the egocentricity and selfishness of individuality, abiding in bliss-consciousness and fully connected with the source of energy, a man can but move about compassionately doing good to all beings.

VERSE 26

कामक्रोधवियुक्तानां यतीनां यतचेतसाम् ।।
अभितो ब्रह्मनिर्वाणं वर्तते विदितात्मनाम् ।।२६।।

Disciplined men, freed from desire
and anger, who have disciplined their
thoughts and have realized the Self,
find eternal freedom in divine
consciousness everywhere.

It should be noticed that verse 24 promises eternal liberation through Yoga, that verse 25 promises it through Sankhya, and that this verse translates the same promise of eternal liberation into

66 See III, 20.   67. See III, 25.   68. See II, 40.   69. See IV, 41.

terms of renunciation. The sequence of these three verses mirrors the sequence of the theme of Chapters III, IV and V. Thus the Lord brings completeness to the philosophy of renunciation.

This verse describes a man in eternal freedom. He is 'disciplined' because he is established in the knowledge of Reality, which gives him a clear understanding of the state of renunciation, or the separation that lies between the Self and activity. By gaining that state he is freed from desire and anger and has disciplined his thoughts. He has 'realized the Self', for he is permanently established in the pure state of Being, or Self-consciousness – he has gained cosmic consciousness. Thus established in divine consciousness he finds eternal freedom everywhere.

The state described in this verse is higher than that described in verse 23, for it has arisen out of the destruction of sins and the dispelling of doubts specified in verse 25.

Verse 23 presented a happy man in Union with the Divine as one 'who is able ... to resist the excitement born of desire and anger'. This implies that it is still possible for the excitement of desire and anger to bubble up in such a happy man united with the Divine, but that he will be able to resist this excitement. The present verse shows that those 'who have disciplined their thoughts and have realized the Self' are freed from any possibility of the excitement of desire and anger arising in them. Such men of fulfilment live eternal freedom in divine consciousness.

'Who have disciplined their thoughts': a disciplined thought is that which is in harmony with the process of evolution of the thinker and of everything around him. It is in accordance with all the laws of nature. When, during meditation, the mind gains the state of transcendental divine consciousness, it becomes the basis of all the laws of nature that govern the process of evolution on every level of creation. On coming out into the field of relative life, its thoughts naturally receive the support of all the laws of nature. Therefore 'have disciplined their thoughts' means living the Being in daily life; it does not mean controlling thoughts.

'Everywhere' means during life here on earth and hereafter.

Arjuna is shown that, to become liberated, it is not necessary to die or to leave the body. If one has known the Self and the mind is inseparably established in It, if the Self is appreciated as separate from activity, then whatever desires or anger arise, the Self remains completely uninvolved and therefore free from them. This is how, when the mind is disciplined in terms of the Self, it remains unconcerned with all activity, even the activity of desire or anger. Naturally, in such a state a man is liberated during his lifetime here on earth and subsequently after death.

It may be recalled that a disciplined life,[70] freedom from desire and anger,[71] discipline of thoughts [72] and realization of the Self [73] are achieved by both Yoga [74] and Sankhya.[75] Therefore it may be inferred from this verse that Yoga and Sankhya are the same so far as these results are concerned. This inference is in keeping with verses 4 and 5, which present the purpose of this chapter.

This verse, together with the three previous verses, establishes the possibility of divine life in the world either through the practice of Yoga or the wisdom of Sankhya. In the following verse, the Lord begins a precise description of the practice which leads a man to achieve that state of cosmic consciousness (jivan-mukti) during his lifetime. This will complete the teaching of the chapter and will provide a sound basis for the wisdom of Chapter VI.

VERSE 27

स्पर्शान् कृत्वा बहिर्बाह्यांश्चक्षुश्चैवान्तरे भ्रुवोः ॥
प्राणापानौ समौ कृत्वा नासाभ्यन्तरचारिणौ ॥२७॥

Having left external contacts outside;
with the vision within the eyebrows;
having balanced the ingoing and outgoing
breaths that flow through the nostrils,

The first point is that the attention has to shift away from the external field of sensory perception. 'Having left external contacts outside' means closing the gates of the senses to any outside

70. See III, 7, 17.　　71. See III, 43.　　72. See III, 43.
73. See III, 43.　　74. See IV, 23, 38.　　75. See IV, 19.

experience and at the same time not thinking about objects of sensory impression.

The second point is that the vision is 'within the eyebrows'. This means that vision is directed outwards from within the eyebrows – it is directed from behind the eyebrows, and this is done with closed eyes. It is the most relaxed and effortless state of the ocular muscles. It is soothing to the entire system and also has the simultaneous effect of leaving 'external contacts outside' and balancing 'the ingoing and outgoing breaths'. This point has been widely misunderstood and the verse misinterpreted as advocating concentration of the vision between the eyebrows. Such a practice may have its value in other systems which depend on effort. Concentrating the vision in this manner involves great strain even with the eyes closed; such a practice has no place in the Bhagavad-Gita, which teaches a simple and effortless method.

The third point is that a state of balance should be established between the outward and inward breaths. This balance means that they should flow evenly, and should cease flowing, in alternating directions, finally coming to a state of suspension.

There are many ways of accomplishing these three aims. In some practices, control of the senses predominates, in others control of thought, in others control of breath. But the practice to which the Lord refers in this verse is one which works on all these aspects simultaneously and results in the state described in the following verse.[76]

VERSE 28

यतेन्द्रियमनोबुद्धिर्मुनिर्मोक्षपरायण: ।।
विगतेच्छाभयक्रोधो य: सदा मुक्त एव स: ।।२८।।

The sage, whose senses, mind and intellect
are controlled, whose aim is liberation,
from whom desire, fear and anger have
departed, is indeed for ever free.

'The sage' (muni): see II, 56, 59.

76. See also commentaries on VI, 13, 14.

'Senses, mind and intellect are controlled' by 'having known him who is beyond the intellect' (III, 43).

'Whose aim is liberation' means that all his efforts are directed one-pointedly towards liberation. He follows unswervingly the sure path trodden by 'the ancient seekers of liberation' (IV, 15). The whole routine of his life is dedicated to the practice of meditation and balanced activity.[77]

As a result of this constant practice, he becomes quite naturally free from desire, fear and anger. 'From whom desire, fear and anger have departed' indicates that he has not done anything to drive them away – they have of themselves departed from him.[78]

The present verse describes an even more perfect state of realization than that portrayed in verse 26. There the expression 'freed from desire and anger' indicates that a man has abandoned them; the expression in the present verse, 'from whom desire, fear and anger have departed', indicates that they have abandoned him.

The reason is that he has arrived at a state where the Self is experienced as separate from activity, and thus he finds himself 'indeed for ever free'. This is the state of perfect renunciation that is gained in cosmic consciousness. Here is the fulfilment of the philosophy of renunciation – everything has been separated from the Self, which has gained in liberation a perfect state of non-attachment.

This apparently marks the peak of renunciation. But the question arises: Is this all that the philosophy of renunciation can offer? If it is, then the philosophy is not complete, because an existence aloof from everything could not possibly be the fulfilment of life. This anxious inquiry is answered in the next verse, which provides for the desired fulfilment of life and shows that fulfilment to be the real pinnacle of the philosophy of renunciation.

77. See commentaries on II, 45; IV, 18, 21.
78. See commentaries on verse 26 and II, 40, 45.

VERSE 29

भोक्तारं यज्ञतपसां सर्वलोकमहेश्वरम् ॥
सुहृदं सर्वभूतानां ज्ञात्वा मां शान्तिमृच्छति ॥२६॥

Having known Me as the enjoyer of
yagyas and austerities, as the great
Lord of all the world, as the friend of
all beings, he attains to peace.

Here is the real glory of renunciation. It discovers the great 'enjoyer': it develops into Union with God.

'Me': whose birth and actions are divine (IV, 9); who am the
refuge of those freed from attachment, fear and anger, unto whose
Being have come those purified by the austerity of wisdom
(IV, 10); who show men favour in the same manner as they
approach Me (IV, 11); who am the author of the fourfold order
of creation, yet remain the non-doer, immutable (IV, 13); whom
actions do not involve and who am without longing for the fruit
of action; knowledge of whom liberates men from the bondage
of action (IV, 14).

'Yagyas': actions supporting life and evolution. These have
been dealt with in detail in Chapter IV, verses 24–33.

'Austerities': means of purification. The performance of yagya
is also considered to be austerity. Verse 10 of Chapter IV describes wisdom in terms of austerity, purified by which one par-
ticipates in the consciousness of the Supreme.

'Having known Me as the enjoyer of yagyas and austerities':
he sees Me as accepting his yagya and austerity; having separated
himself from the field of activity, his activity has been given
over to Nature, which is the Lord's. This is why the Lord says:
'Having known Me as the enjoyer of yagyas and austerities'.

'Having known me ... as the great Lord of all the world':[79]
having raised his consciousness to the level of My consciousness;
that is, having attained God-consciousness. Knowledge of God is
possible only when one has reached the state of God-conscious-

79. See III, 22, 30; IV, 6, 13.

ness. This has been made clear in the commentary on verse 38 of Chapter IV.

'As the friend of all beings': a friend is a source of joy. He brings life-supporting happiness. The purpose of the Lord's creation is the expansion of happiness. Men enjoy His love expressed in creation, each at his own level of consciousness. This is how 'the great Lord of all the world' is also the life-supporting friend, the bestower of happiness on all beings. One who knows Him thus and finds himself close to Him, gains fulfilment: 'he attains to peace', says the Lord.

So that Arjuna's mind may not escape from the present realities of life to an abstract conception of a far-distant friend of all beings, so that he can see the great Lord of all the world close at hand, speaking to him, Lord Krishna shows that He Himself is that Lord. It is only because of Arjuna's complete surrender that He reveals Himself so completely.

This chapter, which lays open the wisdom of the renunciation of action, ends with an exposition of the divine nature of Lord Krishna, so full, friendly and peaceful. This is the glory of the wisdom of renunciation that is uniquely the Bhagavad-Gita's. It does not leave a man in dry detachment, barren and without support. It carries renunciation to the direct realization of the supreme authority, the supreme good, the supreme happiness that are found in rising to the level of the Godhead, to direct communion with God. This humanly inconceivable accomplishment in man's life is the blessing of renunciation. Here is the Lord's invitation to humankind: Enter into the Kingdom of Heaven through the path of action or through the path of renunciation of action. Make your choice.

*Thus, in the Upanishad of the glorious
Bhagavad-Gita, in the Science of the Absolute,
in the Scripture of Yoga, in the dialogue
between Lord Krishna and Arjuna, ends the
fifth chapter, entitled: The Yoga of Action and
Renunciation of Action, Karma-Sanyasa Yoga.*

CHAPTER VI

A Vision of the Teaching in Chapter VI

Verse 1. The performance of right action in the state of non-attachment mirrors the outer and inner life of a realized man.

Verses 2–10. A difference of path is not significant so long as Divine Union is gained. What is important is to know that each path starts from the level of activity and ends in the eternal silence of absolute Being, which develops into God-consciousness. This process is divided into three stages: from the waking state to transcendental consciousness, from transcendental consciousness to cosmic consciousness, from cosmic consciousness to God-consciousness.

Verses 11–28. The practice for rising from the waking state of consciousness to transcendental consciousness.

Verse 29. The practice for rising from transcendental consciousness to cosmic consciousness.

Verses 30–2. The practice for rising from cosmic consciousness to God-consciousness.

Verses 33, 34. How can the mind, which is wavering, be steady on the path?

Verses 35, 36. It is difficult to control the mind directly, but through practice and non-attachment it becomes subdued.

Verses 37–9. What is the destiny of a man who starts faithfully on the path but is not able to reach the goal in this life?

Verses 40–5. Death is no barrier to evolution. In his next life a man continues to evolve from the level gained in this life. If he fails to gain perfection in one life, he will gain it in another; for once set on this path, no one can miss the goal.

Verses 46, 47. The seeker is exhorted to set himself on the path of transcendental meditation, gain Union of the mind with the divine Self in transcendental consciousness, realize that Self as separate from activity in cosmic consciousness, rise to God through devotion, and finally attain complete Union with Him.

THIS chapter stands as the keystone in the arch of the Bhagavad-Gita. It explains in detail what may be called the Royal Yoga of Lord Krishna, which readily brings enlightenment to any man in any age.

The greatness of the theme of these six chapters lies first in the explanation of life in its manifold aspects and then in the synthesis of all these aspects in the Unity of God-consciousness.

It is a divine theme expounding Reality, which assumes newer and newer meanings as man's consciousness grows. It gives significance to life at every level of consciousness and brings fulfilment at every step of man's evolution until eternal fulfilment is gained.

The first chapter showed a great hero overcome by a profound state of suspension, which rendered him unable to act. Presenting this extreme case, it silently demanded a master-cure for all sufferings and sorrows in man's life at any time.

Chapter II gave the vision of the full life by bringing to light the relative and the absolute phases of existence. It suggested a practice by which all problems in the relative phase of life could be solved by adding the value of absolute consciousness to the consciousness of the relative state.

Chapter III expounded the validity of action to make permanent the state of Union experienced in the state of absolute consciousness gained in the transcendental state.

Chapter IV brought knowledge of the state of non-attachment, or renunciation, experienced when the state of Union becomes permanent.

Chapter V showed this state of non-attachment to be common to the paths of both Sankhya and Karma Yoga.

Chapter VI describes the practice that brings about this state of non-attachment, thus fulfilling the teachings on action and on renunciation contained in the third and fifth chapters.

This sixth chapter serves as a commentary [1] on the 45th verse of Chapter II, which contains the central teaching of the Bhagavad-Gita: 'Be without the three gunas.' It develops a simple technique of transcendental meditation leading to a state of consciousness which at all times spontaneously maintains Being and thereby equanimity of mind and behaviour in the field of activity. This technique provides the practical basis for both Sankhya and Yoga and for the very different ways of life associated with these paths, that of the recluse and that of the householder. They virtually cease to be two different paths. But even if they are regarded as different, it can still be said that they develop on a common ground and arrive at a common goal. This is the glory of the practical teaching of the sixth chapter.

VERSE 1

श्रीभगवानुवाच ।
अनाश्रितः कर्मफलं कार्यं कर्म करोति यः ॥
स संन्यासी च योगी च न निरग्निनं चाक्रियः ॥१॥

The Blessed Lord said:
He who performs action that ought
to be done, without depending
on the fruit of action, he is a sanyasi
and he is a yogi; not he who is without
fire and without activity.

The first two expressions of this verse, 'performs action that ought to be done' and 'without depending on the fruit of action', summarize the teaching of the whole discourse thus far. At the same time they indicate that the practice which is going to be explained in this chapter will enable man to live the teachings

1. It also clarifies the teaching contained in II, 48; III, 2, 7, 9, 30, 34, 43; IV, 27, 41, 42; V, 1, 4, 6, 7, 11.

they contain. This practice will enable all men to cultivate that high state of divine consciousness which should be normal to man and which forms the basis of the life of a sanyasi and of a yogi.

It is obvious from the theme of the discourse that what brings fulfilment to life is not a specific way of life, either that of a recluse or of a householder, but experience of Reality and know-ledge about It. This again is obvious from the expressions in the present verse, which describe the state of consciousness common to a yogi and a sanyasi: 'He who performs action that ought to be done, without depending on the fruit of action.'

This verse is a continuation of Lord Krishna's answer to Arjuna's question, in the first verse of Chapter V, about the re-lationship of renunciation of action to the Yoga of action.

In the early stages of His answer, the Lord showed that both ways have an identical end in the state of liberation, that in their aim they are the same. He then made clear the supremacy of the Yoga of action (Karma Yoga) over the renunciation of action (Sanyasa), and this brought out the fact that the two are distinct paths. In the present verse, the Lord establishes that, while there may be certain points of difference between the path of a sanyasi and that of a karma yogi, there is at least one common factor which brings them together: the unattached state of the mind in relation to the fruits of action during activity. The Lord holds this to be the criterion both of a sanyasi and of a yogi, both of the state of renunciation and of the state of Union.

To say that the state of Union is equivalent to the state of renunciation may sound contradictory, but the truth of this state-ment becomes clear in the state of cosmic consciousness. In this state the mind's Union with Being, Self-consciousness, has be-come permanent; this is the state of perfect Union. In this state also the Self is experienced as separate from activity; this is the state of perfect renunciation. This is how renunciation and Union co-exist in the same state of life.

The state of mind which is unattached to the fruits [2] of action is a result of the experience of the Self as separate from activity. This in turn results from the Union that comes from the practice

2. See IV, 19, 20, commentaries; V, 12.

of gaining transcendental bliss-consciousness through the method which the Lord has already given to Arjuna in the 45th verse of Chapter II.

The Lord says to Arjuna: 'action that ought to be done'. By this He intends to save from misinterpretation His teaching about action in the light of non-attachment. Otherwise a misguided man might commit murder or theft and claim that he acted without attachment to the fruits of action.

The doctrine of Karma Yoga is not based on the manner in which a man thinks. It is based upon a state of consciousness, the state of Being. Its purpose is to allow the infusion of Being into the nature of the mind and to make It permanent there. Then It becomes permanent in the whole field of thought, speech and action, in the whole field of man's life. This is brought about very naturally by the practice of transcendental meditation followed by activity that is unforced and without strain.

The purpose of both Karma Yoga and Sanyasa is to establish a man in the state of complete integration of life. Non-attachment to the fruits of action, described here as characteristic both of a sanyasi and of a yogi, is a particular state of mind, not on the level of thought but on the level [3] of Being.

It would be a mistake to make a mood of non-attachment to the fruits of action during activity. It would be sheer hypocrisy to try to hold intellectually, on the level of thought or by mood-making, the idea or feeling: 'I am doing this action for the sake of God, or for the sake of duty, and have no desire [4] for its fruits; I am, indeed doing the action, but actually I am not doing it; I am Brahman, and action is also Brahman, and the fruit of action is also Brahman, so even the fruit is nothing but my own Self, and that Self I am already. What need, therefore, to think about the fruit of action?' This way of thinking has nothing to do with the doctrine of non-attachment in Karma Yoga or Sanyasa, and anyone who tries to live non-attachment on the basis of such thinking is only deluding himself. Yet for many centuries the doctrines of Karma Yoga and Sanyasa have been misunderstood in just this way.

Sanyasa and Karma Yoga are neither of them based on any

3. See IV, 19, 20, commentaries.   4. See IV, 19, 20, commentaries.

manner of thinking, nor on making moods at the conscious level of the mind; they are based on the inner stability of the mind in the state of enlightenment. The way to this is through transcendental meditation. Wihout right meditation and the attainment of the state of transcendental consciousness, and eventually of cosmic consciousness, one's action will always be a means of bondage; no amount of thinking will help to free a man from the binding influence of action.

It is a matter for regret that at the present time a man who is active in the world, but without having gained transcendental consciousness, should consider himself a karma yogi simply because he leads a life of activity, performing certain kinds of action and thinking about them in terms of God or in some other special way. To be a karma yogi, one has first to be a yogi. It is the state of transcendental pure consciousness going hand in hand with activity that constitutes Karma Yoga. Through the practice of transcendental meditation the mind is so steeped in pure consciousness, or Being, that this cannot be overshadowed, however numerous a man's actions, however intense his experience in life. The state of Being together with activity makes him a karma yogi.

The experience of Being is the first prerequisite of Karma Yoga, as it is of Sanyasa. So far as the state of consciousness is concerned, Sanyasa and Karma Yoga are the same.

'Without fire': fire cooks food. By tradition, a sanyasi is not expected to cook food lest it bind him to the needs of the body. Therefore being without fire symbolizes the life of a sanyasi. Again, fire is that which destroys. What destroys the eternal calmness of the ocean? A wind that sets up waves. Eternal unmanifested Being appears as waves of individual life through the instrumentality of desire. That is why desire is considered to be fire for one who chooses the life of silence.

In this verse, the Lord pictures the life of a sanyasi not in terms of non-attachment or desirelessness, but in terms of activity in freedom.

VERSE 2

यं संन्यासमिति प्राहुर्योगं तं विद्धि पाण्डव ॥
न ह्यसंन्यस्तसङ्कल्पो योगी भवति कश्चन ॥२॥

*That which they call Sanyasa, know it
to be Yoga, O son of Pandu, for no
one becomes a yogi who has not
relinquished the incentive of desire.*

'Incentive [5] of desire' translates the Sanskrit word *sankalpa*, which
conveys the idea of a seed which sprouts into desire.

Lord Krishna here makes a most essential point for the student
of Yoga: sankalpa has to be rooted out in order that one may
become a yogi.

The Lord has already established Sanyasa and Karma Yoga on
an equal footing with regard to their results: 'Both renunciation
and the Yoga of action lead to the supreme good' (V, 2); 'He
who is properly established even in one gains the fruit of both'
(V, 4). In this, as in the preceding verse, He puts the two paths
themselves on the same basis, and He does so with great emphasis: 'That which they call Sanyasa, know it to be Yoga.' The
Lord proves this by bringing to light the single quality which
makes a man a sanyasi or a karma yogi. He says: 'no one becomes a yogi who has not relinquished the incentive of desire.' A
yogi is he whose mind is united with the Divine, and in that state
of transcendental consciousness the incentive of desire is rooted
out.

The question arises: If abandonment of sankalpa is necessary
before man can become a yogi and is also the characteristic of a
sanyasi, how in practice is it possible for anyone to become a
sanyasi or a yogi? For life, whether lived in the household or in
seclusion, is full of sankalpa and desires. The answer is that a man
has to create a state of mind in which there is no sankalpa; and
seeing that the Lord's discourse is for the man in the world,

5. See IV, 19, commentary.

it must be possible for everyone to create such a state of mind.

The principle of the technique to make the mind free from san-kalpa was given to Arjuna by the Lord in the 45th verse of Chapter II and will be further expounded in this chapter. During meditation, the mind goes through states of experience which become progressively finer until the finest is transcended. In this way the mind is led to the state of transcendental consciousness and comes completely out of the realm of sankalpa. This is the state of Yoga. It is also the state of Sanyasa, where the mind has renounced everything and is left alone by itself. Thus the technique of transcendental meditation, which helps the mind to transcend sankalpa, is the technique of becoming a yogi or a sanyasi.

As the practice advances, transcendental consciousness becomes permanent in the state of cosmic consciousness, and in this state one has permanently relinquished the incentive of desire.

The following verse considers the activity of an aspirant and the serenity of an accomplished yogi in relation to the state of mind without sankalpa.

VERSE 3

आरुरुक्षोर्मुनेर्योगं कर्म कारणमुच्यते ॥
योगारूढस्य तस्यैव शमः कारणमुच्यते ॥३॥

Action is said to be the means for
the man of thought wishing to ascend
to Yoga; for the man who has ascended
to Yoga, and for him alone, calmness is
said to be the means.

'Means' : course, path, way.

'Man of thought' : this translates the Sanskrit muni. A muni is one whose path of fulfilment is through thought. His practice is in the field of the mind as opposed to the field of bodily activity. In order to make this clear, it must be explained that for the

mind to register any experience a corresponding activity in the
nervous system is necessary. It follows from this relationship of
the mind with the nervous system that any experience can be
stimulated either by the one or by the other. Hatha Yoga is an
approach to realization which trains the physical nervous system
and thereby conditions the mind to gain the state of transcendental consciousness and eventually to gain cosmic consciousness.
On the other hand, the practice of meditation, referred to in these
verses, is an approach to realization which trains the mind and
thereby conditions the nervous system to give rise to the state of
transcendental consciousness and eventually to cosmic consciousness. This mental approach is the way of the muni.

By using the word 'muni', the Lord wants to make it clear that
action is not the means for a man of action only, but also for the
man whose way of approach is through knowledge.

'Wishing to ascend to Yoga' means that he has not yet attained
the state of mind without sankalpa, described in the previous
verse.

'Action is said to be the means': action is the means of cultivating the state of mind without sankalpa. This appears to be a
paradox similar to the one in verse 18 of Chapter IV. The Lord
said there: 'who in action sees inaction'. Here He seems to be
saying: Create calmness through action. There is deep meaning
in the Lord's expression: 'Action is said to be the means'. It
reveals the whole secret of the path of Yoga, the way to create
the state of mind without sankalpa.

This expression may be considered on different levels. First, it
means that the Lord wants the aspirant to perform right action
according to his dharma, thus purifying himself and, through the
increase of purity, maintaining steadiness of mind. This consideration belongs to the surface of life and should be valued for the
inspiration which it gives to a righteous way of living.

The consideration which follows reveals a deeper meaning of
the Lord's words. He wants the aspirant to involve himself in
subtler forms of activity; He wants him to bring the mind from
more gross levels of activity on the common sensory level of
action and experience to the finer levels of thinking and, eventually transcending the finest level of thinking, to arrive at

transcendental consciousness, the state of mind without sankalpa, the state where one 'has ascended to Yoga'.

Thus it is through activity that transcendental consciousness is gained. Moreover, the mind, travelling as it were on the ladder of activity from the relative state of waking consciousness to the silence of the transcendental field of absolute consciousness, and again from there to the activity of the waking state, establishes eternal harmony between the silence of the Absolute and the activity of the relative. This is cosmic consciousness,[6] in which transcendental consciousness, the state where one 'has ascended to Yoga', becomes permanent. This expression of the Lord's also has its meaning therefore on the level of cosmic consciousness. Cosmic consciousness in turn forms the basis for the supreme state of Yoga in God-consciousness, where the eternal Unity of life prevails in the light of God. One who has reached this state has ascended to Yoga in the highest sense of the expression.

Having defined activity as the means of ascending to Yoga, the Lord turns to the importance of that 'calmness' which serves as a means when one has 'ascended to Yoga'.

'The man who has ascended to Yoga': a man whose mind has risen from the waking state of consciousness to the transcendental state of consciousness, in which his mind is in full Union with the Divine. This state of Yoga in transcendental consciousness becomes permanent in cosmic consciousness through increase of calmness, or the infusion of Being into the nature of the mind. That is why the Lord says that calmness is the means when ascent to Yoga in transcendental consciousness has been gained. Again, calmness is the means of ascent from Yoga in cosmic consciousness to Yoga in God-consciousness. In the state of cosmic consciousness, calmness gives the experience of the Self as separate from activity. In God-consciousness, this calmness is transformed into the light of God, in which the experience of the duality of the Self and activity is dissolved.

This eternal silence of God-consciousness is the advanced stage of the silence experienced in the state of cosmic consciousness. It is the living silence of that Unity of life which forms the basis of

6. See III, 20.

cosmic activity and at the same time completely separates God
from cosmic activity. The silence which is experienced in cosmic
consciousness, and which separates the Self from activity, is on an
infinitely smaller scale, for it is on the level of individual existence. The one forms the basis of the activity of the whole of
creation, the other the basis of individual activity. The essential
difference between the two lies in this: in cosmic consciousness
silence and activity co-exist on the same level; whereas the level
of God-consciousness is completely free from duality; it is all the
living silence of eternal life, and Unity pervades all activity as
water every wave. God-consciousness is pure awareness in the
oneness of Being. When the awareness of the Self in cosmic
consciousness develops into the awareness of God in God-consciousness, it develops on the level of silence; the whole process is
one of the transformation of silence. At every step of development
the quality of the silence changes. This is the reason why the
Lord says: 'for the man who has ascended to Yoga, and for him
alone, calmness is said to be the means.'

Thus there are three states of silence: in transcendental consciousness, in cosmic consciousness and in God-consciousness. In
transcendental consciousness, silence is devoid of any trace of
activity. In cosmic consciousness, the silence of Self-awareness
co-exists with activity. In God-consciousness, the co-existence
of activity and silence is transformed into oneness of awareness of
God. This silence of God-consciousness is the most highly
developed state of silence. It is all life on the almighty level of
existence. It is the omnipresent, omnipotent, omniscient silence of
Godhead. It is a completely different state of silence, which has
nothing in common with the silence of cosmic consciousness or
transcendental consciousness.

Any achievement by an accomplished yogi, established in cosmic consciousness or God-consciousness, is brought about by the
power of silence, the eternal silence of absolute Being, which is
the source of all the innumerable laws of nature creating and
maintaining life in the cosmos. The individual life of a yogi being
one with That, he finds that that omnipresent silence works out
everything for him.

By using the phrase, 'for him alone', the Lord makes it clear

that everything will happen without doing [7] – silence will work
as a means for him 'who has ascended to Yoga', but only for him
and for none other. When a man gains transcendental consciousness, his nervous system gains the state of restful alertness which
corresponds with, and is able to reflect, life eternal on the level
of that silence of the Omnipresent. That is why, in this state, the
divine intelligence does everything for him. When transcendental
consciousness becomes permanent and gains the state of cosmic
consciousness, the nervous system permanently remains the instrument of the Divine : Self-awareness is permanently established
throughout life. This blessed state exists in a much deeper sense
in God-consciousness.

In the next verse, the Lord further explains the expression :
'Action is said to be the means'. He shows how the state of non-
action is gained through the means [8] of action. Then, in the verse
which follows, He explains the expression : 'calmness is said to
be the means', showing that the elevation of the self by the Self
is brought about by 'calmness'.

VERSE 4

यदा हि नेन्द्रियार्थेषु न कर्मस्वनुषज्जते ॥
सर्वसंकल्पसंन्यासी योगारूढस्तदोच्यते ॥४॥

Only when a man does not cling to the
objects of the senses or to actions, only
when he has relinquished all incentive
of desire, is he said to have ascended
to Yoga.

Here the Lord describes to Arjuna the state of the mind established in Yoga, the state of Divine Union. When, during meditation, the mind retires from the field of sensory perception, it
becomes disconnected [9] with the outside world. It is turned inwards, away from the field of 'the objects of the senses', away

7. See IV, 38.   8. See III, 4.   9. See III, 4, commentary.

from the sphere of 'actions'. As the mind advances in an inward direction, so it retreats further from the field of gross experience. It continues through increasingly subtle fields of thinking, until it eventually transcends even the subtlest state of thought and reaches the transcendental state of Being. Here it does not in any way 'cling to the objects of the senses or to actions'.

The state of Being is one of pure consciousness, completely out of the field of relativity; there is no world of the senses or of objects, no trace of sensory activity, no trace of mental activity. There is no trinity of thinker, thinking process and thought; doer, process of doing and action; experiencer, process of experiencing and object of experience. The state of transcendental Unity of life, or pure consciousness, the state of Yoga, is completely free from all trace of duality. In this state of transcendental consciousness a man is 'said to have ascended to Yoga'.

Here the Self stands by Itself, Self-illuminant, Self-sufficient, in the fullness of Being. Here one 'has relinquished all incentive[10] of desire', for where there is no duality there cannot be even the seed of desire. But the state of Yoga in transcendental consciousness is not permanent. When the mind comes out of meditation, it will once more cling to the objects of the senses and to actions, even if not so firmly as before, and the incentive of desire will once more play its part. Only when a man has reached the state of cosmic consciousness, where he is ever contented and for ever firmly established in the Self, will the conditions which this verse sets for one who has 'ascended to Yoga' be permanently fulfilled. Naturally these conditions are also satisfied in God-consciousness, which is the fulfilment of cosmic consciousness. Thus, as the previous verse has already shown, the expression 'is ... said to have ascended to Yoga' applies not only to transcendental consciousness but also to cosmic consciousness and God-consciousness.

10. See IV, 19; VI, 2.

VERSE 5

उद्धरेदात्मनात्मानं नात्मानमवसादयेत् ॥
आत्मैव ह्यात्मनो बन्धुरात्मैव रिपुरात्मनः ॥६॥

Let a man raise his self by his Self,
let him not debase his Self; he alone,
indeed, is his own friend, he alone
his own enemy.

Here is a single teaching to show the basic principle of development in any sphere of life, spiritual, mental or material. Every
individual is responsible for his own development in any field.

In the previous verse Arjuna was shown the meaning of realization; now the Lord commands him to reach that state.

'Raise his self': the word used in the original Sanskrit is
uddharet. It means to raise, uplift, elevate, glorify, to free from
bondage. By using the word, the Lord inspires Arjuna to raise
himself from the level of sensory perception and the field of
thought and activity to the state of Self-realization. He not only
inspires Arjuna to cultivate the state of transcendental Self-
consciousness, but instructs him in the direct way of doing so:
'raise his self by his Self'. No help from outside is required. A
man has in himself everything he needs to rise to any height of
perfection. Nothing of the world is needed to elevate the self; no
method is to be adopted, no means to be sought. The self is
elevated by the Self alone.

The question may then arise: How can a man 'debase his Self'
when he has been declared as beyond the reach of anything outside himself? Do not verses 13 to 30 of Chapter II pronounce the
dweller in the body as beyond any influence of time and space?

To understand this one must recall the previous verse. When
the mind attains to transcendental consciousness, it is in the state
of perfect purity; it achieves cosmic status. In the present verse,
the Lord encourages Arjuna to rise to that state, and at the same
time wants him not to fall from it once it has been achieved. For

when the mind comes out of the transcendental state to experience once more the objects of the senses in the world, it regains its limited individual status and falls from that height of universal existence. In order to warn him against this, the Lord says : 'let him not debase his Self', meaning that, once having attained the state of Self-consciousness, he should go on to to rise to the state of cosmic consciousness, as explained in the commentaries on verses 3 and 4.

The expression, 'he alone, indeed, is his own friend', indicates that only in its pure state of transcendental consciousness is the mind helpful to itself. When it comes out of that state of Being, it acts as its own enemy to deprive itself of its cosmic status; but when it continues the practice and rises to cosmic consciousness, then it acts as its own friend to maintain that cosmic status.

This teaching illuminates the whole area of the search for Truth. Nothing in the outside world is relevant to this search. For, the Lord says, there is no friend of the self other than the Self. No particular culture or way of life is especially conducive to Self-realization; no sense of detachment or attachment is conducive or opposed to self-realization. Renunciation of the world, or a recluse way of life, is not especially helpful to the unfolding of the Self, for It unfolds Itself by Itself to Itself. Through meditation a situation is created where the Self is found uncovered, unfolded in Its pure and essential nature with no shadow cast upon It by anything.

Meditation does not unfold the Self – the Self, it must be repeated, unfolds Itself by Itself to Itself. The wind does nothing to the sun; it only clears away the clouds and the sun is found shining by its own light. The sun of the Self is self-effulgent. Meditation only takes the mind out of the clouds of relativity. The absolute state of the Self ever shines in Its own glory.

The Lord's teaching in this verse applies to every level of evolution. This is obvious from the two preceding and the two following verses. It may be interesting to note at this point that the fullest development of the self is through three stages : from the waking state of consciousness to transcendental consciousness, from transcendental consciousness to cosmic consciousness and from cosmic consciousness to God-consciousness. The teaching of this verse is equally applicable to all these stages of one's development. In the first stage, the self evolves by means of the activity of transcendental meditation and realizes the Self. In the second stage, from transcendental consciousness to cosmic consciousness, the state of Self is supplemented by the activity of the self in order to maintain the Self in Its true nature even in the midst of activity. In the third and final stage, from cosmic consciousness to God-consciousness, the Self has to go all by Itself and on the level of silence devoid of any activity. That is why the Lord said in the third verse: 'calmness is said to be the means.' And in the present verse, He says: 'Let a man raise his self by his Self.'

VERSE 6

बन्धुरात्मात्मनस्तस्य येनात्मैवात्मना जितः ॥
अनात्मनस्तु शत्रुत्वे वर्तेतात्मैव शत्रुवत् ॥६॥

He who has conquered his self by his
Self alone is himself his own friend; but
the Self of him who has not conquered
his self will behave with enmity like
a foe.

The acquisition by the mind (the self in its relative aspect) of the state of Self-realization, or transcendental consciousness, is described here as a conquest: the lower self has conquered the higher Self. Through this conquest, the individual mind has gained the status of cosmic mind, or pure consciousness. This cosmic intelligence then becomes the basis of the whole of practical life; it supports and gives strength to all fields of relativity.

The mind, during meditation, reaches the state of transcendental Being and, coming out of the Transcendent into the field of relative life, remains saturated with Being. With constant practice of transcendental meditation, there comes a point where the saturation of the mind with Being becomes permanent and continues without interruption throughout all experiences in the relative world, with the result that the Self is experienced as separate from activity, and the binding influence of action is neutralized. The conscious mind of man, acting in the world, then acts in freedom, supported and protected by Being. This is how the Self, having been conquered by the self, befriends the self.

The lower self and the higher Self belong to the one indivisible Reality, which is inclusive of both the transcendental and relative aspects of life. Like brothers bound by the natural affinity of blood, they support each other in every way. This is one aspect of their relationship. But there is another: when a difference arises between brothers, they can become deadly enemies. This happens when the self has not conquered the Self.

If a man has not begun to meditate and has not consciously realized the Self, if his mind has not reached the realm of transcendental Being, then it will not have attained the status of cosmic intelligence either temporarily or permanently. This means that his lower self is not familiar with the higher Self, and there is no coordination between the two. The one has not accepted the other. They stand opposed to each other in their essential nature, for one is relative and the other transcendental. In the field of relativity they exist as enemies. The lower self is always acting through the senses, encouraging them and enjoying the variety of objective experience, thus preventing the higher Self from being effective in the relative field of existence and allowing It to remain as it were confined in the field of the Transcendent. In return, the higher Self also behaves as an enemy to the lower self. It does not save the self from the fast grip of the ever-changing life of relative existence, but allows it to remain within the cycle of birth and death. The higher Self does not provide the unlimited energy, wisdom, creativity and happiness which alone will give peace and abundance to the lower self.

Conquest of the self by the Self and conquest of the Self by the self amounts to the same thing. It can be understood in either way so long as the conquest denotes the Union of the two, or merger of the one into the other. The merger of the self into the Self takes place in the state of transcendental consciousness and becomes permanent in cosmic consciousness. The self finds itself one with

the Self. This is that state where the self and the Self support
each other so intimately that they do not exist independently of
each other.

The next verse elaborates the inner and outer condition of the
realized man, of one who has 'conquered'.

VERSE 7

जितात्मनः प्रशान्तस्य परमात्मा समाहितः ॥
शीतोष्णसुखदुःखेषु तथा मानापमानयोः ॥७ ॥

For him who has conquered his self,
who is deep in peace, the transcendent
Self is steadfast in heat and cold,
in pleasure and pain, in honour
and disgrace.

In verse 4 of this chapter, the Lord made a distinction between
the realm of worldly activity and that of Being. In verses 5 and 6,
He showed the way to establish coordination between the two.
In the present verse, He describes the condition of the mind in
this state, how one feels within when coordination between outer
life and inner Being is established. The Lord says that one feels
eternally peaceful, being immersed in the glory of the Supreme.
In this state the whole of life, with all its pairs of opposites, is
permeated with the glory of the transcendent Being. This state of
eternal peace in bliss-consciousness cannot be shaken by anything
whatsoever.

This verse emphasizes the resolute nature of the established
intellect.[11] In the following verse, the idea is developed and is
elaborated into a description of the yogi who is united.

11. See II, 56.

VERSE 8

ज्ञानविज्ञानतृप्तात्मा कूटस्थो विजितेन्द्रियः ॥
युक्त इत्युच्यते योगी समलोष्टाश्मकाञ्चनः ॥८॥

That yogi is said to be united who
is contented in knowledge and
experience, unshakeable, master
of the senses, who is balanced in
experiencing earth, stone or gold.

The Lord brings out the two aspects of realization, the two aspects
of becoming a yogi. The first is that of gaining a clear intellectual
conception of the Truth through a proper understanding of
Reality reached by listening, thinking, contemplating and discriminating intellectually between Its various aspects. This, however, satisfies only the mind. The other aspect is that of knowing
Reality by direct experience, which satisfies the heart. This is
gained through transcendental meditation.

The Lord says that when the mind is satisfied by a completely
clear intellectual conception of Reality, and the heart is satisfied
by the direct experience of Its blissful and eternal nature, then a
man gains eternal contentment. Then only does he become firm
in his own state of life. Such an 'unshakeable' nature always
behaves in the field of the senses as a 'master of the senses' and
never as their slave. He 'is said to be united', and he is a yogi
whose life is marked by a balanced state of mind throughout all
experience in the field of diversity.

This idea of balance in life will recur many times during the
discourse. The repetition of this principle at short intervals indicates not only its intrinsic importance, but its relevance to
Arjuna's situation. At the same time it brings home to him that,
whatever method the mind adopts in order to become established
in Reality – be it the path of action or that of renunciation –
once it becomes established, the infusion of Being into the nature
of the mind is the same and brings with it the same balanced

vision. Although they may differ in mode of life and manner of activity, those who are realized have this in common: they always possess balanced understanding and vision.

Having spoken of the realized man's inner state of mind and of his nature during experience of the outer world, the Lord, in the following verse, describes his behaviour towards others in society.

VERSE 9

सुहृन्मित्रार्युदासीनमध्यस्थद्वेष्यबन्धुषु ॥
साधुष्वपि च पापेषु समबुद्धिर्विशिष्यते ॥६॥

*Distinguished is he who is of even
intellect among well-wishers, friends
and foes, among the indifferent and the
impartial, among hateful persons and among
kinsmen, among the saintly as well as the
sinful.*

'Even intellect': because of this inner state of eternal content-ment, the mind of a yogi abides in silence. Based on this silence, his intellect is even. This does not mean that he behaves to everyone in like manner. A yogi does not create confusion in the various fields of relationship by failing to recognize due differ-ences. But among all the variety of relationships his understand-ing, based on the oneness of life, does not waver. He remains 'of even intellect'.

A man who has balanced vision while experiencing objects has been declared a yogi in the previous verse. The balanced vision described in that verse belongs to a yogi, whether he has reached his state through the path of Sankhya or Karma Yoga. The present verse sets the standard for a yogi who is 'distinguished'.

Having so far devoted this chapter to describing all that the practice of meditation can accomplish for man, the Lord, in the following verses, explains the details of the practice.

VERSE 10

योगी युञ्जीत सततमात्मानं रहसि स्थितः ॥
एकाकी यतचित्तात्मा निराशीरपरिग्रहः ॥१०॥

Let the yogi always collect himself
remaining in seclusion, alone, his
mind and body subdued, expecting
nothing, without possessions.

'Collect himself' means meditate. The manner in which the yogi collects himself is mentioned in verse 27 of Chapter V and is detailed in the following five verses of the present chapter.

'Yogi' does not here mean an accomplished yogi. An accomplished yogi no longer has any need to continue the practice necessary for reaching the higher state, for he has already attained it. Because the necessity of practice is being explained, 'yogi' in this context means an aspirant to Yoga. At the same time the word 'yogi' indicates one who has reached a state of Union. The word, therefore, is best understood here as referring to a man who has realized the state of Self-consciousness, or samadhi, but has not yet attained cosmic consciousness – nitya samadhi, or jivan-mukti. Such a yogi has to be intent on practice so that Self-consciousness may become continuous and established in the nature of the mind to such a degree that even when the mind is out in the field of relative experience it is never out of the state of Being. This is the state of cosmic consciousness, the state of an accomplished yogi. To arrive at cosmic consciousness, the yogi has to meditate in silence and then come out into activity.[12] In the present verse, the Lord wants to emphasize that when a yogi meditates he should always do so under the following conditions:

1. remaining in seclusion
2. alone
3. his mind and body subdued

12. See V, 11.

4. expecting nothing.
5. without possessions.

'Seclusion' is essential because the process of transcendental meditation, which is a direct way for the mind to arrive at trancendental bliss-consciousness, is a delicate one. It must be allowed to go its way unhindered. If the place of meditation is not secluded, there is more possibility of disturbance. During meditation the mind engages itself in the deeper levels of the thought-process; if it is disturbed and suddenly made to come out into the gross levels of sensory perception, it will experience a great contrast between the subtle and the gross fields of perception. This sudden contrast will damage the mind's serenity and will upset the nervous system.

'Alone': if a man does not meditate alone, then the feeling of someone being around him or watching him will impede the smoothness of the process of transcending. Any such influence, slowing down the march of the mind towards bliss-consciousness, will bring undue strain to the mind and produce a corresponding stress in the nervous system.

'Mind and body subdued': the word 'subdued' is of special interest. The mind is 'subdued' by the experience of happiness.[13] As the mind, during meditation, experiences ever subtler states of thought, it experiences increasing charm at every step. This increasing happiness keeps the mind unwaveringly on the process of meditation. When the mind is subdued in this manner, the nervous system, following the pattern of the mind, remains unwavering. This is how 'his mind and body' are 'subdued' in a most natural manner.

It would be wrong to conclude here that the yogi has to make constant and strenuous efforts of control in order to have 'his mind and body subdued'.

'Expecting nothing': when the Lord says that the aspirant should 'always collect himself remaining in seclusion', He wants at the same time to warn him against any tendency to expect. This process of collecting oneself should not contain any element of expectation of some further step in the process or, indeed, of

13. See III, 43; V, 21; VI, 21.

any particular experience. It should be free from any expectation
of success in arriving at the goal. This expression brings out the
meaning of verse 47 of Chapter II as applied to meditation: 'You
have control over action alone, never over its fruits.'

The warning against 'expecting' is very significant. When,
during meditation, the mind is engaged in experiencing subtler
states of the thought-process on the way to transcending, it is set
on the path of increasing charm. Any tendency to expect or hope
only serves to pull the mind away from this path. The mind, by
nature, does not cherish this deviation from the path of increasing happiness and is put to strain. 'Expecting', therefore, will only
tend to make the mind miserable, with the result that the body
too will be strained. That is why the principle of 'expecting nothing' [14] during meditation is brought out here.

'Without possessions': [15] meditation is a process which takes
the mind from the consciousness of possessions to the conciousness of Being. In terms of possessions, it is a process of becoming
possessionless: the Self is left by Itself. The mind loses consciousness of the surroundings and the body, leaving the yogi quite
naturally without any consciousness of possessions. The Lord
speaks of being 'without possessions' to indicate that nothing is
helpful for meditation, because it proceeds on the basis of the
mind's natural tendency to go to a field of greater happiness, and
that at the same time the process leaves one in a state where
everything is abandoned of itself.

This expression also conveys that one should sit in meditation
prepared to lose everything. When consciousness of outside
objects begins to be lost, one should not begin to mourn its loss.
The yogi, when he starts his meditation, should not try to hang
on to anything. With a free mind he should go to Being and *be*
– awake in himself and lost to the world. As a result, he will be
possessed of the Self in the midst of the possessions of the world.
The phrase, 'without possessions', expresses the state of Being.

When the Lord says: 'expecting nothing, without possessions',
it is to show Arjuna what actually happens to the mind during
meditation. It would be wrong to *try* not to have any expectations
or desires, not to long for possessions when one sits in meditation;

14. See IV, 21.   15. See II, 45.

for while trying, the mind would be engaged in the thought of
possessions and other objects of desire in order to forget them.
Trying to forget amounts to remembering what one aims to forget.
This should not be done because the process of meditation does
not advance on the basis of forgetting the gross material objective world of possessions, but on the basis of entertaining finer
fields of experience. The attempt to forget is based on hatred and
condemnation, whereas the spontaneous experience of finer fields
of thought during meditation is based on that willing acceptance which is the natural tendency of the mind on the way to
greater happiness, on the path of God-realization.

This verse brings out the essentials of meditation – the practice
which easily leads the mind to transcendental consciousness and
from there, through the spontaneous infusion of Being into
activity, to cosmic consciousness. It must not be mistaken as
teaching a mode of conduct for life as a whole. This verse does not
advocate a monkish withdrawal from life for a yogi. It should not
be understood as teaching that a yogi must always remain away
from society, by himself, aspiring to nothing and possessing
nothing.

If the distinction is not made between the time of meditation
itself and the time spent out of meditation, then this verse and
the succeeding ones may well be misunderstood.

The following verses give further details of the practice.

VERSE 11

शुचौ देशे प्रतिष्ठाप्य स्थिरमासनमात्मनः ॥
नात्युच्छ्रितं नातिनीचं चैलाजिनकुशोत्तरम् ॥११॥

In a clean place, having set his
seat firm, neither very high nor
very low, having placed sacred
grass, deerskin and cloth one
upon the other.

'A clean place' means either that the place is naturally clean or has been made clean and free from dust and insects; that it is, if possible, in surroundings that are pleasant, or at least not unsightly and unpleasant. Both the place and the seat should be conducive to meditation. The meditator should feel comfortable and pleasant.

VERSE 12

तत्रकाग्रं मनः कृत्वा यतचित्तेन्द्रियक्रियः ॥
उपविश्यासने युञ्ज्याद्योगमात्मविशुद्धये ॥१२॥

Seated there on the seat, having
made the mind one-pointed, with
the activity of the senses and
thought subdued, let him practise
Yoga for self-purification.

The first point the Lord wants to make clear is that meditation should be performed in the sitting position and not lying down or standing. Lying down makes the mind dull; standing produces a fear of falling when the mind is drawn deep within. A normal state of mind is needed for starting meditation. The mind should neither be dull nor very active. When it is dull, tending to sleepiness, it loses the capacity for experience. When it is very active, it remains in the field of gross experience, and, as it were, refuses to enter into the field of subtle experience, just as someone very active on the surface of the water does not sink. To meditate is to let the mind sink into the Self. The process of sinking does not start if the mind is too active, as it has to be when the body is standing. The Lord therefore tells Arjuna that he should sit in order to start meditation.

'Having made the mind one-pointed': one-pointedness is most effectively brought about by allowing the mind to become drawn to more and more subtle states of the thought-process.

'With the activity of the senses and thought subdued': all experience arises out of the association of the mind with the objects of experience through the senses. During meditation the mind begins to associate itself with the subtler realms of the senses and in this way goes on experiencing more and more subtle aspects of the object of experience until eventually, associating itself with the subtlest level of the senses, it perceives the subtlest state of the object and then, transcending it, becomes established in the state of Being. In this way the activities of the mind and senses are gradually subdued.

In the state of absolute consciousness, the mind is free from all modes of the relative order and thus gains its most purified state. This is the state of Yoga. The Lord says: 'practise Yoga for self-purification.' Thereby He means that the practice of gaining this state is a means of gaining purification of body, mind and spirit.

When the mind experiences subtle states of the object of meditation, it becomes very sharp and refined. At the same time the breath becomes correspondingly refined, and this soft fine breathing tends to return the nervous system to its normal functioning order; any abnormal functioning is restored to normality. When the mind gains transcendental consciousness, it reaches its most purified state. At the same time the whole nervous system gains a state of restful alertness. In this state the body becomes a living instrument tuned to the divine nature.[16] This is the most purified state of the body.

As for the purification of the spirit, or self, the pure state of the spirit is Being, which is unbounded universal pure consciousness. When, through the practice of meditation, the mind reaches this consciousness, the individual spirit bound by time, space and causation, finds its unbounded cosmic nature. With practice, this state becomes permanent and the Self is experienced as completely separate from activity. This is the most purified state of the self, or the spirit.

This is how the practice of Yoga – that is, transcendental meditation – results in self-purification.

It is interesting to notice that in verse 11 of Chapter V the effect of self-purification was attributed to action performed by a yogi. This teaching becomes significant through the practice of Yoga.

16. See IV, 38.

VERSE 13

समं कायशिरोग्रीवं धारयन्नचलं स्थिरः ।।
संप्रेक्ष्य नासिकाग्रं स्वं दिशश्चानवलोकयन् ।।१३।।

Steady, keeping body, head and
neck upright and still, having
directed his gaze to the front
of his nose, without looking in
any direction.

The art of being steady is described here. When the neck and head are upright, in line with the spine, the path of the breath is clear, inhalation and exhalation are smooth and unrestricted. This eliminates the possibility of any unnatural movement of the body.

Having shown the method of stilling the body, the Lord explains how to still the senses. Sight is the most active of the senses, and if this is stilled the other senses will quite naturally follow it. The sense of sight, like all the senses, functions through the mind. Activity of the mind involves breath. So in order to coordinate the mind, the senses and the breath, the attention is brought 'to the front of his nose', the point where the breath and the normal line of vision meet. The effect of this is to establish coordination between the activities of the mind, the senses and the breath and to remove any abnormalities of these functions. It calms the mind and makes it one-pointed; it quietens the senses and refines the breath.

'Having directed his gaze' means directing it and releasing it, not continuing to gaze.

'Without looking in any direction' means first, not looking here and there; and secondly, not fixing one's look sharply even in the direction of the front of the nose; and thirdly, closing the eyes.

The teaching given here is generally misunderstood in terms of concentration on the tip of the nose. Shankara says that if fixing the gaze on the tip of the nose were meant here, the mind would be left with the nose but without God.

The posture described is free from any strain on the body, mind, senses or breath.

This verse prepares the platform from which the mind plunges into Being. It gives a technique whereby one gathers the attention from the multiplicity of the outside world to a calm and quiet state, while yet remaining in the field of outside experience. From here the process of meditation leads the mind inwards.

VERSE 14

प्रशान्तात्मा विगतभीर्ब्रह्मचारिव्रते स्थितः ॥
मनः संयम्य मच्चित्तो युक्त आसीत मत्परः ॥१४॥

With his being deep in peace,
freed from fear, settled in the
vow of chastity, with mind subdued
and thought given over to Me, let
him sit united realizing Me as the
Transcendent.

'With his being deep in peace' means that the mind is set on the path of increasing charm, bringing greater contentment at every step and filling one's being with ever deeper silence and peace. This is a state where there is no disturbing element. It is not the state of deep sleep because there the sense of being is lost. It is a state where peace is profound and the sense of being is not lost. It is a state of pure awareness. The mind has shifted from the field of sensory experience to the state of the Self, the state of profound peace.

'Freed from fear': on the path of increasing happiness during meditation there is no chance of fear. The Upanishads declare that fear comes with the sense of duality. Freed from fear means freed from the field of duality. The previous verse has seen the mind collected from the field of diversity; in this verse, it is gaining freedom from the sense of duality. The mind, during the inward stroke of meditation, begins to lose the sense of duality, begins to move away from the field of fear. Once begun, this process puts an end to duality and gives rise to transcendental consciousness, in which there is no possibility of fear.

'Settled in the vow of chastity': this does not mean that the practice here prescribed is only for those who have taken a vow of chastity. In the present context, the Lord is not dwelling on any gross aspect of the aspirant's way of life, on whether or not he may have taken any vow of chastity. Every expression in this verse gives deep insight into the state of the mind during the inward stroke of meditation, and it is in this sense that the words 'settled in the vow of chastity' should be understood.

All the energies of a man who has taken a vow of chastity are ever directed upwards, the whole stream of body, mind and senses being channelled towards the higher levels of evolution, with no chance for his energy to flow downwards. Likewise, when the mind of the meditator goes deep within, this too has the effect of directing upwards the life-energy in the different spheres of his body, senses and mind towards the highest level of evolution, at the same time allowing no chance of a downward flow of any mental, sensory or bodily energy. Every aspect of his individuality converges upon universal consciousness in the transcendental field of Being. Because transcendental meditation brings with it a continuous rise of the mind towards the consciousness of eternal Being, it may be compared to the vow of chastity, by virtue of which the whole life-stream of a celibate ever rises towards this supreme consciousness.

It is not, therefore, the act of taking a vow that is emphasized here; rather, it is the secure and safeguarded upward flow of one's energies on the road of the divine quest. This takes place during the process of transcendental meditation and also in the life of a celibate – one becomes 'urdhvaretas', meaning that one's energies flow only in an upward direction.[17]

'With mind subdued': having brought the mind under the influence of eternal Being. This happens in transcendental consciousness and therefore also in cosmic consciousness and God-consciousness. This is the central point of the present verse; all its other expressions follow from this one.

17. The glow appearing on the face during meditation is due to this upward flow of energy.

The expression 'with mind subdued' does not mean that the mind has to be controlled against its natural inclination and forced to go in the direction of the Transcendent. To discipline the mind by trying to control it is not the way to establish the mind in the Self. This verse gives a simple method for the realization of Truth and does not make it in any way complicated or difficult. 'Mind subdued' here signifies both the mind's natural state of calmness in transcendental consciousness and its natural tendency to flow freely in the single channel leading to transcendent bliss because it experiences greater charm at every inward step during meditation. The mind becomes subdued quite naturally, drawn to the Transcendent by increasing charm and not forced by will, pressure of discipline or control.

'Thought given over to Me' means thought surrendered to Me, who am the supreme Lord of all creation.[18] 'Thought given over to me'[19] does not mean thinking of 'Me'. It means surrendering one's authorship of thoughts. This in turn does not mean that one stops thinking. It means entertaining thoughts in the state of non-attachment, where the Self remains unattached to the process of thinking, remains in Its eternal freedom, while all activity is naturally given over to God, who is the basis of the entire life of the cosmos.

In the present context, however, 'thought given over to Me' is best seen as referring to the time of meditation. The Lord's words indicate that when thoughts appear one should not fight them, should not try to control the mind against them or try to run away from them; one should deal with them innocently. Let it be according to the will of God. Proceed on your meditation in a relaxed way and unconcerned with thoughts, as though you had already given them over to God.

During meditation one should not make a mood of surrendering thoughts to God, one should treat them as though they had already been surrendered to Him and did not belong to one any more; one remains completely indifferent to them.

'Let him sit united' : let him be in transcendental consciousness, or let his mind be firmly established in cosmic consciousness or in God-consciousness. The expression 'sit united' has no reference

18. See V, 29.   19. See also IV, 19, 20.

to activity or inactivity; it only means that in the states of transcendental consciousness and cosmic consciousness, the infusion of Being into the nature of the mind is so complete that the mind is totally fixed and embedded in it, and that in the state of God-consciousness, the mind is completely taken over by the Unity of life. In the states of cosmic consciousness and God-consciousness this Union remains the same whether the mind is active or inactive.

'Realizing Me as the Transcendent': this expression makes clear the whole meaning of the present verse, for it brings to light the state of surrender. Surrender has to be on the level of pure consciousness, on the level of life itself, on the level of Being – not on the level of thinking, feeling or understanding.

VERSE 15

युञ्जन्नेवं सदात्मानं योगी नियतमानसः ॥
शान्तिं निर्वाणपरमां मत्संस्थामधिगच्छति ॥१५॥

Ever thus collecting himself,
the yogi of disciplined mind
attains to peace, the supreme
liberation that abides in Me.

'Ever thus collecting himself': this expression refers to the practice explained in the four preceding verses. When the yogi sits to meditate, he continues to collect his mind, that is, he leads it back to the 'subdued' state described in the previous verse.

The Lord's use of the words 'collecting himself', rather than 'collecting the mind', is significant. 'Collecting himself' means collecting all aspects of his being: body, breath, senses, mind. This happens when the mind enters the realm of subtler experience on the way to gaining pure consciousness. All the senses begin to converge and collect themselves in the silent ocean of Being, the activity of the body's inner mechanism begins to sink into that silence, and the breath collects itself on that silent level of cosmic breath. All the different constituents of oneself begin to lie together on that level of pure Being. This comes about automatically and simultaneously for mind, senses, breath and body.[20] The expression 'collecting himself' thus indicates the process of transcendental meditation, which results directly in the state referred to in the Lord's command: 'Be without the three gunas.'[21]

'Ever' means that the yogi's only concern during meditation is to remain collected or engaged in the process of collecting himself. Either he remains collected in the state of pure Being mentioned in the previous verse, or if at any moment the whole structure of collectedness loosens, he has to collect himself again. He has always to be engaged in this manner. The significance of the word 'ever' is restricted to the time of meditation. It does not extend to the whole twenty-four hours of the yogi's day.

'The yogi of disciplined mind': this expression placed immediately after 'collecting himself' gives insight into the technique of 'collecting'. How does a yogi collect himself when he loses the state of collectedness during meditation? By the 'disciplined mind', by a mind which is orderly, smooth and harmonious in its functioning, so that its actions are easy and quiet. The mind is easy and naturally disciplined between 'collecting' and collectedness and again between the state of collectedness and 'collecting'. This means that when the mind goes off the path of meditation, the yogi quietly brings it back without any jerk, without causing strain. The practice, during meditation, of handling all situations in a delicate manner develops discipline in the mind, which then ceases to wander unreasonably and unnecessarily in the outer field of activity.

'Attains to peace': when, during meditation, the mind is collected, it enters into the experience of subtler states of thought. Experiencing increasing charm at every step, it becomes more and more contented, and this brings peace to the mind.

'The supreme liberation': having used the word 'peace', the Lord wants to make clear the nature of this peace in order to distinguish it from such peace as a man may gain through sleep, when the burden of thought has been lifted for a while, or through satisfaction in the various fields of life. He therefore adds that

20. See IV, 38.   21. See II, 45.

this peace is the supreme liberation. One who begins meditation
in the right manner, under the guidance of a qualified [22] person,
certainly develops in himself the state of abiding peace and eternal liberation while leading an active life in the world.

'That abides in Me': the supreme liberation does not lie in
any sovereign power, or power of nature, but in Me, the great
Lord of all creation. By virtue of My Being, this mighty universe
of huge and contrasting elements eternally and spontaneously
exists, while I remain uninvolved. This is 'the supreme liberation
that abides in Me', says the Lord, and this uninvolved state of
mind is developed by the 'disciplined mind' as it grows in
'peace' [23] and attains God-consciousness.

It may be noted that this verse declares the result of practice
to be peace and liberation, whereas verse 28 declares it to be infinite joy. Here no reference is made to this joy because, as verse
28 will show, it is the outcome of a life 'freed from blemish',
and this comes about through the practice described in the present
verse.

VERSE 16

नात्यश्नतस्तु योगोऽस्ति न चैकान्तमनश्नतः ।।
न चातिस्वप्नशीलस्य जाग्रतो नैव चार्जुन ।।१६।।

Yoga, indeed, is not for him who
eats too much nor for him who does
not eat at all, O Arjuna; it is
not for him who is too much given
to sleep nor yet for him who keeps
awake.

'Eats' and 'eat': these words indicate feeding the senses with
their objects. The senses should not be provided with the objects

22. See Appendix: Transcendental Meditation.
23. See verse 3, which says 'calmness' is the means.

of their enjoyment so excessively as to overfeed them, nor should
they be completely deprived of their experience.[24]

'Sleep' means a state where the senses of experience are not
active, while 'awake' denotes the opposite state. It is implied here
that if a man is 'too much given to sleep' or too much given to
keeping awake, then he will find it difficult to rise above the
states of waking and sleeping; and rising above them is absolutely
essential for Yoga.[25]

It is a common axiom that anything in excess is bad. Even
food, which is the source of energy, creates dullness and inefficiency when too much or too little of it is taken. Here the Lord
cautions against excess in either direction. In both cases the mind
becomes dull and fails to reach finer states of experience during
meditation. Remaining in the field of gross experience, it tends
to passivity. This is a waste of precious human existence, which
is meant for the expansion of happiness and the realization of an
integrated state of life, the state of supreme liberation referred
to in the previous verse.

The present verse advocates a normal and comfortable routine
in daily life for success in the practice of Yoga.

VERSE 17

युक्ताहारविहारस्य युक्तचेष्टस्य कर्मसु ।
युक्तस्वप्नावबोधस्य योगो भवति दुःखहा ॥१७॥

For him who is moderate in food
and recreation, moderate of effort
in actions, moderate in sleep and
waking, for him is the Yoga which
destroys sorrow.

Here is the broad principle to be followed by one who wishes to
live a life of inner peace and happiness integrated with successful
activity in the outside world. The body should be given the rest it
needs, and one should engage in activity, but not to a state of ex-

24. See II, 64, 67.   25. See II, 69, commentary.

haustion. Recreation should be taken in due proportion, so that it is neither too little nor too much. The Lord means that life should flow in a regular way, with a proper measure of activity and with each thing given its just value. One should avoid excess in all things and be regular in meditation, for this will result in the state of inner peace and freedom from bondage described in the 15th verse.

'Yoga', Union, is not only a state where the mind is fixed in divine consciousness. It is at the same time a state of individual life where every aspect of being is in perfect harmony with divine life and with life in nature. This state can only become permanent when the physical nervous system is sufficiently cultured to maintain it. The mind, as stated in the commentary to verse 15, is in tune with the cosmic mind, or intelligence of God, while the functioning of the body sets itself in tune with the functioning of cosmic nature. The senses rise to the full height of their capability, in order to experience and enjoy objects on the level of the divine play. But for body, organs and senses to function in their most natural way, in full accord with the laws of nature, it is absolutely essential that the routine of life be moderate, that everything connected with food and activity remain within the limits of moderation, that the happy medium be maintained.

'Moderate in sleep and waking': in its higher sense this expression indicates that one is only moderately involved[26] in the states of sleeping and waking. This means that the waking state, the state of knowing and experiencing the objective world, is primarily maintained by the senses, while the mind is primarily held in Being. And in the sleeping state, the body and the senses are completely withdrawn from activity but the mind is not overtaken by sleep: although detached from all activity it is awake in its awareness. Thus one is 'moderate in sleep and waking' in the sense of not being wholly engrossed in them.

'Moderate in food': in order to be moderate in food it is necessary to keep the whole system functioning normally. With regular meditation morning and evening, the functioning of the inner mechanisms is maintained in a normal condition,[27] and one becomes by nature 'moderate in food and recreation'.

26. See II, 69.   27. See verse 14, commentary.

'Recreation' means re-creation of the normal functioning of the entire system so that it is capable of operating to its maximum capacity. When certain mechanisms of the body have been put to one specific type of activity, they become tired and a man loses efficiency in that activity. When he engages in another type of activity, other mechanisms become active and the tired ones take rest, thereby regaining their efficiency. This is said to be re-creation. Those forms of recreation which are based on a change of activity in the outer field of life do not re-create the whole system at one time and therefore do not renew efficiency to the maximum extent. Transcendental meditation re-creates, in that it produces a state of restful alertness for the entire system and rejuvenates it, thus fulfilling the purpose of recreation.

'Moderate of effort in actions' means that one has not to over-exert when working. This implies first, that one should be strong enough not to get tired – in other words, one should be energetic, alert and free from laziness; and secondly, that the undertaking should be in accordance with one's own dharma,[28] consistent with the laws of nature,[29] otherwise nature offers its silent protest against the effort, and one is compelled to make unduly great 'effort in actions'. The regular practice of transcendental meditation fulfils both these needs because it provides greater energy and produces harmony in nature.

It should not be understood that being 'moderate of effort in actions' is a prerequisite for Yoga. This quality grows as the practice advances. It is not something which can be achieved without transforming the very nature of the man and his surroundings. As the practice of meditation advances, it effortlessly transforms both his inner nature and the influence of his surroundings. This automatically makes him 'moderate of effort in actions'.

Each condition given in this verse lays emphasis on moderation, which is most effectively brought about through the regular practice of transcendental meditation. Therefore transcendental meditation can be regarded as the most effective form of recreation.

'Yoga which destroys sorrow': it has been said earlier that the transcendental state of consciousness is the state of Yoga. This is

28. See I, 1, commentary.   29. See Appendix: Cosmic Law.

undoubtedly a state of bliss, but how does the bliss that lies in the transcendental state help to end sorrow and suffering in the relative field of life? By taking the transcendental bliss and bringing it back to the field of relative existence, bliss begins to dominate the sphere in which sorrows and suffering prevailed. The expression 'Yoga which destroys sorrow', makes it clear that the different points which this verse brings out regarding conduct form an essential part of the practice designed to transform transcendental pure consciousness into cosmic consciousness.[30]

The present verse explains the general mode of conduct which alone will allow the bliss experienced in meditation to be infused into the relative phase of existence. Its entire purpose is to warn the aspirant against laying too much importance on any one aspect of relative life. If only he takes things in their due proportion, every aspect of his life will remain without strain. It is this harmonious level of existence which provides the basis on which the divine Being can be lived in the world. This is further explained by the word 'united' in the following verse.

VERSE 18

यदा विनियतं चित्तमात्मन्येवावतिष्ठते ॥
निःस्पृहः सर्वकामेभ्यो युक्त इत्युच्यते तदा ॥१८॥

When his mind, completely settled,
is established in the Self alone,
when he is free from craving for
any pleasure, then is he said to
be united.

This is a description of the state of mind reached through the practice described in the previous verses.

'His mind completely settled': this refers to transcendental consciousness, where the mind has become an unlimited and silent ocean of pure consciousness without a single wave of thought. It

30. See verse 25.

may also be said to refer to cosmic consciousness, where the calm of the ocean is not disturbed in spite of waves of thought and experience.

It may be argued that it is the very nature of the mind to become completely settled in any object of experience, for was it not said in the 67th verse of Chapter II that a man's intellect is carried away by the senses 'as a ship by the wind on water'? This being the case, does not the mind, drawn by the force of the senses, become completely settled at the contact of the senses with their objects and enjoy the happiness to be derived therefrom?[31]

In order to give no room for such arguments and to avoid misunderstanding, the Lord says: 'established in the Self alone'. This expression has its meaning on two levels: on the level of transcendental consciousness and on that of cosmic consciousness. On the transcendental level there is nothing but the Self alone. The nature of the Self is pure consciousness, cosmic intelligence, cosmic existence, cosmic life, eternal Being, absolute bliss. It is transcendent, ever the same, imperishable. It is 'smaller than the smallest'. it is the silence. The word 'Self' expresses the inexpressible transcendental Truth of life. The mind, coming to this field, loses its individuality and gains its true nature as pure Being.

On the level of cosmic consciousness, the expression 'established in the Self alone' means that in the midst of all behaviour, in the activity or the silence of the waking, dreaming and sleeping states, a man realizes the Self as completely separate from the field of activity and thus remains established in the Self alone. The varied experiences of life fail to overshadow this state of cosmic existence and complete fulfilment which the mind has gained.

Having explained the steadfast and unshakable character of the mind in the state of eternal contentment, the Lord turns to the practical value of such a state of mind; for a principle or a state of mind which has no practical use in daily life is of little importance in the world. The Lord has told Arjuna that the Yoga which He is expounding here was given to the first rulers of the world,[32] thereby placing it on a very practical level. Moreover, throughout the discourse, at the end of any exposition of a highly spiritual

31. See II, 14.   32. See IV, 1, 2.

and abstract nature, the Lord says something to tie it down to practical life. Here He says: 'free from craving for any pleasure'.

'Free from craving for any pleasure' means fulfilled. Craving for pleasure arises from lack of contentment, which may be due to the objects of the senses not being available, or to the inability of the senses to experience the joy that is available.[33] But once a man is established in the state described in this verse, he is eternally contented, and this state of lasting contentment leaves no room for any craving for pleasures.[34]

This state of freedom 'from craving for any pleasure' is on the level of that complete fulfilment of life where the individual being is one with the cosmic Being. It is on the level of 'eternal freedom in divine consciousness';[35] on the level of 'maintaining your consciousness in the Self';[36] on the level of Union and knowledge.[37] It fulfils the aspirations expressed by verse 55 of Chapter II and verse 38 of Chapter IV, and satisfies the level of attainment given in verse 8 of Chapter V.

This state is on the level where the paths of Sankhya and Karma Yoga meet to find fulfilment in a common goal, as brought out by verse 5 of Chapter V.

'United': in verse 8, this word was used to denote evenness of vision; here, as in verse 14, it is given a much wider meaning. It is used in terms of the whole being, encompassing the entire field of the mind, its silence and its desires and activities, the whole field of life that lies between the two extremes of bondage and eternal freedom, between the individual man and the cosmic Divine. It denotes life in cosmic consciousness, which is inclusive of the relative and the Absolute.

33. See II, 59.   34. See III, 17, 18; VI, 2.   35. See V, 24–6; II, 55–72.
36. See III, 30.   37. See IV, 10, 18–24, 35, 41; V, 7, 19–21, 23; VI, 4, 8.

VERSE 19

यथा दीपो निवातस्थो नेङ्गते सोपमा स्मृता ॥
योगिनो यतचित्तस्य युञ्जतो योगमात्मनः ॥१६॥

A lamp which does not flicker in
a windless place – to such is
compared the yogi of subdued thought
practising Union with the Self.

This verse may be compared with verse 69 of Chapter II, which says that in the night of all beings the self-controlled man is awake. But the simile in the present verse is more profound, for whereas the expression in the second chapter is in the context of the senses and their control,[38] the lamp in the windless place represents 'thought', standing by itself, freed from the influence of the senses.

This illustrates the reason for the difference between the discourses of enlightened men at different times. When such men come out to explain the Truth, their manner of expression and depth of thought depend upon the time and surrounding circumstances. Their discourse depends upon the purity of consciousness of those listening to it. At this stage, Arjuna's consciousness has become pure enough to understand with exactness the state of 'the yogi of subdued thought practising Union with the Self'.

It may be noted that any objective experience is due to the mind's association with the object through the senses. For example, if one is meditating on a thought, the experience of the gross and subtle states of that thought are due to the mind's association with the sense of speech.

During meditation the object of experience continues to be perceived in its diminishing states, but when the subtlest state of experience has been transcended, then the mind is free from the influence both of the object and of the sense through which it has been experiencing. As long as the mind is influenced by the senses

38. See II, 68.

and their objects, so long is it like a lamp flickering in the wind, but once out of their influence it becomes steady, like 'a lamp which does not flicker in a windless place'.

As long as the mind is associated with the object, so long is it the experiencing mind; but when the object of experience has diminished to the point where it has disappeared, the mind ceases to be the experiencing mind. Conscious mind becomes consciousness. But during this process of transformation, it first gains the pure state of its own individuality.

It is interesting to see that the verse does not speak of the mind but of 'thought' as being steady. The Sanskrit word used is *chitta*, which signifies that aspect of mind which is a quiet and silent collection of impressions, or seeds of desires. Chitta is like water without ripples. It is called 'manas', or mind, when ripples arise.

When the mind gains this state of chitta, or 'thought', then it stands steady, like 'a lamp which does not flicker in a windless place'. It holds its individuality in the void – the abstract fullness around it – because there is nothing for it to experience. It remains undisturbed, awake in itself.

Imagine a silent wave on a silent ocean, ready to expand and merge into the silence of the deep. The state of the pure individuality of the mind, the pure individuality of the 'I', expressed by this verse, directly merges into transcendental Self-consciousness; this is expressed by the Lord as 'Union with the Self': the mind is united with divine Being.

This state of Divine Union, or Yoga, is defined in its different aspects in the four following verses, after which six verses are devoted to the transformation of transcendental consciousness into cosmic consciousness. Then three verses bring to light the essence of the path from cosmic consciousness to God-consciousness, in which a yogi reaches the pinnacle of achievement.

VERSE 20

यत्रोपरमते चित्तं निरुद्धं योगसेवया ॥
यत्र चैवात्मनात्मानं पश्यन्नात्मनि तुष्यति ॥२०॥

That (state) in which thought,
settled through the practice of Yoga,
retires, in which, seeing the Self by
the Self alone, he finds contentment
in the Self;

This verse describes a further step in the practice. The previous
verses have taken the mind to the state where thought – the
resolute intellect – stands by itself, steady and unmoved. The
present verse says that when, with continued practice, this steady
intellect gains a clear experience of its individuality, it begins to
retire. The process of retiring begins with the expansion of individuality, and when this happens the intellect, losing its individuality, begins to gain universality, begins to gain the
unbounded status of Being. While merging into Being, it cognizes
Being as its own Self and gains bliss-consciousness – the yogi
'finds contentment in the Self'.

The Self, as was said in the commentary on verse 18, is of
transcendental nature; until the mind transcends all experience,
it does not realize the Self. In the process of transcending all
experience, the mind retires from the experience of multiplicity
and gains the experience of Unity in its own individual nature.
Then, transcending its individual status, it expands into cosmic
Being. This state of Being, the state of transcendental consciousness, is referred to by the words, 'seeing the Self by the Self
alone'.

The word 'alone' is significant, for it emphasizes that the transcendental Self Itself forms the content of Its Being and that
nothing which is of relative existence can possibly cognize It. Its
purity, eternal and supreme, is such that even the finest aspect of
individual life, the resolute intellect, is foreign to It and is denied

entry into It. The intellect has to surrender its existence in order to find its place in the eternal Being of the Self.

This is the glory of the nature of the Self. Having come back home, the traveller finds peace. The intensity of happiness is beyond the superlative. The bliss of this state eliminates the possibility of any sorrow, great or small. Into the bright light of the sun no darkness can penetrate; no sorrow can enter bliss-consciousness, nor can bliss-consciousness know any gain greater than itself. This state of self-sufficiency leaves one steadfast in oneself, fulfilled in eternal contentment.

The present verse forms the begining of a long sentence that culminates in verse 23. Nowhere else in the Bhagavad-Gita do we find a sentence of this extended nature. This is because these four verses present Yoga, the state of Divine Union, in its complete glory. The present verse brings to light the state of Divine Union in transcendental consciousness. The following verse depicts it in cosmic consciousness, the third in terms of the supreme gain that is God-consciousness, and the fourth in terms of the elimination of suffering.

VERSE 21

सुखमात्यन्तिकं यत्तद्बुद्धिग्राह्यमतीन्द्रियम् ॥
वेत्ति यत्र न चैवायं स्थितश्चलति तत्त्वतः ॥२१॥

Knowing that which is infinite joy
and which, lying beyond the senses,
is gained by the intellect, and wherein
established, truly he does not waver;

In order to know why the senses cannot experience 'infinite joy', it is necessary to understand the origin of the senses and their objects. Creation begins with prakriti, or Nature, which expresses itself in the three gunas, sattva, rajas and tamas. As the process of creation continues, the three gunas manifest as 'mahat tattva', the principle of intellect. This further manifests as 'aham tattva', the principle of mind, which in its turn manifests as the five 'tan-matras', from which arise the five senses. Then, as the process of manifestation continues, the five tanmatras manifest into the five elements, which combine to constitute the entire objective creation.

The range of sensory experience is limited to the field of creation resulting from these five elements. The senses only enable one to experience the joys of the objective world. The bliss of eternal life lies far beyond the senses and immediately beyond the intellect. It can be appreciated by the intellect but cannot be appreciated by the senses.

The Lord says that infinite joy is of transcendental nature; it is known only when the subtlest aspect of relativity, the intellect, surrenders itself to the transcendental Self, as was explained in the previous verse. Once it is known, one is so captivated by it that one can never again be completely out of its influence.

'Gained by the intellect': although infinite joy comes with the surrender of the intellect, it is even then said to be 'gained by the intellect'. When the crown prince becomes king, the crown prince ceases to exist, but even then it can be said that the crown prince has 'gained' kingship. It is in this sense that the state of transcendental Self is 'gained by the intellect'.

'Does not waver': in the state of transcendental consciousness there is no possibility of activity, but continued practice of transcending the field of relativity cultures the mind so that it remains established in bliss, unwavering even in the field of activity.

This verse brings out the essential characteristic of Yoga in cosmic consciousness: 'infinite joy', 'lying beyond the senses', 'gained by the intellect', 'wherein established, truly he does not waver'.

Details of this state are given in verses 24 to 29.

VERSE 22

यं लब्ध्वा चापरं लाभं मन्यते नाधिकं ततः ॥
यस्मिन्स्थितो न दुःखेन गुरुणापि विचाल्यते ॥२२॥

Having gained which he counts no
other gain as higher, established in
which he is not moved even by great
sorrow;

This is the glory of the supreme state of Yoga; the supreme state of Divine Union in God-consciousness, the blessed oneness of life in which 'he counts no other gain as higher'. This is that state in which the separation of the Self from activity, as experienced in cosmic consciousness, finds its consummation in Unity of life, in the light of God, which knows no duality. Life becomes so at home with this state that 'he is not moved' by all the sorrows and sufferings that go on in the relative aspect of life.

The glory of this discourse of the Lord is found in the words, 'established in which he is not moved even by great sorrow'. Even when the Lord here presents the supreme state of life, 'having gained which he counts no other gain as higher', He keeps it within the range of the human heart, which is exposed to sorrow. Indeed, He extends the very definition of this most blessed state of Divine Union, or Yoga, to the level of human suffering. This is to indicate how even those phases of life in most extreme contrast to Divinity are intimately embraced by this blessed state of Divine Union. The following verse develops this point.

The details of the state of God-consciousness are dealt with in verses 30–32.

VERSE 23

तं विद्याद्‌दुःखसंयोगवियोगं योगसंज्ञितम् ॥
स निश्चयेन योक्तव्यो योगोऽनिर्विण्णचेतसा ॥२३॥

Let that disunion of the union
with sorrow be known by the name
of Yoga (Union). This Yoga should
be practised with firm resolve and
heart undismayed.

This verse brings out the spiritual teaching of the Lord in terms of Union in 'disunion'. He shows that Yoga is universal; it is found even in the field of 'disunion'. He says that even the disunion of the mind with sorrow is Union, and that this Union (Yoga) must be practised with determination and firmness of

mind. The Lord wants everyone to practise this: those who can
practise it in the name of Union should do so; those who cannot
should do so in the name of disunion. The word Union is for those
who can conceive of absolute bliss and wish to possess it even to
the extent of being it. The word disunion is for those who cannot conceive of this bliss, or cannot think themselves capable of
aspiring to it. But these latter are certainly familiar in their lives
with sorrow and will wish to come out of its reach. Let them
therefore begin this practice in order to put an end to sorrow. The
mind must be taken out of the realm of suffering, for there is no
need to suffer in life when there is this centre of happiness within
oneself.

How one may continue to practise this Yoga which puts an end
to all one's suffering is explained in the five verses that follow.

Verses 20 to 23 have been devoted to the definition of Yoga.
The purpose of defining Yoga in four verses is to show that Yoga
is sufficient to fulfil all the four aims of life prescribed by the
Hindu scriptures. These declare the purpose of life to be the fulfilment of 1. dharma, 2. artha, 3. kama and 4. moksha.

1. Dharma is one's natural duty, which includes all moral goodness, right action, freedom, justice and lawfulness – all the
   principles that uphold and support life. All these are completely
   satisfied once a man has realized himself. For in the knowledge
   and experience of the Self, a man attains a level of life which
   is the basis of all morality, virtue and right action, and from
   which he is able to fulfil the laws [39] of nature and do justice to
   all creation. Verse 20, describing the Unity of the mind and
   Being, shows all aspirations of dharma fulfilled.

2. Artha is fulfilled in verse 21. Artha means wealth, business,
   advantage, utility, reward and gain. With the experience of
   eternal bliss, all such aspirations are completely satisfied, for to
   store more and more means of happiness is the only purpose
   of artha in all its aspects.

3. Kama is desire. Desire naturally aims at happiness and the
   removal of suffering. All aspirations on this level are satisfied
   when man realizes the eternal bliss of the Self. When one seeks
   no more and desires no greater happiness, then one is fulfilled

39. See Appendix: Cosmic Law.

from the point of view of kama. Describing such fulfilment, verse 22 presents the summit of the realization of kama. It provides security even against great sorrow and offers supreme happiness.

4. Moksha is liberation. Verse 23 proclaims liberation from all pain and sorrow through Yoga, or Union with the Supreme, as described in verse 20.

These verses, 20–3, form the four pillars of the edifice of Yoga. They stand to remind men of every generation that it is not necessary to suffer in life, that life's goal is easy to attain and that all aspirations are easy to fulfil. The way is by the inward march of the mind, by quietly locating the hidden universal Being, a ray of whose eternal light is sufficient to dispel all the darkness of ignorance and shower down the blessings of almighty God.

These verses, in giving the definition of Yoga, provide a royal road to fulfilment at every level [40] of human life. Fortunate are those who take this highway, who practise transcendental meditation.

It must be made quite clear at this point that the purpose of Yoga does not end in realizing the Self in the transcendental state (verse 20). Although this is the final attainment of the inward stroke of meditation and although it gives a full meaning to Yoga in that it brings complete Union with divine consciousness, it is not complete. The overall purpose of Yoga is not yet satisfied. Unless the divine consciousness, gained in the transcendental state, continues to maintain itself at all times, in a natural manner, irrespective of the different states of waking, dreaming or sleeping, and irrespective of the mind's engagement in activity or in silence, the purpose of Yoga is not fulfilled. Yoga, or Divine Union, attained in the state of Self-consciousness, or Atmananda, has to develop into cosmic consciousness, or Brahmananda, which again is a state of Yoga. This eventually gives rise to God-consciousness, the pinnacle of Yoga, where there is no trace of sorrow or suffering.

40. Refer to *The Science of Being and Art of Living*, by Maharishi Mahesh Yogi (International SRM Publications, 1966).

VERSE 24

सङ्कल्पप्रभवान्कामांस्त्यक्त्वा सर्वानशेषतः ॥
मनसैवेन्द्रियग्रामं विनियम्य समन्ततः ॥२४॥

Abandoning without reserve all
desires from which the incentive
(to action) is born, controlling
the village of the senses on every
side by the mind alone.

Having thus far defined three states of Yoga, the Lord, in this
and the following four verses, describes how the state of Yoga in
transcendental consciousness is transformed into the state of
Yoga in cosmic consciousness.

Such is the marvel of the Lord's expression that in each of these
five verses [41] in sequence He is able to develop not only the theme
of gaining transcendental consciousness, but side by side with
this a second theme: that of the development of cosmic consciousness when transcendental consciousness has already been gained.
The parallel presentation of these two themes is a teaching in
itself. It shows first that the path to cosmic consciousness comprehends the path to transcendental consciousness, and secondly
that cosmic consciousness develops simultaneously with the
growth of transcendental consciousness in the mind.

'The incentive (to action)': the stimulus that a desire produces
in the nervous system, bringing into action the senses of perception and the organs of action. This stimulus is opposed to the
process of gaining that state of restful alertness of the nervous
system which corresponds with transcendental consciousness.
That is why, when the Lord is explaining the whole process of
making transcendental consciousness permanent, He emphasizes
the need for preventing the opposing process from interfering. It
should be borne in mind, however, that even though the Lord
gives this caution He is not advocating a practice of controlling

41. Verses 24–8.

desire. He states as a principle that desires are not helpful [42] on the path because they stimulate the nervous system to external activity and this is opposed to its internal activity, which gives experience of subtle states of thought as the mind proceeds towards the state of transcendental consciousness.

When the Lord says: 'Abandoning without reserve all desires from which the incentive (to action) is born, controlling the village of the senses on every side by the mind alone', He means engage the mind in the process of transcendental meditation and let it enter into the experience of subtle fields of thinking.

Having become familiar with bliss-consciousness in the field of the Transcendent, the mind is very naturally and automatically drawn in that direction if allowed to proceed without distraction. The Lord says: 'by the mind alone', meaning that one does not use any austerity or forcible control to close the gates of the senses. The senses will automatically set themselves quietly to follow the mind as it proceeds to the Transcendent. In the quiet inward stroke of the mind during meditation, desires are automatically abandoned. Here the Lord is only saying that one should let the mind follow its familiar path to the Transcendent in the most natural and normal manner.

'The village of the senses': the place where the senses are housed. This is the structure of the nervous system. The whole nervous system is the village, the individual senses are the villagers and the mind the landlord. Thus, when the Lord says: 'controlling the village of the senses on every side by the mind alone', the principle He wants to bring out is this: control the landlord to influence the villagers, in order to reorientate the village so that its activity, the activity of the nervous system, proceeds in accordance with the laws of nature, while the awareness of the Self maintains its natural state in eternal Being. This places the whole of life in its most natural state: absolute Being and the relative field of activity remain separate and yet integrated in the individual life in the state of cosmic consciousness.

The practice is entirely mental, but it directly influences the whole nervous system, through which the senses function. It should be noted that when the Lord begins the teaching about

42. See III, 37.

gaining cosmic consciousness He speaks of the nervous system, the physical aspect of life, and emphasizes the need for its reorientation. But the human nervous system is of such extreme complexity and refinement that it is not possible to reorientate it through a physical approach. This difficulty is solved by the emphasis that the Lord places on the words 'the mind alone'. Thereby He warns the aspirant against making any attempt to control the senses directly, or to influence the nervous system by any physical means. The reorientation of the nervous system is essential in order to make permanent the state of transcendental consciousness,[43] but it must be brought about by a mental process. If the aspirant tries to control the senses on their own level, or if he attempts to control them by a mental process which goes against their natural tendencies, the result will be strain. The practice taught in this verse is absolutely free from any possibility of strain.

'Controlling the village of the senses on every side' : this expression indicates the technique of controlling all the senses at one and the same time, without offering them any resistance individually on the level of the senses themselves, and without attacking their natural tendency to lead the mind towards their objects. This aspect of the teaching is of the utmost value. When the senses are turned inwards during the inward stroke of meditation, and outwards during the outward stroke of meditation, then they are becoming reorientated in a most natural way so that their every activity is spontaneously in accordance with the laws of nature.

This process of reorientation will be strained if the senses are restricted. Only if a situation is created in which the senses have a free inward and outward activity motivated by their own nature to enjoy is it possible for man to realize that the greater intensity of happiness lies in the inward direction. And with this realization, the habit of remaining under the influence of the bliss of Being is built up, to give rise to cosmic consciousness.

43. See IV, 38.

VERSE 25

शनैः शनैरुपरमेद्बुद्ध्या धृतिगृहीतया ॥
आत्मसंस्थं मनः कृत्वा न किञ्चिदपि चिन्तयेत् ॥२५॥

Let him gradually retire through
the intellect possessed of patience;
having established the mind in the
Self, let him not think at all.

This verse clarifies the words 'retires' (verse 20) and 'abandoning' (verse 24). It emphasizes that the process of retiring should be gradual and adds 'possessed of patience' to make quite clear that nothing should be done to hasten or modify this process. Once begun, it should be allowed to proceed by itself.

The points about patience and gradualness are highly important. If a man becomes impatient and tries to push the mind into the Transcendent, then many disadvantages arise. The intensity of thought is very great at that subtle level of thinking where the mind is slipping out of thought and is about to lose the experience of the relative field. If the process is not disturbed and is allowed to go by itself in a very innocent manner, then the mind slips into the Self. If, on the other hand, pressure or force is applied in any way to check the mind or to control the process, the mind will be thrown off the course on which it is naturally set and off-balance into agitation and a feeling of discomfort. That is why the process has to be allowed to take place quietly and patiently, without any anxiety or hurry.

One must not exert oneself in order to transcend. Exertion of any kind only retards the process of transcending. The mind naturally proceeds towards the Self because in that direction it is attracted by ever-increasing happiness. So the Lord says it should be allowed to come in that direction naturally and innocently.

'Intellect possessed of patience' has an inner meaning, apart from the obvious one of advocating patience on the part of the intellect. It is that the intellect should not function during the process. What is happening should not be watched and analysed or scrutinized by the intellect. No critical scrutiny of the process is needed. The intellect only needs to be receptive and appreciative and not in any way discriminative or on its guard. It has only to accept experience as it comes.

'Let him gradually retire': so that the mind, as it fathoms the deeper levels of the thought-process, may simultaneously become refined in order to experience further subtler states and may proceed onward in an innocent manner. If a man standing in bright light suddenly rushes into a dark cave, his eyes may not be able to see what is there inside the cave; but if he enters slowly, his eyes become used to the lesser intensity of light, and then he is able to see. The mind, when it retires deep within, goes from the more gross to the subtler levels of experience. Therefore it is essential for the mind not to rush in suddenly but to go gradually and patiently.

Again, when the individuality of the intellect begins to gain the state of Being, it is absolutely necessary that the process be slow. Only then will the bliss be within the range of experience.

'Let him not think at all': the Lord says that when the mind is established in the Self one should not try to think, because the transcendental state of consciousness lies beyond the mind's ability to think. Any attempt to think in that state will not succeed. This is the state where one just enjoys being there. It is not on a level where thought can find a place. The Lord informs the aspirant of its nature so that he may not expect some good thoughts to come in that state.

The Lord says: 'Do not think at all.' This state of not thinking is a natural consequence of the mind's being established in the Self; and it holds good only during meditation. It does not mean that a man should not think of anything when he is out of meditation, for a habit of not thinking will make his life dull and useless.

The mind, coming out of the Self, out of the state of transcendence during meditation, alights on a thought; what is then to be done is explained in the following verse.

'Let him gradually retire through the intellect possessed of patience': this expression also presents a teaching which is important on the way to cosmic consciousness when transcendental consciousness has already been gained. When, through the practice of transcendental meditation, the mind gains familiarity with the state of Being, one begins to feel as if uninvolved while engaged in activity. This experience of non-attachment grows in intensity with practice. This is what the Lord means by 'gradually retire', in the context of gaining cosmic consciousness. He adds that during this process the intellect should be 'possessed of patience' so that it may not hurriedly and wrongly interpret the experience. It should be noted that when this sense of non-attachment is appreciated by the intellect, activity becomes much more effective and fruitful in the outer world. In the absence of a proper interpretation of this expression of non-attachment, one might become bewildered, and this great blessing of life might become a liability.

'Having established the mind in the Self, let him not think at all': when the mind has permanently gained transcendental Self-consciousness, then it is no longer required to embark upon any mental activity, the necessity of which was implied by the previous verse. When the mind is permanently established in the Self, the purpose of the teaching of the previous verse has been accomplished: cosmic consciousness has been gained.

The expression, 'let him not think at all', brings out the essential features of cosmic consciousness. First, this state of life is not maintained on the basis of thinking or feeling: it is lived naturally on the level of Being. Secondly, the Self in this state has separated Itself so completely from the field of activity that, even when the mind entertains thoughts, the Self remains completely free [44] from the process of thinking. This is that state of life referred to in verse 3: 'for the man who has ascended to Yoga, and for him alone, calmness is said to be the means.'

The previous verse described the value of mental activity during the inward stroke of meditation. The following verse shows how to direct mental activity when the mind comes out of the transcendental state of consciousness.

44. See V, 7–9.

VERSE 26

यतो यतो निश्चरति मनश्चञ्चलमस्थिरम् ।।
ततस्ततो नियम्यैतदात्मन्येव वशं नयेत् ।।२६।।

*Whatever makes the fickle and
unsteady mind wander forth, from
that withdrawn, let him bring it
under the sway of the Self alone.*

'Withdrawn': the word in the text is *niyamya*, which means
having regulated or disciplined. Here it means having turned
back to the Self.

This is the art of successful meditation. It is natural that when
the mind has taken a dive into the Self and comes out to the relative field again, it should be brought back to the medium of
meditation in order to begin a second dive. In the early stages of
meditation, however, it is generally found that with the outward stroke of meditation the mind comes on to some thought.
The Lord therefore says that the mind should be brought back
from a foreign thought to the medium of meditation, so that it
comes once more to the established channel and, experiencing the
finer states of the medium in a natural way, comes again to the
Transcendent.

The Lord says: Turn the mind towards the Self. This in no
way suggests difficulty. Unfortunately for the student of the
Bhagavad-Gita, commentators have stated that the mind needs to
be controlled and disciplined, which implies that the whole
approach is strenuous and difficult. There is, however, no idea of
control or discipline of the mind in the Lord's teaching. True,
He has used two adjectives to qualify 'mind': 'fickle' and 'unsteady'. But we have to remember that the Lord is here describing the process of leading the mind to the Self, whereas these
adjectives apply to the mind when it is subjected to the outward
stroke of meditation. It is quite right for the mind to enter a
wavering state when it comes out of the field of transcendental

Unity, like waves beginning to appear on the still surface of the ocean. So when at times the mind is found on a foreign thought during meditation, this should be regarded – if the process of meditation is a right one – as the outward stroke of meditation. It should not be taken as evidence that the mind is by nature 'fickle' and 'unsteady', though commentators have supposed it to be so.

If one notices that the mind is going out into thoughts even when it has not reached the transcendental Being but is only on the way to It during the inward stroke of meditation, this again should not be ascribed to the innate weakness of the mind. It may be due to the nervous system being under strain, or it may be due to lack of proper guidance. It can be the result of inefficiency either on the part of the teacher or of the pupil, but usually the inadequacy is found to be on the part of the teacher.

The Lord, then, teaches that if it happens that the mind is distracted by something external, one should quietly bring it back to the channel which leads to the Self. It is the nature of the mind to go to a field of greater happiness. When, during meditation, the mind begins to experience the finer states of the object of attention, it begins to experience increasing charm at every step. There is then no chance for it to go anywhere except in the direction which leads to the Transcendent.

This is true of the system of transcendental meditation, which is the main concern of these verses.

The significance of this verse in relation to cosmic consciousness lies in its emphasis on the necessity of alternating the inward and outward march of the mind. This is to allow the infusion of Being into the nature of the mind so that all its activity may become supported and enriched by divine value, and so that finally the whole of life may become divine in cosmic consciousness.

The following verse brings to light the nature of cosmic consciousness in terms of supreme happiness and summarizes the essential features of the way.

VERSE 27

प्रशान्तमनसं ह्येनं योगिनं सुखमुत्तमम् ॥
उपैति शान्तरजसं ब्रह्मभूतमकल्मषम् ॥२७॥

For supreme happiness comes to the
yogi whose mind is deep in peace,
in whom the spur to activity is stilled,
who is without blemish and has become
one with Brahman.

The Lord made a similar statement about supreme happiness in
the 21st verse; but from the 24th verse He has been intent upon
describing the method by which supreme happiness is to be
attained. During meditation the mind, as it experiences the finer
aspects of the object of meditation, eventually transcends even
the subtlest experience, and then there is no activity. This is
what the Lord means when He says that the 'spur to activity'
(rajas) 'is stilled'. This is the field of the Transcendent, the state
of pure consciousness, stainless, sinless. Here the individual mind
ceases to be; it gains the status of divine intelligence. Having gone
beyond the limits of an individual mind's wanting and desiring,
it is fully established in deep peace and attains supreme happiness.

The faculty of experience becomes extinct when the mind loses
its individuality. The state of Being knows no knowing; it is a
state that transcends all knowing or experiencing. But if this is
so, how can it be said that the mind experiences supreme happiness? First, it should be noted that the Lord uses the word 'up-
aiti', which means 'comes to'; the word 'experiences' is not used.
However, even if the word 'experiences' were used, it could be
regarded as valid. The mind does have the ability to experience
when it is on the verge of transcending, at the junction of relativity and the Absolute. It is at this point that the mind experiences the nature of absolute bliss-consciousness. This has
been brought out in the Upanishads, where it is stated specifically

that Reality is experienced by the mind alone. Experience of Reality by the mind is always at the junction-point: while it is about to transcend at the end of the inward stroke of meditation, and while coming out of transcendence at the start of the outward stroke of meditation.

'Deep in peace': see verses 7, 14 and 15 of this chapter and verses 70 and 71 of Chapter II. The Lord means peace that is not overshadowed even by activity – the eternal peace that is gained when one 'in action sees inaction' (IV, 18); 'the supreme peace' (IV, 39); 'lasting peace' (V, 12).

The nature of the 'spur to activity' (rajas) was explained in the commentary on verse 45 of Chapter II.

'Who is without blemish': who is established in the absolute purity of Being, completely separate from the field of activity. His actions being completely in accordance with the laws of nature,[45] they are free from blemish.

'Has become one with Brahman': has gained cosmic consciousness.

It is interesting to see how this one verse describes both the state of cosmic consciousness itself and the path by which it is reached. It makes clear that supreme happiness is gained in cosmic consciousness and that there are three prerequisites to gaining it: the mind must be 'deep in peace', 'the spur to activity' must be 'stilled' and one must be 'without blemish'.

The teachings of the three previous verses, which have defined in detail the nature of the path to cosmic consciousness, are represented by individual phrases in this verse. 'Mind is deep in peace' refers to verse 24; 'in whom the spur to activity is stilled' refers to verse 25; 'who is without blemish' refers to verse 26.

The flower of divine wisdom of this verse comes to full bloom in the following five verses.

45. See V, 25.

VERSE 28

युञ्जन्नेवं सदात्मानं योगी विगतकल्मषः ॥
सुखेन ब्रह्मसंस्पर्शमत्यन्तं सुखमश्नुते ॥२८॥

Ever thus collecting himself,
the yogi, freed from blemish,
with ease attains contact with
Brahman, which is infinite joy.

Here the Lord brings out quite clearly that realization of cosmic
consciousness is not at all difficult. It is easily attained.

'Ever thus collecting himself' gives expression to the points
brought out in the previous four verses.

'Ever' here does not signify continuity of time. It means regularly, as part of the daily routine. It is directly connected with
'thus', which indicates that whenever the yogi collects himself
he should do so in this particular manner.

'Freed from blemish': for any experience there must be a corresponding state of the nervous system.[46] The most normal state
of the human nervous system is that which can support 'contact
with Brahman', the omnipresent Reality. It must necessarily be a
state of extreme refinement and flexibility, and this is possible only
when the nervous system is entirely pure. Such purity demands
that the functioning of the nervous system should be in no way
contradictory to the laws of nature. The influence that it produces should support all life, fulfilling the cosmic purpose.

It is interesting to note that the first half of verse 15 has the
same text as the present verse, except that the yogi is 'of disciplined mind', whereas here he is 'freed from blemish'. This important difference brings correspondingly different results: in the
earlier instance the outcome is 'peace' and 'liberation'; in the
present it is 'infinite joy'.

It is clear from this comparison that if the nervous system is
not freed from blemish, even though it may give the experience
of peace and freedom it cannot give rise to infinite joy.

46. See IV, 38.

The repeated practice of 'collecting' oneself and arriving at transcendental consciousness continues to refine the nervous system until it becomes so pure that it is capable of giving rise to a state of consciousness described as 'contact with Brahman'.

'With ease attains': because the practice is easy and the way of life that is prescribed is also easy and comfortable. The practice is easy because it represents the movement of the mind in a direction which it follows quite automatically, that is, towards bliss. This teaching of a way that is easy both recalls and supplements the teaching in verse 40 of Chapter II, where the Lord declared this method to be free from any resistance.

It has been made clear that the practice of transcendental meditation, by leading the mind to transcendental consciousness, also brings purity to all aspects of life and sets it in tune with nature. One practice accomplishes all this.[47] The practice itself is in accordance with the very nature of the mind, and this is what makes 'contact with Brahman' easy.

'Contact with Brahman': it was stated in the commentary on verse 20 that in the transcendental state of consciousness the mind becomes Being. When Being is retained in a natural manner even while the mind is out in the relative field, then 'contact with Brahman' is realized. Such contact means harmony between the absolute and the relative states of consciousness. With the practice described in the previous verses, and with an easy manner of life, this highly developed state of consciousness says the Lord, is attained 'with ease'. The result is 'infinite joy'.

It should be noted that it is the 'contact' that is infinite joy, and not Brahman Itself. Brahman, which is an all-pervading mass of bliss, does not exhibit any quality of bliss. It may be likened to a mass of energy – matter – which does not exhibit any quality of energy. This verse emphasizes the glory of 'contact'; it does not set forth the nature of Brahman.

Brahman is that which cannot be expressed in words, even though the Upanishads use words to educate us about Its nature. In the field of speech, Brahman lies between two contrary statements. It is absolute and relative at the same time. It is the eternal imperishable even while It is ever-changing. It is said to be

47. See Appendix: Transcendental Meditation.

both this and That. It is spoken of as a Sat-Chit-Ananda but includes what is not Sat, what is not Chit and what is not Ananda.[48]
It is beyond speech and thought, yet the whole range of thought
and speech lie within It. 'Within It' and 'without It' are just
expressions, and like any other expressions about Brahman they
do justice neither to Brahman nor to the speaker nor to the listener.
Brahman is lived by man with ease but cannot be spoken of, in
the sense that words are inadequate to encompass That which
is the unlimited fullness of transcendental Being and the fullness
of active life at the same time. Verse 29 of Chapter II speaks of
It as a 'wonder', for it is not anything that can be conceived
of intellectually; it is not anything that can be appreciated by
emotion.

This verse and its expression 'with ease' give added meaning
to earlier verses about Brahman: 'This is the state of Brahman,
O Partha. Having attained it, a man is not deluded. Established
in that, even at the last moment, he attains eternal freedom in
divine consciousness';[49] 'his self joined in Union with Brahman,
he enjoys eternal happiness';[50] 'being one with Brahman, attains
eternal freedom'.[51]

Brahman is the value of our life, and the truth about It is that
It is lived 'with ease'.

The glory of this verse is also the glory of the Bhagavad-Gita.
The eternal glory of the goal of human endeavour is that one
'with ease attains contact with Brahman, which is infinite joy'.

VERSE 29

सर्वभूतस्थमात्मानं सर्वभूतानि चात्मनि ॥
ईक्षते योगयुक्तात्मा सर्वत्र समदर्शनः ॥२६॥

He whose self is established in
Yoga, whose vision everywhere is
even, sees the Self in all beings,
and all beings in the Self.

48. Sat, eternal; Chit, consciousness; Ananda, bliss.
49. II, 72.   50. V, 21.   51. V, 24.

This verse portrays the state of Brahman and at the same time gives a practical meaning to the 'contact' of which the previous verse speaks.

The nature of Brahman is expressed in two phrases placed together : 'Self in all beings' and 'all beings in the Self' [52] – the Absolute and the relative, one within the other. This makes Brahman seem incomprehensible. Even taken separately, the relative and the Absolute, the diversity of creation and the Unity underlying it, are each too much for the mind to grasp; how much more so when they are found integrated in Brahman! It is the glory of the Lord's discourse that we are enabled to comprehend the incomprehensible so clearly and are shown how to live it 'with ease'.

The quality of experience depends upon the state of one's consciousness. If the mind is cheerful, everything is found to be cheerful; if the mind is sad and miserable, one's outlook is gloomy. When the state of Being becomes infused into the nature of the mind during meditation, then this infusion makes the mind divine. And when this infusion becomes permanent, the mind begins to live Unity throughout the whole field of diversity. The whole field of diversity is then appreciated in the light of the inner divine Unity. When the mind becomes filled with divine Being, the vision is naturally full and even. It is steady and undistorted by the diversity of life in the world. This is the vision of a man who has gained 'contact' with Brahman.

It must not be lost to sight that evenness of vision is the result of 'contact with Brahman'. It should not be regarded as a path to realization of Brahman. If an unrealized man tries to cultivate evenness of vision in life, he will only create confusion for himself and for others. Such attempts result in strange moods and stranger behaviour. And responsibility for this lies with those commentators who have deduced from this verse the value of mood-making in the name of understanding the Reality and living It.

The glory of this verse is beyond description. Most lucidly, it expresses the inexpressible Brahman and at the same time lays

52. See also IV, 35.

It open to the level of human vision. It is this that has made the Bhagavad-Gita the 'milk' of the Upanishads.

The following three verses take this blessed vision to its consumation in God-consciousness.

VERSE 30

यो मां पश्यति सर्वत्र सर्वं च मयि पश्यति ॥
तस्याहं न प्रणश्यामि स च मे न प्रणश्यति ॥३०॥

He who sees Me everywhere, and sees
everything in Me, I am not lost to
him nor is he lost to Me.

When a man has gained the oneness of vision described in the previous verse, when the fullness of Being overflows through the mind into the fields of perception, when spiritual Unity prevails even on the level of the senses, when the oneness [53] of God overtakes life, then is that state attained where perception of anything whatsoever is perception of the Being made manifest. Then his consciousness finds a direct relationship with the Lord, with Being made manifest, who becomes a living Reality for him on that supremely divine level of consciousness. Then he and his Lord are not lost to one another.

This direct relationship of man with God is first established on the level of Being and then comes to be on the level of feeling; from there it enters the field of thinking and then finds its way on to the sensory level of experience. God thus overtakes all the levels of man's life. Man lives in the sanctuary of God. His life is in love, in bliss, in wisdom, in God-consciousness. He lives in the realm of universal existence. He moves on earth and he lives in the land of God, in the divine ground of Being far above human vision and far beyond human thought.

The way to cultivate this blessed state is to transcend thought. Continuing to think about it has its own value – it fills the mind with a pleasant thought – but fails to create the desired

53. See IV, 35.

state. Transcending thought is infinitely more valuable than thinking.

Therefore let the mind transcend thought and enter that realm of absolute purity which is the abode of God. Thinking about it is wasting time on the surface of life. A thought keeps the mind away from that blessed realm. A thought of bread neither gives the taste of bread nor fills the stomach. If you want bread, go to the kitchen and get it instead of sitting outside thinking about it. We remain thinking of God, or trying to feel Him, only so long as we lack knowledge of Him, so long as we do not know how to break through the phenomenal field of experience and enter the realm of transcendental bliss, the pure kingdom of the Almighty.

The records that history has brought us of the direct communion of saints and sages with God reveal their blessed lives, but the secret of the success of such lives lay in their transcending the fields of thought, emotion and experience. The secret of God-realization lies in transcending the thought of God. Thought that remains thought obscures God-consciousness. Emotions likewise hide the blessed bliss. The thought of God finds fulfilment in its own extinction. And emotion too has to cease in order to let the heart be full in the unbounded love of God.

The state of consciousness that knows the glory of the great Lord of all beings is divine. It is developed through constant and regular practice of meditation and the experience of transcendental Being, which eventually brings cosmic consciousness, the state in which the heart and mind are fully matured. This full development of the capacities of heart and mind enables a man to understand and live the divine Being. The relationship that exists between the unmanifested Absolute and the manifested Being unfolds itself. The personal God comes to be experienced on the sensory level. He becomes the living Reality of daily life. Every object in creation reflects the light of God in terms of one's own Self.

Philosophers call this a mystical experience, but it is no more mysterious than is the working of a clock for a child. On one level of consciousness it is normal, on another it is mysterious, and again on another it is impossible. The intensity of God-realization in its personal and its impersonal aspects depends upon the level of Being, or the purity of consciousness (verse 28). It is not possible to conceive of God-consciousness through any state of consciousness that is not God-consciousness itself; but it is possible for everyone, at any level of human consciousness, to rise to the realization of God-consciousness through the practice of transcendental meditation, which is a simple and direct way of developing pure consciousness.

The overpowering sweetness of the Lord's assurance in this verse gives expression to the glory of life. It has been, it is and it will continue to be the source of inspiration and the guiding light to many an ardent seeker of Truth, to many an ardent devotee of God. It is given to such men to enjoy the love of the Almighty and the protection that He offers. This is their good fortune; they share their life with God. The oneness that they live from moment to moment is the Union of the oneness of the Absolute, the oneness of eternal life in the multiplicity of crea-tion – the great oneness symbolized in the Divine made manifest, the almighty personal God.

The Lord's assurance in this verse is restated in the following verses with even deeper truth and greater glory.

VERSE 31

सर्वभूतस्थितं यो मां भजत्येकत्वमास्थितः ॥
सर्वथा वर्तमानोऽपि स योगी मयि वर्तते ॥३१॥

Established in Unity, he who worships
Me abiding in all beings, in whatever
way he lives, that yogi lives in Me.

To live through the various phases of man's life on earth while abiding in the worship of God is the character of a particular level of consciousness. In order to make clear that its basis is not thought about God, the Lord says: 'in whatever way he lives'. This is that fullness of life in God which knows no varia-tion, however the mind or senses may be engaged, whatever the different modes of activity. When a man looks at things through green spectacles, no matter what he sees the green is there. For a devotee, no matter what he is doing God is there in his consciousness; He is there in his vision and in his being.

The word 'worships' is of great significance. It expresses devotion, dedication, dependence and surrender. From the ordinary level of consciousness this is hard to understand, and to explain the nature of God-consciousness is still harder. But some idea may be gained by making clear the difference between levels of consciousness.

A child takes delight in toys; his consciousness grows and books take their place; as he develops farther his career in the world begins to interest him. As his consciousness grows, so does he rise to different levels of interest and understanding. Similarly, when a man's consciousness has grown to cosmic status, the supreme level of creation becomes his normal field of interest. God, the manifested Being on the supreme level of creation, begins to draw him to Himself; he begins to rise to God-consciousness. Remaining in the world of his fellow men, he begins to live in the world of God. And when he is permanently established in this blessed state, he is included within this loving expression of the Lord's: 'in whatever way he lives, that yogi lives in Me.'

In order to make clear the nature of worship, the Lord adds to the words 'worships Me' the phrase 'abiding in all beings'. The sense of worship holds the devotee to his God; it expresses a personal relationship. What is impersonal and universal from the point of view of ordinary human consciousness becomes intimate and personal in this state of consciousness; for it is at the level of harmony between the unmanifested Absolute and the manifested Being, the Lord of all creation. It would be wrong to understand from the Lord's words here that the yogi tries to see the personal God in all things. This would not only be impractical but would result in strain, to say the least. The divine Being is worshipped through the most natural way of living, based on God-consciousness. Trying to see one's God here, there and everywhere is an act of the imagination which is far from the truth of this verse, and farther still from the practicalities of life.

When the individual consciousness has developed into cosmic

consciousness, then this state of fullness of divine consciousness
develops into God-consciousness. It is in this established state of
God-consciousness that the Lord is worshipped 'abiding in all
beings'. Every thought is then a flower at the feet of God, every
word a prayer and every action an offering to Him. The scriptures
sing the glory of God in the glory of such a devotee, of whom
the Lord says he 'lives in Me'.

Having shown that the realized man attains His level of existence, the Lord, in the following verse, establishes the evenness
of such a man's vision in life.

VERSE 32

आत्मौपम्येन सर्वत्र समं पश्यति योऽर्जुन ॥
सुखं वा यदि वा दुःखं स योगी परमो मतः ॥३२॥

He who sees everything with an
even vision by comparison with the
Self, be it pleasure or pain, he
is deemed the highest yogi, O Arjuna.

This verse brings out the practical value of God-consciousness
and extends the dignity of this enlightenment to everything
around the realized man.

Verse 29 expressed the state of realization in terms of impersonal Being; verse 30 expressed it in terms of the personal. Verse
31 brought the personal God into intimate contact with the
realized man and kept alive the bond of devotion in order to
maintain that blessed state of Union with Him. The present verse
dissolves the bond of devotion, for this can no longer exist when
intimacy becomes complete. While devotion served as a link to
maintain Union, this remained in some degree on the level of
formality. The formality of worship is a pleasure which overtakes
the devotee's heart and his whole being, which gives meaning
to his life and glorifies it on all levels; but the joy of such devotion is the joy of Union at a distance. As the Union grows more
complete, the link of worship, of adoration and devotion, finds

fulfilment in its own extinction, leaving worshipper and worshipped together in perfect oneness, in the oneness of absolute Unity. Then he and his God are one in himself. Then himself has become Himself; his vision is in terms of Himself, his pleasure and pain are in terms of Himself.

'By comparison with the Self': in terms of his own Self.[54] In the state described in the previous verse, the Unity of the devotee with God has reached such fullness that his life is the life of God. Everywhere and in everything he lives God. He sees everything in terms of God. This exalted state of Union with God becomes yet more glorious in the present verse, where the Lord says: 'with an even vision by comparison with the Self'. Here the difference between the devotee and God, which was alive in the state described by the previous verse, is found no more. His Union with God, which was of an order that still permitted worship of Him, has become a Union of much greater intensity. Now his God is one with himself; the supreme divine Unity prevails in him. In his individuality, the eternal glory of the Divine shines brightly and in such fullness that It exists not only on the level of his Being but is infused into his feeling, his thinking, his vision, his whole field of experience. His vision, which before was coloured by his devotion to the Lord, now stands clear in terms of his own Self, permeated by his own eternal Being; in that Being the glory of God resides, sustaining It and maintaining the eternal freedom that His beloved devotee has gained in Him.

In that perfect liberation he leads the life of fullness and abundance. His vision is such that it quite naturally holds alike all things in the likeness of his own Self, because he himself and the vision that he has are the expression of the Self.

The Lord uses the words 'pleasure or pain' to show that the pairs of opposites – and indeed the whole diversity of creation which his individuality offers him – fail to present their differences to the yogi's vision. His is a vision of life in totality. The pairs of opposites, such as pleasure and pain, which present great contrasts on the lower levels of evolution, fail to divide the evenness of his vision. To make such a vision more comprehensible to the

54. See IV, 35.

ordinary level of consciousness, it may be compared to a father's even vision towards a variety of toys which, to the vision of his child's undeveloped consciousness, will present great differences.

This verse shows the height of realization, which is to realize the supreme oneness of life in terms of one's own Self. No diversity of life is able to detract from this state of supreme Unity. One who has reached It is the supporter of all and everything, for he is life eternal. He bridges the gulf between the relative and the Absolute. The eternal Absolute is in him at the level of the perishable phenomenal world. He lives to give meaning to the paean of the Upanishads: 'purnamadah purnamidam' – That Absolute is full, this relative is full. One who lives this supreme Reality in his daily life 'is deemed the highest yogi', says the Lord. Yoga in this state has reached its perfection; there is no level of Union higher than this that he has gained. He stands established on the ultimate level of consciousness.

It may be of interest to those who like to dwell on the metaphysics of Union with God that two states of Union have been clearly portrayed in the present context. That described in this verse is only a more advanced state of Union than that of the preceding verse. The union where the devotee still holds to the supremacy of his God passes very naturally into a much more intimate Union with Him. The principle of Union is not affected. This is not a matter which can be decided by metaphysical speculation or theological understanding. Unless one's consciousness is actually raised to that level of God-consciousness, any description or understanding of the difference between the two states of Union will always fall far short of truth for, as has already been said, the truth about a more advanced state of consciousness cannot be rightly evaluated from a lower level.

Fortunate are they who live in Union with God. They are man's guides on earth, furthering the evolution of all creation. They are above the limitations of religion or race. Whether they play with God or hold Him as one with their own Being is a point to be settled between them and God. They live as devotees of God or they become united, become one with their Beloved – it is a matter between them. Let it be decided on that level of Union. One view need not exclude the other. It is a sin against

God to raise differences over the principle of Union. Let the followers of both schools of thought aspire to achieve their respective goals and then find in that consciousness that the other
standpoint is also right at its own level.

VERSE 33

अर्जुन उवाच ।
योऽयं योगस्त्वया प्रोक्तः साम्येन मधुसूदन ॥
एतस्याहं न पश्यामि चञ्चलत्वात् स्थितिं स्थिराम् ॥३३॥

Arjuna said:

This Yoga described by Thee as
characterized by evenness,
O Madhusudana, I do not see its
steady endurance, because of
wavering.

Arjuna has understood the Lord's teaching concerning the cul-
tivation of God-consciousness. Now he brings up a point which
arises out of the Lord's exhortation in verse 26 about 'the fickle
and unsteady mind'. The question is that if the mind is indeed
'fickle and unsteady', as the Lord Himself has said, then how
is it possible to maintain 'an even vision'[55] in the oneness of
God-consciousness?

Arjuna's question does not imply any doubt about the possibility of cultivating God-consciousness, even with a wavering
mind. What he doubts is its steady endurance when the mind
is wavering.

That has been the story of many seers and devotees of God.
Having felt occasional flashes of divine radiance, they become
miserable because it is not there all the time. But they miss it
when their attention wavers only because they have cultivated
it on the level of attention. It is wrong to think that the steady
endurance of God-consciousness is based on attention. If it does
not endure, this is only due to lack of Being. For the basis of

55. See verse 32.

God-consciousness is that oneness of life which develops on the
solid foundation of cosmic consciousness. This the Lord is going
to explain in answer to Arjuna's question. The following verse
completes that question.

VERSE 34

चच्चलं हि मनः कृष्ण प्रमाथि बलवद्दृढम् ॥
तस्याहं निग्रहं मन्ये वायोरिव सुदुष्करम् ॥३४॥

For wavering is the mind, O Krishna,
turbulent, powerful and unyielding;
I consider it as difficult to control
as the wind.

The nature of the senses has already been accepted by the Lord
in Chapter II [56] as 'wavering', 'turbulent', 'powerful and unyielding'. It is in the nature of things that the mind, on the level
of the senses, is never steady. Arjuna reminds the Lord of this
fact.

There is no reason to think that Arjuna missed the Lord's
essential teaching that it is easy [57] to cultivate God-consciousness,
irrespective of the wanderings of the mind in the field of the
senses and regardless of the dragging influence of the senses
on the mind. He is only afraid of losing it when the mind is
drawn by the senses. So he wants to know some method which
can bring the mind under control and thus enable him to cultivate
and enjoy evenness of mind in God-consciousness. His question
is really about the control of the mind on the level of the senses,
and it is in regard to this level that the Lord's answer is given.

Arjuna's question in these two verses has been widely misunderstood to mean that God-consciousness is difficult of attainment because of the wavering nature of the mind. This has resulted either in restraining enthusiasm for cultivating God-consciousness or in leading seekers to practise strenuous methods
of controlling the mind and steadying the attention. This pitiable

56. See II, 60, 67.   57. See II, 40.

state of affairs in the exalted field of God-realization has come about only because one essential principle has been missed : that God-consciousness is based on the level of Being in cosmic consciousness and not on any thinking, understanding or fixity and continuity of attention.[58]

It should be noted that when the Lord, in answer to Arjuna's question, emphasizes the need for practice, such practice is for the purpose of developing transcendental consciousness into cosmic consciousness and then into God-consciousness, and not at all for gaining the ability to maintain the attention.

VERSE 35

श्रीभगवानुवाच ।
असंशयं महाबाहो मनो दुर्निग्रहं चलम् ॥
अभ्यासेन तु कौन्तेय वैराग्येण च गृह्यते ॥३५॥

The Blessed Lord said:
No doubt, O mighty-armed, the mind
is hard to control, it is wavering,
but by practice and non-attachment
it is held, O son of Kunti.

The Lord accepts the difficulty of controlling the mind on the level of its wandering, because the nature of life is such that the mind has to attend to a variety of things. If the mind is channelled only in one direction, other phases of life will suffer. It wanders of necessity, and this is what makes it difficult for the mind to remain steady at any one place. It is unnatural to try to keep it steady. Steadiness does not belong to the relative field of life. That is why the Lord accepts that 'the mind is hard to control'.

It should not be lost to sight, however, that even when the mind is wavering and wandering 'it is held' by the experience of happiness. This fact about the nature of the mind enables the Lord to show Arjuna a way of keeping the mind 'held' wherever

58. See II, 45; III, 43.

it may be, to show him something which will give the mind steadiness even when it continues to waver.

By saying that the mind 'is held' through practice and non-attachment, the Lord does not mean that the mind will cease its wandering and will always remain fixed and steady, for this would be impractical in daily life. He only means that practice and non-attachment will provide a steady field of omnipresent Being, by virtue of which the mind will be permanently held in the bliss of its own essential nature.

'Practice and non-attachment' means regular practice of transcendental meditation and an easy comfortable routine of daily life after meditation. Practice is not recommended for gaining the ability to keep the mind fixed and steady. It is for cultivating Being. The state of non-attachment helps Being to be infused into the nature of the mind.

'Non-attachment' signifies a simple, easy and unstrained way of life with a proper sense of values, giving no undue importance to anything; for attachment restricts life by laying stress on one particular aspect. Non-attachment does not mean refraining from the responsibilities of life, but rather giving all aspects of practical life their due, while spontaneously maintaining the Self as separate from activity. This happens as transcendental consciousness grows into cosmic consciousness. The state of non-attachment is meant here and not the practice of gaining that state.

'Practice' brings the mind in contact with transcendental Being, while the unstrained life of 'non-attachment' helps Being to be lived in the field of activity, eventually giving to God-consciousness that steady endurance which was Arjuna's main concern in verse 33 and which is the goal of all Yoga.

Cosmic consciousness is the complete state of non-attachment. Practice has to be continued in that state of non-attachment in order to gain and maintain God-consciousness. Practice at this stage means devotion.

VERSE 36

असंयतात्मना योगो दुष्प्राप इति मे मतिः ॥
वश्यात्मना तु यतता शक्योऽवाप्तुमुपायतः ॥३६॥

For an undisciplined man, Yoga is
hard to achieve, so I consider;
but it can be gained through
proper means by the man of endeavour
who is disciplined.

'Yoga' in this verse refers to the state of Yoga in God-conscious-ness, for Arjuna's question, here answered by the Lord, concerns this state.

'An undisciplined man' in this context is he who has not disciplined himself according to the teaching of verses 24 and 25; he who has not gained cosmic consciousness.

The Lord here names three prerequisites for success in Yoga: 'proper means', [59] 'endeavour' [60] and a 'disciplined' [61] life.

'Through the proper means' refers to 'practice and non-attach-ment' in the previous verse.

The expression 'man of endeavour' indicates that the state of Yoga in God-consciousness is not for dull and lazy people: it is for men of responsibility and of a dynamic nature. Thereby the Lord dismisses Arjuna's fear of losing God-consciousness when the mind is engaged in different fields of life (verse 33).

'Who is disciplined': this means a man who has a proper sense of values, who does not confuse the activity of relative life with the Self, or absolute Being. It means the man who has realized cosmic consciousness.

It should not be thought that one has to strain in order to keep life disciplined. There are two ways of disciplining a dog. One way is difficult, the other easy. Run after the dog, try to catch it and then tie it down at the door – this is one way of controlling the dog. Do not run after it, do not try to catch it, do not try to tie it at the door; rather, leave the dog quite free to

59. See verse 3.   60. See verse 1; III, 8, 9.   61. See V, 26.

go anywhere it wants, only put some food outside the door, just what the dog likes to eat. The dog will be found always at the door and as often as you wish. This is a simple way of gaining control over the dog without controlling it. We want to discipline the mind, and the easy way is not to try to put restraint upon it. It is attracted by fields of greater happiness; then lead it towards some field of greater happiness in life and it will be found to stay there through its own desire to enjoy that happiness. The practice of transcendental meditation, bringing contentment through the experience of Being, naturally establishes cosmic consciousness and thus gives a disciplined pattern to life. This is the simple way of gaining a disciplined state of mind.

In this verse, the Lord is not advocating any particular way, either simple or difficult; He is only bringing out the principle of success in Yoga: the need for discipline in life. The principle which the Lord sets out is indisputable: 'for an undisciplined man, Yoga is hard to achieve.' The mind is undisciplined when it is not contented and at the same time has the whole field of the senses laid open for it to explore. It becomes disciplined when it gains contentment through the permanent experience of transcendent absolute bliss [62] in cosmic consciousness. The word 'disciplined' indicates that, even if the mind associates itself with the senses to enjoy their objects, it does not lose the equanimity which has become permanent through the realization of the Self as separate from activity.

VERSE 37

अर्जुन उवाच ।
अयतिः श्रद्धयोपेतो योगाच्चलितमानसः ॥
अप्राप्य योगसंसिद्धिं कां गतिं कृष्ण गच्छति ॥३७॥

Arjuna said:
What goal does he reach, O Krishna,
who is not perfected in Yoga, being
endowed with faith, yet lacking effort,
his mind strayed from Yoga?

62. See II, 59.

The roots of this question lie in the Lord's teaching in verses
24 to 28, which proclaim attainment of cosmic consciousness
through practice, through 'effort'.

The immediate stimulus to the question, however, is given
by the words of the previous verse: 'It can be gained through
proper means by the man of endeavour who is disciplined.' The
three conditions thus set out for gaining supremely divine evenness of mind [63] make it seem to Arjuna as if he had a long way to
go. The Lord has told him earlier that 'in this Yoga no effort
is lost and no obstacle exists. Even a little of this dharma delivers
from great fear'.[64] So when He now puts three conditions upon
it, Arjuna wants to make sure whether or not there will be any
advantage in starting on this path, bearing in mind that one may
not be able to arrive at the goal in this life.

There is yet another implication in this verse. When Arjuna
hears about the three prerequisites for the attainment of the
state of Yoga in God-consciousness, he wants to know if there is
any short cut. He wants to know how far faith can help a man
on this path, for he probably thinks that it may be easier to
succeed in God-realization through faith alone. Such a question
from Arjuna, a very practical man, comes as no surprise. It does
not arise from any wish on his part to avoid effort: it arises
from the very practical quality of his understanding. Wise are
those who understand the nature of a path from beginning to
end before they enter upon it, and wiser still are they who take
a short cut to accomplish the goal. Arjuna's question reflects his
seriousness and the great alertness with which he is following the
Lord's discourse.

Arjuna asks: 'What goal does he reach?' What is his destiny,
where does he go? His concern with this problem springs from
his knowledge of the universe. His statements at the beginning
of the discourse about dharma, about his ancestors, about hell
and heaven, and about the structure of society have revealed his
precise knowledge about life and the world. A man of such learning will naturally be anxious to understand the goal of an aspirant on the path of Yoga. And he has all the more reason to ask
because the Lord is speaking to him about attainments in those

63. See verse 32.   64. See II, 40.

abstract regions of consciousness which seem very far removed
from practical everyday life in the world – or the urgency of a
battlefield.

In the following verse he makes his question clearer.

VERSE 38

कच्चिन्नोभयविभ्रष्टश्छिन्नाभ्रमिव नश्यति ॥
अप्रतिष्ठो महाबाहो विमूढो ब्रह्मणः पथि ॥३८॥

Deluded on the path to Brahman,
O mighty-armed, without foothold
and fallen from both, does he not
perish like a broken cloud?

'Deluded on the path to Brahman' means fallen from the regular practice of transcendental meditaton, which develops cosmic
consciousness. The question is about a man who starts the practice[65] but who for various reasons is unable to continue it. The
word 'deluded' indicates that the reason for giving up the practice
lies with the aspirant. There exists nothing on the side of God
or on the path to Him that might encourage or impel the aspirant
to stop his practice. If he does so, it can only be as a result of
his own delusion. This, in turn, may be due to lack of knowledge
about the goal or to doubt about his own ability to reach it;
or it may be due to lack of proper estimation of its worth. All
this may be due to lack of proper guidance. Whatever the cause,
if a man stops the practice it can only be because he is deluded.
Arjuna's use here of the word 'deluded' reveals the depth of
his understanding of the Lord's teaching. Even though he is
asking a question about the man who falls from practice, he
wishes to show that he already regards such a man as deluded.

'Without foothold': Arjuna is aware of different levels of
consciousness and of the different states of life that correspond
to them. He is also aware that when a man's consciousness evolves

65. See II, 45.

from one level to another, the life of the previous level becomes
useless to him. His question is about one who, as the result of a
certain amount of practice, has risen above the level of ordinary
human consciousness but who has not yet attained cosmic consciousness, which ensures liberation and is the foundation of
God-consciousness. Such a man has lost ground on the human
level but has as yet no foothold on the divine level. He is neither
here nor there. This is what Arjuna expresses with the words
'fallen from both', and he thereupon presents a terrible picture
of destruction with the words 'perish like a broken cloud'.

Arjuna wants to understand the destiny of the deluded man
who has fallen from practice. The question sounds simple but is, in
fact, extremely complex, because there can be innumerable levels
of consciousness between that of the ignorant and that of a fully
liberated, realized man. As Arjuna recognizes in the next verse,
the precise answer can come only from Him who knows the whole
range of life and all the possibilities that exist between ignorance
and the realized state of consciousness.

VERSE 39

एतन्मे संशयं कृष्ण छेत्तुमर्हस्यशेषतः ॥
त्वदन्यः संशयस्यास्य छेत्ता न ह्युपपद्यते ॥३९॥

Thou art able to dispel this
doubt of mine completely,
O Krishna. Truly, there is
none save Thee who can dispel
this doubt.

Having listened to the Lord, Arjuna is by now convinced of
the immeasurable depth of His wisdom. The words 'there is none
save Thee' indicate that Arjuna, even while raising the question,
feels that this is not the right moment for it, the battlefield being
no place for metaphysical discussion. But he justifies his question
by pointing out that if he does not ask it now he may never have
another chance, since no one else can answer it. It appears that

the discourse in verses 28–32 has convinced Arjuna of the limitless wisdom that lies at the feet of Lord Krishna.

When the disciple expresses appreciation of the wisdom of the
master, then the wisdom flows from the master in a more delicate
atmosphere of kindness and love. This is clear from the first word
of Lord Krishna's answer in the following verse and from the
great flood of knowledge that He pours out in response to this
question of Arjuna's.

VERSE 40

श्रीभगवानुवाच ।
पार्थ नेवेह नामुत्र विनाशस्तस्य विद्यते ॥
नहि कल्याणकृत्कश्चिद्दुर्गतिं तात गच्छति ॥४०॥

The Blessed Lord said:

O Partha, there is no destruction
for him in this world or hereafter;
for none who acts uprightly, My son,
goes the way of misfortune.

If someone has begun to wash a cloth and for some reason can
rinse it only once, he has at least succeeded in removing some of
the dirt, even though the cloth is not completely clean. Certainly
he has not made it more dirty. A man begins the practice of
meditation and, even if he meditates only a few times and transcends only once or twice, whatever purity the mind has gained
thereby is his.

VERSE 41

श्राप्य पुण्यकृतां लोकानुषित्वा शाश्वतीः समाः ॥
शुचीनां श्रीमतां गेहे योगभ्रष्टोऽभिजायते ॥४१॥

Having attained the worlds of the
righteous and dwelt there for countless
years, he that strayed from Yoga is
born in the house of the pure and
illustrious.

'He that strayed from Yoga' means either he who could not complete the practice of meditation during his lifetime and has therefore not been able to attain cosmic consciousness, which ensures
liberation, or he who has lost interest and has abandoned the
practice of Yoga after some time.

Purity follows from meditation in proportion to practice. Increased purity leads to a better and happier level of consciousness
here, which continues hereafter.

During meditation the mind reaches the state of transcendental consciousness and becomes free from any shadow of relativity.
It attains to its real status of cosmic existence, unstained by any
shadow of ignorance. This is the purified state of the mind, which
is completely free from the influence of sin. Having attained it,
the mind gains the status of universal Being so perfectly that, on
returning to the field of relativity, it brings contentment into the
whole realm of thought, speech and action. This quite naturally
makes a man's behaviour righteous in every aspect of life, and as
a result he attains to the worlds of the righteous, which are said
to comprise different planes of existence above the human.

When righteous people who have not been able to gain cosmic
consciousness die, they enter one or other of these planes, for
human life is regarded as the gateway to them all. Here life is
longer and very much happier because these planes correspond
to higher levels of consciousness. The highest level of consciousness is absolute Being, which has eternal life. At the other end

of the scale, where purity is least, life is infinitely short. The level
of purity determines the span of life on each plane and also the
degree of happiness.

The Taittiriya Upanishad describes the various degrees of happiness enjoyed by the different beings in creation. All the different planes of life are gained in accordance with the principle
of action and its results. The degree of righteousness in this world
is the criterion for determining which of these higher planes of
life is reached.

The worlds of the righteous are therefore the worlds of greater
happiness, where beings enjoy much greater harmony and freedom than man enjoys on earth. But they no longer engage in the
practice of Yoga. For that they have to come back to earth. Coming
back here they are born 'in the house of the pure and illustrious',
which provides a congenial atmosphere for Yoga. They resume
their practice and attain final liberation.

VERSE 42

अथवा योगिनामेव कुले भवति धीमताम् ॥
एतद्धि दुर्लभतरं लोके जन्म यदीदृशम् ॥४२॥

Or he is born in an actual
family of yogis endowed with
wisdom, though such a birth
as this on earth is more
difficult to attain.

The Lord wishes to impress upon Arjuna that to be 'born in the
house of the pure and illustrious' is easier than to be born into a
'family of yogis endowed with wisdom'. There are two reasons
for this: not only are such families of yogis scarce in the world,
but one also needs to attain a great degree of purity before one
can be born into the holy atmosphere of a yogi's family. For
having been born into that atmosphere one gains a chance of
quickly realizing God-consciousness.

VERSE 43

तत्र तं बुद्धिसंयोगं लभते पौर्वदेहिकम् ॥
यतते च ततो भूयः संसिद्धौ कुरुनन्दन ॥४३॥

There he regains that level of Union
reached by the intellect in his former
body, and by virtue of this, O joy of
the Kurus, he strives yet more for
perfection.

'There': in the atmosphere of the 'family of yogis endowed
with wisdom' (verse 42), or 'in the house of the pure and illustrious' (verse 41).

'He regains' : he starts his life from 'that level of Union reached
by the intellect in his former body'. This may be understood
from an example. Suppose that a cloth needs dipping a hundred
times in dye before it is fully coloured, and that after it has been
dipped ten times the factory closes. The cloth will then be taken
to another factory. The second factory can only start from the
eleventh dipping. Thus, even though the cloth could not be fully
coloured by a continuous process in one factory, the degree of
colour attained in the first factory determines the starting-point
in the second. When a man begins to meditate, Being begins to
grow into the nature of his mind. If, after a certain degree of
infusion, he stops the practice in this life, or if his body perishes,
whenever he again resumes his practice he will do so at that
level of purity of consciousness which he had obtained through
his former practice. The degree of purity gained in this life is
not lost because of the death of the body.

VERSE 44

पूर्वाभ्यासेन तेनैव ह्रियते ह्यवशोऽपि सः ॥
जिज्ञासुरपि योगस्य शब्दब्रह्मातिवर्तते ॥४४॥

By that former practice itself
he is irresistibly borne on.
Even the aspirant to Yoga
passes beyond the Veda.

'By that former practice itself': by the practice of meditation in
the life that is past. The word 'itself' indicates that the strength
of that former practice is in itself sufficient to set a man on this
path of Yoga. Nature becomes favourable to him, and circumstances mould themselves in favour of his resuming the practice.

'Irresistibly borne on' means that, whether he makes a conscious effort to start the practice or is unconsciously drawn by
the accumulated effect of the practice performed in his previous
life, he resumes meditation.

The Lord means that no temptation held out by any other
aspect of life is able to keep him from resuming his path. He is not
held back by anything, not even by the promise of various gains
through Vedic rites and rituals.[66] One-pointedly he sets himself
on the path of Yoga and, being intent on it, quickly attains the
goal.

'Passes beyond the Veda': transcends the field of relativity
and arrives at transcendental consciousness. The Lord means that
even 'the aspirant', the beginner in Yoga, transcends the field of
relative life because, as has already been brought out in verse 40
of Chapter II, there is no difficulty for the mind in reaching absolute transcendental consciousness. Here is a great hope for the
student of Yoga, whether learned or otherwise.

66. See II, 42, 43.

VERSE 45

प्रयत्नाद्यतमानस्तु योगी संशुद्धकिल्बिषः ॥
अनेकजन्मसंसिद्धस्ततो याति परां गतिम् ॥४५॥

But the yogi who strives with zeal,
purified of all sin and perfected
through many births, thereupon
reaches the transcendent goal.

The present verse has been the cause of great misunderstanding
and discouragement, for many people have inferred that the
Lord here enunciates the principle that attainment requires many
lifetimes. This comes from a failure to understand the true meaning of the word 'birth'. Birth means taking a new body. If we
analyse what happens when the individual mind gains cosmic
status in transcendental consciousness, we find that the individual
ceases to exist – he becomes pure Existence. On coming out from
the Transcendent, individual life is regained. Birth means this
regaining of individual existence. Failure to understand the language of the Scripture of Yoga is due to lack of experience of the
state of Yoga and to lack of knowledge of the details concerning
the practice of Yoga. In this situation misinterpretations are bound
to arise.

Three states of Yoga [67] have already been referred to : Yoga in
transcendental consciousness, in cosmic consciousness and in God-
consciousness. The expression 'perfected' shows that the present
verse refers to God-consciousness. The Lord says: 'perfected
through many births.' By this He means perfected through the
continued practice of repeatedly gaining transcendental consciousness and thus being re-born to the world many, many times
until cosmic consciousness is gained. This state of cosmic consciousness, which the Lord says is attained 'with ease', [68] forms
the solid foundation upon which God-consciousness grows.

Of this growth of God-consciousness from the state of cosmic

67. See verse 3, commentary.   68. See verse 28.

consciousness, the Lord says: 'in time finds this within himself'.[69]
It should be noticed that the Lord's expression 'in time' contains
no suggestion whatever of many lifetimes. Thus there is absolutely no reason to suppose that the expression 'many births'
means many lifetimes. The teaching is that by the practice of
transcendental meditation one readily gains transcendental consciousness, and that through constant practice of gaining transcendental consciousness, one rises to cosmic consciousness
'without long delay'[70] and then to God-consciousness.

We may interpret 'many births' in the superficial sense of the
expression as many lives, but it is clear that this meaning will
apply only to those who are 'not perfected in Yoga' in this life
through 'lacking effort' and because their 'mind strayed from
Yoga'.[71] Even they, the Lord says, attain the transcendent goal
by gradually purifying themselves through practice in many
lives.[72] This is the glory of Yoga, that once it has been started it
will have its effect. If it does not bring complete fulfilment in
this life, owing to lack of practice, then it will have its influence
in future lives, bringing a man back to its practice and eventually to liberation.

'Transcendent goal': the goal of transcendental consciousness.
When transcendental consciousness becomes permanent in cosmic
consciousness, the goal that lies ahead is God-consciousness.

VERSE 46

तपस्विभ्योऽधिको योगी ज्ञानिभ्योऽपि मतोऽधिकः ॥
कर्मिभ्यश्चाधिको योगी तस्माद्योगी भवार्जुन ॥४६॥

A yogi is superior to the austere;
he is deemed superior even to men
of knowledge. A yogi is superior
to men of action. Therefore be a
yogi, O Arjuna.

69. See IV, 38.   70. See V, 6.
71. See verse 37.   72. See verses 43, 44.

BHAGAVAD-GITA   466

In this verse the Lord denies the value of all doing, of all strain-
ing and of all effort for the sake of enlightenment. The man of
austerity strains both body and mind. The practice of Yoga refines the nervous system in a gentle way and, removing all strain,
leads to transcendental consciousness. Therefore austerity is inferior to Yoga from every point of view.

The man of knowledge in this context is one who has theoretical knowledge about the three gunas, the Self and God, but has
not directly experienced them. Certainly he is inferior to the
yogi, who knows their nature through direct experience.

The path through activity is taken by one who strives for
purification of the body, mind and soul by the ritualistic performance of righteous action, by charity and by the exercise of
a proper sense of duty, by any kind of action aimed at refining
his mind and reaching enlightenment. This path again is inferior
to Yoga, which enlightens the mind in an easy and direct way.

It is certainly true that all such practices have a purifying
effect, thus helping the mind to grow in sattva. Becoming more
pure in this way, the mind will eventually reach the status of the
Self. The theory of all these paths is right, but they are inferior
to Yoga. Not only do they take a very long time, but they are
confined within the field of which the Lord has said 'action is ...
the means'.[73] Whereas the yogi is established in the field of which
the Lord has said 'calmness is . . . the means'.[74] This is a very
much more advanced state of life.

The superiority of a yogi lies not only in his realizing the
Supreme quickly and easily but also in his realization of Its fullest glory, the glory of the manifested Being in the absolute
existence of God. This is the glory of God-consciousness in man's
life, a glory beyond the excellence reached through austerity or
knowledge or action.

73. See verse 3.   74. See verse 3.

VERSE 47

योगिनामपि सर्वेषां मद्गतेनान्तरात्मना ॥
श्रद्धावान्भजते यो मां स मे युक्ततमो मतः ॥४७॥

And of all yogis, I hold him most
fully united who worships Me with
faith, his inmost Self absorbed in Me.

Here is an exposition of the highest state of evolution. The Lord
says: 'of all yogis'. By this He means that there are various types
of yogi, the hatha yogi, gyana yogi, karma yogi, and so on. All
these have four levels of attainment: the first is realization of
Self-consciousness (verses 10–18); the second, realization of
cosmic consciousness (verses 24–9); the third, realization of God-
consciousness (verses 30–2), and the fourth, realization of all
creation in God-consciousness (verse 32). When the Lord says:
'of all yogis ... his inmost Self absorbed in Me', He is referring
to the man who has established within himself a natural and
permanent bond of Union with the Lord of all beings and with
the whole creation. This happens on the level where devotion is
fulfilled.

Infusion of the state of Being into the nature of the mind, in
such fullness and so permanently that no experience of relativity
can overshadow it, characterizes cosmic consciousness. One who
has reached this state is ever contented in himself. But though
this contentment is positive and actual, it is wholly abstract in
its essential nature, for it is, after all, a sign of the infusion of
transcendental Being into the nature of the mind. This infusion
does not cause Being to be experienced on the level of the senses.
The eyes cannot see Being, the tongue cannot taste It, the ears
cannot hear nor the hands touch It. It is the process of devotion
in faith which brings this about.

Devotion is always on a personal level. So, when the Lord
says: 'of all yogis' he 'who worships Me with faith', He means
one who, established in cosmic consciousness, attaches himself to

the manifest expression of cosmic existence, to cosmic existence made individual in God, for the sake of devotion and worship. Then the eyes enjoy the abstract eternal Being made manifest – all the senses enjoy It as their object of experience. This is the way of devotion which glorifies even one who has gained cosmic consciousness and enables him to enjoy the Transcendent, the Supreme, on the level of the senses. Religious history records individuals – men like Shukadeva, King Janaka and others – who, established in Reality, were devoted to the Lord and enjoyed Him by every means of experience, by the senses, by the mind, by the intellect and by the soul. Such fortunate beings, the Lord says, are 'most fully united'.

This is the verse which puts an end to any misunderstanding about the highest state of Union. The Lord shows that in Him rests 'absorbed' the 'inmost Self' of the highest yogi. This is an explanation from His side, but the expression which He gives to that state from the side of the devotee is different: the devotee worships Him 'with faith'. This is the glory of Union with the Lord. The Lord embraces the devotee and makes him one with Himself, and the devotee holds fast to the Lord in worship. This is the state of oneness where each upholds the other.

This is the duality and the Unity in the Great Union.

Thus, in the Upanishad of the glorious
Bhagavad-Gita, in the Science of the Absolute,
in the Scripture of Yoga, in the dialogue
between Lord Krishna and Arjuna, ends the
sixth chapter, entitled: The Yoga of
Meditation, Dhyana Yoga.

JAI GURU DEVA

APPENDIX

THE HOLY TRADITION

The following verse records the cherished names
of the great masters of the holy tradition
of Vedic wisdom:

Nārāyanam Padmabhavam Vashishtham
Shaktim cha tatputra Parāsharam cha
Vyasam Shukam Gaudapadam mahāntam
Govinda Yogīndra mathāsya shishyam
Shri Shankarāchārya mathāsya Padma-
Padam cha Hastāmalakam cha shishyam
Tam Trotakam Vārtikākaram-anyān
Asmad Gurūn santat māntosmi.

Shruti-smriti-purānānām-
Ālayam Karunālayam
Namāmi Bhagavat-pādam
Shankaram loka-shankaram.

Shankaram Shankarāchāryam
Keshavam Bādarāyanam
Sutra-bhāshya-kritau vande
Bhagavantau punah punah.

Yad-dvāre nikhilā nilimpa-parishad
Siddhim vidhatte-anisham
Shrimat-shri-lasitam Jagadguru-padam
Natvātma triptim gatāh
Lokāgyana payoda-pātan-dhuram
Shri Shankaram Sharmadam.
Brahmānanda Sarasvatīm Guruvaram
Dhyāyāmi Jyotirmayam.

Transcendental Meditation:
The Main Principle

When a wave of the ocean makes contact with deeper levels of water, it becomes more powerful. Likewise, when the conscious mind expands to embrace deeper levels of thinking, the thought-wave becomes more powerful.

The expanded capacity of the conscious mind increases the power of the mind and results in added energy and intelligence. Man, who generally uses only a small portion of the total mind that he possesses, begins to make use of his full mental potential.

The technique may be defined as turning the attention inwards towards the subtler levels of a thought until the mind transcends the experience of the subtlest state of the thought and arrives at the source of the thought. This expands the conscious mind and at the same time brings it in contact with the creative intelligence that gives rise to every thought.

A thought-impulse starts from the silent creative centre within, as a bubble starts from the bottom of the sea. As it rises, it becomes larger; arriving at the conscious level of the mind, it becomes large enough to be appreciated as a thought, and from there it develops into speech and action.

Turning the attention inwards takes the mind from the experience of a thought at the conscious level (B) to the finer states of the thought until the mind arrives at the source of thought (A). This inward march of the mind results in the expansion of the conscious mind (from W_1 to W_2).

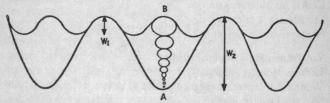

The technique is described as transcendental meditation.

Its practice is simple. There are no prerequisites for beginning the practice, other than receiving instructions personally from a qualified teacher.

It should be noted that transcendental meditation is neither a matter of contemplation nor of concentration. The process of contemplation and concentration both hold the mind on the conscious thinking level, whereas transcendental meditation systematically takes the mind to the source of thought, the pure field of creative intelligence.

COSMIC LAW, THE BASIC LAW OF CREATION

The ever-changing creation of infinite variety seems to be grounded on some stable plane of existence. The rhythm of nature seems to conform to a definite pattern. The infinite number of the galaxies in the vast structure of cosmic space seem to move according to a definite plan. The creation, evolution and dissolution of all things seems to follow a definite procedure. Things change, but the incessant change itself seems to have some unchanging basis.

Hydrogen and oxygen are gases. They combine to form water, H_2O. The qualities of gas change to the qualities of water, but hydrogen and oxygen remain H and O. Again, when water freezes and is transformed into ice, the qualities of water change to those of ice, but hydrogen and oxygen, the essential constituents, remain the same. This means that, while there are certain laws responsible for changing the qualities of gas to water and water to ice, there is some force, some law, which maintains the integrity of hydrogen and oxygen.

The law that does not allow hydrogen and oxygen to change into anything else is itself the unchanging basis of the laws responsible for changing gas into liquid and liquid into solid. The cosmic law is that law which maintains the integrity of the essential and ultimate constituent of creation – absolute Being. Being remains Being by virtue of the cosmic law, which gives rise to different laws responsible for different strata of creation. Although these varied laws of nature are directly responsible for the maintenance and evolution of the universe, their basis is the eternal cosmic law at the plane of Being.

When, during transcendental meditation, the mind transcends the subtlest state of thought and attains the state of Self-consciousness, or pure Being, it attains the level of cosmic law. Coming out of that state, its position is like that of a man entering the office of the President and coming out endowed with his good-will; all the subordinates begin to be in sympathy with him and give him their full support by directing his activities towards a successful end.

When the mind comes out from the field of Being, the plane of cosmic law, into the relative field of activity, which is under the influence of innumerable laws of nature, it automatically enjoys the support of the cosmic law, and this makes possible the accomplishment of any aspiration and the ultimate fulfilment of life.

This is how the life of a man who has risen to cosmic consciousness is eternally established on the level of cosmic law and receives spontaneous support from all the laws of nature.

THE SIX SYSTEMS OF INDIAN PHILOSOPHY

Knowledge is true only when it is acceptable in the light of each of the six systems of Indian philosophy. The truth of every statement in the Bhagavad-Gita can be tested and proved in this way. The second [1] verse of Chapter I is analysed below to illustrate this perfection of Vyasa's exposition. The systems are presented in their classical sequence.

The first system, Nyaya, analyses the correctness of the procedure of gaining knowledge. Having arrived correctly at the object of investigation through Nyaya, one turns to the second system, Vaisheshika, which sets forth the criteria for analysing the special qualities which differentiate the object from other objects. When Vaisheshika has identified the object of inquiry beyond any doubt, the third system, Sankhya, enumerates the different components of the object. Yoga, the fourth system, then offers a way for the direct cognition of the object. Knowledge of the modes of activity of the object and of its components is pro-

1. The first verse presents a question. The truth of a question does not need to be verified as does the truth of a statement which presents the answer. That is why the first verse has not been analysed here. The answer begins from the second verse and its validity is open to verification in the light of the six systems of Indian philosophy.

vided by the fifth system, Karma Mimansa. These five systems
having analysed the different aspects of the object of inquiry
from the point of view of relative existence, the sixth system,
Vedanta, shows that the ultimate Reality of the object, which underlies all its different phases, is absolute in nature. Thus it is
clear that the six systems taken together make knowledge complete by considering every possible aspect of the object.

It should be noted that each system is so thorough in itself
that it appears to be sufficient to give complete knowledge for
liberation. Many scholars have thus been dazzled by one particular system and blinded to the value of the others. It therefore seems
that the very perfection of each system has robbed Indian philosophy of its wholeness and made it weak. In order to be complete,
knowledge requires the support of all six systems.

The following analysis illustrates how the various words of
the second verse of Chapter I give expression to each of the six
systems in detail.

It will be recalled that the verse runs as follows:

Then Duryodhana the prince, seeing
the army of the Pandavas drawn up
in battle array, approached his
master and spoke these words

Nyaya

Nyaya, the science of reasoning expounded by Gautama, presents
sixteen points by which to test the procedure of gaining knowledge:

1. THE MEANS OF VALID KNOWLEDGE (PRAMANA)

There are four means of valid knowledge:

i. *Perception (pratyaksha)* The lesson on perception [2] is given
by the word 'seeing'.

ii. *Inference (anumana)*. 'Seeing ... battle array': seeing the army

2. Transcendental meditation, which forms the central teaching of
the Bhagavad-Gita, is a means of direct perception, a direct means
of gaining knowledge.

in battle array, Duryodhana inferred that it was time to fight, and this made him approach his master.

iii. *Comparison (upamana)*. This is a means of gaining knowledge of something by comparing it with another well-known object. Here the word 'prince' is used with reference to Duryodhana.

iv. *Verbal testimony (shabda)*. 'These words': the words of a prince are authentic.

2. THE OBJECT OF VALID KNOWLEDGE (PRAMEYA)

The object of knowledge is that about which the inquiry is made, or that which is approached, in this case the 'master'.

A point to be noted here is that when Vyasa teaches the lesson of prameya, he presents as the object of knowledge the master, who is the source of all knowledge.

3. DOUBT (SAMSHAYA)

The 'approach' to a 'master' is made in order to remove doubts and gain clarity.

4. PURPOSE (PRAYOJANA)

The words 'drawn up in battle array' demonstrate the purpose of the army.

5. EXAMPLE (DRISHTANTA)

'Duryodhana' gives the lesson on drishtanta. In the previous verse, Dhritarashtra asked about the actions of his sons. Duryodhana being the eldest, his actions may be taken to exemplify the actions of all the hundred sons of Dhritarashtra.

6. ESTABLISHED PRINCIPLE (SIDDHANTA)

It is an established principle that the master is always approached by the disciple. Duryodhana 'approached his master'.

7. PARTS OF A LOGICAL ARGUMENT (AVAYAVA)

'Seeing ... approached ... spoke.'

8. THE PROCESS OF REASONING (TARKA)

Duryodhana 'approached his master' in order to gain an authori-

tative decision which would leave no possibility of error or sup-
position. The lesson on reasoning given here is highly practical.

9. THE ART OF DRAWING CONCLUSIONS (NIRNAYA)

Seeing the army, Duryodhana judged the situation and immediately acted upon the conclusion he had drawn: he 'approached
his master'.

10. DISCUSSION (VADA)

Discussion consists of the interplay of two opposing sides for the
purpose of arriving at a decisive conclusion. The lesson on discussion taught by this verse is of a very perfect nature. One man seeing both sides 'approached' the 'master', the knower of Reality,
to find a solution. In teaching the lesson of discussion, of the
interplay of two opposing sides, this verse at the same time teaches
the lesson of harmony.

11. POLEMICS (JALPA)

Polemics is argument for the sake of victory, as opposed to discussion for the sake of arriving at the truth. In the present verse,
the lesson on polemics is given by 'spoke these words'. The battlefield is the place for action, but instead of taking action Duryodhana engages in speech. Further, the opposing army is silent, and
against that silence Duryodhana 'spoke these words'. Therefore
in this verse action is pitted against speech and speech challenges
silence. Here is a lesson on polemics in its most extreme form.

12. CAVIL (VITANDA)

This verse places 'the army' on one side and 'words' on the other
and thereby lowers the dignity of the army. This is the purpose
of cavil – to lower the dignity of the other side. It is the beauty
of this verse that it teaches a lesson on cavil without using the
language of cavil.

13. FALLACIES (HETVABHASA)

Fallacies are of five types:

i. *The inconclusive (savyabhichara)* – reasoning from which more
   than one conclusion can be drawn. This verse leaves us in

BHAGAVAD-GITA   476

uncertainty about what Duryodhana said, even though it uses
the word 'these', which indicates definiteness.

ii. *The contradictory (viruddha)* – where the reasoning contra-
dicts the proposition to be established. In the face of 'the army
of the Pandavas ... in battle array', the reasonable thing to
be established by Duryodhana was that the fighting should
begin. But instead of starting to fight, Duryodhana 'approached
his master'.

iii. *The equivalent to the question (prakaranasama)* – where the
reasoning is such that it provokes the very question that it is
designed to answer. The lesson on this fallacy is found in
'these words'. The word 'these' is definite in its character, but
here its use is such that it provokes a question about the
definiteness of the 'words'.

iv. *The unproved (sadhyasama)* – where the reason given in order
to establish a conclusion is not different from what is to be
proved and itself stands in need of proof. The reason for
Duryodhana's approach to his master needs proof or justification, because at the time of battle Duryodhana could have
had a reason for going to the commander-in-chief but not for
going to his master.

v. *The belated (kalatita)* – where the reason is advanced when
the time for it is past. The master is consulted in order that
he may give his judgement on the correctness of an action. The
reasonable thing would have been for Duryodhana to approach
his master before coming on the battlefield.

14. EQUIVOCATION (CHALA)

Equivocation is of three types:

i. *Verbal (vakchala)* – assuming a word to have a meaning other
than that intended by the speaker. The sequence of words in
the original text is such that the word 'prince' (raja) can also
be taken to qualify 'words'. It would then mean that Duryodhana spoke princely words, that he spoke like a king – implying that he was not a king but spoke like one. This use of 'prince'
with reference to 'words' gives the teaching on verbal equivocation.

ii. *Generalizing (samanyacchala)* – challenging the possibility of a statement because of the impossibility of the whole situation. Duryodhana's words had never been as responsible as those of a prince, so the use of the word 'prince' could be taken ironically. It would then mean that Duryodhana is being ridiculed here. This is a teaching on the second type of equivocation.

iii. *Figurative (uparacchala)* – misinterpreting a word which is used figuratively by taking it literally. As Duryodhana was not a true ruler, the use of the word 'prince' (raja) with reference to him may be regarded as figurative. When it is taken literally, it gives a lesson on this type of equivocation.

15. FUTILE ARGUMENT (JATI)

This means argument based merely on similar and dissimilar characteristics. There is similarity of nature between 'Duryodhana' and 'prince'. There is dissimilarity of nature between 'the Pandavas' and their 'army ... in battle array', because the Pandavas are by nature peaceful.

16. DISAGREEMENT ON FIRST PRINCIPLES (NIGRAHASTHANA)

This arises from mistaken ideas or from a complete lack of understanding. A master is approached when one needs some clarification, and clarification is needed to eliminate error or misunderstanding. The lesson with regard to disagreement on first principles is exemplified by the 'master', in whom all disagreements are dissolved.

This is the perfection of the teaching of Gautama's Nyaya in the Bhagavad-Gita : even the lesson on disharmony is taught from the centre of all harmony, so that the student of Nyaya is not left on the dry plains of reason.

Vaisheshika

Vaisheshika, the system expounded by Kanada, analyses the special qualities (vishesha) which distinguish an object from other objects. In the present verse, the word 'prince' brings out a special quality which distinguishes Duryodhana from other men. 'His' specifying 'master' and 'these' specifying 'words' serve a similar purpose. Here we have a general lesson on the Vaisheshika philosophy.

According to Vaisheshika, there are nine substances which form the basis of all creation. The special qualities of these substances are responsible for the varying qualities of the multitude of objects in creation. The nine ultimate substances are : earth (prithivi), water (apas), fire (tejas), air (vayu), space (akasha), time (kala), direction in space (dik), soul (atman), mind (manas).

The first four ultimate substances are distinguished from one another by the special qualities of their paramanus, or atoms. There are four such special qualities : odour (gandha), taste (rasa), form (rupa), touch (sparsha). Earth possesses all four of these qualities; water possesses flavour, form and touch; fire possesses form and touch; air possesses touch only.

1. EARTH (PRITHIVI)

The lesson on the earth element is given by the word 'Duryodhana'. As odour is inseparable from earth, so a princely fragrance is inseparable from Duryodhana, the prince, or master of the earth.

2. WATER (APAS)

Taste is the essential quality of the water element. The sense of taste dwells in the tongue, which is also the organ of speech. Therefore the word 'spoke' may be said to give the lesson on the water element.

3. FIRE (TEJAS)

'Seeing' gives the lesson on the fire element, because the sense of sight relates to the fire element.

4. AIR (VAYU)

'Approached' gives the lesson on the air element, because touch is the inseparable quality of the air element. The process of approaching culminates in touch.

5. SPACE (AKASHA)

The fifth ultimate substance, space, is characterized by sound. Therefore the lesson on space is given by 'words'.

6. TIME (KALA)

Time is indicated by such concepts as sequence, simultaneity, speed and slowness. 'Seeing ... approached ... spoke' gives a lesson on all these concepts.

7. DIRECTION IN SPACE (DIK)

Direction in space is indicated by expressions such as here, there, far, near, above, below. The lesson on direction in space is given by 'army ... in battle array' and 'approached'.

8. SOUL (ATMAN)

According to the Vaisheshika Sutra, the existence of the eighth ultimate substance, soul, is indicated by the ascending life-breath (prana), the descending life-breath (apana), the closing of the eyelids (nimesha), the opening of the eyelids (unmesha), life (jivana), mental activity (manogati), the inner changes in the field of the senses (indriyantara-vikara), pleasure (sukha), pain (duhkha), desire (iccha) and effort (prayatna).

The lesson on soul is given by:

i. The ascending and descending life-breaths join to bring forth speech: 'spoke these words'.

ii. The closing and opening of the eyelids relate to vision: 'seeing'.

iii. Life is indicated in Duryodhana by the words 'seeing ... approached ... spoke'.

iv. Mental activity is inherent in the sequence of 'seeing ... approached ... spoke'.

v. Pleasure is inherent in 'approached his master'.

vi. Pain is inherent in 'seeing the army of the Pandavas ... in battle array'. The lesson on pain is taught without recourse to any obvious reference to pain.

vii. Duryodhana's desire is indicated by the word 'these'. Vyasa, in giving a lesson on desire, uses an expression which indicates the principle of desire without specifying any particular desire lest the mind be drawn away from the central point under consideration. Here is an example of Vyasa's great precision of language in his teaching on the different systems of Indian philosophy.

viii. The lesson on effort is given by the word 'approached'. For any man the process of approaching involves effort, all the more so for a prince, who wields the power to summon anyone at any time.

It is clear that in order to verify the special qualities of the soul, the soul must be 'approached'. In the verse under consideration, 'approached' is the result of some mental activity following upon the sensory activity of 'seeing'. Likewise, in order to approach the soul, it is necessary to go from the experience of the field of sensory activity to that of mental activity until, transcending the subtlest mental activity, one approaches the field of pure Being, which is pure consciousness, the basis of all activity. Only through this process, known as transcendental meditation, can the mind realize intimately the subtle fields of relative existence, which Kanada indicates as constituting the special qualities of the soul, and this fulfils the purpose of the Vaisheshika teaching.

9. MIND (MANAS)

The ninth ultimate substance, mind, is the faculty responsible for giving knowledge to the soul upon the soul's contact with the senses and their objects. The lesson on mind is given by the thought that lies between 'seeing' and 'approached' and 'spoke'.

Sankhya

Sankhya means pertaining to number. This system of philosophy, expounded by Kapila, holds that knowledge of an object will not be complete without the knowledge of its components. In its analysis of life and creation, Sankhya establishes twenty-five categories as lying at the basis of the entire creation and of the process of cosmic evolution. The teaching concerning these categories can be verified by direct experience through the practice of transcendental meditation, in which the mind travels through all the gross and subtle levels of creation to the state of pure transcendental consciousness.

1. PURUSHA

Purusha, or Cosmic Spirit, is the transcendental Reality which comes into direct experience during transcendental meditation at the point where even the subtlest level of creation is transcended and pure transcendental consciousness alone remains. Purusha forms the basis of the subjective aspect of life. He is the eternal silent witness of all that was, is and will be.

In the verse under consideration, the teaching about Purusha is found in the word 'Pandavas'. The expression 'army of the Pandavas' indicates that while the army belongs to the Pandavas, the Pandavas themselves may not necessarily form a part of the army; they may remain, as it were, uninvolved. Even though the whole of nature functions under His will, Purusha remains a silent witness to its activity.

2. PRAKRITI

Prakriti, or Nature, is the primal substance out of which the entire creation arises. Its constituents are the three gunas,[3] sattva, rajas and tamas. They are responsible for all change and form the basis of evolution.

Whereas in the present verse 'the Pandavas' represent Purusha, 'the army' represents prakriti. Furthermore, the phrase 'army . . . drawn up in battle array' represents prakriti laid out in its different constituents, ready to be active. Without specifically mentioning the three gunas, Vyasa fully conveys the nature of prakriti. As long as the three gunas are in equilibrium, they do not present themselves as three, they do not demonstrate any activity, and there is no process of creation and evolution; when they have begun to be active, they appear in a whole multitude of permutations and combinations.

3. MAHAT

Mahat is that first state of evolution where the previously undifferentiated primal substance, prakriti, begins to move towards manifestation, begins to take a specific direction. It is the cosmic will in operation, satisfying the urge for manifestation that has

3. See II, 45, commentary.

been created by the disturbance of the perfect equilibrium of the three gunas.

The lesson on mahat is given by the word 'approached', which depicts the first stir in the situation presented by the verse – a movement in a specific direction.

4. AHAMKARA

Ahamkara is the principle responsible for the individuation of mahat.

The teaching of ahamkara is to be found in the word 'his', which presents an example of the principle of individuation, the individuation of the general term 'master'.

5. MANAS

Manas is the cosmic mind which provides the object for the individuating principle, ahamkara. In the state of manas, the urge of prakriti towards manifestation becomes clearly defined.

The lesson on manas is given by the phrase 'these words', which gives definite shape to the situation created by the first stir, mahat, indicated by the word 'approached'.

6–15. THE INDRIYAS

The next ten principles are called indriyas, or senses: five senses of perception (gyanendriya) and five organs of action (karmendriya). They connect the mind with the manifested world of objects.

The lesson on the senses of perception is given by the word 'seeing', taking the sense of sight as representative of the five senses of perception.

The lesson on the organs of action is given by the word 'spoke', the organ of speech being taken as representative of the five organs of action.

16–20. THE TANMATRAS

The tanmatras constitute the five basic realities, or essences, of the objects of the five senses of perception. They express themselves in the five elements which go to make up the objects of

APPENDIX

the senses and which provide the material basis of the entire objective universe. Thus the essence of sound (shabda tanmatra) expresses itself in space, the essence of touch (sparsha tanmatra) in air, the essence of form (rupa tanmatra) in fire, the essence of taste (rasa tanmatra) in water, and the essense of smell (gandha tanmatra) in earth.

The lesson on the tanmatras is provided by the Sanskrit word 'tu', omitted in the translation, meaning 'only after' seeing. This expression draws a dividing line in the sequence of events. Likewise the tanmatras mark the dividing line between the subjective and objective creation. In the process of evolution, as the influence of tamas [4] increases, the subjective creation comes to an end and the objective creation begins. The tanmatras, forming as they do the basis of the five elements, lie in the grossest field of the subjective aspect of creation.

21–5. THE MAHABHUTAS

The five mahabhutas, or elements out of which material creation is constituted, are space (akasha), air (vayu), fire (tejas), water (apas) and earth (prithivi).

The lesson on the mahabhutas has already been made clear while dealing with Vaisheshika.

It may be noted that the whole teaching of Kapila's Sankhya can be verified by direct experience through transcendental meditation, because in order to reach the state of transcendental consciousness the mind has to traverse all the gross and subtle levels of creation.

Yoga

The purpose of Yoga is to gain knowledge by direct perception. Yoga is a practical science of life which lays open to direct experience not only the field of absolute Being but all the different levels of relative creation as well.

The very first word of the verse in the original text, 'drishtva'

4. See II, 45, commentary.

(literally 'having seen'), gives a lesson both on the purpose of Yoga and the way to its fulfilment.[5]

Patanjali, in his exposition of Yoga, divides life into eight spheres in order to deal thoroughly and completely with the subject of Yoga:

1. The entire field of creation lying outside the individual but constantly influenced by his thoughts and actions. The state of Yoga, or perfect harmony, is found established in this field when man's life is naturally upheld by the five qualities of observance (yama):

i. Truthfulness (satya).
ii. Non-violence (ahimsa).
iii. Non-covetousness (asteya).
iv. Celibacy [6] (brahmacharya).
v. Non-acceptance of others' possessions (aparigraha).

These qualities are represented by 'the Pandavas', the five virtuous sons of Pandu.

2. The physical structure of the individual body and nervous system. The state of Yoga is found established in the field of the body and nervous system when man's life is naturally upheld by the five rules of life (niyama):

i. Purification (shaucha).
ii. Contentment (santosha).
iii. Austerity (tapas).
iv. Study (svadhaya).
v. Devotion to God (Ishvara-pranidhana).

These five qualities again are represented by 'the Pandavas'.

3. The different limbs of the body, the sphere of posture (asana). The state of Yoga is found established in the sphere of the limbs of the body when there is a perfect functioning of all the limbs in good coordination with each other. In this state, the body is

5. The phrase 'a little of this dharma' in verse 40 of Chapter II gives expression to the principle of direct perception.
6. A state of the individual where the life-force is always found directed upwards.

capable of remaining in a steady posture for any length of time.

The lesson on asana is given by 'drawn up', for in the state of Yoga, the state of transcendental consciousness, all the limbs of the body are in perfect accord with each other, fully alert, but not yet set in action.

4. The sphere of the individual breath, the sphere of breathing exercises (pranayama). In the state of Yoga, the activity of breath comes automatically to rest.

The lesson on pranayama is given by 'the army of the Pandavas, drawn up in battle array'. 'The Pandavas', or five sons of Pandu, represent the five breaths – prana, apana, vyana, udana and samana – functioning in different parts of the body. 'The army of the Pandavas drawn up in battle array' represents the steadiness of all the five breaths in the state of Yoga.

5. The sphere of life which lies between the senses and their objects. The state of Yoga in this sphere is marked by complete self-sufficiency on the part of the senses so that they are no longer projected outwards towards their objects. Yoga here means retirement from the field of the objects of the senses.

The lesson on the turning away of the senses from their objects (pratyahara) is given by the word 'seeing' (literally 'having seen'), which shows that Duryodhana's vision, having fallen on the army of the Pandavas, was thereupon withdrawn.

6. The sphere of life that lies between the senses and the mind. The state of Yoga in this sphere is marked by the withdrawal of the mind from the realm of the senses.

The lesson on steadiness of mind (dharana) is given by the expression 'drawn up', which indicates that the mind is steady, that it is no longer associated with the senses.

7. The sphere of life that lies between the mind and Being. The state of Yoga in this sphere is marked by the refining of the mental impulses until the most refined state of mental activity is transcended and the mind gains the state of pure consciousness, absolute existence, or eternal Being.

The lesson on this process of meditation (dhyana) is given by the words 'approached his master', the master representing the state of Being.

A close scrutiny of Patanjali's exposition of Yoga reveals that the actual process of attaining the state of Yoga belongs not only to dhyana, or meditation, which alone appears to result directly in samadhi, or transcendental consciousness, but also to all the other limbs of his eightfold Yoga. Each limb presents the principle underlying the practices that bring about the state of Yoga in the sphere of life pertaining to that limb.

For hundreds of years these different limbs of Yoga have been mistakenly regarded as different steps in the development of the state of Yoga, whereas in truth each limb is designed to create the state of Yoga in the sphere of life to which it relates. With the continuous practice of all these limbs, or means, simultaneously, the state of Yoga grows simultaneously in all the eight spheres of life, eventually to become permanent.

It seems necessary to point out here that even samadhi, which is already the state of Yoga in the sense of transcendental consciousness, serves as a means to the ultimate state of Yoga, cosmic consciousness. In the state of cosmic consciousness, transcendental consciousness has become permanently grounded in the nature of the mind or, to speak in Indian terms, kshanika (momentary) samadhi has become nitya (perpetual) samadhi. It is in this sense that Maharishi Patanjali has placed samadhi along with the other seven limbs, or means, of Yoga.

In order to connect the principle of dhyana with practice it may be mentioned that the most valuable practice in the sphere of dhyana is the simple system of transcendental meditation. Transcendental meditation belongs to the sphere of dhyana, but at the same time transcends that sphere and gives rise to the state of transcendental consciousness, samadhi. After this state has been gained the attention returns to the sphere of dhyana, which is a sphere of activity. This regular passing of the attention from one sphere to the other enables transcendental consciousness to be maintained even during activity, first at a very subtle level and later in the gross activity of daily life, so that it may eventually become permanent. In this way the simple system known as transcendental meditation, which is a specific type of practice, forms the most effective working tool of these two spheres of life, dhyana and samadhi.

8. The sphere of absolute Being, the state of transcendental consciousness (samadhi).

The lesson on samadhi is given by the word 'Pandavas'. In this verse, the use of the word 'Pandavas' indicates that the Pandavas possess the army and, as its masters, are separate from it. Similarly, in the state of samadhi the self is experienced as the Transcendent, uninvolved with anything.

Karma Mimansa

Mimansa means investigation, close consideration. Karma Mimansa is concerned with the close study of action, because action forms the basis of the existence and evolution of the individual. The very first sutra of Jaimini's Karma Mimansa begins an inquiry into dharma, the invincible force of nature which upholds the entire creation. The main quest of Karma Mimansa is for that action which will be spontaneously in accord with dharma. The influence of every action is so far-reaching[7] as to be beyond human understanding. Therefore the criterion by which the rightness of an action should be judged can be no other than the verbal testimony (shabda) of the Vedas.

Jaimini establishes the eternal nature of shabda by logical argument and removes all doubts concerning it. The lesson on this is given by the expression 'approached his master', because the master is approached to remove all doubts.

Having established the eternity of shabda, it was necessary for Jaimini to establish that the Veda is divine revelation at the time of creation. The lesson on this is found in the word 'then' – at the time of creation.

Jaimini also proves that the words of the Veda, even though impulses of the Divine, are not meaningless notes or rhythms. They have a meaning and therefore a specific purpose just like any spoken sound (word) in any language. Every word and every phrase of the verse under consideration offers a lesson on this point.

7. See IV, 17, commentary.

Because he held the Veda to be the final authority on dharma, it was necessary for Jaimini to devise a definite method of investigation of the Vedic text. This he did by analysing the contents of the Vedas as follows:

1. VIDHI (PRECEPTS OR INJUNCTIONS)

The lesson on this is given by the sequence 'seeing ... approached ... spoke'.

2. MANTRA (KEY-WORDS)

Mantras are key-words which help one to remember the different steps of the yagyas.[8]

The 'master' (acharya) is the custodian of the knowledge of the mantras and is there to answer all objections raised against them. The mantras exist to help the performance of the yagya: there is a different mantra at every step. During the process of the yagya, the master speaks the mantra, and in accordance with that others perform actions. Duryodhana 'approached his master' in order to receive the right word (mantra) of action from him.

3. NAMADHEYA (PROPER NOUNS)

The lesson on namadheya is given by 'Duryodhana' and 'Pandavas'.

4. NISHEDHA (PROHIBITIONS)

Nishedha is the opposite of vidhi.

The lesson on nishedha is given by 'approached his master' and 'spoke these words'. The procedure in accordance with precept (vidhi) is that after approaching the master one should at once prostrate oneself. But instead of prostrating himself, Duryodhana began to speak.

5. ARTHAVADA (EXPLANATORY PASSAGES)

'The prince' gives a lesson on arthavada.

The Mimansakas, following the Sanskrit grammarians, divide Vedic substantives into three types:

1. *Rudhi*, a simple non-compound word with a conventional

8. See III, 9, commentary.

acceptation which we learn from a teacher or other authority.

The lesson on rudhi is given by 'words'.

2. *Yaugika,* a compound word made up of two or more words, each of which has its independent meaning and contributes to the meaning of the whole.

The lesson on yaugika is given by 'army of the Pandavas' (pandava-anikam).

3. *Yogarudhi,* a word which, though compound, has its own conventional meaning.

The lesson on this is given by the word 'Duryodhana' (Dur-yodhana).

Jaimini points out that substantives are not self-sufficient but require a verb to convey the purpose of speech. Verbs introduce the element of action, which is classified by Jaimini according to whether its effects are mainly visible or invisible. Those actions with mainly invisible effects (apurva) are called principal (pradhana), and those with mainly visible effects are called secondary (gauna).

The lesson on actions which are pradhana is given by the word 'spoke', because the effects of Duryodhana's speech are not visible in this verse. The lesson on actions which are gauna is given by the word 'seeing', because the effect of seeing is immediately apparent in 'approached his master and spoke these words'.

In order to permit a thorough scrutiny of the Vedic texts in accordance with the principles of interpretation laid out above, the Vedas are considered in two sections: 1. The Samhitas, those parts which deal with the mantras; 2. The Brahmanas, those parts which deal with ritualistic performances and explanatory passages.

1. THE SAMHITAS

These are divided into three sections:

i. *Rik* – verses collected in a group and marked by their metrical arrangement. The lesson on this is given by the metrical quality of the present verse.

ii. *Sama* – verses sung at the conclusion of the yagya. The lesson on sama is given by the word 'then'. This word places the

situation portrayed in the verse at the end of some other happening.

iii. *Yajus* – mantras in prose. They are of two types:

    a. those which are spoken aloud (nigada). The lesson on this
    type of mantra is given by all the words of this verse since
    they are spoken aloud.

    b. those which are pronounced silently (upamshu). 'These
    words' refer to words that are not pronounced in this verse.
    This gives a lesson on the mantras which are pronounced
    silently.

2. THE BRAHMANAS

Shabara, in his commentary on the Mimansa Sutra, mentions ten
ways of analysing the Brahmanas:

i. *Hetu – motive.* The lesson on this is given by the word 'seeing'. It was 'seeing' which caused Duryodhana to approach his
master and speak.

ii. *Nirvachana – explanation or expression.* The lesson on this
is given by 'drawn up in battle array', an expression which
explains what is seen.

iii. *Ninda – deprecation.* The lesson on deprecation is taught by
the fact that the word 'Pandavas' remains unqualified, whereas
Duryodhana is called a prince.

iv. *Prashansa – praise.* The lesson on this is taught by the phrase
'drawn up in battle array', which expresses the dignity of the
army.

v. *Samshaya – doubt.* 'Approached his master' gives a lesson on
doubt, because the master is always approached in order to remove doubt.

vi. *Vidhi – precept.* As explained earlier, the lesson on this is
given by 'seeing ... approached ... spoke'.

vii. *Parakriya – the action of an individual.* The whole verse is
concerned with Duryodhana's action: 'seeing ... approached
... spoke'.

viii. *Purakalpa – past events.* The lesson on this is given by 'army
drawn up in battle array'.

ix. *Vyavadharana kalpana – meaning according to context.* The
word 'then' teaches this lesson.

APPENDIX

x. *Upamana – comparison.* This helps to gain knowledge of a thing by comparison with another well-known object. The lesson on upamana is given by the word 'prince', used with reference to Duryodhana.

It is important to note that the practice of transcendental meditation spontaneously fulfils the quest of Karma Mimansa for action in accordance with dharma. Transcendental meditation brings the mind to the state of Being. Being is eternal; It forms the basis of creation and therefore upholds the entire universe. When the mind gains the state of Being, it simultaneously gains the level of dharma. Therefore action by a mind held in Being is automatically in accordance with dharma. Transcendental meditation thus brings fulfilment to the teaching of Karma Mimansa.

Vedanta

Vedanta means end of the Veda, final knowledge of the Veda. The system of Vedanta is also known as Uttara Mimansa, meaning that it is an investigation into the last chapter of the Veda, the Upanishads. Whereas Jaimini's Karma Mimansa, or Purva (earlier) Mimansa as it is sometimes called, considers that portion of the Veda which is concerned with action, Vyasa's[9] Uttara (later) Mimansa, or Vedanta, considers that portion of the Veda which is concerned with knowledge. The main purpose of Vedanta is to educate man in the truth that complete knowledge of life is no other than life itself as it is lived naturally on the level of Being.

From a cosmic standpoint, Vedanta explains the relationship of the unmanifested absolute Reality (Brahman) with the manifested relative aspect of life by introducing the principle of maya. The word maya means literally that which is not, that which does not exist. This brings to light the character of maya: it is not anything substantial. Its presence is inferred from the effects that it produces. The influence of maya may be under-

9. Vyasa, the author of the Bhagavad-Gita, also expounded the system of Vedanta.

stood by the example of sap appearing as a tree. Every fibre of
the tree is nothing but the sap. Sap, while remaining sap, appears
as the tree. Likewise, through the influence of maya, Brahman,
remaining Brahman, appears as the manifested world.

On the individual level, Vedanta explains the relationship of
the absolute Self (Atman) and the relative aspect of individual
life by the principle of avidya. Avidya, or ignorance, is nothing
but maya in a coarser form. If maya can be likened to clear water,
then muddy water is avidya.

Under the influence of maya, Brahman appears as Ishvara, the
personal God, who exists on the celestial level of life in the subtlest field of creation. In a similar way, under the influence of
avidya, Atman appears as jiva, or individual soul.

The lesson on Brahman is given by the word 'master'. The
master, possessing the whole wisdom of life, is established in
brahmi-sthiti, the state of Brahman, or cosmic consciousness.

The lesson on maya is given in this verse by the word 'raja',
which means 'prince' or 'king'. A rightful king Duryodhana was
not.

The lesson on Ishvara also is given by the word 'raja', or king.
The king wields the highest authority on the human level.

The lesson on Atman is given by the word 'Pandavas'. The
phrase 'army of the Pandavas' expresses that the Pandavas are not
necessarily part of the army even though they are the masters
of it. Likewise, Atman is separate from and not involved with
the world of activity.

The lesson on avidya is given by 'seeing ... approached ...
spoke'. Avidya, or ignorance, is at the basis of all the activity of
individual life.

The lesson on jiva is taught by 'Duryodhana', of whom it is said
that he saw, approached and spoke. It is the jiva which partici-
pates in activity.

The exposition of knowledge about life in Vedanta is so perfect that the ordinary level of human intelligence is unable to
comprehend it. Therefore, as a necessary prerequisite for gaining
knowledge of Vedanta, the level of consciousness must be raised.
In order to become capable of understanding Vedanta, one's life
must be lived on the level of the four qualities:

1. VIVEKA (DISCRIMINATION)

The lesson on this is taught by 'seeing the army' and 'approached his master'. It was through the power of discrimination that Duryodhana, on seeing the army, decided to approach the master and present to him the situation before finally plunging into battle.

2. VAIRAGYA (NON-ATTACHMENT)

The lesson on this is found in the word 'Pandavas'. The Pandavas were on the battlefield, yet the expression 'army of the Pandavas' depicts them as separate from the army, as though uninvolved with it. This makes it clear that the teaching of vairagya, according to this verse, does not involve abandonment of the activities and responsibilities of life. It is enough to remain uninvolved with one's possessions. Abandonment of possessions is no criterion of non-attachment.

3. SHATSAMPATTI (THE SIX TREASURES)

1. *Shama – control of mind.* The lesson on this is given by 'seeing the army' and 'approached his master'. Had Duryodhana not possessed this quality of shama, he could not have had the presence of mind to approach and consult his master.
ii. *Dama – control of senses.* The lesson on this is given by the expression 'army ... drawn up in battle array'. The army of the senses is drawn up, capable of functioning but not yet active. This indicates that the alertness of the senses does not discredit the principle of control of the senses.
iii. *Uparati – abstinence.* 'Approached his master' gives a lesson on abstinence. It suggests that the path to the state of enlightenment is true abstinence – abstinence from ignorance and bondage. This word has commonly been misunderstood to mean abstinence from activity.

The practical aspect of abstinence is transcendental meditation, because this practice is a direct way to transcendental consciousness, the state of enlightenment. After gaining transcendental consciousness by the inward stroke of meditation, the mind comes out to engage in activity. This process of repeatedly gaining transcendental consciousness and then engag-

ing in activity results in making permanent the state of enlightenment. It is therefore clear that the teaching on uparati, or
abstinence, in no way involves falling into inactivity or abandoning activity altogether.

iv. *Titiksha – endurance.* The lesson on this is given by 'army
... drawn up in battle array'. The army, whose function it is
to fight, endures non-activity. The essence of endurance is to
take all things as they come.

v. *Shraddha – faith.* The lesson on faith is given by 'approached
his master'.

vi. *Samadhana – mental equilibrium.* The unmoved state of the
'master' presented in this verse gives a lesson on mental equilibrium.

4. MUMUKSHUTVA (DESIRE FOR LIBERATION)

The lesson on this is taught by 'approached his master'.

This analysis of the second verse of Chapter I serves as an
illustration showing that every verse of the Bhagavad-Gita is
valid and its truth verifiable in the light of the six systems of
Indian philosophy. At the same time it has been shown that the
aims of each system are fulfilled through the practice of transcendental meditation.

JAI GURU DEVA

Shankaracharya Nagar,   Mahashivaratri
Rishikesh, U.P.   18 February, 1966

MORE ABOUT PENGUINS
AND PELICANS

Penguinews, which appears every month, contains details of all the new books issued by Penguins as they are published. From time to time it is supplemented by *Penguins in Print*, which is a complete list of all titles available. (There are some five thousand of these.)

A specimen copy of *Penguinews* will be sent to you free on request. For a year's issues (including the complete lists) please send 50p if you live in the British Isles, or 75p of you live elsewhere. Just write to Dept EP, Penguin Books Ltd, Harmondsworth, Middlesex, enclosing a cheque or postal order, and your name will be added to the mailing list.

In the U.S.A.: For a complete list of books available from Penguin in the United States write to Dept CS, Penguin Books Inc., 7110 Ambassador Road, Baltimore, Maryland 21207.

In Canada: For a complete list of books available from Penguin in Canada write to Penguin Books Canada Ltd, 41 Steelcase Road West, Markham, Ontario.

THE UPANISHADS

Translated and selected by Juan Mascaró

The Upanishads represent for the Hindu approximately what the New Testament represents for the Christian. The earliest of these spiritual treatises, which vary greatly in length, were put down in Sanskrit between 800 and 400 B.C.

This selection from twelve Upanishads, with its illuminating introduction by Juan Mascaró, whose translation of the *Bhagavad Gita* is already in the Penguin Classics, reveals the paradoxical variety and unity, the great questions and simple answers, the spiritual wisdom and romantic imagination of these 'Himalayas of the Soul'.

'Your translation ... has caught from those great words the inner voice that goes beyond the boundaries of words' – Rabindranath Tagore in a letter to the translator.